Mirror On

1939

ISBN: 9781790807178

INDEX

INDEX - 2

INDEX - 3

INDEX - 4

DAILY MIRROR, WEDNESDAY, JAN. 4, 1939

Daily Mirror

No. 10,945   ONE PENNY

Registered at the G.P.O. as a Newspaper
Geraldine House, Fetter-lane, E.C.4.
HOLBORN 4321.

Picked the Lock

Lock of hair of Charles, Lord Queensberry, a duchess's wedding ring, a toothpick, were among articles of value stolen by thieves who raided Orsett Hall, Grays, home of Lieutenant - Colonel Whitmore, Essex's Lord-Lieutenant.

Thieves spent an hour boring forty holes in front door panel to get in.

FATHER IS 'DOCTOR' TO HIS 15 LB. BABY

BY A SPECIAL CORRESPONDENT

WHILE his twelve children waited on the landing outside the door ready to obey their father's slightest request for towels and hot water, Michael Taylor, of Salisbury-road, Anfield, Liverpool, yesterday successfully acted as midwife to his wife for the birth of their thirteenth child.

He was unable to get a doctor or a nurse in time, and before this, a husband and father's greatest ordeal, he prayed earnestly for help.

" As he is our thirteenth child we are going to call him Lucky—for luck certainly came our way to-day," the smiling father told me last night.

Prompted by whispered instructions from his wife, he got through the ordeal, and a perfect baby was born weighing 15lb.

And when it was all over the nurse who came to see Mrs. Taylor said:—

" Mr. Taylor managed splendidly. I couldn't have done better myself. Fortunately there were no complications. The baby is perfect, and Mrs. Taylor is comfortable."

Roused Children

The baby was not expected for another two or three weeks.

Mrs. Taylor awoke in pain early yesterday and her husband, a case-maker for the British and American Tobacco Co., roused his two eldest children and sent them for a doctor and nurse.

Time passed, and they did not arrive. Mrs. Taylor's agony increased.

Mr. Taylor, who has never been present at the birth of any of his twelve children, set about preparing for the birth of the baby.

A whisper from his wife told him that medical aid would be too late. So, white-faced, he muttered a prayer.

His wife remained conscious throughout the birth, and Mr. Taylor carried out her instructions implicitly.

"It Was Nerve-Racking"

" As time went on and no one arrived I saw that the life of my wife and our new baby lay in my hands alone," said Mr. Taylor.

" Praying that I should do nothing wrong, I acted instinctively.

" It was a nerve-racking experience. The rest of my children were grouped outside the door.

" When the birth was over they crowded in and were thrilled at the sight of their new baby brother.

" I have trained them to carry out my orders promptly, and they certainly worked like Trojans, keeping me supplied with hot water and the other essentials.

" The nurse arrived ten minutes after it was all over," he added.

Katherine, the eldest child, said that she went to five surgeries to find a doctor before she was successful.

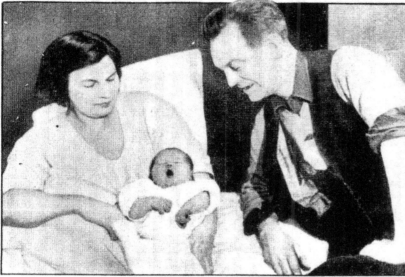

Looking proudly at the " lucky thirteenth " he brought into the world . . . Mr. Michael Taylor with his wife and their 15lb. baby boy

SHOT SERGEANT SAVED BY P.-C.

shooting   with   Police - Sergeant Sidney Cranfield.

Two miles up the river a sporting gun was accidentally discharged and Cranfield was wounded in the thigh. An artery was severed and blood poured from the wound.

BY A SPECIAL CORRESPONDENT

GRASPING the control wheel with one hand and staunching the blood flowing from a companion's wounded thigh with the other, a constable steered a police launch safely to Brightlingsea pier, Essex, yesterday.

Constable Greengrass, of the River Colne police, had been duck-

Greengrass covered the wound with his hand, laid his friend on the floorboards of the launch.

He then guided the launch through the choppy water until he saw a small boat.

Signalled for Help

He signalled for help and two men in the boat transferred Sergeant Cranfield into their craft with great difficulty while Greengrass still held his fist in the wound.

The boat was then hoisted on to the Brightlingsea landing stage while onlookers telephoned for an ambulance.

In great pain, the thirty-seven-year-old sergeant was hurried six miles to hospital. Late last night his condition had improved.

Sergeant Cranfield is married and has one child.

An onlooker told me : " It was a magnificent display of heroism on the part of Police-Constable Greengrass. Without his prompt action the sergeant would have bled to death."

GIRL LASHED WITH WHIP IN STREET

AN attacker with a whip struck the legs of a girl clerk as she walked home from work at Southall, Middlesex, last night.

Rene Adamson, twenty, was near her home in Lancaster-road, when she was struck.

Mrs. M. Edwards, a neighbour, who was walking with Rene, told the Daily Mirror:—

" As she came to say 'good night,' a man who had apparently been following us passed by and I heard the swish of a whip. There were weals across the backs of her legs above the ankles.

" The man turned and ran down the street."

Cake He Won't Eat

Most treasured possession of Mr. C. H. Bartle, disabled ex - Service pensioner, of Prospect Cottages, Metchley - lane, Harborne, Birmingham, is a piece of fruit cake which he will never eat.

It was iced by Princess Elizabeth and sent to him " with the season's compliments " by the Queen.

" With other ex-Servicemen I received the cake at a dinner in Birmingham," he told the " Daily Mirror." " I shall keep the piece of cake until I die."

WIFE LEAVES "THE KID"

FROM OUR SPECIAL CORRESPONDENT

NEW YORK, Tuesday.

BLONDE Betty Grable has gone home to mother until her harassed young husband, Jackie Coogan, can get his financial affairs settled.

" They've had no trouble and are still in love," said Betty's mother, Mrs. Lilian Grable, announcing that the handsomest couple in Hollywood had decided to live apart until The Kid, who earned a million dollars in child star roles, can support her daughter in a style that he wishes.

£100,000 Suit

" There isn't any talk of divorce, but it's just a sensible arrangement," said Jackie. " It's true we've separated. As to divorce, that's all very indefinite, but I still love Betty."

Betty's mother thinks everything will be all right as soon as Jackie's pending suits against his mother and stepfather, Arthur Bernstein, are settled.

He is suing for the recovery of about £100,000.

DAILY MIRROR, SATURDAY, JAN. 7, 1939.

Daily Mirror

No. 10,948   ONE PENNY

Registered at the G.P.O. as a Newspaper
Geraldine House, Fetter-lane, E.C.4.
HOLBORN 4321.

WONDER LOVER WINS BACK WIFE

They're across the frontier. . . . Mr. Brian Grover and his wife, pictured as they reached Poland from Russia last night.

Mr. Grover, "England's greatest lover," made a perilous journey by 'plane, was thrown into gaol by the Soviet Secret Police—in his attempt to win back the bride he had not seen for four years.

Even Russia's stern rulers gave way before the story of his love flight. He was set free, trudged for miles across the snow to claim his wife.

"This is a lesson to all lovers," said Mrs. Grover.

Their story—page 15.

18-IN. MAN IS STOLEN

A MAN, 18 INCHES HIGH, KNOWN AS PRINCE DOMLING, HAS VANISHED FROM BERTRAM MILLS'S CIRCUS, OLYMPIA. IT IS FEARED HE HAS BEEN KIDNAPPED.

Mr. G. S. Tuncke, his manager, lost him in the cloakroom. Later Prince Domling was reported to have been seen in the arms of a tall man.

The police were informed. An inspector and a sergeant from Hammersmith Police Station were in conference with officials of the Fun Fair at Olympia until 3 a.m. this morning.

His disappearance was discovered just before midnight, and when a search of the premises proved fruitless the police were called in.

"Quite Self-Possessed"

Says His Manager

"He would not have wandered away without telling me," Mr. Tuncke said. "He is such a self-possessed little fellow, although he is so very tiny.

"I am worried. The 'Prince' was seen with a stranger . . and no one is allowed to pick him up except myself. . . ."

"Prince Domling," eighteen inches high, is probably the smallest midget ever on show in England.

LONDON FARES GOING UP

ALL fares in London—rail, tubes, trams, buses and trolleybuses—may be increased in the next few months.

The fares of the four main line companies—Great Western, L.M.S., L.N.E.R., and Southern —may be increased by five per cent. Those of the London Passenger Transport Board services by a figure yet to be announced.

Notice will be made in the London Gazette next week of the railway companies' intention to apply to the Railway Rates Tribunal for the increase.

Before increases may be granted the Tribunal must hold an inquiry.

The London Passenger Transport Board may increase its fares up to five per cent increase without sanction of the Tribunal.

CONVENT GIRL LOST AT SEA

BY A SPECIAL CORRESPONDENT

"WOMAN overboard!" rang out in the steamer Princess Astrid on the way from Ostend to Dover yesterday, when a girl travelling with a party of nuns fell from the deck into the sea.

At once the ship stopped and a boat was lowered, but it searched for half an hour before the girl was picked up—dead.

A British passport in her possession revealed the name Miss Margater Finaghty and her age as twenty-four.

Only a few hours before she had said farewell to the Sisters of Charity at the Convent of St. Vincent de Paul in Ghent, to travel to the Sisters of Charity St. Francis College Letchworth (Herts) to continue her training.

"A Beautiful Girl"

Last night, after a gendarme had broken the news to the convent, I spoke on the telephone to one of the sisters.

"The party for Letchworth was so happy when we wished them good-bye this morning," she said. "It seems impossible to believe she has been drowned.

"Margater was a beautiful girl, with a wonderful nature. She was hoping to enter the Order. She was quite young."

As we talked there came faintly over the wires the slow tolling of a bell. The Sisters were already mourning the passing of Margater Finaghty.

Miss Finaghty was believed to come from Southern Ireland.

The accident occurred about two miles off the Goodwins, and when her body was recovered it was brought to Dover.

Maternal Rings Now

The "maternal" ring, introduced to commemorate the birth of a child, is the latest fashion in jewellery.

This completes the trio of rings symbolising the most important events in a woman's life—engagement, marriage and motherhood.

Husbands already often make gifts of jewels to their wives on the birth of her first child. The maternal ring has originated from this idea.

These rings will consist of precious stones set in either platinum or gold.

There will be rubies for baby boys and sapphires for girls.

Twin and triplet rings can be made to order. Well-to-do mothers of twin boys and girls can wear a cluster ring of rubies and sapphires.

Already some London jewellers have had orders for maternal rings.

KING AND QUEEN TO VISIT QUINS

FROM OUR OWN CORRESPONDENT

MONTREAL, Friday.

THE King and Queen will make a quiet, unofficial visit to the Dionne Quintuplets at Callendar during royal tour in Canada, it was learned here to-night.

The visit was not mentioned in the official itinerary because the place would have been so full of sightseers that the royal visitors would have been hampered.

A "Rest" Period

It's understood that the King and Queen will slip off quietly from a Sudbury, Ontario, where they are to arrive on June 5, and be driven to Callendar.

The next few days are scheduled as a "rest period," but they may spend the time with the quins.

BLACK-OUT BABY NAME IS TWILIGHT

BY the light of torches and candles, a baby was born at Blackpool last night during an electricity failure.

Several Lancashire towns were plunged into darkness.

The baby, a boy weighing more than 6lb., has been named Twilight by nurses at the hospital. His mother is Mrs. George Henderson, of Belmont-avenue, Blackpool.

An attendant and an elderly woman passenger were trapped in a lift for twenty minutes between two floors of a departmental store when the current failed.

The black-out lasted two and a half hours, though some areas had a partial restoration of supply after about ten minutes.

Nurse Works by Torchlight

Two surgeons were operating to remove a woman's appendix in Fleetwood Hospital when the light failed.

Emergency lighting apparatus was hurriedly brought into use, and by the light of three small bulbs connected to a 12-volt battery, the operation was completed.

A nurse then stitched the incision by the light of an ordinary pocket electric torch.

From a sick bed, Preston borough electrical engineer, Mr. G. A. Robertson, directed his staff in efforts to restore the supply.

The black-out was caused when, simultaneously with a cable breakdown, fire occurred in the switch room at the Blackpool sub-station.

Firemen had to crawl on their stomachs through thick smoke to the seat of the outbreak which they got under control with carbon dioxide gas in half an hour.

DAILY MIRROR, MONDAY, JAN. 9, 1939.

Daily Mirror

No. 10,949   ONE PENNY

Registered at the G.P.O. as a Newspaper.
Geraldine House, Fetter-lane, E.C.4.
HOLBORN 4321.

FED BABY: THEN SHOT

BY A SPECIAL CORRESPONDENT

A YOUNG mother, Mrs. Gladys Dinham, rose at dawn yesterday to feed her baby boy. Carefully she tended him and wrapped him up warm in his crib.

A few minutes later her parents heard a shot and found her dead—her father's sporting gun at her side.

Mrs. Dinham, who was twenty-eight, lived at Wilks Farm, Doynton, near Chipping Sodbury. She had been ill since the birth of her baby six weeks ago and had returned to the home of her father, Mr. Edgar L. Webb, Lodge Farm, Mangotsfield, near Bristol, to recuperate.

She Worried

Her father told the *Daily Mirror*:—

"She was worried to death about the baby—and he's the picture of health. We reassured her that young William was fine and dandy, but she worried just the same.

"She came to us four weeks after the baby was born and was pretty weak for a while. On Saturday she was up for the first time, and we were so pleased.

"Early to-day I was up and out milking. My wife and Gladys' three sisters were still asleep. They were awakened by the shot.

"We found her dead—the gun beside her.

"We called the doctor and I jumped in my car and drove four miles to her husband, and brought him back with me. He's heartbroken." The couple had been married two years.

SEYMOUR HICKS A GRANDDAD

SIR SEYMOUR HICKS and Lady Hicks yesterday became grandparents. A son was born to their only daughter, Mrs. Betty Stuart of Wellington-square, London.

Mother and baby are "going on well."

Mrs. Stuart is the wife of Captain Donald Stuart, of the Gordon Highlanders, whom she married in April, 1937.

THE GOWN FITTED

BY A SPECIAL CORRESPONDENT

WEARING a dress made for her by a sister-in-law in Hungary whom she has never seen, Miss Ferdinanda Hager, a Viennese, aged twenty-three, was married yesterday to Joseph Hoffer, Soho's famous Hungarian restaurateur.

Although the sisters-in-law have never met they know each other well—so well that Mr. Hoffer's sister was able to make a Hungarian national costume for the wedding. It fitted perfectly.

◆ ◆ ◆

Miss Hoffer knows as much about her pretty new Viennese sister-in-law as if she had met her.

For the five years her brother Joseph has been in England he has written home regularly—and always his letters were filled with news of his fiancee.

His family knew she was the only girl for Joseph, and so the wedding-dress was made.

Yesterday the couple were married at St. Patrick's Church, Soho-square.

The bride's Hungarian costume consisted of a flared white brocade skirt and dainty bodice of blue velvet, decorated with gold cord, and puff lace sleeves.

◆ ◆ ◆

Her head-dress was of field flowers, poppies and corn, resting high on her golden curls.

A Hungarian wedding breakfast was held at the bridegroom's Soho restaurant in Dean-street. Best man was the bridegroom's business partner. They had two wedding cakes.

"It was my mother's wish for my wife to be married in Hungarian style. My sister made the wedding-dress and sent it to us from Hungary," Mr. Hoffer told me.

"In the summer we are going to Hungary for a holiday. For our honeymoon we are going to Paris."

SHOT FOR HIS PANTS

FROM OUR OWN CORRESPONDENT
NEW YORK, Sunday.

A NEW YORK manufacturing tailor, Archangelo Difronzo, had made a fortune from his own specialised line—the making of coats.

He recently decided to manufacture trousers and waistcoats.

"Stop or You Die"

Mysterious warnings reached him. "Stop making trousers or you die!" the messages said. Archangelo ignored them.

As his employees were streaming from the factory, yesterday, at the end of the day's work, Archangelo fell dead in his cutting-room with three bullets in his chest.

The assassin escaped.

In the bridal dress made for her by a sister-in-law she has never seen, Miss Ferdinanda Hager, wearing her Hungarian national costume of blue velvet, white brocade, and lace, at the reception after her wedding.

BISHOP ON 'PHONE 'O.K. TO WED'

BY A SPECIAL CORRESPONDENT
BILLERICAY (Essex), Sunday.

A BRIDAL party looked helplessly at the water-surrounded church here for more than an hour while the twenty-year-old bride pleaded with the vicar and the vicar coaxed his Bishop into Britain's first "telephone consecration."

The wedding took place in the church hall, after the Bishop had been asked by the vicar for a "definite answer within a minute."

The Bishop gave his sanction by saying "Go ahead!"

Miss Doreen Allen, of The Dairy, Gardiner's-lane, Billericay, was waiting for her sweetheart of four years, Frank Fawcett, of Basildon, Billericay, when she was told that the church, which stands in a hollow, was cut off by floods.

"It's All Off," Then . . .

A car tried to break through, but failed. While the guests were saying "It is all off," Miss Allen rushed to the vicar's home, a mile away, and asked him if anything could be done to avoid cancelling the wedding.

The vicar, the Rev. Francis Trousdale, thought of the Church Hall, All Saints Chapel-of-Ease. It was erected so that if floods threatened the church, evening service could be held there.

The chapel had been dedicated, but it was not consecrated for marriage.

While the twenty guests stamped their feet to keep themselves warm, the vicar rang up Dr. Wilson, Bishop of Chelmsford, and asked him if it were permissible to hold a marriage there.

"I knew that such a thing had not been done before," Mr. Trousdale told the *Daily Mirror*, "and I would not move an inch without the Bishop's express permission.

"At first Dr. Wilson would not give a definite answer, but I alternately coaxed and pressed him.

"Go Ahead"

"'There are twenty people waiting outside,' I pointed out, 'and if you do not give me a definite answer within a minute or two the wedding will be cancelled. I dare not take the responsibility of marrying the couple myself. The marriage would not be valid without your permission.'

"The Bishop questioned me very closely about the banns and the register. I was able to reassure him that they were valid.

"'All right,' he said suddenly, in a kindly manner. 'Go ahead with the marriage.'"

While the Bishop was giving his consent Police-Constable Hales made three attempts to wade through the flood. He swore that if he could get over the flood he'd "carry every member of the party to the church and back again for the wedding." But the water was too deep for him.

"Billericay has never seen such a celebration as there was after the wedding," Mr. George Allen, brother of the bride, said.

9

Daily Mirror

No. 10,953   ONE PENNY

Registered at the G.P.O. as a Newspaper
Geraldine House, Fetter-lane, E.C.4.
HOLBORN 4321.

ROME TALKS FREEZE: BOTH SAY 'NO'

THEY WED ON 13TH

WHEN Mr. Arthur Bailey, of Guildford, Surrey, asked his fiancee Alma Phair, of Godalming, to name the happy day she answered without hesitation: Friday, January 13.

And when they marry at Guildford Registrar's office to-day, the 13th, the bride will wear green, there will be thirteen wedding guests, and thirteen decorations will adorn the bridal cake.

Mr. Bailey was born on January 13, 1915. He met his bride on December 13. Their engagement lasted thirteen months.

He has been in his present job for thirteen months. He left home to live in Godalming thirteen months ago.

Advised by Spirits

And they have been advised by the spirit world, they say, to marry on the 13th.

"Alma and I met for the first time on December 13, thirteen months ago," Mr. Bailey said last night. "We both were attending our first spiritualist meeting. We have both grown extremely interested in the activities of the private circle we attend.

"Our wedding date might have been January 12, but at a meeting of our circle a message came through the control from my dead grandfather, directing that the wedding be postponed until January 13.

"We changed the date immediately. My birthday falls on the thirteenth. There are thirteen children in my mother's family.

Bride and bridegroom are both twenty-three years old . . . and somehow their ages seem ten years out.

Laugh at the 13th—See page 18.

Clara Is Home From the Sea

Clara, the heifer who ran away to sea, came back yesterday a sadder and wiser adventuress.

While being unloaded from a truck in Middlesbrough goods station on Tuesday, she ran to the wharves, dived into the Tees and swam out of sight.

Yesterday she was found wandering along a road on the opposite side of the river, and taken home.

THE diplomatic talks between Mr. Chamberlain and Lord Halifax and Mussolini and Count Ciano ended in Rome last night. Although the conversations were cordial they ended in stalemate.

Mr. Chamberlain and Mussolini both stated their views at length, but no possible line of agreement was found.

Mussolini emphatically told the British statesmen:

1. Italy refuses to withdraw troops from Spain until belligerent rights have been granted to Franco.

2. The Italian attitude towards France will not be altered.

The Premier and the Duce talked for seventy-five minutes last night, and Count Ciano, Mussolini's son-in law Foreign Minister, is understood to be working out a communique, which will be revised and issued to-day.

Mr. Chamberlain has a slight cold, and is looking rather tired.

That cold may provide the opportunity, if it is wanted, to confine the next talk to a formal leave-taking.

As it became clear in Rome last night that the talks had done nothing to help the appeasement of Europe, foreign observers believed that Mr. Chamberlain will now be forced to take a firmer line with the dictators.

It is certain that the Premier formally requested the Duce to withdraw from Spain, and received a blunt refusal.

Duce Sees Envoys

The Italian people will regret it. Already 244 Italians have been killed and 1,300 injured in the new Spanish offensive, according to an official Rome statement.

Two moves behind the scenes in Rome caused a sensation, particularly because of efforts to keep them secret.

Before the talks were resumed last night it became known that the Duce, who has rarely received Ambassadors since Count Ciano took over the Foreign Secretaryship, saw the Ambassadors of Germany and Japan, co-partners in the axis.

It was revealed, too, that Mussolini talked with Mr. Toshio Shiratori, Japanese Ambassador, for ninety minutes before the talks with the British statesmen opened on Wednesday.

Then Herr von Mackensen was with the Duce for an hour.

Children on Parade

Lord Halifax saw Count Ciano yesterday morning for fifty minutes before he and the Premier lunched with King Victor Emanuel.

They were with the King half an hour before the luncheon

During a Fascist Youth gymnastic display watched by Mr. Chamberlain and Lord Halifax at the Mussolini Forum yesterday afternoon, fifty children, aged from six to eight years, marched and counter-marched across the arena, doing rifle drill like soldiers on parade.

Finally, they flung themselves on the ground in front of Mr. Chamberlain's stand and took direct aim at the Prime Minister with their rifles—much to his amusement.

Daily Mirror, Reuter and British United Press messages.

Arthur Bailey and Alma Phair drink to their lucky thirteen . . . a photograph taken last night.

FOUND BOY HURT WAS HIS BROTHER

RUNNING home white-faced to his mother last night, Stephen Pope, aged twelve, of Lombard-road, Battersea, London, told her: "A little boy has been run over by a trolley bus in York-road. He was crying so dreadfully I could not look to see who it was."

"How terrible," his mother told him. "It only shows how careful you must be when crossing the road."

A few minutes later there was a knock at the door . . . and a policeman told Mrs. Pope that the victim of the accident was her younger son Peter, aged eight.

Both his legs had been run over. Mrs. Pope went with Peter in the ambulance to hospital, where his condition was last night stated to be "critical."

FELL UNDER TRAIN —AND LIVED

FALLING under an electric train at New Malden (Surrey) last night, as crowds of business people were returning home, a company director escaped with head injuries.

He was Mr. Albert Winterbottom, of Langley-grove, New Malden.

An eye-witness told the *Daily Mirror*: "I heard a scream and saw the man slip from the platform under the train.

"It seemed certain that he must be dead, but the ambulance men gave him first-aid on the platform before taking him to hospital at Kingston."

DEARER FARES FOR 8,000,000

EIGHT million people in Greater London face a demand for higher fares on train, tube, bus, coach, tram and trolley bus services.

Cheap day return, workmen's, scholars', midday and season tickets will all be dearer, it is proposed.

Saying that the need for more revenue is "imperative," the London Passenger Transport Board and the main line railway companies announced last night that they are to apply to the Railway Rates Tribunal for permission to increase fares by five per cent. on suburban lines.

"Many of the fares on the Board's railways are now below the Board's standard of a penny a mile," it is stated, "and it is proposed to increase some of these fares to conform more closely to that standard, especially in those cases where the mileage rate is exceptionally low.

"There will also be an adjustment of certain fares to avoid anomalies."

Workmen's fares on the Board's railways will still be determined upon the existing standard of single ordinary fare for a return journey where that basis now applies, and therefore will only be increased where the ordinary single fare is increased.

Cheap day return tickets will be on the basis of the single ordinary fare plus one-half.

Season ticket rates will be increased where they are now below the scale of charge adopted by the Board, but the increases will, as far as

(Continued on back page)

DAILY MIRROR, SATURDAY, JAN. 14, 1939.

Daily Mirror

No. 10,954   ONE PENNY
Registered at the G.P.O. as a Newspaper
Geraldine House, Fetter-lane, E.C.4
HOLBORN 4321.

GANG GAOL

Dearer Light for London

Central London Electricity Company last night announced an increase of 7½ per cent. on all charges for current.

This will take effect from February 1, except where a supply is taken under the two-part tariff system, when the increase will operate when the current period of the contract expires.

Central London Electricity, Ltd., supplies the City of London, the City of Westminster, the Borough of Chelsea, and parts of the boroughs of Holborn and Kensington, the authorised area of supply being about eight square miles.

GASSED GIRL EXILE'S FEAR

BY A SPECIAL CORRESPONDENT

EIGHT days before she was to have been married, and shortly before her licence to remain in this country expired, Leni Stolt, twenty-three-year-old German art student was yesterday found gassed at her lodgings in King's-road, Chelsea.

She wrote to her fiance on Thursday asking him to call at her flat yesterday.

He arrived a few hours after the girl had been found, dressed in yachting clothes, lying gassed on the bed in her flat. When the news was broken to him he collapsed.

Blanket Muffled Door

Leni was very unhappy because her permit to stay in England was on the point of expiring and she was afraid to go back to Germany, he told the police.

"Miss Stolt told me on Wednesday that she was going to be married in ten days' time," Mr. Reny de Meo, of the Pheasantry Club, King's-road, Chelsea, said last night.

The girl's body was found by Mr. Anthony Sagar, an actor living in the block of flats.

The door had been muffled with a blanket and all cracks were blocked up.

Upset by Visit

Some hours after the girl had died an official-looking letter from Berlin arrived for her.

Mr. G. Martin, who was a neighbour, told me: "Yesterday I helped Leni to arrange her back room. I found that she had stuffed up all the cracks in the floor with paper and bits of metal.

"She had done this, she told me, because she was afraid of mice.

"A week ago two official-looking men called on her. After they had gone she was very upset."

One of her frequent visitors was a young German, Mr. George Muller. Their mutual interest apparently was in political books

LEADER SHOT AS BREAK

FROM OUR OWN CORRESPONDENT
NEW YORK, Friday.

MACHINE guns fired mercilessly by guards patrolling the sea and shore forced five desperate convicts, making an amazing attempt to escape from Alcatraz Prison—America's " Devil's Isle "—to surrender.

One notorious kidnapper, Arthur (Doc) Barker, fell, groaning, severely wounded in the head and legs.

Another life-sentence kidnapper, Dale Stamphill, fell with a bullet in a leg.

The three others raised their arms in surrender and to-night lie chained in dungeons of the island off the coast of San Francisco.

To-night all the convicts on the island are under a special guard. It is feared the news of the attempted escape may encourage them to mutiny.

Sawed Through Bars

Barker and his four companions, miserable from the iron discipline of the island, are believed to have made plans to escape months ago.

This morning, when The Rock, as Alcatraz is called in the underworld, was enshrouded in fog, they decided their chance had come.

With a saw they had smuggled into their cell they cut through the bars, crept along prison corridors, eluded the guard, and made their way into the open.

Then they prepared to dash to the beach and attempt to swim through treacherous currents to the mainland.

Suddenly the alarm sounded, revealing that their disappearance had been noticed. Prison Warden Johnson flashed the order to all police boats off the island and all stations ashore to watch for the escaped men.

Then Barker and his companions made their dash towards the sea.

Guards in watch towers and machine-gunners in the fleet of police cutters which now surrounded the island, spotted them as the fog lifted.

Powerful searchlights were trained on to the convicts as they ran, hoping to reach the sea and swim to the mainland.

They were easy targets to police in watch towers and boats.

Guns in the watch towers and cutters spluttered.

Barker fell with a groan, then Dale Stamphill fell.

The others seeing escape was impossible, threw up their arms. They were speedily seized and thrown into irons.

Long-Term Men

They are negro William Martin, a post office robber with thirty-five years' sentence, who was badly grazed from sliding down rocks; Henry Young, a bank robber with twenty years' sentence; Rupert McCain, with a life sentence for robbery and kidnapping.

"They got out at 4 a.m." said Warden Johnson, America's strictest prison chief.

"I don't know exactly how they did it. They were first seen crawling down to the beach over rocks."

The only escape from America's "Devil's Isle" was made in 1937 by two convicts. They were never seen again. It is believed they were drowned in trying to swim to the mainland.

A meeting like this brought them romance. . . . Lord Lisle and his bride-to-be, Miss Mary Helen Purgold, riding in Rotten Row.

WAR MINISTER IN RAIL ESCAPE

MR. Hore-Belisha, the Minister for War, was a passenger in a train which had a narrow escape from accident yesterday.

He was returning from an engagement in Nottingham, and caught the train to Marylebone Station which was due at 6.38.

It did not arrive until 7.25, however, because at Helmdon, in Northamptonshire, a goods truck came off the rails.

The truck turned over the points at the line crossing and the London train was stopped in its progress, or a serious accident might have occurred.

The express was held up while the points were put right.

—And Time Marches On

TWO HUNDRED men a week will be suspended from Woolwich Arsenal, it was announced last night, because of temporary shortage of work in the royal filling factories.

The suspensions will last for five or six weeks. The shortage, it is stated, follows the opening of new filling factories elsewhere in the country. The ordinary part of the Arsenal is not affected

SIGNOR MUSSO-LINI is planning to send 32,000 Italian workers into Germany this year to help in the harvest and the German arms drive.

Hungary yesterday formally joined Germany, Italy and Japan in the anti-Comintern Pact.

French reports last night say that Germany is about to take military measures on the Dutch frontier.

PEER'S RIDING SCHOOL BRIDE

BY A SPECIAL CORRESPONDENT

A ROMANTIC meeting in Rotten Row has led to the engagement of John Nicholas Horace Lysaght, Baron Lisle, to a riding school mistress, Miss Mary Helen Purgold.

They will be married at a London register office to-day. Lord Lisle is thirty-five, his bride thirty-three.

Lady Lisle's decree nisi for the dissolution of her marriage was made absolute on Wednesday.

When Lord Lisle was adjudged bankrupt in 1934 he took a £2 a week job as riding master at a Marble Arch school.

Miss Purgold was then in charge of a Knightsbridge riding school. They met in Rotten Row every morning, but it was not until Lord Lisle advertised a horse for sale that they spoke to each other.

Miss Purgold bought the horse, and they became firm friends. "He has helped me to buy and sell many horses since then." Miss Purgold told me yesterday

"I Am Very Happy"

"We got on so well together that we decided to amalgamate. We became partners, and for the past four years have run the Albion Riding School, Knightsbridge, together.

"Now we are free to marry ... am very happy. Lord Lisle has had ... trying time, and I hope our marriage will bring him happiness."

Miss Purgold's hobby is writing thrillers, which she circulates among her friends in manuscript form.

Her Irish peer fiance is the seventh Baron Lisle, a title created in 1758. He succeeded his grandfather in 1919.

In 1928 he married Vivienne, daughter of the Rev. M. Brew.

DAILY MIRROR, TUESDAY, Jan. 17, 1939.

Daily Mirror

No. 10,956   ONE PENNY

Registered at the G.P.O. as a Newspaper.
Geraldine House, Fetter-lane, E.C.4.
HOLBORN 4321.

Stevenson-square, Manchester, the scene of an explosion that killed Albert Ross, twenty-seven, as he waited for his brothers on his way to work. They were late—and escaped.

SPURNS £10,000 TO GIVE UP GIRL

A MINER, Alexander F. ederick Powell, twenty, of Blaina (Mon), whose fiancee, aged eighteen, a maid, vanished on the day fixed for their wedding, told yesterday how he had scorned an offer of £10,000 from a wealthy Indian to renounce his love for the girl.

He received a cheque for £10,000 but tore it up and threw the pieces in the river.

Powell's bride was to have been Phyllis May Britton, a miner's daughter, of High-street, Blaina. They were to have been married at Tredegar (Mon.) Register Office on Saturday.

Powell who works at a Blaina colliery was working on the night shift on Friday night. Soon after he left Miss Britton, who was staying with his parents, went out to buy him a pair of shoes.

She did not return. With her maid, Olga Bailey, aged fifteen, she left the district and yesterday was in Surrey.

Until six weeks ago Miss Britton had a flat in Cardiff and Olga was her maid there.

Mr. Thomas Britton, her father, would not

(Continued on back page)

Alexander Powell and (below) Miss Elsie Phyllis May Britton. They were to have wed on Saturday.

ARMED MEN GUARD GRID

POLICE guards, many of them armed, were ordered out last night to patrol every power station and principal reservoir in Britain following the series of bomb explosions that rocked seven areas of England yesterday.

As warnings were flashed to all police chiefs reports of new explosions reached London.

At Birmingham a bomb burst at the base of one of the huge cooling towers of the city's electrical power station at Hams Hall.

Near Alnwick, in Northumberland, an explosion wrecked the base of a pylon, left undamaged the main electricity line bearing supplies to Scotland.

All the outrages occurred at exactly the same time, just before six o'clock yesterday morning.

At that moment bombs burst in two parts of London, in Southwark and in Harlesden.

At the same time three manholes blew up in Manchester, killing Albert Ross, a porter; an ex losion took place at Crosby, near Liverpool, and another at Brimsdown, in Middlesex.

ALL CLUES POINT TO THE EXPLOSIONS BEING THE WORK OF POLITICAL GANGS, PROBABLY WORKING UNDER THE DIRECTION OF THE IRISH REPUBLICAN ARMY.

Beneath the bridge at Harlesden, where a home-made bomb failed to destroy the electric cable at which it was aimed, scorched scraps of paper were found.

They bore the typewritten words:

". . . remain as . . . Ireland, Labour in . . . by a thousand . . . terests of the prop . . . rather than risk . . . enting war . . . Madame McBride means . . . it is true . . . banking systems . . . financiers . . . way of usury . . ."

The name "Madame McBride" occurs about four times.

Madame Maude Gonne McBride has been

(Continued on page 19)

Man Who Lived by Night —Page 3

DAILY MIRROR, Thursday, January 19, 1939.

Daily Mirror

No. 10,958   ONE PENNY

Registered at the G.P.O. as a Newspaper.
Geraldine House, Fetter-lane, E.C.4.
HOLBORN 4321.

FOOD, WATER & WAR

By THE EDITOR

SIR AUCKLAND GEDDES, speaking officially, on behalf of the Government, has urged the housewives of the country—rich and poor alike—to " store a little extra food in their cupboards and to keep bottles of water in case Government food plans fail in war time."

He has aroused the fear in the minds of thousands that we are on the brink of war.

The *Daily Mirror* states emphatically that war is not imminent.

We have never concealed the menace of war; we have been in the forefront of those who have warned the nation of that menace, and our opinion has not changed.

But again we say

WAR IS NOT IMMINENT.

We expect the Government to deny any necessity for the individual storage of food and water, for Sir Auckland is inadvertently accusing the Government of criminal negligence, and we do not believe any Government could so betray its people.

For the storage and safeguarding of food and water in time of national emergency is a task for the Government, and for the Government alone.

Even if some reservoirs are in danger, there are thousands of wells in the country which the Government could control and protect.

Do not, therefore, be panicked into buying food you cannot afford, and storing water you will never drink.

Once again, war is not imminent

NOR IS IT INEVITABLE

GEDDES GETS A COLD SHOCK

THE Metropolitan Water Board last night poured cold water on Sir Auckland Geddes's advice to householders to store water in bottles to be prepared for an emergency

" The question of conserving water in small doses in bottles has not been considered or contemplated," said an official of the Board.

He pointed out that already domestic cisterns contained enough water to last twenty-four hours or longer with care, that the Board had taken steps to ensure that any damaged mains were repaired without delay, and that alternative sources of supply were available wherever possible.

On Sir Auckland's advice to householders to buy a little more food, especially tinned stuff, the secretary of the Retail Distributors' Association said it was more important that adequate supplies of fresh milk, meat, butter, flour in bulk, and vegetables should be available, and for these the average householder would have to depend on the steps taken by the Food Defence Department of the Board of Trade

KID BERG AND WIFE PARTED

Jack (Kid) Berg, former British light-weight champion, who arrived at Los Angeles yesterday to train for his fight with Baby Breese on February 3, revealed that he and his actress wife, Bunty Pain, had had a " little quarrel " and were now separated. He denied, however, that there was to be a divorce.

"It's just a friendly separation," he said. " We will be together again in a few days."

Bunty Pain (right), a vivacious blonde, was a London cabaret girl before her marriage to Berg five years ago.

TRAPPED 7 HOURS IN LIFT

FOR nearly seven hours yesterday Miss Nora Shepherd, a maid, was imprisoned in a lift in the house where she is employed at Cheyne-walk, Chelsea.

She was alone in the house and went into the lift during the afternoon.

The lift became wedged between two floors.

She was not released until last night, when another maid returned to the house and discovered her plight.

The fire brigade had to be called to move the lift. Miss Shepherd suffered shock.

P.-C. IS HIT IN DEATH DROP

BY A SPECIAL CORRESPONDENT

A CAMBRIDGE undergraduate who fell 85ft. to death from the fifth story of a West End block of flats last night struck a policeman who was taking the numbers of parked cars.

Quiet and studious, the young man, Martin T. Krasny, aged twenty-two, seldom spoke to women, yet two nights before he died he entertained a beautiful blonde to dinner.

A few minutes after his death a friend, Mr. James Shewan, rang him up at the flat in Quebec-street, W.

Police took the call and asked Mr. Shewan to see them.

After he had answered the detectives' questions Mr. Shewan told me:—

" I met Martin when I was up at Cambridge with him. He was a very secretive sort of fellow.

" As regards women, he had a great inferiority complex. We went to the Chelsea Arts Ball with a party, and he was accompanied by a blonde girl called Peggy, whom I had not seen before.

" But he never spoke about his love affairs.

"Left Me a Pen"

" He left five letters for me before he died, calling me a good friend and giving me a valuable fountain pen.

" It was a great shock to hear what had happened, because he was due to come round to see me at two o'clock to-day.

" I 'phoned him several times when he did not arrive, and the last time the police answered the telephone and told me of his accident.

When Krasny fell his outflung arm struck the policeman on the leg.

" He was popular and seemed quite happy at college," his Cambridge landlady, Mrs. A. Sampson, of Jesus-lane, said, when she was told of the tragedy.

" He should have got back to Cambridge for the new term last Monday, but he did not turn up. He was an Austrian Jew.

" The porter at the block of flats told me of the blonde's visit on Monday evening.

" That is the only woman we ever saw him with," he said.

MYSTERY CLUE IN LOVE NOTE

A LETTER from a girl named Margi, making peace after a lovers' quarrel may identify an unknown, good-looking young man who is suffering from loss of memory at Lewisham Hospital, S.E.

The letter was found in the lining of his coat. It reads:—

" Dear Billy,—I am willing to go back if you can please let me know if it is okay.

" I am sorry if I offended you. Please meet me to-night at 7.30 at Gairbraid-avenue and try to bring someone for Elsie, as I will bring her.

" Get someone good-looking or at least good appearance. You can bring Nifty if not someone else. Please do not let me down.

" With tons of love, from MARGI XXXX."

DAILY MIRROR, Saturday, January 21, 1939.

Daily Mirror

No. 10,960   ONE PENNY

Registered at the G.P.O. as a Newspaper
Geraldine House, Fetter-lane, E.C.4.
HOLBORN 4321.

Gunners on All Ships

All British merchant ships are to have members of the crew trained as gunners in peacetime.

This was announced last night by the Admiralty which describes the scheme as a further development of the defence courses for merchant navy officers which were first commenced in August, 1937, and which have proved very popular and successful.

The officers already receive training in gun control at the merchant navy defence courses, but the value of this experience is greatly reduced if the crew of a gun lacks training.

The new courses will ensure that each ship has a proportion of seamen trained in gunnery. Details of the scheme and the date on which training will begin will be announced soon.

CRASH AT 91 SPOILS RECORD

FROM OUR OWN CORRESPONDENT

ILFORD (Essex), Friday.

THE first woman in three generations to die before reaching 100 has been killed by a motor-car at the age of ninety-one.

Mrs. Julia Maria Waring, of Second-avenue, Manor Park, was sure she would live to be at least 100 years old. In the past 300 years no woman member of her family has failed to reach the hundred.

The average life of all the family in the past three centuries was 102.

And Mrs. Waring herself was healthy and active. Despite her great age she loved to go shopping alone.

As she was going home, two days ago, after a visit to a relative in Dulwich, she was knocked down by a car in Romford-road, Ilford, and killed. An inquest was opened to-day and adjourned.

The family is proud of its record of long lives.

"Father Was 88

Bomb Killed Him"

"We used to keep a family tree going back to the days of William, Prince of Orange," Mrs. Waring's son said to me to-night. "The family could be traced back even to earlier days, if one took the trouble to go through the records in Ireland. We came originally from Co. Down.

"Except where they met their deaths on battlefields the people who have died under the age of 100 could be counted on the fingers of the hand.

"My mother paid regular calls on friends at Dulwich, Elm Park and Streatham, and always travelled by bus—usually alone.

"My father died as a result of shock when a bomb hit the house in which we still live in Seventh-avenue, Manor Park, during the last war. He was eighty-eight at the time."

FOOD CHIEF GOES AWAY

BY A SPECIAL CORRESPONDENT

LONDON'S recently-appointed wartime Food Dictator — seventy-year-old Major - General Sir Reginald Ford—has gone to live in Belgium.

His "beat" in an emergency will be the capital and the Home Counties, but though he has made his home in a foreign country, two hundred miles away, I was assured yesterday that he is "within easy access of Whitehall."

"If an emergency arose," it was stated at his Government department in Westminster yesterday, "he could be in London very quickly. He is within a few hours of London."

Major-General Ford was appointed last August to the position of Chief Divisional Food Officer for London and the Home Counties.

At that time his addresses were stated in reference books to be in the Haymarket, S.W., and in Upper Warren-avenue, Mapledurham, Oxford, while in the telephone directory his address was given as Newton Court, Church-street, Kensington, W.

Current reference books now give his address as care of a bank in Oxford-street, W.

"Hate To Be Rung Up"

"Sir Reginald left here a month or so ago," I was told at Newton Court. "We are not allowed to give his new address, but all correspondence will be forwarded."

The Haymarket address is that of an employment agency, and here, too, they declined to say where Sir Reginald now lives.

"I am sure he would hate to be rung up by the Press," I was told. "Oh, yes, he is in London quite frequently. How often? Very often."

Sir Reginald is attached to the Food (Defence Plans) Department of the Board of Trade. An official of the Department agreed when I asked whether Sir Reginald lived in Brussels.

"He is a retired soldier, and he has no day-to-day executive duties in peace time." it was added.

"His function is mainly co-ordinating so far as other divisional officers are concerned. There are three divisional officers for London and the Home Counties under him."

"Constantly in Touch"

"Sir Reginald attends here for conferences and we keep constantly in touch with him.

"He is within easy access if an emergency arose."

Sir Reginald retired in 1920 after a distinguished Army career. He was awarded the D.S.O. during the Boer War, and thrice mentioned in dispatches.

In the Great War he was eight times mentioned in dispatches and received many foreign decorations. He was Deputy Quartermaster-General, later commanded the Royal Army Service Corps, and in 1931 was appointed Southern Area Traffic Commissioner.

Few men have so wide an experience of the transporting of food supplies.

Sir Reginald Ford, London's recently-appointed war-time food dictator. He lives "within easy access of Whitehall"—in Belgium.

WOMAN RACER IN DEATH COLLISION

MRS. KAY PETRE, the famous racing motorist, was seriously injured last night in a crash in which her companion, Major R. Calvert Empson, was killed.

Their car, in which they were driving to the Monte Carlo car rally, was wrecked in collision with a lorry near Villefranche, on the Lyons-Macon road.

Major Empson, who was a motor-racing journalist, was killed when taken from the wreckage.

Mrs. Petre, who had been driving, was unconscious, her head critically injured. She was taken to a nursing home, where a major operation was performed.

This morning, says the Exchange, she had recovered consciousness. Her life was no longer in danger, though her condition was still serious.

(Continued on back page)

SHE'S SORRY THEY'VE BEEN TROUBLED

BY A SPECIAL CORRESPONDENT

THE £100 pearl necklace, missed after its owner had sent a boxful of cheap trinkets to a Girl Guides' Christmas bazaar, has been found.

The cheap necklaces were sold by Santa Claus at 2d. a time.

Then Mrs. Davies-Scourfield, of Tongham Manor, near Farnham, the donor of the jewels, found that her £100 necklace was gone. She was in Switzerland when she discovered her loss. She telephoned to Mrs. G. M. Birch, of Tongham, Surrey, the organiser of the bazaar.

Mrs. Birch at once went to work to find the missing neck ace.

Notices were posted in the village. All purchasers of twopenny necklaces were asked to return them for inspection

Necklace in Drawer

The Girl Guides went into action. They circulated news of the loss; they traced some of the new owners of the necklaces, who readily presented their pearls for inspection.

All of the trinkets were found to be imitation.

Now Mrs. Davies-Scourfield has come home to Tongham Manor. And there yesterday, in a drawer of her dressing-table, she found the missing necklace.

Mrs. Birch did not know of the find until a Daily Mirror reporter told her last night. She said: "I am so pleased. It has been a lot of trouble and worry."

And Mrs. Davies-Scourfield said: "I am sorry if it has caused any trouble."

DRESS-SUIT FIREMEN

Firemen in evening dress, with top boots hastily pulled on, rescued terrified horses from a fire at a Buckhurst Hill, Essex, riding school at midnight. Loughton brigade rushed from their annual dinner to the blaze.

LONDON HUNT FOR LUNATIC

BY A SPECIAL CORRESPONDENT

POLICE searched London last night for a dangerous lunatic who had escaped from Friern Mental hospital, New Southgate, earlier in the evening.

His two male attendants hurried to the man's home address in Hackney, E., as soon as the alarm was given.

His mother, aged sixty-three and almost deaf, tramped the streets in search of him.

The man, who is of very powerful build, was kept in the Refractory Ward. He has been a patient seven or eight years.

He is described as a "dangerous suicidal and homicidal maniac."

Nearly 6ft. tall, he is of swarthy complexion and wears horn-rimmed glasses.

It Was Sweet Nothing

A man with a "whispery" voice had to read the oath three times in the witness-box at Romsey, Hants, yesterday.

The first time he gabbled it off. Ordered to read it again, he admitted he could not read.

The third time he got it correct by repeating it after the magistrate's clerk.

The chairman of the magistrates, Brigadier-General E. Cuthbertson, now somewhat exasperated, asked him: "Now, my man tell us what you have to say."

The Witness: Nothing, sir.

14

DAILY MIRROR, Wednesday, January 25, 1939

Daily Mirror

No. 10,963   ONE PENNY
Registered at the G.P.O. as a Newspaper
Geraldine House, Fetter-lane, E.C.4.
HOLBORN 4321.

Home Army Drive To-day

"To ensure peace we must be strong" — the Premier in the National Service Handbook.

Britain's campaign for a civilian army, 1,800,000 strong, opens to-day. It is described on page 2.

Women as well as men are asked to volunteer.

The special work they may do is also outlined on page 2.

The National Service Handbook will tell you how best you can serve.

Half of Britain's man-power comes within the scope of trades and professions "reserved," exempt from the national fighting services.

These are listed on page 25.

FRANCO A MILE AWAY

Barcelona is in the battle front. The Moors are only one mile from her southern suburbs. Her airfield has been captured.

Franco's big guns are firing into the streets. German and Italian 'planes in constant relays rain bombs on houses and factories.

The last line of defence is down. The rebels yesterday swept across the Llobregat river.

In the north-west their army captured Manresa, key city of 50,000 people, then wheeled round to complete the encirclement of Barcelona.

And the City has taken to the trenches. Girls in jumpers and slacks are marching up to fill sandbags. Mothers are preparing their children for flight, then taking the places among the labour battalions.

As night fell columns of troops marched to the city's outskirts. Girls tramped beside them, carrying rolled blankets. Again the cry was heard: " No Passaran."

Hundreds of Tanks Lead Advance

The city streets, which had been thronged all day by streams of refugees were deserted at dusk by all except the marching troops and the columns of army lorries.

The traffic kept on the move, despite the almost incessant bombing of raiding 'planes.

But the roads leading out of Barcelona were still crowded with refugees. Peasants' carts, loaded with household goods, children and old women, rumbled towards the French frontier.

For nothing now can stop the rebels. They are headed by hundreds of German and Italian tanks. Fascist aeroplanes have reduced the harbours to a mass of rubble and wreckage.

Women of the British Embassy staff have been taken off in the destroyer Greyhound and are on their way to Marseilles.

The Government have left Barcelona for an unnamed town in the north. A skeleton Cabinet has been left to carry on.

Messages from British United Press, and Reuter correspondents.

600 M.P.H. Dive

All speed records have been smashed by an American warplane, estimated to have exceeded 600 m.p.h., it was claimed yesterday.

In a free dive, near Buffalo, New York, it went beyond the speedometer's limit of 575 m.p.h.

H. Lloyd Child, the pilot, confessed later that he had no idea that he was travelling faster than any man in history.

FRANCE SEEKING NAZI ASSURANCE

M. Bonnet, the French Foreign Minister, is seeking to obtain assurances from Germany about her attitude towards Italian claims against France, according to reports in Paris.

Left political circles say he has approached the Reich in accordance with the Franco-German peace declaration of December 6 with the object of restricting Germany's support for any Italian demands.

Field-Marshal Goering and Herr von Ribbentrop, the Foreign Minister, addressed a number of German generals yesterday. Goering spoke "on the armed forces," and von Ribbentrop on foreign politics, says Reuter.

POLICE GUARD CASTLE BRIDE

BY A SPECIAL CORRESPONDENT

Twenty C.I.D. men and five Flying Squad cars will form part of the guard for the Hon. Anne Wigram, daughter of Lord Wigram, when she is married in St. George's Chapel, Windsor Castle, to-day, to Mr. John Harvey.

Scotland Yard has taken this precaution to prevent attempts to mar the ceremony.

The detectives, picked for their knowledge of Mayfair's "Who's who," will scrutinize the faces of the 2,000 guests as they arrive at the Castle gate.

Immaculately clad in morning dress, the detectives will move among the guests and watch more than a thousand wedding presents, which include valuable jewels.

Public Disappointed

The King and Queen are not able to be present.

Among those who attend will be many high officials of the Court and distinguished men in diplomatic circles.

The Archbishop of Canterbury will perform the ceremony.

Members of the public who have not been issued with tickets of admittance will not be allowed inside the Castle grounds.

Police guards outside the Castle will turn them back.

Thousands of Windsor people who expect to catch a glimpse of the bride and bridegroom as they leave St. George's Chapel will be disappointed.

The public may stand only at the entrances to the drives of the King Henry VIII Gate and the Royal Mews four hundred yards from the Chapel.

Only 150 people from Windsor who applied for permission to stand outside the Chapel will see the couple as they leave.

Typists' Luck

Windsor Castle officials announced recently that a certain number of tickets were available to permit members of the public to stand in the Lower Ward near the Chapel.

Hundreds of applications were refused because of the restriction of space.

Typists, shop assistants and clerks will be among the lucky 150 to-day.

Thousands more will wait outside the walls of the castle hoping that they will catch a glimpse of the guests as they shoot past in cars.

The last wedding in St. George's Chapel took place twenty years ago.

The Hon. Anne Wigram and Mr. J. L. Harvey photographed yesterday at the head of the Grand Staircase in Windsor Castle. Theirs will be the first wedding in St. George's Chapel for twenty years. Wedding presents picture on page 14.

DAILY MIRROR, Tuesday, January 31, 1939

Daily Mirror

No. 10,968   ONE PENNY
Registered at the G.P.O. as a Newspaper.
Geraldine House, Fetter-lane, E.C.4.
HOLBORN 4321.

HITLER'S TRADE THREAT AS HE PROMISES PEACE

MEN RACE RISING RIVER

FROM OUR OWN CORRESPONDENT

WINDSOR, Monday.

WORKMEN, called from their homes, rushed to the Thames-side at Windsor to-night to build an emergency wall to prevent water from flooding into the town.

Windsor Corporation had ordered an emergency floodbank to be built at this vulnerable point after another day during which the level of the Thames rose rapidly.

It is now 4ft. 7in. above normal and within a few inches of the top of the wall. To-night men have been building a clay bank, 200yds. long and 2ft. high, on top of the flood wall.

At the other end of the town the £30,000 flood defences built three years ago are holding out against the rising river, and Windsor, although it has water all round it, has no floods in the streets.

The river at Windsor Ferry is now three miles wide.

Eton, on the other side of the river, is now surrounded by water and many of the roads are flooded.

To-night the floods crossed the main road to Dorney and a temporary footbridge was erected for pedestrians, as this road is the only one that serves the villages of Dorney, Boveney and Eton Wick.

The Thames Conservancy officials stated to-night that they thought the peak of the flooding had been reached.

Floods in the Fens.—Page 5.

IGNORES DREAM, IS INJURED

RICHARD OWENS, fifty-eight, ironstone miner, of Wellingborough, awoke yesterday and told his wife that in a dream he had seen himself injured in a road accident.

Mrs Owens advised her husband that the dream was a warning for him not to cycle the six miles to work.

He set out and four miles from home he was seriously injured in a collision with a car driven by Mr. C. W. Coleman, of The Strand, London, managing director of a mining equipment firm.

Wendy Hiller, star of the film, "Pygmalion," gave birth to a daughter in London last night.

Miss Hiller is the wife of Mr. Ronald Gow, the author, whom she married in 1937.

A Lancashire girl, she won stage fame in a night by her performance in the play Love on the Dole," in 1935.

Mr. Gow told the "Daily Mirror" last night: "Mrs. Gow and the baby are doing fine.

"What does the baby weigh? I have been too excited to find that out.

"We haven't thought of a name for baby yet."

At the nursing home the "Daily Mirror" learned that the baby weighs 7lb. 6oz.

KING'S SHIP: GUNS TO STAY

WHEN the King and Queen sail for Canada in H.M.S. Repulse in May, the battle-cruiser will carry her full complement of armaments.

An Admiralty announcement last night stated:—

"The plans for the accommodation of their Majesties in H.M.S. Repulse for their forthcoming visit to Canada originally involved the removal of some of the ship's anti-aircraft armament.

"It has now been decided that the arrangements in the ship for their Majesties and their suite shall be modified in such a way as not to interfere with her fighting efficiency."

Repulse is undergoing extensive alterations at Portsmouth to provide better accommodation for the Royal party.

An extra deck is being built into her aft superstructure.

A special orchestra and military band will provide music.

HITLER'S TWO AND A QUARTER HOUR SPEECH TO THE REICHSTAG IN BERLIN LAST NIGHT PUZZLED EUROPE.

He demanded Colonies—without war. He claimed friendship with Britain—and threatened her with an economic and propaganda war.

He promised Italy the complete support of Germany in her territorial claims—and HE PROPHESIED A LONG PERIOD OF PEACE.

Hitler made it clear that he had no immediate territorial ambitions in Europe; no designs on Holland or Switzerland. But his pledge to Italy was emphatic.

"If Italy is involved in a war it is absolutely certain that Germany will be on the side of Italy. Fascist Italy and Nazi Germany will secure European civilisation."

It was for civilisation, too, he said, that Germany and Italy supported General Franco in his fight "against Bolshevism."

But Hitler admitted that Germany was faced with economic difficulties. "But we will win this struggle"—his voice rose—"I tell you we have already won it."

"IF We Are Threatened"

He warned Germany that exports must be increased, that there could be no increase in wages. "We must export or die . . . and the German people will not die."

He replied to the threat of economic war uttered by Mr Hudson in the House of Commons with a counter-threat.

"If foreign statesmen threaten us with economic counter-measures I can only assure you that in such a case a desperate economic war will begin which will be easier for us than for other over-saturated nations."

And he attacked again the leaders of Democratic countries who oppose his policy—Mr. Eden, Mr. Duff-Cooper, Mr Ickes the U.S. Secretary of State.

The B.B.C. broadcasts have amazed Germany, and the recent appeal to the German people inspired this passage in the Fuehrer's speech:—

"I WISH TO MAKE THE FOLLOWING WARNING PUBLIC: IF THE BROADCASTS SENT FROM CERTAIN COUNTRIES TO GERMANY DO NOT CEASE WE WILL SOON ANSWER THEM."

He reaffirmed his friendship with Japan: "It would be folly to assume that a defeat of Japan could be of value to Europe. It would

(Continued on back page)

Unazimous

Before Herr Hitler's speech began a member of the Reichstag said: "I propose to re-elect Field-Marshal Goering President of the Reichstag, and Herren Kerrl Esser and Von Schaussen Vice-President.

"The vote will be taken by every member rising to his feet."

The whole Reichstag rose.

They agreed that the powers of the Government to legislate have been extended for a further period of four years.

"WE'D CLOSE OUR RANKS"

—Earl Baldwin

IF ever the time comes when war is inevitable, I know this: that our people will brace themselves to stand that first shock and that whether it be short or long, there can be but one result.

"This country, with a cause to fight for—the liberty of the human spirit—will fight with a unanimity of all classes and all ranks that has never been seen in any war that has yet taken place."

Earl Baldwin said this last night at a Worcester meeting of women to encourage National Service recruitment.

He declared: "We are an extremely difficult people for foreigners to understand.

"There are two very dangerous illusions about us in parts of the Continent of Europe.

"One is that we are afraid of war, and the second is that our people will never make the sacrifices that are necessary to organise themselves in the event of war."

Munitions Race Tragedy

"They are dangerous because, it believed, they may lead people to take a course which they would not take if they knew that their belief was wrong."

He said that while he knew that unless the will to peace existed in the hearts and souls of all the leaders in Europe, there might come a time when war would be inevitable.

After commending things done for their people by Hitler and Mussolini, Lord Baldwin said: "To me it is so sad to see them compromising the opportunity of their own class to improve a low standard of living by keeping them at work making munitions for a bloody war."

He revealed that before he retired from the Premiership, he discussed with Mr. Chamberlain Britain's "new diplomacy" of personal contact between heads of States, and said to him: "I wish I could have done it myself, but my bolt is shot." He added: "We shook hands on it."

DAILY MIRROR, Thursday, February 2, 1939.

Daily Mirror

No. 10,970   ONE PENNY
Registered at the G.P.O. as a Newspaper.
Geraldine House, Fetter-lane, E.C.4.
HOLBORN 4321.

Lost Number

BY A SPECIAL CORRESPONDENT.

"I have a pound note," I said yesterday to the Principal of the Issue Department, Bank of England.

"Congratulations," the Principal gravely replied.

"But," I said, "it has no number in the top right-hand corner."

"WHAT; No serial number!" The Principal of the Issue Department, Bank of England, had very nearly shrieked.

Then he found his composure and in the best tones of Threadneedle - street said: "That's most unusual . . . most unusual.

"Occasionally a faulty note gets out and yours must have been missed. Notes are subject to the most careful examination . . . most careful."

I pocketed my note. I have a use for it. If ever things get a bit dull I shall stroll along to the bank, plank my pound on the counter and demand, "What do you know about that?"

SAFE IN VAN CUT IN TWO BY A TRAIN

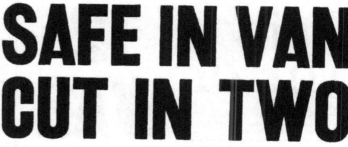

HIS VAN CUT IN TWO BY A FORTY-MILE-AN-HOUR EXPRESS, THE DRIVER, A YOUTH OF SEVENTEEN, WAS LEFT SITTING UNHURT AT THE WHEEL... BUT WITH NO FRONT WHEELS TO DRIVE.

One wheel was yards up the line . . . the engine, torn clean from the chassis, lay at the side of the track. A bit of tangled metal was all that remained of what was once the bonnet.

White with the shock of the crash, the driver, George Thompson, of Sand Hutton, near Thirsk (Yorks), sat at his wheel unable to move until the train was pulled away from the wreckage of his van.

Freed, he walked up to the engine-driver, said, with a smile: "That was a narrow squeak," and then ran off to tell his employer —not of his narrow squeak, but of the damage to his van.

The crash occurred as Thompson was driving over a level crossing on the Northallerton-Hawes railway at Ainderley Steeple, near Northallerton.

The express, racing along at forty miles an hour, smashed into the van near the windscreen and cut it clean in two.

A shower of metal and glass was thrown into the air and horrified railway officials ran forward, expecting to find the driver dead. But he sat at his wheel, unhurt.

"Opened the Gates"

Later, Thompson told the *Daily Mirror*: When I got to the crossing and opened the gates there was no train in sight.

"I had just set off across the lines in the van when the train came round the corner and crashed into the front of the van.

"Another few inches and it would have cut me in halves, as well as the van.

"I was too surprised to realise what it felt like to have such a narrow escape.

"No, it didn't shake me up all that much. Anyway I kept at work all day."

DEAD GIRL: MAN CHARGED

FROM OUR SPECIAL CORRESPONDENT

ROMFORD, Thursday.

LEONARD Richardson was charged at the police station here this morning with the murder of Pamela Coventry, the nine-year-old Hornchurch girl, whose body was found in a ditch on January 19. Richardson will appear in court this morning.

He is aged thirty, and lives in Coronation-drive, Hornchurch. He is married and has one child, aged three weeks.

Late last night police paid a surprise visit to a house in Hornchurch, and Richardson went with them in a patrol car to the police station here for questioning.

Chief Inspector Bridger, of Scotland Yard, Divisional Detective-Inspector Baker and Superintendent Totterdell were present at the police station.

Last night's moves followed a conference at Scotland Yard between Chief Inspector Bridger and Chief Constable Horwell, the head of the C.I.D.

The dead child lived in Morecambe-close, Hornchurch.

Her body, unclothed, bound with 15ft. of insulated flex, was found in a 5ft. deep ditch in Wood-lane.

Police and 200 R.A.F. men from Hornchurch station searched for six miles around to try to find her clothes.

Thousands of people were questioned by the police.

Sir Bernard Spilsbury, the pathologist, said at the opening of the inquest, that Pamela had been strangled.

RANG CHANGES ON HER 2s.

A TWOPENNY bus fare cost Mrs. Jack Soulal, of Linden-gardens, London, W., exactly 1s. 8½d.

She gave the conductor 2s. and received 1s. 10d. change. Still her fare cost her 1s. 8½d.

When she reached home she found a Kruger shilling of 1892, an Australian sixpence, an Irish penny and an Indian halfpenny in her bag.

The Australian sixpence is the only one of the four worth anything. Coin experts valued it at 3½d. So Mrs. Soulal is 1s. 6½d. out.

MOST NOBLE MOTHER IN BRITAIN

Mrs. Emelia Bibby, of Hull, is mother of the boy who couldn't grow up. For seventeen years she did not have a single night's unbroken sleep. On page 15 you will see the story of her devotion.

COUNTESS WED COACHMAN

FROM OUR OWN CORRESPONDENT

HOVE, Wednesday.

THE Countess who ran away with James, her coachman, died at Hove yesterday. She was ninety-three.

Countess Ravensworth, the beautiful, brilliant leader of Edwardian society, was widowed when her second husband the Earl of Ravensworth, died in 1903.

A year later, when she was fifty-seven, she married James William Wadsworth, the handsome, genteel coachman who had always driven the Earl and Countess.

The runaway marriage shocked English society, and ended the Countess's social career. James didn't care. He scorned the idle life of the aristocracy, but remained the loyal servant of his wife faithfully carrying out M'lady's wishes.

He was asked once why they had married. "It was m'lady's wish," James answered. That had been enough for him.

But the Countess couldn't remain in England with the doors of society closed to her. They went to America. Soon the Countess

(Continued on back page)

DAILY MIRROR, Friday, February 3, 1939.

Daily Mirror

No. 10,971   ONE PENNY

Registered at the G.P.O. as a Newspaper.
Geraldine House, Fetter-lane, E.C.4.
HOLBORN 4321.

12 WAR DICTATORS IN BRITAIN

BRITAIN, in the event of war, will be divided into twelve areas, each of which will be ruled by a Commissioner with the powers of a dictator.

The plan, which will be completed in every detail by the end of this month, covers the possibility of any one area being completely cut off from the rest of the country and from the centre of Government.

"In that event," said Sir John Anderson, the A.R.P. Minister who disclosed the plan last night, "it will be necessary for the Commissioner to exercise the full authority of the Government."

The area dictators will have full powers to act under the Defence of the Realm Act, will have full staffs a free hand to spend money.

The men have yet to be chosen. "We want big names," Sir John Anderson adds. "Men with something behind them."

The plan is described on page 6.

You May Store Food

The Government will not object if householders store about a week's supply of food to hold in case of war Mr. Oliver Stanley, Board of Trade President, announced in the House of Commons yesterday.

But, he made it clear, that does not mean that hoarding of big supplies would be encouraged, nor must you make a last-minute rush to buy stocks in an emergency.

You must buy in normal times.

And you need not store water. The supply in your household tanks is sufficient reserve to keep.

Mr. Stanley said that accumulation by householders in peace time of small reserves would be a useful addition to the total stocks of the country. It would not be taken into account by the Government in seeing that adequate supplies are available to all in an emergency. "I must make it clear," he said, "that in an emergency household reserves might be requisitioned by the Government.

But No Hoarding

"There is a clear distinction between the accumulation of small stocks in peace time and food hoarding in war."

Britain's defence gaps are being filled, but greater effort is still needed. That is the conclusion of the Advisory Panel on Rearming who have been studying the problem for the past month.

"In some cases," the report says, "practically new industries are being established."

Germany has now officially informed Britain that she intends to build submarines until she has as many as Britain.

AND HE NEVER SENT THE WIRE!

AMERICAN pole-squatters and dance marathon champions have a rival—a non-stop writer.

At 8 a.m. yesterday a tall, dark man entered Fleet-street Post Office, E.C., went to the telegram cubicle and started to write. And he went on writing all day.

Only once did he look up—when a reporter asked him if he was writing a book.

He smiled and said: "My name is Smith, and I am trying to get through some private work. That is all there is to it."

Some time after 6 p.m. a member of the staff noticed that he had gone. The assumption is that he decided on reflection not to send a telegram!

IN CAR CRASH —BUT DANCED BEFORE QUEEN

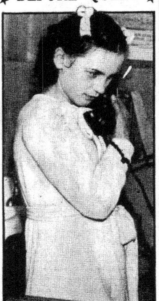

Mina Jordan, aged thirteen—you see her in this picture—is a ballet dancer. She was chosen to dance before Queen Mary at Sadler's Wells Theatre, Islington, last night.

On the way to the theatre, the car she was in crashed into another and Mina was badly bruised.

But she danced before Queen Mary all the same. You'll find the full story on the back page.

A dozen men at the bar, drinking lunchtime beer . . . peace in the Crown Hotel, Leiston (Suffolk).

His back to the fire stands stoker Albert James Goodwin, mug in hand.

✦ ✦ ✦

Suddenly a loud Pop! and stoker Goodwin goes up in flames!

A pint bottle of petrol in his coat pocket had burst.

✦ ✦ ✦

"In a moment," says the landlord, "the whole bar was alight. Goodwin sprang on a table, over it went, tipping over a lighted oil stove, and that made matters worse. His lighted clothes dropped from him and set fire to the floor boards."

✦ ✦ ✦

Goodwin was taken outside by a man named Larter and rolled in an overcoat on the pavement. Larter said: "I heard a pop as if a cork had blown and Goodwin burst into flames."

Goodwin was seriously burned. Larter and two other men were burned helping him and at one time the whole hotel was threatened by fire.

The Stoker Went Up in Flames

SPREES SAVED HIM £31

WHEN Benjamin Charles Richards, now twenty-four, of Penarth-road, Cardiff, went out with a bachelor friend, his companion made a mental note of anything Ben paid when he did not contribute.

This arrangement had been in force secretly for five years, and always these expenses—an odd drink, a bus fare—were jotted down.

When he married Miss Maud Turner, of Cardiff, his friend, shaking him by the hand as he offered his congratulations, gave him an envelope with "Here's something for the wedding, Ben. Hope it will do."

Tearing open the envelope, commercial traveller Benjamin Richards, who had just sold his car to help set up home, found a cheque inside for £31 10s.

"Why all this?" he asked.

Then his friend explained.

"Surprising how it mounts up," Ben's friend said. "Often you have paid for something when I had no change, and instead of paying you back immediately, I kept it in my mind and after all these years, £31 10s. is the total."

Made It His Hobby

Mr. Richards refuses to reveal the name of his friend. "It would hurt his feelings if I did," he told the "Daily Mirror" last night. "He was to have been my best man, but owing to his work could not arrive in time.

"He first thought of the idea about five years ago and made a hobby of it right up to the time I married.

"I always used to buy our tickets for football matches in Cardiff, so I suppose he put that down every week.

"Scores of times during the past five years I have paid small bus fares, but I never dreamed my pal was keeping a regular check.

"When I tackled him about the money after the wedding, he told me that each night he wrote down the items on the back of an envelope, totted up the total at the end of the week, then entered it in his diary."

400 M.P.H. DIVE TO 20FT. 'TOMB'

ROARING down from 2,000ft. like a shell, a Hawker Hurricane monoplane crashed into a field in a 400 m.p.h. power dive last evening and dug a 20ft. tomb for the pilot.

Like a projectile the 'plane came down. People two miles away saw fragments burst away and fall.

Earth slipped back over the buried pilot and his machine. For hours workmen dug before they could reach him.

Only a few struts pointed above the ground. The dead pilot, Terence Hugh Knapp O'Brien, of the 87th Fighter Squadron attached to the R.A.F. station at Debden, Essex, was still in the wrecked cockpit when he was found.

The 'plane buried itself within 200 yards of the farmhouse of Mr. and Mrs. Ketley, of Pamphillia Farm, close to the Debden flying field.

It is understood that the pilot's family live in Kenya.

DAILY MIRROR, Saturday, February 4, 1939.

Daily Mirror

No. 10,972   ONE PENNY
Registered at the G.P.O. as a Newspaper.
Geraldine House, Fetter-lane, E.C.4.
HOLBORN 4321.

ONE-ARMED, SHE HAS TWINS

FROM OUR OWN CORRESPONDENT
NEWTON ABBOT (Devon),
Friday.

WITH a smile, a mother to-day began the greatest task in the life of a woman with a handicap which would drive thousands to despair.

Twins have been born to her, making a family of three children—and the mother has only one arm.

To-day Mrs. Ellen Good, of Hill Crest, Stoke Gabriel, Devon, came downstairs for the first time since the twins were born.

You see her, in the picture on the left, holding the twins on her shortened arm, while her eighteen-month-old daughter, home once again after staying with friends, peeps at the new arrivals.

Though born without a left forearm, Mrs. Good is happy with her family around her. Feeding, bathing, dressing, mending—problems to many a mother—do not beat her.

"I shall not fail to see that my three children are as well cared for as other children," she told me.

"Nothing I Cannot Do"

"It is the first time I have been on my own, but I bathed the twins this morning and fed them. There is nothing I cannot do for them."

Holding her twins, David and Diana, born on January 20, on her shortened arm and with auburn-haired Rosemary holding her dress, Mrs. Good fed one and then the other of the twins from tiny bottles as capably as any normal woman.

"Don't you like their clothing?" she asked. "That is all my work. I can knit, sew and stitch on buttons without any difficulty."

Villagers of Stoke Gabriel praise Mrs. Good, and District Nurse V. Baker told me: "You could go into many houses here, run by women with both hands and without children, and not find them as neat and trim."

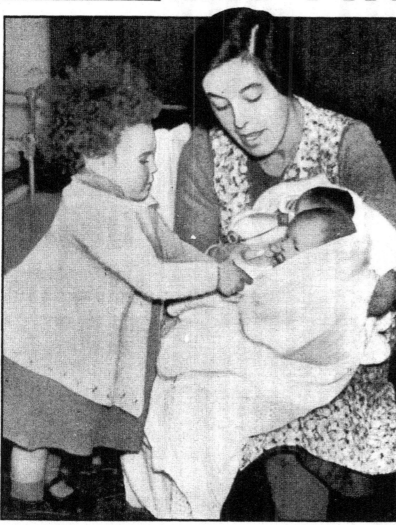

7 BOMBS FOUND

SEVEN hand grenades were found by C.I.D. officers in the garden of a house in Fairholt-road, Stoke Newington, N., late last night. Four of them were charged.

The discovery was made after a day of intense activity by hundreds of policemen seeking the terrorists whose bombs wrecked the luggage rooms of two Underground stations yesterday.

At King's Cross an anonymous telephone caller warned officials: "Remove all parcels deposited since one o'clock. There may be bombs . . . I am a member of the gang." A search was made. No bombs were found.

An hour later a shot was fired at a signalman in his box on the L.N.E.R. line between East Finchley and Highgate Stations.

Police were called. They searched along the line and in the nearby Highgate woods. The signalman was not hit.

Armed detectives in Manchester raided thirty houses in the city this morning. One man was detained for questioning at police headquarters.

All last night police guards patrolled every Underground station in London.

Chief attention centred on stations of the North London line where, early yesterday, two time-fused bombs rocked Tottenham Court-road and Leicester-square stations, injuring seven people.

(Continued on back page)

GARLIC FOR THE DUCHESS

FROM OUR OWN CORRESPONDENT
NEW YORK, Friday.

THE Duke and Duchess of Windsor have adopted a special diet in which garlic is a prominent feature, according to a health expert who has arrived here from Paris.

The expert is Dr. Benjamin Gayelord Hauser. The diet he prescribes includes garlic, juices of spinach, carrots and celery as an aid to health.

"The Duke and Duchess," he said, "are probably the most slender and the healthiest couple in world.

"I met the Duchess when Lady Mendl invited twelve of the most glamorous women of the world to tea.

"I told them the damage caused by wrong eating and how they could retain their glamour for a much longer time."

Mr. Herman Rogers, the friend of the Duke and Duchess, who arrived here to-day, confirmed that they were on a special diet.

MAN WHO BEAT FORGERS

A receiving order has been made on a creditor's petition against Lieutenant-Colonel Vladimir Mansfield, the handwriting expert and bane of forgers, of Flodden-road, Camberwell, S.E., according to last night's "London Gazette." Colonel Mansfield, in 1932, perfected a new means of detecting forgeries by ultra-violet ray photography. His discoveries interested Scotland Yard, and he was called as a witness in famous cases.

Irish, Ticked Himself Off

A Japanese student and an Irishman gave good-natured Mr. Harry Skinner, of Oakington Manor-drive, Wembley, who is retiring from the Information Bureau at Euston Station, the biggest laughs of his forty years' service with the L.M.S. He told the "Daily Mirror" yesterday:

"The Japanese student, text book in hand, addressed me with a ceremonial bow and said: 'Dear sir or madam, as the case may be——'

"The Irishman, asking for the time of a train for the second time, said: 'I am not asking for myself this time, but for my brother.'"

DAILY MIRROR, Monday, February 6, 1939

Daily Mirror

No. 10,973   ONE PENNY

Registered at the G.P.O. as a Newspaper.
Geraldine House, Fetter-lane, E.C.4.
HOLBORN 4321.

Cutting Out the Dead Wood

Lord Chatfield, the new Minister for Co-ordination of Defence, who arrived from India by air during the week-end. He stayed with his son-in-law, Mr. Patrick Donner, M.P., and his daughter, Mrs. Donner (seen with him in this picture), at their home near Whitfield (Hants).

To-day he starts on his new job. He is expected to CUT QUITE A LOT OF DEAD WOOD AWAY DURING THE NEXT FEW WEEKS !

BEATEN ARMY QUIT TO FRANCE

THE war in Catalonia is over. To-day the Republican Army that retreated before the Franco advance on Barcelona will march in formation over the frontier into France.

There they will lay down their arms. A huge concentration camp has been prepared by the French authorities near St. Cyprean. The defeated army will be interned in the camp until arrangements can be made for their return.

Three Republic Presidents—Azana, the President of the Republic, Luis Companys, Catalan President, and Antonio de Aguirre, the ex-footballer President of the Basques—fled over the frontier yesterday.

Behind them came 4,500 caribineers, the first of the fighting men to be allowed to enter France.

And at eight o'clock this morning the march of the defeated army will begin.

The Spanish Government has gone. Its destination is said to be Madrid, but in France it is understood that they will establish their headquarters in Valencia.

The Government, according to an unofficial statement, has offered to come to terms with the rebels. Franco refuses. Unconditional surrender, he says, is the only way to peace.

Meanwhile France, alarmed at the approach of Italian troops on her Spanish frontier, has appealed to Franco.

The rebel chief last night announced that he had withdrawn the only Italian division operating near the frontier.

Eighty-six Spanish Republican warplanes are reported to have crossed the frontier between Spain and France.

Twenty-five of the machines landed at Carcassonne, in the Aude department, sixty miles from the Spanish frontier.

The French authorities fear that, as fighting

(Continued on back page)

Ice Girl on £166 a Day Trip

FROM OUR OWN CORRESPONDENT

New York, Sunday.

The Normandie has left New York on the most luxurious cruise ever planned. There are 743 passengers. All are wealthy; most of them are millionaires. They have paid £200,000 in passage money.

When the ship reaches Nassau in the Bahamas, Sonja Henie, the skating film star, will come aboard with her party. She has booked a suite that cost £1,500.

Sonja has six guests, including her mother and brother and two servants. Their fares cost Sonja £1,800—and her £3,300 bill does not include special entertaining.

The Normandie is bound for South America and the West Indies and the £200,000 cruise will last only twenty-four days.

In that time gallons of champagne and expensive wines will be consumed; rare food cooked by the most famous chefs afloat will be served. For the number of millionaires is the largest that has ever filled a passenger list.

Sonja Henie can afford to eat, drink and make merry on the millionaire standard. At twenty-six, she has an income of £1,000 a week. Her recent " personal appearance " tour of U.S.A. brought her in £80,000.

During that tour her hosiery bill was £500. While she skates she wears silk tights that cost £7 a pair—and she changes five times a day.

The cruise will cost Sonja about £166 a day, which is not much more than she earns every day.

FOUGHT 'DROME RAIDER

A POLICEMAN was wounded last night while preventing what is believed to have been an attempt to blow up Rochester Aerodrome.

Police-constable H. Ovenden was on motor-cycle patrol on the Chatham-Maidstone road when he saw a man dart into the shadow of a hanger of the Rochester Naval Auxiliary Flying School.

Ovenden jumped from his motor-cycle, leaped a fence, and ran towards the hangar, from which a man dashed into the grounds of Rochester Airport.

Escaped in Car

Ovenden overtook him and grappled with him. After a struggle of several minutes the man was almost overpowered, but a second man came to his help. Ovenden was struck on the back of the head and pulled to the ground.

As he got up, dazed, blood streaming from his head, Ovenden saw the men escaping in a large car.

He ran to the flying school, phoned Chatham police, and an S O S was immediately circulated throughout the area.

House Raided

Rochester, Gillingham and Maidstone mobile police joined in a search of the district. Motorists were stopped and questioned.

Flying school officers and men searched the hangars. The police guard at the school was doubled and armed detectives patrolled the grounds.

Special precautions are also being taken at Rochester Airport, where Messrs. Short Brothers have aeroplane works employing 1,300 men, and Messrs. Pobjoy have an aeroplane engine factory.

Police last night raided a house at Ilford, where they found fifteen sticks of gelignite.

Midnight threat to works—Page 3

JOHN GOES TO SEA

ALL his life John Elliott longed to go to sea. As a boy his parents killed his secret ambition by putting him to work in an insurance office, and they nearly broke his heart.

John did well at his job. But the spell of the sea never died in him.

When at last he retired from business he was too old to answer the call—but not too old to dream of what-might-have-been.

Although he was now eighty-six, and almost blind, this ex-insurance official spent hours on Newcastle quayside watching ships come and go.

At the week-end John Elliott left his home at Hedley-street, Gosforth, near Newcastle saying, as usual, that he'd be back soon.

Two Riddles . .

Fourteen hours later a log raft was seen floating down the Tyne towards the sea. And on the raft lay the old man—dead. But he had not been drowned; only his legs were wet.

How the old man reached the spot and exactly how he died are questions which are puzzling the police.

They believe that he got on the raft—one of hundreds tied alongside one or other of the saw mills on the bank—and that the rising tide carried it away into midstream.

So John Elliott, his eyes still on far horizons set out at last for the sea. . .

DAILY MIRROR, Thursday, February 9, 1939.

Daily Mirror

No. 10,976.   ONE PENNY.
Registered at the G.P.O. as a Newspaper.
Geraldine House, Fetter-lane, E.C.4.
HOLBORN 4321.

BRITAIN SENDS

H.M.S. Devonshire, which dashed with General Franco's envoys to a peace parley at Minorca.

SHIP TO SETTLE SPAIN WAR

BY OUR POLITICAL CORRESPONDENT

A MESSAGE, flashed from the Admiralty yesterday, sent the British cruiser Devonshire on a dramatic peace mission to the Mediterranean island of Minorca.

The Devonshire lay off Majorca, the Franco-controlled island largely occupied by Italian troops and airmen.

Her captain—Captain G. C. Muirhead-Gould—received his orders as soon as yesterday's British Cabinet meeting ended at 10, Downing-street.

With envoys from General Franco on board the Devonshire sailed for Minorca.

There, on board the cruiser, Franco's men met the representatives of the loyal garrison who hold Minorca for Government Spain.

If the talks are successful, Minorca will be spared the bloodshed of a sea and air bombardment and the horrors of a long siege.

That can be achieved only if Minorca surrenders and Britain is urging the garrison to adopt this course.

Captain Muirhead-Gould has been charged with the task of bringing the two sides together—a delicate diplomatic task seldom entrusted to a naval officer.

Italy Calls Up Men

It is believed in Whitehall that an island truce will now be arranged and that this may lead to the greater achievement of bringing peace throughout Spain.

Mr. Chamberlain in the House of Commons yesterday was asked if the British Government's view was that the Italian Government had undertaken to withdraw troops as soon as hostilities cease in Spain.

Mr. Chamberlain said : " Yes."

In Rome last night it was unofficially reported, says British United Press, that officers and specialists had been hurriedly called to the colours.

At the same time 50,000 to 80,000 Italian soldiers are being assembled in certain ports owing to "reported French troop movements in Tunisia."

The Italian Supreme Defence Council was stated to have discussed details of the new preparedness programme, including the question of calling up more reservists

Signor Mussolini, who presided over the council, said Italy must inform the world that she is speeding up her preparations.

WIVES LACK WORK

SUBURBAN nerviness, that state of mind which makes a wife worry herself into illness, is due to too many labour-saving devices and too little work, a doctor declared yesterday.

And the doctor was a woman, Dr. Elizabeth Sloan Chesser, who was addressing the New Health Club, in London.

She said that at least one-third of the illness in this country was due to nervous trouble.

Some psychologists, she said, declared that it resulted from an attempt to retreat from life. A person would argue: "If I am too ill I cannot be expected to visit my mother-in-law."

So he or she developed a headache, and it was a real headache, too.

Mental Age—18

Dr. Chesser said that she did not believe any of those listening to her were mentally over eighteen years of age. She told one wife recently that her husband had the mentality of a public schoolboy of fifteen.

"Fifteen," replied the wife, "he's two.'
"She was quite right but I was trying to soften it for her," added the doctor. (Laughter.)

Referring to the type of nervy persons who wanted all the time to talk about themselves and their love affairs and emotional feelings, Dr. Chesser said: "The best secretary is the person who can forget her own nerviness and think of that of her employer."

Dog Acts as Cupid

Dorothy Russell, twenty-one, of Rathmoor Hall, Sheffield, thanks her fox terrier, Dinah Leigh, for bringing her the man of her dreams.

Two years ago, after she returned from America with her dog, Dinah Leigh developed distemper. She took it along to the vet, gave it in charge of a handsome young surgeon, twenty-four-year-old David W. Caldwell.

He fell in love with Dorothy at sight and on February 18 they will be married.

Miss Russell told the " Daily Mirror " yesterday: " I liked David from the start, and a few months later when he asked me to marry him I accepted. Then he proclaimed Dinah Leigh to be fit again.

" In fact, she seemed to be very encouraged by our engagement. A few weeks after we announced our engagement, Dinah Leigh presented us with a pup—we called her Carolina."

You see Dorothy and David, with Dinah Leigh—and Carolina—in the picture below. They'll all meet at the wedding, too.

'GET OUT !'

shouted 600 women to two men at Ilford Town Hall last night Then they threw them out.

The women were listening to an A.R.P. address by Lady Reading when the two men rushed on the platform.

They unfurled a banner, "Let unemployed men build A.R.P. shelters." Then the women surrounded them and hustled them out.

'STAY IN !'

shouted a dozen women to the district officer at the Nottingham Unemployment Assistance Board yesterday.

They tried to lock him in his office as a demonstration against " intolerable conditions." But he pacified them and they let him go.

Treat yourself to a Guinness

Daily Mirror

No. 10,977.   ONE PENNY

Registered at the G.P.O. as a Newspaper.
Geraldine House, Fetter-lane, E.C.4.
HOLBORN 4321.

The Queen's Sister-in-Law Fined

The Hon. Mrs. Elizabeth Margaret Bowes-Lyon, sister-in-law of the Queen, and wife of the Hon. Michael Bowes-Lyon, of Gastlings, Southill (Beds), was fined £2 at Stevenage (Herts) yesterday for exceeding the speed limit in her motor-car at Knebworth on January 17.

Her licence was endorsed.

SPAIN 'CEASE FIRE'

BY OUR POLITICAL CORRESPONDENT

BUGLES will sound the "Cease Fire" in Spain next week and the civil war that has been fought for nearly three years will end.

To-day a meeting of Cabinet Ministers in London will decide, in concert with France, to recognise General Franco as the ruler of Spain.

It is proposed that representatives of the two sides will attend a peace conference at which Britain and France will act as mediators.

The British Government urged Dr. Negrin, the Spanish Premier, to end hostilities at once and to recommend a plebiscite of the people to decide how they shall be governed.

Franco will be urged to grant an amnesty, to order the withdrawal of volunteers and military advisers and to guarantee not to hand over any territory to foreign Powers.

Whitehall is confident that these terms will be accepted.

When they are, Britain proposes to offer a loan to Franco to help in the reconstruction of war-battered Spain.

Negotiations will also be begun to ensure that Britain's trade with Spain is not handicapped.

New Move by Axis?

General Miaja, the hero of the Madrid defence, has already been given British and French passport visas, and a British cruiser will be at his disposal to take him to a place of safety.

It is generally expected that Miaja will capitulate in order to avoid further bloodshed.

Dr. Negrin has telegraphed appointing him Generalissimo of the Republican land, air and sea forces in Central and Southern Spain.

Anxiety is felt in diplomatic circles as to Rome-Berlin reactions to Franco coming to an agreement with Britain and France.

Concentration of troops is reported from Italian ports, Genoa and Spezzia.

Twenty German submarines are at present in Mediterranean waters.

The Rome-Berlin axis may launch a new adventure to prevent the Spanish war ending in circumstances favourable to British and French interests.

HELEN HAYES BITTEN

Stage and screen star Helen Hayes was bitten on the face, arms and hand in New York yesterday when she went to the rescue of her tiny Yorkshire terrier attacked by three big dogs.

Again and again she threw herself into the fray, despite three bites from one dog. Doctors ordered her to bed and said the bites would leave no permanent scars.

THE KING MAKES BOY OF 5 'SIR'

A BOY aged five was created a baronet last night with the special approval of the King.

He is Sir Andrew Hills. Death robbed his father of the title that would have been bestowed on him in the last New Year's Honours.

And as they told Sir Andrew of his new rank last night he sat up in bed and asked:

"MUMMY. WHAT IS A BARONETCY. IS IT SOMETHING TO EAT?"

His cousin Stella—" she's my sweetheart

(Continued on back page)

Sir Andrew Ashton Waller Hills . . . a baronet at five.

"BOMB" WAS A FIREWORK

SIRENS screaming, three police cars and a radio car raced into Macdonald-road, Walthamstow, E., last night. Officers poured out, questioned everybody in sight.

Someone had dialled "999" and said "bomb."

But it wasn't a bomb—it was a firework.

Walthamstow was having a big A.R.P. demonstration.

About 1,000 auxiliary firemen, first aid workers, decontamination squads and other helpers were taking part in rescue operations of Boy Scout and Girl Guide "victims," gassed, wounded or trapped in imaginary blazing houses wrecked by imaginary bombs.

Rang Scotland Yard

In the middle of it all someone let off the firework near a factory engaged on Government contract work.

A watchman heard, rang Scotland Yard and said he thought there was another I.R.A. outrage. Hence the excitement.

THE POPE: GRAVE FEARS

THE condition of the Pope, who has been ill for several days, was stated this morning to be "very serious" following two heart attacks during the day.

After the second attack he was unable to speak. His entourage fear the worst.

He is reported to be suffering from cardiac asthma and bronchial pneumonia.

Dr. Filippo Rocchi, who is attending the Pope while Professor Aminta Milani, his usual physician, is ill, again spent last night in the Pope's room. Four Franciscan monks were acting as nurses.

Rome's churches last night were thronged with crowds of the faithful, mostly women, praying for the Pope's recovery.

Reuter and British United Press

DAILY MIRROR, Wed., February 15, 1939

Daily Mirror

No. 10,981   ONE PENNY

Registered at the G.P.O. as a Newspaper
Geraldine House, Fetter-lane, E.C.4
HOLBORN 4321.

Faced Death on Their Honeymoon

They faced death for one and a half hours yesterday, the couple in this picture.

They're Mr. and Mrs. Altmann, just returned by air from their honeymoon in Austria to make their home in Liverpool. You see them here at Croydon Airport.

When the 'plane reached Croydon, the landing gear jammed. The machine circled round for an hour and a half while the crew tried to get it free . . . and Mr. and Mrs. Altmann joked with the other five passengers.

✦ ✦ ✦

Eventually the pilot brought the 'plane down with one wheel out of action . . . and landed without any of the occupants being injured and with no serious damage to the 'plane.

★ Full story and dramatic pictures are on page 14.

ABSENTEE FOOD CHIEF IS PAID £5 A WEEK

SIR Reginald Ford, the retired soldier who will control London's food supplies in the next war, lives in Brussels, has no staff, does no work—and gets 250 guineas a year for doing it.

His appointment was assailed in the House of Commons last night when M.P.s demanded to know why Sir Reginald lived abroad—a fact first revealed in the " Daily Mirror."

" Is the fact that he lives in Brussels likely to inspire public confidence," asked Mr. Bellenger, M.P. for Bassetlaw.

He quoted Sir Reginald Ford as saying that he could " Hop into an aeroplane and get from Brussels to his office in Westminster in three hours, or in less time than if he lived in Scotland.

" That attitude," said Mr. Bellenger, " is an insult to public opinion and it is an affront to those well-meaning people who have the interests of their country at heart and are responding to the country's call."

He Has No Staff

Mr. Oliver Stanley, the President of the Board of Trade, said the duties of the divisional food officer in peace time were not very great. The payment of a retaining fee was not so much a payment for his services in peace time as to ensure that when war started he would be able to take up the post of divisional officer.

He had no responsibility for the preparation of plans for rationing and preparing for emergency distribution of food.

He had no staff—the 130 people who had been described as his staff were in fact the staff of his (Mr Stanley's) Food Defence Department

Action To Be Taken

The retaining fee was not payment for services rendered at the moment.

Mr. Ellis Smith (Lab., Stoke-on-Trent): Compare it with what the unemployed receive.

Mr. Oliver Stanley: Compare it with what Mr. Ellis Smith is drawing.

Mr. A. V. Alexander said that many people had given their time, their brains and their staffs to the service of the country for nearly three years. Then three months ago the Government appointed to this position a retired Army officer of General rank and therefore in receipt of a pension of well over £1,000 a year.

The attack had its effect. When Mr.

(Continued on back page)

SHOT RECLUSE : MAN CHARGED

GEORGE HENRY WILLIS, aged about twenty-eight, of Braywick Cottages, near Maidenhead, was taken to Ascot Police Station late last night and charged with murdering Frederick James Paul, eighty-five-year-old recluse, who was found shot dead in a pond at Winkfield, near Wokingham, last Saturday.

Police went by flying squad car to a hamlet on the outskirts of Maidenhead, where they interviewed Willis at his home.

Willis will appear before the magistrates this morning.

He is unmarried.

The inquest on Paul was opened yesterday and adjourned until March 7.

'Blackmailed' by Girl of 6

A mother told East London magistrates yesterday that her six-year-old daughter persistently spread rumours that she was going about with other men when refused extra pocket money.

The child was stated to be beyond control, but when the Bench dismissed the case the mother, who is separated from her husband remarked, " I will kill her if she does not behave herself."

Sleep on this!

Imagine it's bed time. You've had a hard day. You're tired out, so off you go to bed. But as soon as your head is on the pillow, you find yourself suddenly wide awake. By some strange paradox you're *too tired to sleep*. And so you lie awake — hour after hour after hour — worrying about all the little things that went wrong today and the other little things that are sure to go wrong tomorrow. If this happens to you, it's serious. Have you tried a glass of Guinness before you go to bed? The value of Guinness for promoting sound refreshing sleep is well known to doctors. One writes* :—

" In insomnia, I personally have found Guinness invaluable."

Another says* :—

" In simple insomnia, Guinness accomplishes marvels."

Try a Guinness yourself to-night and see if you don't agree with these doctors tomorrow.

*These letters from doctors are quoted with their special permission.

G.E.853

23

DAILY MIRROR, Wed., February 22, 1939.

Daily Mirror

No. 10,987   ONE PENNY
Registered at the G.P.O. as a Newspaper.
Geraldine House, Fetter-lane, E.C.4.
HOLBORN 4321.

Hitler Has Sent for Her

She's nineteen-year-old Marian Daniels, American acrobatic dancer. Hitler wired her yesterday to come and dance at his party at Munich last night.

Marian flew to answer the summons—a German 'plane took her from Cannes, where she is now appearing. She danced for Hitler's guests and to-day the 'plane will take her back to Cannes in time for her performance to-night.

NEW DEAL FOR HOUSE BUYERS

A new charter for the small house owner to free him from the profiteering builder and an intensified drive to put Britain to work are part of the Government's plans to help the little man.

Mr. Chamberlain, alarmed at the failure of his Minister of Labour, Mr. Ernest Brown, is to set up an inquiry into unemployment. Mr. Eden is forecast as the next Labour Minister.

MISS Ellen Wilkinson introduced in the House of Commons last night the Building Societies Bill which will protect those buying by hire purchase houses valued up to £1,000.

If the buyer finds, after occupation, that the house is not properly built he will have the right to demand from the local authority a survey and a certificate showing the house's defects.

The owner can then go to the building society who must put right the faults.

If the society refuses, the owner may go to a county court and get authority to withhold all payments until the work has been completed.

Even should Miss Wilkinson's Bill not become law, there will be a new Act involving the building societies.

For Sir John Simon, Chancellor of the Exchequer, announced yesterday that, after the issues raised by the "Tenants' K.C.," Mrs. Elsy Borders, in her case against a society, new building society legislation would be introduced.

ARE THERE ANY MORE?

SIR REGINALD FORD, London's Food Controller, has resigned. This was announced yesterday (as reported on Page 4) by the President of the Board of Trade in the House of Commons. Sir Reginald requested that no further payments be made to him.

This was the obvious, indeed the only, solution to a deplorable situation.

The one miserable grain of credit in the whole outrageous affair was, at the last moment, snatched by the aged General with the speedy way in which he extricated himself from an untenable position.

The "Daily Mirror," which was the first newspaper to reveal the facts, gets little satisfaction from the inevitable retreat.

But what it does condemn and detest is the appalling ineptitude that led to this appointment. Who was responsible? What possible excuse was there for seeking out an elderly military gentleman, who stubbornly refused to be domiciled in the country that employed him?

If Sir Reginald Ford was the deliberate official choice for our butter—WHAT ABOUT OUR GUNS?

What guarantee is there that we are not being exposed to this same abysmal outlook in other fields?

There is a time in national affairs when mere stupidity can become criminal lunacy. Is it not enough that we should have to guard against the enemy —let alone the folly of our friends?

ARE THERE ANY OTHERS?

GIRL ON ROOF SCREAMS FOR HELP

SCREAMING "Help! Help!" a pretty girl yesterday afternoon climbed from a three-storey window on to the roof of a building in Leicester-place, Leicester-square, London.

It seemed to the quickly-gathering crowds as though she were going to jump. But Mr. Barnett Cohen, a shopkeeper on the ground floor of the building, shouted to her: "Stay where you are! I'll get the police."

Two police cars drove up within a few minutes. Three policemen ran up to the top floor and helped the girl through the window.

Four coloured men were driven away in a police car and later three men were charged. They will appear to-day at Bow-street Police Court.

The girl who had been on the roof, and another girl who was also in the top floor flat, went away with women police in a car.

The girls, who were aged about eighteen, told the police they had come from Sunderland.

Died of Fright

By mistake, a "knocker-up" rattled at the wrong bedroom window. In the room was Beryl Dronsfield, aged two years, ten months. Terrified, she trembled all over, became delirious and died. Verdict at the Oldham (Lancs) inquest yesterday: Death from natural causes, accelerated by excitement or fright.

GORDON HARKER: OPERATION

Comedian Gordon Harker is absent from the cast of "Number Six," the Edgar Wallace thriller at the Aldwych Theatre.

He has undergone a minor throat operation in a London nursing home, and his place is being taken by his understudy. Mr. Harker is expected to resume in a few days.

DOLE FIGURES ALARM M.P.s

GOVERNMENT M.P.s from the North of England have warned Mr. Chamberlain that they cannot hold their seats until the unemployment problem is tackled.

And the Premier has decided to act at once. He will set up an inquiry into the whole problem of unemployment.

He is anxious to go to the country in October with a complete plan to put Britain back to work.

Mr. Ernest Brown's failure in the Ministry of Labour, writes the Daily Mirror Political Correspondent, has become more apparent every week.

Mr. Chamberlain, it is now believed, will reconstruct his Cabinet after the General Election, which he is convinced will return him to power.

In the new Ministry Mr. Eden will be offered the Ministry of Labour—an appointment which will be popular with the Opposition.

GREASE IN CAR TO TRAP 'HUBBY'

SUSPECTING that her husband was taking out another woman, a wife smeared the back seat of his car with grease.

Later she found that some of the grease was on her husband's clothing.

She also discovered a hairnet in the back of the car, and a pattern of the net on one of the windows.

The wife herself told all this to magistrates yesterday, when she summoned her husband, alleging persistent cruelty, and applying for maintenance.

But the magistrates, after hearing the evidence, decided that there was no case.

DAILY MIRROR, Saturday, February 25, 1939

Daily Mirror

No. 10,990   ONE PENNY
Registered at the G.P.O. as a Newspaper.
Geraldine House, Fetter-lane, E.C.4
HOLBORN 4321.

William Buck, aged sixteen. . . . For two years his mother kept him in a darkened room . . . he never went out.

His face was white and waxy, his hair hung down his back like a schoolgirl's. An N.S.P.C.C. official found him in "a filthy and deplorable condition."

KEPT BOY 2 YEARS IN ROOM

BY A SPECIAL CORRESPONDENT

FOR two years William Buck, now aged sixteen, of Newport, Mon, was imprisoned in a darkened bedroom by his mother. Never once was he allowed out.

His fair hair grew down his back like a schoolgirl's. His face turned white and waxy. He became effeminate and frightened. An overcoat, reaching to his feet, hid his ragged clothing. His shoes were several sizes too small for him.

For neglecting and ill-treating her son like this, the mother, Mrs. Gladys Buck, thirty-nine, of Courtybella-road, Newport, and her husband, William, a boatman, were sentenced to three months in gaol at Newport yesterday.

The boy was not present in court. He was in Woolaston Public Assistance Institution, Newport. I saw him there last night.

He had had a hair cut. His hair was parted neatly on the left. Colour was returning to his cheeks. He was smiling.

"She Never Hurt Me"

"What has happened to mother?" he asked. When I told him she has been sentenced to three months' imprisonment he murmured:

"Oh, no sir. My poor mother. She never hurt me. She was good."

Then in a soft voice, almost timid, he told me about the last two years of his life and what he hoped to do for the future.

"My time in the bedroom was spent reading." he said. "My favourites are books about

(Continued on back page)

'First Night' Sky Show

The aurora borealis, or Northern Lights, last night gave Britain a wonderful free show.

It formed a mighty arc across the sky and from it rose a marvellous reddish curtain. In some districts it was visible for hours.

Reports that the lights had been seen came from places as far apart as North Wales, Devon, Suffolk, Leuchars, Fifeshire, Acklington, near Newcastle, and Ross-on-Wye, Herefordshire.

Ross-on-Wye first saw the lights at seven o'clock, but London had to wait for another three hours.

Mrs. Buck, sent to prison—with her husband—for three months.

FRANCO GETS HIS OWN WAY

MR. CHAMBERLAIN will announce in the House of Commons on Monday Britain's recognition of the Franco Government in Spain. A simultaneous announcement will be made by France.

Thus Franco will be recognised without Britain and France insisting on a truce in Spain.

To forestall the Opposition, the Government will move a vote of confidence in their Spain policy. This will be carried by a big majority.

A full day's debate on the Spanish situation will be held, writes the Daily Mirror political correspondent

Appointment of a British Ambassador to Spain will also be announced on Monday. Lord Londonderry is regarded as almost certain to be Britain's representative.

In the French Chamber last night M. Daladier announced that he proposed to ask the Council of Ministers on Monday to grant de jure recognition of the Nationalist Government in Spain.

"We have been officially advised by the British Government," said M. Daladier, "that the hour has come to recognise General Franco, and that the moment should not be allowed to slip by."

DAILY MIRROR, Monday, February 27, 1939.

Daily Mirror

No. 10,991 ONE PENNY
Registered at the G.P.O. as a Newspaper.
Geraldine House, Fetter-lane, E.C.4.
HOLBORN 4321.

POLICE BREAK NO. 10 MARCH

CHILD, ASLEEP FELL 9ft. UNHURT

FROM OUR OWN CORRESPONDENT

COVENTRY, Sunday.

A BOY, aged three, walked in his sleep during the night, and, still sleeping:

Climbed out of his bedroom window,

Slithered down a sloping roof,

Dropped 9ft. to the ground, and crawled for a mile in a cold wind along the side of a canal.

A policeman found him at 3 a.m. huddling in a shop door, and his flashing torch awoke the boy.

"I'm Dennis," he told the policeman who took him into a bakery to get warm, then carried him to hospital.

↑ Dennis Richards, none the worse for his lventure, looks up at his bedroom window. The broken line shows you how far he fell when he climbed out in his sleep.

Neighbours Joined in the Search

Three hours later the boy's mother, Mrs. Richards, of Sydnall-road, Coventry, found that Dennis had vanished.

She searched the house, the railway line, the nearby canal. Neighbours joined in the hunt.

Then, frantic with fear, she telephoned to the police.

Dennis had been put to bed with his brother Leonard, aged eight, at eight o'clock last night.

"I awoke at 6 a.m. to-day and went straight into the kiddies' bedroom, as I always do," Mrs. Richards told me.

"Leonard was awake. He thought I had taken Dennis into my bedroom during the night.

"Then I saw the open window.

"I was horrified. I looked out, expecting to see Dennis lying on the concrete below.

"Then I searched the house, but could not find him. My husband was away on night work. I thought of the canal. Dennis always had a liking for the water.

"I Was Horrified"

"I ran and awoke my mother, who lives a few streets away. With a few neighbours we searched the banks. Whichever way he had gone he had to pass along the canal.

"I kept picturing him in my mind's eye, walking along the edge and then falling in. It was horrible.

"I kept calling out: 'He's been drowned I know it.' We searched the railway bank.

"When I 'phoned the police and they said they had taken a little boy to hospital who might be Dennis, I shouted: 'It's got to be Dennis.'

"When they described him to me, and said he had not a scratch or a bruise, I would have collapsed had not a neighbour held me."

At his home this morning Dennis was the least perturbed of the family.

Mr. Richards said:

"It is the first of my children that has sleepwalked, but I think it is hereditary.

"All the members of my family have walked in their sleep at some time or another.

"We shall take precautions to see this doesn't happen again.

How to Check It

A medical authority told the Daily Mirror:

"Sleepwalking is not hereditary, but a nervous system could be inherited which might show itself in this way.

"It is the first time I have heard of a child so young sleepwalking.

"People subject to it always avoid obstacles.

"They rarely get through windows or go into the open. Usually they walk around the house and then go back to bed, still asleep.

"Locked windows and doors are the best method to prevent them coming to any harm.

"The child should be taken to a clinic or specialist, who might check this."

MOUNTED police broke up a Whitehall demonstration against recognition of Franco last night. When hundreds of people marched on Downing-street they found the way barred by scores of police and three fire engines.

There were shouts of " Are you going to turn the hoses on us ? " but the fire-engines were soon driven away.

They had been on the spot because shortly before the demonstrators arrived someone set in action the fire alarm at the corner of Downing-street and Whitehall. It was a false alarm, and was entered in the fire brigade books as a "malicious call."

As the crowd blocked Whitehall traffic and chanted "Arms for Spain," "No recognition for Franco," and "Chamberlain must go," a double cordon of police, sixty strong, was drawn up across the entrance to Downing-street.

Mounted police suddenly appeared from nearby turnings, and there were reinforcements of foot constables.

A roar of boos arose as the mounted men forced their horses through the crowd and gradually marshalled the demonstrators in a block in the middle of the road and on the pavements, clearing the way for traffic.

Some of the demonstrators attempted to break the cordons of constables, and the guard across Downing-street was increased.

Morrison Shouted Down

About 200 men and women, led by buglers and banners of the International Brigade, marched up and down Whitehall, disorganising the traffic, and several times mounted police broke up the procession.

The demonstration lasted an hour and a half. Then the police were able to "move on" the crowds.

They had marched from a Trafalgar Square mass meeting organised by the National Council of Labour, and during the Whitehall demonstration a deputation delivered a letter to No. 10, Downing-street.

Mr. Herbert Morrison, M.P., was shouted down at the meeting. "We want Cripps" was the cry.

Mr. Morrison argued with the crowd when he shouted ten minutes, then shouted: " I am not going to waste my voice by trying to get over interruptions organised by the Communist Party. Let it be recorded that the Communist Party are enemies of free speech."

The meeting passed a resolution which "viewed with shame and abhorrence" the Government's non-intervention policy and condemned the Government for having "acquiesced in the murder of innocent women and children and of British seamen, and for

(Continued on back page)

NORMA SHEARER IMPROVING

The condition of Miss Norma Shearer, the film star, who is in a Hollywood hospital with throat infection, was much improved yesterday, says Reuter.

He Marched To "Tipperary"

FROM OUR OWN CORRESPONDENT

WARSAW, Sunday.

Signor Gayda — "Mussolini's mouthpiece"—stalked angrily out of a night club here to-night when the orchestra played "It's a Long, Long Way to Tipperary."

Other Italians, diplomats accompanying Gayda during Count Ciano's visit to Poland, also refused to listen to the wartime British song, and walked out after Gayda.

"Long live England!" the night club crowd gleefully shouted after them. A fight started and one man was arrested.

WOMEN TRAPPED IN CAR WRECK

SKIDDING in a narrow winding lane at Fingest, Bucks, yesterday, a car driven by Lady Francis Allen, widow of Sir Francis Raymond Allen, Bt., who died a month ago, struck a bank and overturned.

The car was wrecked, trapping Lady Allen and her companion, Miss Joan Cavendish, aged twenty-five.

They were pulled out by a passing motorist. Miss Cavendish was suffering from concussion and was detained in High Wycombe Hospital, but Lady Allen was only bruised.

Lady Allen was formerly Mrs. Althea Joan Black, daughter of Mr. O. L. Hanks, of Wallasey Bay, Essex.

Sir Francis, who was twenty-nine, died at their home in Ibstone, Bucks, three years after their marriage.

Lady Allen.

VICAR'S GUEST DIES IN STREAM

Two men walking through Flood Meadows, Alton, Hants, last night, saw a hat, coat and handbag on the bank of a stream which feeds watercress beds.

Then they found a drowned woman lying face downwards in the stream, which is only about 18in. deep.

The woman was Miss Mabel Griffin, fifty-five, a cousin of the Rev. T. N. Rathbone Griffin, vicar of St. Lawrence Church, Alton.

She had been staying with him for the last few weeks, had been ill for some time.

DAILY MIRROR, Thursday, March 2, 1939.

Daily Mirror

No. 10,994   ONE PENNY
Registered at the G.P.O. as a Newspaper.
Geraldine House, Fetter-lane, E.C.4
HOLBORN 4321.

BRITAIN HAS ANSWERED THE CALL

IN THE FIRST THREE WEEKS OF THE NATIONAL CALL TO SERVICE, 371,000 MEN AND WOMEN IN BRITAIN ENROLLED FOR SOME FORM OF SERVICE.

"A remarkable figure," commented Mr. Ernest Brown, when he announced it in the House of Commons last night.

He said that from the day the National Service Guide was issued—January 25—until February 18, there had been 218,000 applications through the Ministry of Labour, 52,000 for service in the Army, 41,000 for the Royal Air Force, and 60,000 for Civil Defence.

"All who remember August, 1914," said Mr. Brown, "when the first 100,000 was not completed, in war, until the end of the month, will agree that the present figure is magnificent."

In the three weeks of this year 28,000 women enrolled; ninety-five per cent. of the country's doctors and eighty-five per cent. of the dentists registered.

These figures give some idea of the spirit of patriotism stirring in this country," added Mr. Brown.

There is one service which still needs "the greatest stimulation." The auxiliary fire services are still under-manned.

Mr. Herbert Morrison had one solution for the problem of recruiting women—a smart uniform.

He revealed how the Home Office had asked him, as L.C.C. chief, to recruit 5,000 women auxiliary ambulance drivers then they suddenly increased the number to 17,000.

"There are only 40,000 women drivers in London," Mr. Morrison added, "and it is very difficult to get them, unless I can give them a uniform.

"Cynics may say a uniform is unnecessary. Believe me, a smart uniform would enormously ease the burden."

Sir John Anderson, Britain's A.R.P. chief

(Continued on back page)

Sonja Earned £175,000 Last Year

SONJA HENIE earned £175,000 last year—about £3,650 a week—it was stated yesterday. Her income was seventeen times that of Mr. Chamberlain, who receives £10,000 a year, and two and a half times that of Greta Garbo.

Sonja is now cruising in the liner Normandie.

The skating star and her party are occupying a suite costing £1,500.

With her are her mother and brother and two servants. When the twenty-four days' cruise to South America and the West Indies is over she will have spent £3,500—not including her special entertaining bill aboard.

At twenty-six "the Pavlova of the ice" recently toured the U.S. and netted £80,000.

When she skates she wears silk tights that cost £7 a pair—and she changes five times a day.

Sonja began to skate when she was eight; in 1936 she became Olympic champion. A year later she took Hollywood by storm, and without previous film training starred in two pictures that earned £1,000,000.

HE WALKED TO HIS DEATH

Peter Redlich, three-year-old son of the rector of Little Bowden (Leics), toddled happily down the rectory garden, just as you see him in this picture.

There's a stream at the end of the garden and a tree trunk across it. Fearless Peter climbed out on the tree trunk. But his little feet slipped. He fell into the water.

On a railway embankment a few feet away thirty platelayers were at work. None of them saw Peter fighting for his life below them. And so—with help close at hand—Peter was drowned.

FLOOD BID BY BOMB

AN explosion that was heard ten miles away wrecked the parapet of the Grand Union canal aqueduct over the North Circular-road, Stonebridge Park, Willesden, N., this morning.

The explosion is believed to have been caused by a bomb intended to blow a hole in the canal bank and flood the area.

Masonry dislodged by the explosion blocked the North Circular-road, but the canal bank was undamaged.

Nobody was injured.

Scotland Yard rushed a number of police cars to the area, which was cordoned off.

PILOT ILL— LANDS WIFE IN SAFETY

THE pilot of a private aeroplane, Mr. Michael Border, aged twenty-eight, ground engineer, of Westbourne-court, London, W., was taken ill while flying with his wife and her dog from North Weald to Romford, Essex, yesterday.

He told his wife Their only chance was to find a safe landing-ground and get down before he collapsed.

Anxiously his wife waited. They found a spot near Gallows Corner, Romford.

The machine circled three times while Mr. Border fought the weakness that was sapping his control

Then he made a safe landing

BABY BORN ON WAY TO RECORD

RUSHING in an ambulance yesterday to Edinburgh's new maternity hospital, attached to the Royal Infirmary, Mrs. David Vance, Parkhead-crescent, West Calder, believed her baby would be the first to be born there.

The hospital opened only on Monday and, as no babies have been born there yet, the child would have qualified for a special gift from Edinburgh's Lord Provost.

But when the ambulance was racing through the suburban streets, Mrs. Vance's baby, a girl, was born.

The child is at present the sole occupant of a special air-conditioned nursery.

DAILY MIRROR, Friday, March 3, 1939.

Daily Mirror

No. 10,995   ONE PENNY

Registered at the G.P.O. as a Newspaper.
Geraldine House, Fetter-lane, E.C.4.
HOLBORN 4321.

With Daddy at the Zoo

Prince Edward and Princess Alexandra had a day at the Zoo yesterday with father; a tiring day, too, for the Duke of Kent had to carry his little daughter—as most daddies have to do at the end of the afternoon.

Their mummy wasn't there, but soon the Duchess will hear all about the Zoo, for she is now on her way home.

She left London more than a month ago to visit Athens—and she and the Duke have never before been so long parted.

It was first announced that the Duchess would stay in Athens for about eight days, and would then be joined by the Duke.

Instead, the Duke stayed at home, and the Duchess went on with her sister, Princess Paul, to Belgrade.

Princess Paul, speaking from her Belgrade home yesterday, said to a " Daily Mirror " representative :—
" The Duchess of Kent is not here now. She has left for London, and will be there this week-end."

MURDER IN CITY, CALL TO BOY

A LONDON business man was murdered last night in his office in deserted St. Paul's Churchyard—and this morning the police announced that they wished to interview a fifteen-year-old boy in connection with the discovery.

The dead man was Albert John Rea, aged fifty-four, who lived at Danvers-road, Priory-lane, Muswell Hill.

The boy's description was given as:
Height 5ft. 9½in., slim build, hair light brown

(Continued on back page)

Another Happy Picture of the Duke and His Children on Page 18

DAILY MIRROR, Wednesday, March 8, 1939.

Daily Mirror

No. 10,999.　　ONE PENNY.
Registered at the G.P.O. as a Newspaper.
Geraldine House, Fetter-lane, E.C.4.
HOLBORN 4321.

HAVING A RIGHT ROYAL TIME

To a children's fancy dress party given by Viscountess Astor in St. James's-square, London, went the Princess Elizabeth and Princess Margaret Rose.

The Princesses became submerged in the party spirit.

Two little girls thoroughly enjoyed themselves; and here's Princess Margaret Rose blowing one of the squeakers that young 'Arriet blows on Hampstead Heath on fete days!

Both Princesses wore dresses like those of Queen Elizabeth's Court. Princess Elizabeth—you see her behind her younger sister and in the picture below—was in a magnificent grown-up gown, with high collar and rich brocade . . . just like those of the great Queen whose name she bears.

15, He Eats in State

These reports were given on two boys at Newark, Notts, Juvenile Court yesterday.

One, aged fifteen: "He has not had his meals with his parents for the past two years. He insists on having them alone, with the wireless on."

Of the other, aged fourteen: "He cannot even wash himself properly. His mother has to do it for him."

Accused of stealing cigarettes and chocolates, the boys were sent to an approved home and nautical school for three years.

DOG ILL, SO SHE BROKE HONEYMOON

A TELEGRAM sent to a bride when she was on her honeymoon made her leave her husband, jump into her car, and race from London to her home at Southsea. The telegram said: "Fisher is seriously ill." Fisher is her pet dog.

She was so anxious to be at her pet's side that her car's speed touched 53 m.p.h. in a "limit" area and drew the attention of the police.

In Reading Police Court yesterday the just-wed wife—Mrs. Diana Wright, of Castle-road, Southsea—was fined £1 and had her licence endorsed for exceeding the speed limit.

She drove, said the police, at speeds varying from 45 to 53 m.p.h.

Her solicitor told the magistrates about Fisher's illness. "Unfortunately," he said, "she did not notice her speed."

"I Love Him Dearly"

At her home last night Mrs. Wright told the *Daily Mirror*:—

"It was just after we had been married that I received the telegram about the dog's illness.

"My husband and I were honeymooning in London and, without any more thought, I jumped into the car and drove home to Southsea.

"There I found Fisher, my six-month-old Alsatian dog, seriously ill with gastritis.

"I love him dearly, and while I was getting
(Continued on back page)

JUG THROWN AT AN M.P.

FIREWORKS and smoke bombs were exploded, fire hydrants turned on, and chairs thrown at a Labour meeting in Shoreditch Town Hall last night.

Police were called and five arrests were made after the platform had been rushed by Fascists.

A jug and a glass were thrown at Mr. Ernest Thurtle, Labour M.P. for Shoreditch, who was the principal speaker.

"The jug was smashed by the microphone into which I was speaking," said Mr. Thurtle. "The thrower then seized the glass and flung it at me, but Mr. R. Willis, secretary of the London Trades Council, who was sitting beside me, held up a chair, and the glass smashed against that."

DAILY MIRROR, Saturday, March 11, 1939.

Daily Mirror

No. 11,002   ONE PENNY
Registered at the G.P.O. as a Newspaper.
Geraldine House, Fetter-lane, E.C.4.
HOLBORN 4321.

John Glenn.

FIVE MEN GET 20 YEARS, GIRL GETS 7, IN I.R.A. TRIAL

FIVE MEN EACH RECEIVED SENTENCES OF TWENTY-YEARS' PENAL SERVITUDE AND A GIRL OF TWENTY-TWO GOT SEVEN YEARS, IN THE MANCHESTER TRIAL OF IRISH REPUBLICAN ARMY EXPLOSIVES CHARGES, LAST NIGHT.

In one hour, Mr. Justice Stable, one of the youngest Judges, appointed only five months ago, passed sentences totalling 205 years on seven people found guilty. These included concurrent sentences, and the time actually to be served is 121 years.

The Judge showed no emotion. But as the men in turn looked at his stern face, heard him pronounce sentence, each cried "God save Ireland!"

After the first cry, warders tried to stifle the succeeding cries. Hands were clapped over the men's mouths. Several struggled. One was lifted bodily out of the dock.

But the girl, Mary Glenn, was calm. She smiled as she heard the sentence pronounced in a voice which had not softened.

"God save Ireland," she said quietly, and she was smiling as she walked down the steps from the dock and vanished from the sight of the crowded courtroom.

The first time the Judge's lips framed the words "Twenty years"—the man then in the dock was twenty-one-year-old Michael Rory Campbell—a woman's voice screamed "Rory! Rory!"

"If there is any further disturbance in the court, the person who makes the disturbance will be committed to prison," said the Judge sternly.

When the Judge his task done, left the court, a heavy police guard was waiting.

Gripping his red gown about him, he hesitated for a few seconds on the top of the steps leading to the courtyard, then slowly descended to his waiting car.

Police stationed every three yards along the pavement turned their backs on the Judge and watched the opposite side of the road.

The nearest man to Mr. Justice Stable was

(Continued on page 27)

PIRATE FOILED BY NAVY

H.M. Destroyer Intrepid, steaming full speed on Admiralty orders, rescued the British steamer Stangate from a Franco blockade warship at 1 a.m. to-day.

The Franco warship had swooped to arrest two British ships twenty-three miles off Cape San Antonio—the Stangate, which beat the blockade to take food to Valencia, in Republican Spain on Thursday, and the Bellwyn.

The Bellwyn's master sent out radio messages to "any British warship" saying that he had refused to submit to arrest, that his own ship was being left alone, but asking for help for the Stangate, which was being taken to Palma Majorca.

The Admiralty ordered the destroyers Intrepid and Impulsive to go to the rescue. This call for Navy action against the blockade came hardly twenty hours after Lord Halifax's announcement that British merchant ships would get full protection.

The Intrepid intercepted the Franco warship, and under her nose took the Stangate away. Now the destroyer is escorting the merchant ship to Gibraltar.

The blockade warship had been waiting for the Stangate since she left Valencia yesterday morning, bound for Almeria to load oranges for London.

Her master, Captain Dibbings, who has a crew of twenty-four, went on to beat the blockade on Thursday after a British warship had warned him of the danger.

Britain has not granted belligerent rights to Franco, and any action taken by him against our foodships will be regarded as an act of piracy.

HAD £250 'SPECIAL' FOR HIS SICK WIFE

A LONDON man chartered a special train to take his sick wife home from Plymouth last night.

While returning from a cruise to the West Indies, Mrs. Pamela Tennyson-D'Eyncourt (prettiest debutante of her year), of Hyde Park-square, W., had been taken seriously ill.

Although Mrs. Tennyson-D'Eyncourt would have had to wait only two and a half hours for an ordinary train, her husband had the special train brought to Millbay Dock.

It cost him about £250. A saloon coach and a guard's van were drawn by the engine, and the services of three railwaymen, a driver, fireman and guard, were entailed.

Mrs. Tennyson-D'Eyncourt had disembarked on the outward journey at Barbados, and rejoined the ship on her homeward journey.

Mr. Justice Stable.

THIS JUDGE HAS PITY, TOO

SIR WINTRINGHAM STABLE, the Judge who yesterday passed sentences ranging from seven years to twenty in the I.R.A. trial at Manchester, who did it coldly and sternly, is a very human individual.

This man, at fifty, has all the prestige that becomes one of the youngest Judges of the King's Bench, a King's Counsel and a knight. His salary as a Judge is £5,000 a year.

He is the squire of his village at Plas Llwyn Owen, Llanbrynmair, amid the hills of Montgomery.

Last week, at the same Manchester court, he showed that his voice could soften.

Before him was a woman on whom he had to pass a death sentence—his first. It was the pathetic case of a mother who had killed her invalid son.

"You need not be alarmed," he smiled to the woman. "You most certainly will be reprieved. . . ." Then he told warders to make her comfortable and give her tea. Within twenty-four hours she was reprieved.

Again yesterday he faced an unpleasant duty. But there was no softening of his voice. "Conspiracy of a diabolical character. . . ." He rapped the words out. Then the sentences. So much for the Judge.

And the man—at home? Wintringham Stable is the country gentleman. He rides, shoots, fishes. His villagers love their great man.

When he was raised to the Bench they came to his manor Welsh fashion. They sang verses to the twanging of a harp.

***

★ Answer to Terrorists ★

By THE EDITOR

The public will agree with the sentences on the Irish terrorists. They are heavy, the maximum that can be given. But confronted with such callous brutality, justice cannot be tempered with mercy.

These criminals were willing to imperil the lives of innocent persons in a vain passion to destroy the law as it is.

Can there be anything more cowardly and cruel than to strike out at anybody and everybody in the hope of adjusting what is, after all, a personal grievance?

Terrorism is a method that will never intimidate British feeling. And far from winning adherence to a cause, it alienates all sympathy.

The appeal to open force in itself is bad enough, but the kind of terrorism employed recently in Britain is the weapon of an assassin working in the dark.

Such methods must be stamped out. May these sentences be a lesson and a warning.

DAILY MIRROR, Friday, March 17, 1939.

Daily Mirror

No. 11,007   ONE PENNY
Registered at the G.P.O. as a Newspaper.
Geraldine House, Fetter-lane, E.C.4.
HOLBORN 4321.

'ARREST 10,000'

That was the order after Hitler had held this conference in Prague yesterday . . . first taste of Nazi "protection" the Czech people had.

They got it from the spectacled man with the grim smile—Herr Himmler, head of the Gestapo, Germany's Secret Police. "We have 10,000 arrests to carry out," said Himmler . . . more than 3,000 had been made before Hitler left the city. (See page 2.)

BRIDE FEARS FOR MISSING TAXI-DRIVER

FROM OUR OWN CORRESPONDENT
Portsmouth, Thursday.

BRIDE of a fortnight, Mrs. Henry Cotton, of King-street, Portsmouth, waited anxiously to-night for news of her husband, a young taxi-driver, who has been missing since picking up two fares at the Portsmouth Aerodrome last night —three days after returning from his honeymoon.

Mr. Ernest Wyatt, proprietor of Citax Taxis, told me to-night:

"We received a message from Portsmouth airport about 7.10 last night asking for a car to be sent to pick up two passengers.

"Cotton was sent and left the airport with his fares about 8.15 p.m. From the conversation with the two men at the airport it appeared that they wanted to go to Heston.

"When I found Cotton had not returned this morning I 'phoned to Heston airport and found that there was no trace of either the car or passengers.

Mystery 'Phone Call

"I got into touch with the police at once and an S O S was put out from Scotland Yard.

"About three o'clock this afternoon we had a 'phone message from Earl's Court, London, purporting to be from Cotton stating that he was returning to Portsmouth.

"The message added, 'Please tell my people.' We have heard nothing since."

The telephone operator who took the message said that she was certain it was Cotton who spoke to her.

But Mrs. Cotton said she had grave fears that the message was not genuine.

"My husband knew where I worked and I am sure he would have telephoned direct to me to say that everything was all right.

"We have known each other ever since we were boy and girl together, and he has never given me a minute's anxiety before."

The police search was called off this afternoon when the message from Earl's Court was received, but late to-night when Cotton had not arrived back at the garage grave fears were entertained for his safety.

If no further news is received to-morrow morning an all-stations S O S will be put out by Scotland Yard.

Cotton was formerly a chauffeur in Portsmouth and had been employed by Citax for about six months.

GINGERING-UP THE BLONDES

'IT is not enough to put behind the drapery counter the bright young thing whose head is full of the boy she is going to meet when the shop closes," said Miss Ellen Wilkinson, M.P., addressing the Incorporated Sales Managers' Association in London last night.

"I can say, as an older woman, that the views of the bright young platinum blonde on what will suit me and what I think will suit me are entirely different," added Miss Wilkinson, who has red hair.

Miss Gladys Burlton, director of the Burlton Staff Training Institute, gave amusing examples of answers offered her by shop assistants. For instance:—

"Will this tarnish?" "Oh, yes. It will tarnish beautifully!"

"Does pasteurisation destroy the vitamins?" 'Oh, yes Destroys everything, ma'am."

ARMY SERVICE FOR ALL IS M.P.s' DEMAND

THESE are the chief events that emerged yesterday as Germany grew still greater:

1. A dramatic move was made in London to form a Council of State to advise on foreign affairs.

2. **Conservative M.P.s called for a measure of conscription in Britain.**

3. Britain is expected to recall her Ambassador from Berlin as a protest against the Czech annexation.

4. **Slovakia, after forty-eight hours of independent existence, was wiped out. It becomes part of Germany.**

5. Hitler left Prague for a secret destination. believed to be Brunn. From there he will go to Bratislava and Vienna.

6. Signor Gayda, Mussolini's spokesman, announced that Italy is delighted at the success of her friend and is "awaiting her turn."

HERO BRINGS US ARMS PLANS

General Sirovy

GENERAL SIROVY, one-eyed national hero of Czechoslovakia, has arrived in London. He was one of the eleven secret passengers who arrived in Croydon on the last 'plane out of Prague

And Sirovy—he was Minister of War in the last Czech Ministry—has brought with him the latest secrets of the great Skoda arms works.

Documents relating to new models of guns and cannons, perfected by Czech experts, will be handed over to the British Minister of War.

Sirovy's fellow passengers in the escaping 'plane were M. Beran, the Prime Minister; M. Fescher, Minister of the Interior, and highly-placed officials of the Skoda works.

MR. EDEN IS PRESSING THE GOVERNMENT TO FORM AN ALL-PARTY COUNCIL OF STATE TO ADVISE ON FOREIGN AFFAIRS.

The plan was at first rejected by Mr. Chamberlain. but Lord Halifax supported it, as did other influential Conservatives.

NOW THE PREMIER IS BELIEVED TO HAVE GIVEN WAY. HE WILL MAKE AN IMPORTANT ANNOUNCEMENT WHEN HE SPEAKS IN BIRMINGHAM TO-NIGHT.

The Council of State would include, it is anticipated, Mr. Attlee and Mr. Greenwood, the Labour leaders; Sir Archibald Sinclair, the Liberal Chief, and Mr. Lloyd George and Mr. Winston Churchill.

Meanwhile the important Foreign Affairs Committee of Conservative M.P.s met last night and decided to urge the Premier to introduce a Military Service Bill, writes the Daily Mirror Political Correspondent.

More than 130 M.P.s attended. They

(Continued on back page)

The Booty

German Storm Troops appeared at the Czech National Bank in Prague yesterday afternoon and, according to eye-witnesses, drove off with sixteen lorry loads of gold, says British United Press.

How to treat your wife

DAILY MIRROR, Monday, March 20, 1939.

Daily Mirror

No. 11,009.   ONE PENNY
Registered at the G.P.O. as a Newspaper.
Geraldine House, Fetter-lane, E.C.4.
HOLBORN 4321.

GERMAN TROOPS MARCH ON AS CAROL MANS FRONTIER

BY OUR DIPLOMATIC CORRESPONDENT

LATE LAST NIGHT THE GERMANS WERE STILL MARCH-
ING, THROUGH SNOW AND SLEET, TO THE SOUTH-
EAST.

Their destination is a closely-guarded secret. Last news of them
was that they were concentrating on the Carpatho-Ukrainian border,
now the new frontier of Hungary.

King Carol, faced with the knowledge that Hitler is determined to
seize his oil wells by "negotiation" or by force, has called up half a
million men to defend Rumania's frontiers.

And Carol waits, too, to learn what help he may expect from the
democracies should the German troops sweep into Rumania.

If Britain, France and Poland promise him assistance, he can resist. If they refuse he must be the
next victim of the "Drive to the
East."

In London, a Cabinet meeting has been
called for this morning. Sir Nevile Henderson, the recalled Ambassador, arrived
from Berlin and reported to Lord Halifax.

Premier Sees The King

Mr. Chamberlain, after a prolonged meeting
with his inner Cabinet, went last night to
Buckingham Palace where, for an hour he had
an audience with the King.

To-day's Cabinet will discuss the threat to
Rumania and the pressure on the Government
to introduce conscription.

ALL SECTIONS OF POLITICAL
OPINION ARE NOW STRONGLY IN
FAVOUR OF A CONSCRIPTION BILL,
IF ONLY AS A GESTURE OF BRITAIN'S
STRENGTH.

Lord Halifax will make an important statement on compulsory national service in the
House of Lords to-day.

Meanwhile Britain and France are consult-
ing through diplomatic channels with all the
Governments of Central and Eastern Europe.
They are anxious to make sure which of
Rumania's allies—she has pacts with Poland,
Yugoslavia, Turkey and Greece—will honour
their obligations.

It is possible that Britain and France, with a
view to ensuring peace, will promise support to
any victim of aggression which is ready to defend herself and her neighbours.

Russia Denounces Hitler

And as Britain prepares events in Europe
are hastening to a climax.

In Hungary the Government newspaper Uj
Magyarsag, of Budapest, in an important announcement signed by its editor-in-chief,
says:

"Slovakia will sooner or later be merged
with Hungary. The destiny of Hungary is
bound up with the Rome-Berlin axis.

"Germany will not oppose the merger between the two countries. A world conflict is
inevitable. Hungary must be actively on the
side of the axis Powers."

An alliance between Hungary and Germany
would leave the way clear for the German
army to swarm through Hungary towards
Rumania and Yugoslavia.

Russia, in a stern Note, told Germany that
the rape of Czechoslovakia cannot be
recognised.

The invasion by German troops, the Note
says, was "arbitrary, violent and aggressive."

Lord Halifax was told of Russia's protest
when M. Maisky, the Soviet Ambassador, called
at the Foreign Office last night.

(Continued on back page)

★ HE GOES

Two trains approached and passed
each other between London and the
South Coast yesterday. . . .
In ten seconds.
Ten seconds of drama.

In one sat Sir Nevile Henderson,
Britain's Ambassador in Berlin, hurrying to see our Cabinet, which had recalled him.

In the other sat Dr. von Dirksen,
Germany's Ambassador in London,
racing to the coast on his way to tell
Hitler how Britain stands—at long last
—against the bullying of Germany.

You see the two Ambassadors in
these pictures . . . on the left Dr. von
Dirksen, leaving the German Embassy
in London for Berlin . . . below, Sir
Nevile Henderson stepping from the
train on his arrival at Victoria Station.

Rushing wind, rattle of rails, and the
trains had passed.
The Parting of the Ways?

HE COMES

DAILY MIRROR, Saturday, March 25, 1939.

Daily Mirror

No. 11,014   ONE PENNY
Registered at the G.P.O. as a Newspaper.
Geraldine House, Fetter-lane, E.C.4.
HOLBORN 4321.

DODGED AN ARMY, DIES RAIDING BANK

FROM OUR SPECIAL CORRESPONDENT

NEW YORK, Friday.

THE man who held up an avenging army for a week while he sniped at them from his mountain lair, killed himself with his last bullet to-night as he was trapped raiding a bank.

Earl (Tarzan) Durand, a 6ft. 2in. rancher, shot his way out of prison a week ago. He killed two men in his getaway, and made for the Wyoming mountains beyond the town of Powell.

And for seven days Durand became a national sensation as he dodged the army of 300 men, equipped with howitzers and trench mortars, who pursued him into the mountains.

Army officers, Sheriffs and State troopers trundled their heavy weapons over the mountainous region where Durand hid.

From his rocky fortress he defied them. His rifle shot down two more men. Then the troops began to encircle his lair.

At dawn to-day the Army advanced. Above them an aeroplane dipped and roared. There was no sign of Durand.

And the Army was unsteady. Durand's skill with the rifle had made him more feared than a hundred men. He had fired only five times—and four times he had killed.

"Has Me Scared"

William Garlow, a nephew of the late great Buffalo Bill and a member of the Army confessed. "Oh boy, oh boy. Durand has me scared."

And British born Sheriff Blackburn, of Powell, encouraged the troops with an impassioned speech against defeatism.

Blackburn was weighed down with weapons. He carried a rifle, two revolvers swung at his hips; he had pouches full of ammunition. With fourteen bloodhounds, he led the attack up Bear Tooth mountain, where Durand hid.

They fired a fusillade at his cave. The State troopers, with their fingers on their triggers, crept in.

The cave was empty. Durand, who had vowed he would never be taken alive, had escaped again.

The troopers advanced. As they went they fired at every moving object they saw.

But Durand was in their rear. He had crawled through bushes and scrub to the main road.

There he found two armed policemen in a car. He crept up behind them, jumped into the car, pushed his rifle into their backs and ordered them to drop their guns.

Man Used as Shield

He forced them to drive him into Powell. At the outskirts of the town the car pulled up. Durand jumped out and vanished.

Now his position was desperate. He had no money, he was hungry—although he had boasted he could live for days on raw deer's meat—and the whole town was organised for his capture.

With the boldness of a crazy man Durand marched into the First National Bank and ordered its president to hand over the money.

At once the alarm was given. Before the bandit could seize the notes the doorway was filled with armed men.

Durand was trapped. He grabbed a bank clerk who was standing near him with hands raised, and using him as a shield tried to shoot his way out.

He killed the bank clerk—his fifth victim. Then as the police levelled their guns he fell dead with his own last bullet in his heart.

The pursuers emptied their guns into his lifeless body.

And Tarzan Durand, the twenty-six-year-old poacher who defied an army, had kept his vow.

BRIDGE ARSON THEORY

BY A SPECIAL CORRESPONDENT

THREE quick flashes were seen to shoot from under the new partly-built Waterloo Bridge last night. Then flames leapt up among the bridge structure.

The fire is believed to have been started deliberately in an attempt to damage the bridge or the temporary bridge which carries road traffic.

A man who saw the start of the fire told me: "There was no sound of an explosion, but just three blinding flashes. Then the flames began to shoot up the structure."

The fire started in a carpenter's hut on a wooden gantry standing out of the water adjoining the centre pier. The hut had contained tools, coats and other stores. It was practically burned out.

All the workmen had gone home four hours before the outbreak.

Traffic over the temporary Waterloo bridge was promptly diverted, and was not resumed until police had made a thorough examination.

A policeman in a taxi was the first to cross the bridge. He told the police cordon at the other end that traffic could pass.

The alarm was given by two seventeen-year-old members of the auxiliary fire brigade—Sidney R. Hillier, of the Brompton-road Fire Station, and B. W. Doe, of the Clerkenwell Station.

Hillier said: "When we got near the centre
(Continued on back page)

BOUVERIE Was a Good WORKMAN

He gave the Grand National winner at

100 to 8

They Call Her "Carrots"...

. . . because that's what she mostly eats. Myra Stephens is her name. Described as "America's most perfectly formed girl," she reached London yesterday with a troupe of girls for London cabaret.

"My secret," she said, "is that I always eat a quarter-of-a-pound of raw carrots every day, and other raw vegetables. Mother brought me up that way—and mother was right."

Want to know the measurements of the most perfectly formed girl? Here they are:—Height 5ft. 8in., waist 25in., hips 36in., bust 34in.

FRENCH CABINET WELCOMES LEBRUN

The entire French Cabinet, headed by M. Daladier, the Premier, was at the station to welcome M. Lebrun, the President, when he arrived back in Paris last night.

His visit to Britain is hailed in France as having considerably reinforced the Franco-British entente.

The French Press described the visit as "a moving demonstration of the union of the peoples."

President's Farewell Kiss—Page 8.

DAILY MIRROR, Monday, March 27, 1939.

Daily Mirror

No. 11,015.   ONE PENNY.
Registered at the G.P.O. as a Newspaper.
Geraldine House, Fetter-lane, E.C.4.
HOLBORN 4321.

"More guns, more ships, more aeroplanes.." Mussolini making his "Might is Right" declaration yesterday from a lofty platform in the Mussolini Forum.

BOYS ON GALE-TORN CLIFF 5 hrs.

WHILE breakers snatched at their feet and spray from the gale-lashed sea drenched them, two Broadstairs boys yesterday clung for five hours to a slippery chalk ledge, high up the cliff face, waiting for the tide to go down.

A police-constable knelt at the cliff top, shouting encouragement to them and hot coffee and sandwiches were lowered to them in a bucket.

The boys were John King, aged thirteen, of Normand-road, St. Peter's, Broadstairs, and Thomas Briggs, aged fourteen, of Victoria-avenue, Broadstairs.

They were walking along the sands, between North Foreland and Broadstairs, when they were cut off by the tide.

They scrambled up the cliff face to a chalky ledge just beneath Bleak House, once the home of Charles Dickens.

Below them was a sea lashed by a seventy-mile-an-hour gale; every second breakers threatened to tear them from their perilous hold.

It was too rough for a boat to reach the spot and the boys had to wait until the tide receded, when they climbed down and reached the jetty.

Coffee Lowered

Mr. H. Moreland, of Coastguard Bungalow, Broadstairs, told the *Daily Mirror*: "I telephoned for the police when I saw the boys' plight from the cliff top. There was a biting wind blowing and I was afraid that the boys might suffer from exposure and lose their hold.

"My wife made hot coffee and sandwiches and I lowered these down the cliff face in a bucket."

Police-Constable Weston, of the Broadstairs police, remained on duty at the cliff top and kept up the boys' courage by shouting to them until the tide receded and they were able to reach safety."

John, the younger boy, said last night: "It was a terrifying experience, and we had all the thrills for a long time."

Channel Gale

Last night the Channel was being lashed by a seventy-mile-an-hour gale. Cross-Channel steamers had the worst crossings of the year and were delayed in reaching port.

In mid-Channel the full force of the storm was experienced, and while the S.S. Biarritz, one of the Southern Railway steamers, was crossing from Boulogne to Folkestone with 460 passengers, one tremendous sea struck the ship and lifted passengers off their feet.

Small coasting vessels put into harbours for shelter, while along the south-easterly coast the sea defences and promenades were swept by tremendous seas.

The part of the coast affected most was from Yarmouth to Beachy Head. At Yarmouth a number of ships sought shelter in the Roads. Heavy seas swept over the promenades at some seaside towns.

At Lympne (Kent) the wind reached 60 m.p.h. at times and light aircraft was unable to take off.

Londoners shivered in the cold wind and gusts of 45 m.p.h. were registered on the roof of the Air Ministry building. In parts of Kent there were snow showers and sleet fell at Cromer.

Kenneth Lock, aged seventeen, of Northfield-terrace, West Thurrock, was drowned in the Thames at Dartford Creek yesterday when his canoe overturned owing to the strong wind and swell.

POLES 'READY —AND WAITING'

"The whole civilised world stands on the eve of events of tremendous importance. To-day, as in 1914, the world has ceased to believe in German promises, which have been disproved by facts;

"Poland is to-day the only strong barrier in the way of German progress eastward, and in this historic moment the Polish nation, fully prepared, calmly awaits the order to march."

AMID a storm of cheers, this fighting resolution was yesterday passed at a general meeting of 7,000 members of the Polish ex-Servicemen's organisation at Lodz.

The resolution continued:—

"We declare that a complete union of the whole nation, under the command of the President and the Chief of the Army, is the urgent need of the moment. Poland must become a fortress.

"Every Pole, rifle in hand, must stand on his post. This is the slogan of the present day."

The resolution was passed with great enthusiasm and greeted with loud and prolonged cheers.

Housewives of Teschen, Poland—a former Czech town—deserted their homes last night to stage an anti-German demonstration.

Polish officials in Danzig yesterday refused to comment on movements of their troops, although German sources there estimated that "more than 10,000" took positions in the harbour city of Gydynia, on Danzig's western border.

MUSSOLINI SHOUTS: 'WOE TO THE WEAK'

"Woe to the weak; woe to the unarmed.

"In Italy, the order of the day is this: more guns, more ships, more aeroplanes, at whatever cost and by whatever means, even if we have to wipe out completely what is called civilian life."

SIGNOR Mussolini, from the high platform of the Mussolini Forum in Rome, screamed down to the 100,000 Fascists below.

"Duce, Duce, Duce," shouted the crowd until Mussolini silenced them with an imperious gesture and cried:

"Events are moving. We desire that nothing more shall be heard of brotherhood, of sisterhood, of cousinhood or other bastard relations, because the relations between States are the relations of force, and force determines our policy."

Behind him, celebrating yesterday's twentieth birthday of Fascism, were Germans waving a gigantic swastika flag, and delegates from General Franco.

There were fresh cheers as Mussolini thundered the Fascist belief:—

"When one is strong he is cherished by his friends and feared by his enemies. From prehistoric times the strong have risen above the waves of centuries and generations."

"Italy Claims from France"

Through the cheering came the chant from the crowd: "Tunisia—Nizzia (Nice)—Savoia" —the "colonies" Italy claims from France.

But Mussolini did not mention Nice or Savoy. Instead:—

"In the Italian Note of December 17, 1938," he said, "the problems outstanding between France and Italy were clearly stated.

"They were problems of a colonial character. These problems have a name, and they are called Tunis, Djibouti, and the Suez Canal.

"The French Government is perfectly free to refuse even to engage in the simple discussion of these problems as it has done with its too-often reiterated 'Never, Nevers.'

"But they will not be in a position to complain if the trench which divides the two countries becomes so deep that the task of crossing it will become most arduous if not impossible."

The Duce had an early sneer against Britain

(Continued on back page)

Secret Talk with France

Secret talks between Italy and France on Mussolini's colonial claims have been going on for some weeks, says a British United Press Rome message. Italy's terms are:—

Italy must be dominant in the Mediterranean;

The Tunisia, Djibouti, Suez claims must be met on Italy's terms.

Official negotiations are expected to open as soon as Madrid falls.

DAILY MIRROR, Thursday, March 30, 1939.

Daily Mirror

No. 11,018   ONE PENNY
Registered at the G.P.O. as a Newspaper.
Geraldine House, Fetter-lane, E.C.4.
HOLBORN 4321.

FALL IN !

MUSSOLINI PROVED A LIAR

—Says Daladier

" We will not yield one acre . . . " M. Daladier.

SIGNOR MUSSOLINI'S ANNOUNCEMENT THAT ITALY HAD MADE DEFINITE CLAIMS FOR COLONIES TO FRANCE WERE REVEALED AS A LIE BY M. DALADIER, THE FRENCH PREMIER, IN A BROADCAST SPEECH FROM PARIS LAST NIGHT.

In a frank statement he told how Italy had suggested and Mussolini had confirmed the impression that demands for rights in Tunisia, Djibouti and the Suez had been made in a letter from Count Ciano last December.

Daladier's strong voice trembled as he nailed that lie. " There was no question in that letter of Tunisia, Djibouti and Suez."

He paused for a moment before pronouncing the Duce's name, then declared: " Signor Mussolini has left a false impression on the world."

"Not an Acre . . ."

He promised France that not one acre of land would be yielded. " not a single one of our rights."

(M. Daladier's speech is on page 4.)

In Paris, where Lord Gort is in consultation with French military leaders, the speech was regarded as a strong answer to Italy, and a general strengthening of the anti-aggression front.

In Rome, disappointment was the first reaction. Surprise was expressed that M. Daladier's speech proved a stronger reply than expected to Signor Mussolini's Sunday address.

Berlin newspapers this morning give little space to the speech, though the general tone is " Daladier says no; shrinks from the initiative."

A.R.P. Workers to "Sign Up"

BY OUR POLITICAL CORRESPONDENT

A.R.P. and other National Defence workers will, before Easter, be asked to agree to serve their country for a definite period.

An announcement to this effect will be made in the House of Commons.

At present, all groups of defence workers are giving their services voluntarily; they are under no legal obligation to attend classes or parades.

Under the new system, it is proposed to ask workers to agree to serve as long as the crisis exists.

HEARD SOS ON JOURNEY

BY a million to one chance a dramatic B.B.C. SOS last night brought a father to the bedside of his daughter, who lay dangerously ill in hospital.

Travelling by car to Whitstable, Mr. Cecil Puttock, of Tankerton (Kent), chanced to stop for a few minutes before the time of the broadcast.

His heart missed a beat when he heard his own name repeated by the announcer

" Will Cecil Puttock, of Tankerton, travelling in a grey car, No. A.J.G. 507, and who may be in the neighbourhood of West Wickham, go to the Hospital for Sick Children, Great Ormond-street, where his daughter Shirley is dangerously ill and may have to undergo a blood transfusion," ran the SOS.

Mr. Puttock rang the hospital, told them that he was on his way to London.

But while he was driving to London, a blood donor for the child had been found. When he reached the child's bedside, he found that his wife was already there.

Mr. Puttock was given a room in the hospital so that he could be near his daughter through the night.

EXPLOSIVES CHARGES

Two men were charged at Bow-street Police Station last night under the Explosives Substances Act and will appear in court to-day.

A third man who was taken to Hammersmith Police Station left after he had made a statement.

GREAT NEW CITIZEN ARMY

MOVES to form the greatest peace time Citizen Army in Britain's history were made last night when telegrams were sent from the War Office to Territorial Associations ordering the immediate enrolment of 40,000 of the men who had been refused because units were over strength.

This followed the announcement in the House of Commons yesterday by Mr. Chamberlain, the Premier, that Britain is to double the war strength of the Territorial Army (to 340,000), and immediately to increase its present strength from 130,000 to 170,000.

The Premier had said that an immediate intensive recruiting campaign " will be necessary." and that " in time there will be double the number of divisions available " for overseas service

Democratic Officers

As speakers in the recruiting campaign. M.P.s, irrespective of Party, will, in the next few weeks, carry the call to Britain's manhood into every town and village in the country

It was emphasised last night that officers will, as far as possible, be promoted from the ranks.

The Government hopes that the majority of the officers will serve as privates and N.C.O.'s Retired officers and N.C.O.s of the Regulars will help in the training of the new Citizen Army

But there will be no elderly dug-outs as there were during the last war.

" It's the biggest thing ever." declared Sir Walter Kirke. Director-General of the Territorial Army last night.

" Now,' he said, " it is a case of carrying out Nelson's historic message—' England expects that every man this day will do his duty '—and the duty of every young man in Britain lies in the fighting forces."

Sir Walter added that the immediate plan

(Continued on back page)

DAILY MIRROR, Friday, March 31, 1939.

Daily Mirror

No. 11,019   ONE PENNY
Registered at the G.P.O. as a Newspaper.
Geraldine House, Fetter-lane, E.C.4.
HOLBORN 4321.

BRITAIN PLEDGES AID TO POLES

M.P.s May Sit Through Easter

M.P.s' Easter holiday may be cut short. Normally the House of Commons would rise next Thursday for twelve days. But, if the crisis grows more tense, Parliament may remain in continuous session.

The Speaker has authority to recall M.P.s by wire, 'phone or radio.

A quorum of M.P.s could be recalled within two hours, and everyone could be back in the House within twenty - four hours.

Few M.P.s will go far afield this Easter. All Cabinet Ministers are expected to remain near London.

HE TOOK A BUS —PANIC

BY A SPECIAL CORRESPONDENT

WHILE the driver and conductor were away, a middle-aged man jumped into the driving-cab of a double-decker Maidstone and District bus at Gravesend yesterday and drove off at a furious speed through the crowded main street.

He ignored traffic lights, several times the bus mounted the pavement, and in Windmill-street it crashed into a small saloon car and tore off part of the side of the car.

Mr. H. A. Young, estate agent, gave chase in his car.

Zig-zagging from side to side, the bus was overtaken about two miles out of the town and Mr. Young, aided by an A.A. scout, tried unsuccessfully to stop it at the Toll Gate cross-roads at Watling-street.

The driver ignored their signals, and skidded to a standstill in avoiding a collision with a lorry.

Then he drove off again at high speed.

Police cars took up the chase and six miles away, in Princes-road, Dartford, the runaway driver was hemmed in and stopped and taken to Dartford police station.

He is now under medical observation

"WE HAVE MOST WAR SUPPLIES"

THE claim that the British Empire and the U.S.A. control 75 per cent. of all materials necessary for war was made by Mr. A. Edwards, M.P., in the House of Commons last night.

Could the Board of Trade tell, he asked, to what extent Germany, Italy and Japan had to draw their materials from the British Empire?

A CODE WIRE WAS FLASHED TO WARSAW FROM LONDON LAST NIGHT, GIVING A PLEDGE BY BRITAIN AND FRANCE TO PROTECT POLAND AGAINST UNPROVOKED AGGRESSION BY GERMANY.

The pledge, writes the "Daily Mirror" Political Correspondent, is conditional. It is believed that special conditions operate for the ex-German territories of the Polish Corridor and Danzig.

But if any other part of Poland is attacked, Britain and France promise to take immediate military action.

The Poles alone may decide to fight for the corridor. There they have built from a fishing village the great seaport of Gnydia, their only outlet. once Danzig falls, to the sea.

Mr. Chamberlain will make a statement in the House of Commons to-day, when he will reveal the progress of the democratic line-up against aggression.

Surprise Cabinet

Colonel Beck, the Polish Foreign Minister, is due in London on Monday. It may be that, as the result of last night's message, his visit will be postponed.

The decision to inform Poland of the attitude of Britain and France was taken at the surprise Cabinet meeting at 10, Downing-street yesterday, when Ministers discussed reports of German troops massing on Poland's frontier.

The Cabinet is likely to be in constant session during the week-end, although it is believed that Hitler will not immediately order his men to march.

In Warsaw yesterday, Ministers met the military leaders to discuss the German threat.

It was decided to strengthen the Polish forces on the frontier.

Now, says the Daily Mirror Warsaw correspondent, there are over half a million Polish troops on the German frontier and in the Corridor.

German submarines arrived in Danzig yesterday and German submarine chasers have been seen in the Baltic near Danzig.

Poland believes that the German activity on the frontier is aimed at preventing the visit of Colonel Beck to London.

The German Foreign Office and the Warsaw Government denied last night that a twenty-four-hour ultimatum had been presented to Poland. "There is not a word of truth in the report," it was said in Berlin.

Late last night the gravity of the situation was indicated by a visit paid to the Premier by three Labour leaders, Mr. Greenwood, Dr. Dalton and Mr. A. V. Alexander.

They stayed with Mr. Chamberlain for more than half an hour and left just before midnight.

Colonel Beck.

NEIGHBOUR DIES AFTER EXPLOSION

BY A SPECIAL CORRESPONDENT

A MAN in a house opposite collapsed and died after an explosion in an unoccupied flat in Trafalgar-road, Moseley, Birmingham, late last night.

He was Frederick Harris, a bricklayer, who had been suffering from bronchitis.

Detectives, led by Chief Detective-Inspector Richardson, of Birmingham C.I.D., searched the flat and the rest of the house.

The flats are a few yards from a large tramway depot.

No one was injured in the flat, but the tenants of the other flats in the house were told by police to leave.

The block was placed under an all-night police guard.

Frederick Harris's landlady, Mrs. Alice Wakelam, told the Daily Mirror: "I was sitting in the kitchen with Mr. Harris when there was a terrible bang which shook the house.

"My dog dashed out of the room in terror.

"Mr. Harris jumped out of his chair and exclaimed, 'My God. That was a shock.'"

Mrs. Wakelam said that soon afterwards her lodger became ill and died.

The only damage to the flat which can be seen from the road is a blown out window.

Bomb Near Shops

Shop windows were blown out by the explosion of a crude bomb at midnight in Bold-street, Liverpool, fashionable shopping centre.

The bomb was apparently placed outside an optician's. The windows of these premises and of others on the opposite side of the road were shattered.

No one was injured.

BRIDGE SCARE

Police officers were rushed in cars to the L.N.E.R. bridge at Gainsborough-road, Leytonstone, last night, after two men wearing mackintoshes and carrying a small suitcase had been seen acting suspiciously.

"The last break . . . The last straw . . ." So ran a passage in a letter written by Mrs. C. Grahame-White (Ethel Levey, the stage star) and read in the Divorce Court yesterday.

Subject of the letter was the association of her husband, Mr. Claude Grahame-White, with Miss Phœbe Lee, former chorus girl, whom you see in this picture.

Mrs. Grahame-White was granted a decree nisi. See story on page 4.

DAILY MIRROR, Saturday, April 1, 1939.

Daily Mirror

No. 11,020.   ONE PENNY
Registered at the G.P.O. as a Newspaper.
Geraldine House, Fetter-lane, E.C.4.
HOLBORN 4321.

Symbol of the stand at last made against German aggression.

The flags of Britain and of France . . and with them the eagle of Poland on its ground of red and white.

HITLER FURIOUS AT BRITISH PLEDGE —U.S. PLEASED

PREMIER: ALL SUPPORT IN OUR POWER

THE Prime Minister's statement in the House of Commons yesterday was:

" As I said this morning, his Majesty's Government have no official confirmation of the rumours of any projected attack on Poland, and they must not therefore be taken as accepting them as true.

" I am glad to take this opportunity of stating again the general policy of his Majesty's Government. They have constantly advocated the adjustment by way of free negotiation between the parties concerned of any differences that may arise between them.

" In their opinion there should be no question incapable of solution by peaceful means, and they would see no justification for the substitution of force or threats of force for the method of negotiation.

Assurance to Poles

" As the House is aware, consultations are now proceeding with other Governments.

" In order to make perfectly clear the position of his Majesty's Government in the meantime, before those consultations are concluded, I now have to inform the House that during that period, in the event of any action which clearly threatened Polish independence and which the Polish Government accordingly considered it vital to resist with their national forces, his Majesty's Government would feel themselves bound at once to lend the Polish Government all support in their power."

" They have given the Polish Government an assurance to this effect.

" I may add that the French Government have authorised me to make it plain that they stand in the same position in this matter as do his Majesty's Government."

Soviet Consulted

In reply to Mr. Arthur Greenwood (for the Labour Opposition), Mr. Chamberlain said that his statement was meant to cover an " interim period," that the Government was consulting other Powers, including the Soviet Union, and that the Soviet Ambassador and the Foreign Secretary had had a very full discussion.

" I have no doubt," added the Premier, " the principles on which we are acting are fully understood and appreciated by the Soviet."

When Colonel Beck, the Polish Foreign Minister, comes to London, added Mr. Chamberlain, there will be discussion of further measures."

Mr. Greenwood pressed this question:—
" Could the Prime Minister say whether he would welcome that maximum co-operation from all the Powers, including U.S.S.R. ? "

" Yes, we should welcome the maximum amount of co-operation," said the Premier.

Debate, page 27.   Hore-Belisha says " Join the Ranks," page 7.

FOR THE FIRST TIME SINCE 1914, BRITAIN TOLD THE WORLD YESTERDAY THAT SHE WAS READY TO FIGHT IN EUROPE TO STOP FURTHER GERMAN AGGRESSION.

Mr. Chamberlain, speaking with the knowledge and approval of America, France and Russia, said in the House of Commons:

" In the event of action which threatened Polish independence and which Poland considered it vital to resist, Britain would feel bound at once to lend the Polish Government all support in her power."

The Premier added: " The French Government have authorised me to make it plain that they stand in the same position as do His Majesty's Government."

That declaration had immediate reaction throughout the world.

It enraged Hitler, who tore up the speech he had prepared to make to-day at Wilhelmshaven.

There was great excitement in the Berlin Foreign Office and the Chancellery.

Hitler sent for his secretary, says Reuter, and re-dictated entirely those passages of his speech dealing with foreign affairs.

In Warsaw it is reported that military talks between the General Staffs of Britain, France and Poland have already begun.

Some British and French warships, says Associated Press, may be loaned to Poland.

What of Danzig?

And as the news spread through Warsaw that Poland would not fight alone, there was general rejoicing. It means " equal peace for east and west," was the official comment. One spokesman said:

" The matter is simple. If Germany does not respect our frontiers, we fight."

The special position of Danzig and the Polish Corridor as they are affected by the British pledge has not yet been made clear.

German newspapers last night reflected the anger of the Nazi leaders. A violent anti-British campaign was soon in full blast.

" It is absolutely incomprehensible how Mr. Chamberlain came to make such an announcement out of the blue," says a statement issued by the official German News Agency.

" One can only regard this statement by the British Premier as a laughable attempt to stir up unrest and sow mistrust of Germany in the concert of the nations.

" The whole thing gives the impression that Britain can only make the small Powers, if any, believe she is prepared to take action. In

(Continued on back page)

BOMB IN PARK LANE

EXPLOSION of a bomb blew out the window of a lingerie shop in Park-lane, W., early to-day.

Women in evening dress from the mannequin ball at the Dorchester, fifty yards away, ran into the street, believing that an entire building had blown up.

Extensive damage was done to the lingerie shop, which is next door to a bank, in a recently opened block of flats. But no one was injured.

About an hour before a bomb had shattered the windows of the " News-Chronicle " offices in Fleet-street.

Parts of the window were hurled by the force of the explosion right across the street, and there was a gaping hole in the masonry underneath the glass.

The explosion is believed to have been caused by a fuse bomb which was lit only a few minutes before.

Daily Mirror

No. 11,921   ONE PENNY

Registered at the G.P.O. as a Newspaper.

Geraldine House, Fetter-lane, E.C.4.

HOLBORN 4321.

PITY ME

LOAN TO ARM THE POLES

COLONEL BECK, POLAND'S FOREIGN SECRETARY, PASSED THROUGH BERLIN BY TRAIN LAST NIGHT ON HIS WAY TO LONDON.

He did not leave his coach during the twenty minutes his train was in Berlin, and only a minor official of the German Foreign Office was sent to greet him.

His talks with Mr. Chamberlain and Lord Halifax will begin to-morrow. They will be followed almost immediately by joint military, naval and air conversations between Britain, France and Poland.

A British guarantee to Rumania, similar to that given to Poland, is expected to be announced this week.

During Colonel Beck's visit a big British loan, probably for £25,000,000, will be negotiated, to enable Poland to strengthen her army and air force.

Other pressing Polish problems will be discussed, among them the refugee Jews from Germany.

King Carol has authorised Colonel Beck to discuss with Britain the possibility of finding space in Britain's colonies for thousands of Rumania's Jews.

In Warsaw it is believed that Hitler, checked in his drive against Poland, is now seeking to better his relations with Russia.

Hitler's Saturday speech (it is reported, with world comment, on page 18) is not considered in London to have given any grounds for believing the danger is over.

It will be discussed in the Foreign Affairs debate in the House of Commons to-day, when Mr. Chamberlain is expected to allay Russian suspicions of his Polish pledge.—See page 2

Pact to Outlaw War

During Parliament's Easter recess the Government's "long-term" peace policy will be announced.

This will invite every peace-loving nation to join a pact to resist aggression and to outlaw war.

To-day M. Guy le Chambre, the French Air Minister, arrives in London. He will discuss with Air Minister Sir Kingsley Wood the joint British and French air preparations.

Viscount Gort, Chief of Britain's Imperial General Staff, inspected at the week-end the French fortification system.

There has been a sudden quickening of military preparation in Holland, where frontier garrisons have been reinforced by coast troops.

All leave has been cancelled. The frontier complement is now at full strength.

In Rome it is reported that Britain and Italy are working "behind the scenes" for general European appeasement.

MISSING A.-A. PLANS FOUND

A TRAVELLING-BAG, containing secret anti-aircraft plans, for which Scotland Yard men had been hunting for twenty-four hours, was handed in last night at Bow-street Police Station.

The man who handed in the bag was unaware of the importance of its contents.

The bag belonged to a young officer. He was going to Somerset, and on Saturday, while in London, where he was breaking his journey to stay with friends, discovered his loss.

This is the third occasion during recent weeks on which Government papers have been reported missing. C.I.D. men are still searching for the papers in the other two cases.

MYSTERY LIGHTS SEEN AGAIN

FLARES and flashing lights at sea, which have puzzled the Sussex police for nearly two years, were seen again last night from the coast between Brighton and Shoreham.

Shoreham lifeboat searched the Channel for more than three hours in vain.

A suggestion was that the lights were signals of boats trying to smuggle refugees.

No, no. You've got us all wrong. We're not making him say "Pity me—triplets," but "Pity Me triplets." What he's really thinking is "Don't pity me. . ."

The plain facts are that they're the triplet girls of Mr. and Mrs. Wilfred Richardson (that's father carrying the babies) photographed after their christening yesterday as Mary, Frances and Norah.

And Mr. and Mrs. Richardson live in the County Durham village of Pity Me.

Since their birth in November their father has had to put up with the leg-pulling of his pals, but he doesn't mind.

Proudly he said yesterday: "Pity me? No fear! They are grand lasses."

And Mrs. Richardson chimed in: "It's me you should pity. I have got to look after them."

With all the villagers out to cheer them, the triplets were taken in two cars to Framwelgate Moor Church for the christening.

Mr. and Mrs. Richardson have two other children aged six and two years.

GUNMAN HID IN BED

2 THERE ALREADY

FROM OUR OWN CORRESPONDENT

NEW YORK, Sunday.

A PRIEST to-day saved an elderly couple from being shot dead by a crazed desperado who forced his way into their apartment here, climbed into bed with them to hide and then held them as hostages.

While 200 police, armed with machine-guns and tear-gas bombs surrounded the apartment building where the desperado, John Naumo, twenty-three, held the couple prisoners, a priest, Father Francis Flynn, climbed the fire-escape to the apartment window.

By a moving plea, he dissuaded Naumo from killing Merton Nicholas, sixty-three, and his wife, sixty-one.

The drama ended when Naumo handed Flynn his revolver, saying: "Take my gun from me father."

Battle with Police

Naumo had been pursued by police in a running gun battle which followed a restaurant hold-up, in which Naumo and two companions lined twenty customers against the wall and robbed them of £100.

Naumo forced his way into the Nicholas home. Mr. and Mrs. Nicholas, lying in bed, screamed for mercy when he jumped in with them and prodded them with a revolver warning them to be silent.

Hearing police at the door, which he had

(Continued on back page)

DAILY MIRROR, Wednesday, April 5, 1939.

Daily Mirror

No. 11,923   ONE PENNY
Registered at the G.P.O. as a Newspaper.
Geraldine House, Fetter-lane, E.C.4.
HOLBORN 4321.

CONSUL KILLED BY MOB

A MOB in Mosul, Iraq, yesterday stoned to death Mr. G. E. A. C. Monck-Mason, the British Consul, as he faced them on the steps of the Consulate.

The death of King Ghazi had been announced. Agitators moved among the mourners, inciting them to fury by declaring that he had been killed by the British.

Mr. Monck-Mason bravely went to the Consulate steps and tried to pacify the mob. He told them the truth, that the young King had been killed in a car crash. But they would not listen.

They swept on, killed him, and fired the Consulate.

Troops were called out, and four men alleged to be responsible for the murder were arrested. Martial law was declared and order was restored within a few hours.

The four men are to be tried by a special court.

Back from Holiday

The Prime Minister of Iraq called on the British Charge d'Affaires at Bagdad and expressed the regrets of the Iraq Government. The Premier added that the incident had come as a terrible shock to himself and his colleagues.

The news of the assassination unleashed a sensational Wall Street decline, to which fears of a new international crisis also contributed.

The close, however, was slightly stronger.

Mr. Monck-Mason, who would have been fifty-three next week, had been married twice and his second wife is now living in Station road, Hessle, near Hull.

"Until four years ago," she said last night. "I travelled with my husband to all the countries to which he was appointed as Consul.

"Then I had to return to England and live here so that my four children could be educated.

"Last September we had just returned from a long holiday in Sweden when the crisis started, and my husband was sent to Mosul

"This is not the first riot that my husband has been in. He was in an anti-British riot in Syria, and again in Armenia in 1912-1914."

Mr. Monck-Mason was educated at Dover College.

Promoted

He became Acting Vice-Consul at Uscub (now Skoplje) in 1911 and at Adana from that year until 1914.

He was promoted to be Vice-Consul at Diarbekir in October, 1914, and when Great Britain and Turkey went to war in November that year he was employed at Alexandria and later at Salonika and Kavalla.

In 1920 he returned to Salonika as Acting Consul-General and in 1921 he was appointed Vice-Consul at Suez. He had also served at Istanbul, Port Said, Constanza, Aleppo, Syria and Tetuan.

Reuter, Exchange, Associated Press and "Daily Mirror" messages.

How King Ghazi Died—page 31.

Lord Stanhope, First Lord of the Admiralty.

Speech by First Lord Censored

AN amazing statement made by Lord Stanhope, First Lord of the Admiralty, last night, and later cancelled by officials at the Admiralty under the Official Secrets Act, is to be the subject of a question in the House of Commons to-day.

Lord Stanhope was speaking on board the aircraft-carrier Ark Royal at Portsmouth at the inauguration of the Royal Navy Film Corporation.

An hour later his statement was cancelled in Britain, but by then the news agencies had flashed it to all parts of the world, and could not recall it.

Mr. Arthur Greenwood, Deputy Leader of the Opposition, will this afternoon ask the Government for a full explanation of Lord Stanhope's statement.

"V.C." WIDOW OF PEER DIES

GERTRUDE, Lady Decies, who was awarded the French equivalent of the V.C. for her nursing work in the Great War, died yesterday in a London nursing home. She was aged over seventy.

Lady Decies was the widow of the late (fourth) Baron and sister-in-law of the present, Lord Decies.

Lady Decies was one of the greatest animal lovers in England.

She invented "jumpers" for dogs. She designed them firstly to protect her valuable Pekinese dogs against cold

They were properly-shaped jumpers with four "sleeves"

ITALY REPLIES: SENDS HER TROOPS TO ALBANIA

ITALIAN TROOPS ARE EXPECTED TO LAND IN ALBANIA WITHIN THE NEXT FORTY-EIGHT HOURS. ALREADY ITALIAN AIR SQUADRONS HAVE ARRIVED.

That is the German-Italian reply to Britain's effort to raise a Grand Alliance against aggression.

An Italian army in Albania is a direct threat to Yugoslavia and an indirect threat to Greece.

It is interpreted, writes the "Daily Mirror" Diplomatic Correspondent, as a warning to the small nations, to keep out of the British line-up.

Britain yesterday strongly hinted to Signor Mussolini that if Italy seizes Albania the Anglo-Italian pact will be regarded as violated.

If the occupation takes place "at the request" of King Zog of Albania, then Britain and France would stand aloof.

There was general alarm in Rumania last night. King Carol cancelled his engagements and the Rumanian Foreign Secretary called off his projected visit to Turkey, Paris, London and Rome.

Rumania yesterday sent infantry reinforcements to the Bulgarian frontier following reports that Bulgaria had asked German support for her claim to ex-Bulgar territory lost to Rumania after the Balkan war of 1913.

Landings Denied

In Albania reports of a landing of Italian troops were still denied last night, but in Rome it was admitted that King Zog "had asked that the 1927 agreement be brought up to date."

One clause of that agreement provides that each nation shall provide the other with military and financial help when called upon.

The Italian Government radio station at Bari announced last night, says Associated Press, that negotiations were under way to strengthen Albania's military alliance with Italy.

Mr. Chamberlain and Colonel Beck, Polish Foreign Secretary, confirmed last night their reciprocal pact against aggression.

Negotiations between the two Governments are proceeding satisfactorily, but as yet Rumania has not entered into the pact with Britain, France and Poland.

Rumania's hesitancy causes some concern.

Premier Ridiculed

Hitler arrived back in Berlin yesterday after his week-end cruise in the Strength Through Joy Liner Robert Ley. He plans to go to Berchtesgaden as soon as he can.

The reserve of the German Press towards Mr. Chamberlain, which has been wearing thin since Munich, has now, says Reuter, largely disappeared.

He is caricatured as a governess with a prayer-book under his arm and the five-pointed Jewish star round his neck.

The newspapers all claim that the British Press has been officially inspired to deny that the British policy is one of encirclement against Germany.

DAILY MIRROR, Saturday, April 8, 1939.

Daily Mirror

No. 11,025.   ONE PENNY

Registered at the G.P.O. as a Newspaper.
Geraldine House, Fetter-lane, E.C.4.
HOLBORN 4321.

ITALY LAUNCHES AIR, SEA AND LAND ATTACK ON ALBANIA

★ The Bruiser Is Crushing Child ★

"A prize-fighter, to show his skill, has knocked down a child."

That was how the Italian invasion was described yesterday by the Albanian Minister in Washington.

Here the Italian "prize-fighter's" measurements are compared with infant Albania:—

	ITALY	ALBANIA
Population	44,000,000	1,000,000
Army	600,000	13,000
Navy	4 battleships	6 gunboats
	22 cruisers	
	110 destroyers	
	82 submarines	
Air Force ..	3,000 'planes	2 'planes

MUSSOLINI, ACTING ON TELEPHONED INSTRUCTIONS FROM HIS AXIS-PARTNER HITLER, INVADED THE LITTLE KINGDOM OF ALBANIA, YESTERDAY, BOMBING AND SHELLING DEFENCELESS TOWNS AND VILLAGES TO GAIN A BASE, IT IS BELIEVED, FOR AN ATTACK ON YUGOSLAVIA.

IN the brutal attack the Italians used 400 'planes, 170 warships and 35,000 troops. But they met with a magnificent resistance.

Mussolini's excuse for unprovoked aggression was that "armed bands had imperilled the personal safety of Italian residents in Albania."

Actually, both Hitler and Mussolini are believed to be planning a combined drive in Eastern Europe.

King Zog rejected an ultimatum which would have violated his country's integrity, and said he had decided on armed resistance.

To the entire civilised world Albania broadcast an appeal for help, saying she would fight to the last man.

Lord Halifax, Britain's Foreign Minister, was on duty at the Foreign Office all day and saw a stream of callers. He cancelled his Yorkshire holiday.

With Albania in her possession, Italy will hold the entrance to the Adriatic . . . cut off Yugoslavia from outside aid, and add another front for attack on that country, already beset by Germany, Hungary and Bulgaria. After Yugoslavia, Rumania. . . .

BRITAIN WATCHES, WAITS

BRITAIN has no direct interest in Albania," said the Prime Minister in the House of Commons on Thursday, "but we have a general interest in the peace of the world. His Majesty's Government, are watching developments."

Lord Halifax, only Cabinet Minister on duty in London when the news came yesterday, did the watching.

He had long telephone talks with Mr. Chamberlain in Scotland.

A special meeting of all available Cabinet Ministers has been called for early to-day. The meeting will include the three Ministers for Defence, with their officials.

The Rumanian Minister was nearly the whole afternoon at the Foreign Office yesterday, and other callers included the French Ambassador (M. Corbin) and the Albanian, Turkish, Polish, Greek and Italian representatives.

Shortly before the evening train in which he was to have travelled to Yorkshire was due to leave, Lord Halifax cancelled his trip.

Lord Halifax

Lord Perth, the British Ambassador in Rome, saw Count Ciano yesterday.

Mr. Chamberlain continued to enjoy his fishing holiday

Early yesterday morning 400 Italian warplanes roared over Albania dropping leaflets asking for surrender and warning the people that any resistance would be crushed.

Bombs followed the leaflets when the Albanians refused to crumple in the face of the threat.

The Italian troops were met with a fierce defence when they landed troops at Durazzo, Valona, Santi Quaranta and San Giovanni di Medua.

"We Fight—Inch by Inch"

Late last night the Albanians admitted that the first three of these towns had fallen, but declared that heavy fighting was still going on.

At San Giovanni di Medua the Italian troops thrust their attack as far as the heights of Kakarrique, but after fierce counter attacks by the Albanians they fell back again.

San Giovanni di Medua is in ruins.

Durazzo was bombed twice, shelled four times from the sea, and invaded seven times, before the Italian troops gained a foothold.

Rome last night claimed a nine-mile advance beyond Durazzo. At this point the Albanians blew up a bridge over the river Shijak.

"The Gendarmerie and civilian population are continuing to defend their country inch by inch," said an Albanian communique.

"Bloody battles are taking place and the struggle is continuing to the bitter end."

The peasants are hiding in the hill country and sniping the invaders, who are calling on warplanes to bomb any groups which machine guns cannot wipe out.

The King, having decided, with his Cabinet, to resist a great Power's aggression with arms, issued to his million people a proclamation which said: "I call upon the Albanian people to be united with their hearts and to defend the Fatherland to the last drop of their blood!"

Asked whether a British warship had been sent to Albania to take off any British nationals who might want to leave, an Admiralty official said last night: "No action has been taken on the part of the Admiralty to-day."

(British United Press, Reuter, Exchange, Associated Press.)

ZOG SAVES HIS QUEEN AND BABY

QUEEN GERALDINE, with the baby Crown Prince—born only last Wednesday—and the Queen's mother, last night arrived in the Greek town of Florina, near where the Greek Yugoslav and Albanian borders meet.

Queen Geraldine was in a very weak state and had to be carried on a stretcher from her car into the hotel, which had been taken over for the royal party. She was immediately put to bed.

The royal party had travelled from Tirana in two cars, escorted by Albanian soldiers. They left Tirana at five in the morning and had travelled fourteen hours through the Albanian mountains into Greece

Hotel Guarded

The hotel is being guarded by soldiers, and no one is permitted to enter. None of the party would give details of what happened in Tirana before they left, says British United Press

It was at first stated that Queen Geraldine had taken refuge in the United States Legation in Tirana.

Later it was reported that King Zog had fought for time in face of Mussolini's threat, until his Queen could travel out of the country.

Two of Zog's five handsome sisters have arrived in Florina. The remaining three are to raise an Amazon Corps in Albania.

NEW FOOD DEFENCE CHIEF

Mr. W. S. Morrison, Chancellor of the Duchy of Lancaster, who, the Prime Minister announced in the House of Commons, is to take over responsibility for the Food Defence Plans Department, already answers in the Commons for Lord Chatfield, Minister for Co-ordination of Defence, and assists him generally.

DAILY MIRROR, Saturday, April 15, 1939.

Daily Mirror

No. 11,031   ONE PENNY
Registered at the G.P.O. as a Newspaper.
Geraldine House, Fetter-lane, E.C.4.
HOLBORN 4321.

BRITAIN ASKS RUSSIA TO JOIN PACT

Summer - time begins at 2.0 a.m. to-morrow—so before you go to bed to-night put your clocks **FORWARD** one hour.

LOVE BUG BIT GIRL IN BUS

TRAVELLING on a bus three weeks ago a twenty-three-year-old shorthand-typist was bitten by a love bug.

Tall, bespectacled Leslie Haskell, musician and expert on insects, of Dalston-road, London, N.16, sat next to Trudie Morriss, of Northwold-road, N.16, in a crowded bus.

Under his arm he carried glass cases full of insects.

The bus jerked. Leslie's cases crashed on the floor.

Trudie politely bent down to help the stranger pick them up.

An insect bit her. She screamed in panic.

Leslie was full of apologies. They got off at the same stop, talked and joked, and made a date. Now they are engaged.

"A Good Turn"

"That insect certainly did me a good turn," twenty-seven-year-old Mr. Haskell told the *Daily Mirror* last night.

"I should never have spoken to Trudie had it not been for the insect.

"When we got off the bus I apologised for the bite. Trudie seemed annoyed at first, but she isn't now."

Miss Morriss said: "I was shocked when the strange young man grabbed me by the arm and began to search for the insect that had bitten me.

"At first I wanted to slap Leslie's face, but he was so apologetic that I had to forgive him.

"He asked me to marry him a few days later."

(Picture on back page.)

30,000 Curse Mussolini

Demonstrations of protest against the Italian occupation of Albania took place yesterday after Mahomedan prayers in the principal towns of Syria and Lebanon.

In Damascus, 30,000 Mahomedans marched through the town shouting: "There is only one God, and Mussolini is his enemy."

The Arab Press is urging a boycott of Italian goods.

Moslems demonstrating at Casablanca last night shouted: "Hooray for France," and "Down with Germany and Italy."

According to an unconfirmed report, Ethiopians have attacked the railway station at Kojjo, forty-five miles from Addis Ababa, and killed the Italian garrison, and burned buildings, food depots and ammunition stores.—Reuter and Associated Press.

M.P. SUING HEIRESS WIFE FOR DIVORCE

BRITAIN HAS DECIDED TO SEEK A MUTUAL PACT WITH RUSSIA TO RESIST AGGRESSION.

Sir William Seeds, Britain's Ambassador in Moscow, has been instructed to call to-day on M. Litvinoff, Russia's Foreign Minister, and to ask him to agree to a mutual military, naval and air defensive agreement.

Russia, says the "Daily Mirror" Diplomatic Correspondent, is expected to state at once the conditions on which she will enter the pact, and Britain is confident that a mutually acceptable treaty can be negotiated.

France, which already has a pact with Russia, will seek an agreement on the same lines as the Anglo-Soviet undertaking.

The British plan is that, while Britain and Russia will promise each other full support if either is attacked by the dictator Powers, the Russian air force would be available to help Poland, Rumania, Greece or Turkey.

This would remove the objections of the smaller States to Russian troops operating in their territory.

If the treaty is signed Russia will probably suspend all sales of oil and by-products to Germany and Italy.

Litvinoff for London

Russia, so far, has announced her opposition to the plan of granting guarantees to individual nations, but has constantly expressed her readiness to take part in any scheme for collective security.

The British decision to seek Russian help is a dramatic reversal of policy. M. Maisky, the Russian Ambassador, saw Lord Halifax at the Foreign Office yesterday.

It is possible that M. Litvinoff will visit London at Lord Halifax's invitation during the first week in May.

BY A SPECIAL CORRESPONDENT

THE Hon. Mrs. Mary Ashley, £90,000-a-year wife of Captain A. S. Cunningham-Reid, M.P., is being sued for divorce by her husband.

M. Henri Garat, the French film star, has been cited as co-respondent. The action is due for hearing before Whitsuntide.

Captain Cunningham-Reid is the Conservative M.P. for St. Marylebone. Last year he figured with his wife in an action concerning the financial arrangements said to have been made between them.

A settlement of the case was announced during the hearing. The action was brought by Mr. Cunningham-Reid and a counter action by his wife was withdrawn

Back to Maiden Name

Before her marriage in 1927, Mrs. Ashley, who is thirty-two, was the Hon. Ruth Mary Clarisse Ashley. She is the daughter of Lord Mount Temple.

She announced last March that she was no longer using the name Cunningham-Reid and that she would in future be known by her maiden name.

Last night a friend told the *Daily Mirror*: "Mrs. Ashley has been on a yachting cruise for the last three weeks. I last heard from

Captain A. S. Cunningham-Reid, M.P. (left), and his heiress wife (centre), whom he is suing for divorce. M. Henri Garat (right), the French film star, is cited as co-respondent.

her from Palestine. I believe that she will shortly be returning to London."

M. Henri Garat, the French film star, was voted recently the most handsome film actor in France. He was paid £1,000 a week for his role in the film of "The Girl in the Taxi," made here in 1937.

Mrs. Cunningham-Reid was co-heiress with her sister, Lady Louis Mountbatten, to £6,000,000 left by their grandfather, Sir Ernest Cassel.

CANADA SPEECH BY KING

The B.B.C. announces that the King will broadcast an Empire Day message from Winnipeg, Canada, on May 24, at 8.0 p.m. (B.S.T.). His speech will provide the climax to a "Round the Empire" programme in course of preparation by the Canadian Broadcasting Corporation.

This will be the only occasion during the Canadian tour that a speech by his Majesty will be relayed outside the Dominion

FRANCO'S MARCH POSTPONED

IN Spain, where troops are still arriving in towns on the Gibraltar boundary, chief interest lies in the date of Franco's march of triumph into Madrid.

It was originally fixed for May 2 and Mussolini has promised that Italian troops will leave immediately afterwards.

But in Burgos last night it was reported that the date had been postponed to May 15.

And the Agence Radio from Madrid

(Continued on back page)

Inside—

DAILY MIRROR, Tuesday, April 18, 1939.

Daily Mirror

No. 11,033. ONE PENNY.
Registered at the G.P.O. as a Newspaper.
Geraldine House, Fetter-lane, E.C.4.
HOLBORN 4321.

Crisis Latest

Soviet army aid for Rumania: Back Page; Other crisis news: Page 2; How to beat bombs: Page 25: Cook too Small for the W.A.T.S.: Page 17

YOUR FOOD IS SAFE: CONTROL OF PRICES, NO QUEUES

FOOD SUPPLIES OF EVERY HOUSEHOLD IN BRITAIN ARE SAFE AGAINST THE THREAT OF WAR.

Government plans are now so far advanced that in the first moment of an emergency all food distribution will come under State control.

THERE WILL BE NO FOOD SHORTAGE, NO QUEUES, NO PROFITEERING. SUPPLIES WILL BE AVAILABLE IN ALL PARTS OF THE COUNTRY WITHOUT INTERRUPTION THROUGH ENEMY ACTION.

Prices of almost everything except luxuries will be controlled.

Food rationing cards will be issued and, immediately on the outbreak of an emergency, meat, bacon and ham, butter and margarine, lard, dripping and sugar will be rationed.

Hard Work—More Food

To deal with retail food supplies 1,400 local committees would be set up at once. Food executive officers for each committee —usually the clerks to the local authorities—have already been named.

They now have locked up in their safes the household application forms for distribution to householders and ration cards for distribution to every person in the country.

Altogether 19,000,000 forms and 60,000,000 ration cards have already been sent out to the local food control offices, where they are being kept waiting for the word "go."

Different types of workers will be given different rations. A miner, for instance, will have more substantial provisions than a shop assistant or a clerk

Oil, Wheat Reserves

The scheme has been prepared by the Food (Defence Plans) Department, which, in the event of war, would become the nucleus for a separate Government department similar to the Ministry of Food in the great war.

Distribution will remain in the hands of private traders, wholesale and retail, since it is believed that the task can be done only by existing trade organisations.

Food supplies produced at home or abroad will be bought and shipped by the Government, who will use existing importers or wholesalers as their agents.

The department are holding reserves of wheat, sugar and whale oil, and these will be used where necessary to tide over any dislocations in the flow of supplies.

All raw materials, whether imported or produced at home, will be distributed under con-

(Continued on back page)

SOUGHT TRIAL —WON

BY A SPECIAL CORRESPONDENT

DETERMINED to prove that she had not stolen money from a friend, Mrs. Phyllis Allen, eighteen, of Princes Park-close, Hayes, Middlesex, went to the local police station and insisted that she should be charged and that her fingerprints and history should be taken, just as if she had been a thief.

At Uxbridge yesterday she was found Not guilty of stealing 6s. 6d. from Mrs. Elizabeth Calderwood, of Holmbury-gardens, Hayes, Middlesex.

Mrs. Calderwood told the Court:—

"Mrs. Allen was in my house having a cup of tea with me. My handbag was in a glass dish on the sideboard.

"We had been looking at a photograph when I left the room. Later, after Mrs. Allen had left, I noticed my handbag had been opened and 6s. 6d. was missing from my purse inside.

"I Bear Her No Malice"

I went round to try to see Mrs. Allen, but she was out. I saw her sister and after a lot of arguing she gave me 6s. 6d."

In the witness-box Mrs. Allen said: "After having a cup of tea with Mrs. Calderwood I invited her to my flat to tea. I certainly did not touch her handbag.

"After hearing she had accused me of being a thief, I went to her house to get back the 6s. 6d. my sister had given her.

"Then I insisted on going to the police station to have my name cleared."

Outside the court Mrs. Allen met Mrs. Calderwood, who returned the 6s. 6d. to her.

"She did not want to press the charge," Mrs. Allen told me later.

"It was only because I was determined to clear my name that I went to court.

"It was a terrible ordeal in the police station. My husband stood bail for me, and I had no legal advice and wanted no one to speak for me.

"It is the first time I have been in the police court, but I was not a bit afraid because I was not guilty.

"I feel sorry for Mrs. Calderwood and bear her no malice.

"She promised to come and have a cup of tea with me this week-end. I hope she will."

Mrs. Phyllis Allen, aged eighteen, of Hayes (Middlesex). She insisted on being charged with stealing in order to clear her name.

WIFE AND BABY FOUND DEAD

A MAN rushed into his fish-frying shop in Lough-road, Holloway, N., last night shouting: "My wife and baby—they're drowned!"

One of the customers, Mr. Albert Thorogood, of George's-road, Holloway, followed him to the bathroom.

In the bath were Mrs. L. Johnson and her four-month-old baby. Both were dead.

"The door of the bathroom was open when I got there," Mr. Thorogood told the *Daily Mirror*. "The husband was crying: 'Oh, my baby! Oh, this is horrible!'"

PRINCE BRINGS HIS KITE

A large kite, which he carried himself and declared at the Customs, was among the luggage of Prince Abhas Bhanubandh, of Siam, when he arrived at Folkestone Harbour from France yesterday.

DAILY MIRROR, Saturday, April 22, 1939.

Daily Mirror

No. 11,937.   ONE PENNY
Registered at the G.P.O. as a Newspaper.
Geraldine House, Fetter-lane, E.C.4.
HOLBORN 4321.

CANDY GIRL TO FILM STAR

BY A SPECIAL CORRESPONDENT

IF these film fellows had their way you wouldn't be able to read anything about Skipper.

He is four years old and a film actress's baby. And according to all the rules of the film game, motherhood and glamour don't mix.

But Ellen Drew, ex-candy girl, threw a spanner in the works when she arrived in London from Hollywood yesterday.

Because this lovely young thing with the corn-coloured hair is proud of her son Skipper and she doesn't care who knows it

When she was seventeen she went from a Chicago suburb to Hollywood. She had just won a beauty contest, but she had no flighty ideas about local-girl-makes-good.

Instead she went to serve behind the counter of an ice-cream parlour—and there met her husband and the film chance she had never sought. A year in films has brought her to stardom.

Ate Fudge to Win Her

"Skipper is the most wonderful person in the world," she told me at the Savoy Hotel last night. 'I'd have brought him along, only I thought strange food and surroundings might not be too good for him.

"So he's way back in Hollywood, being looked after by a young fellow who has taken a great liking to him."

With Miss Drew is her husband, Fred Wallace, make-up expert turned actor, a quiet young man who had to eat his way through oceans of hot chocolate fudge to win his bride!

"He went into her ice-cream parlour one day for a hot chocolate fudge, and it very nearly became my staple diet after I saw the girl who was serving it," he told me with a laugh

Put Love First

Hot chocolate fudge also melted the heart of a film agent, who asked Ellen Drew if she would like a job.

She said "No," because she wanted to marry But after Skipper arrived, she thought she'd see whether the offer still held good. It did.

Miss Drew has come to England to play in Paramount's new picture, "French Without Tears,"

Ray Milland, who will also play in "French Without Tears," also arrived on the Aquitania yesterday. He was met by Tommy Farr, the heavy-weight boxer.

They knew each other as boys in Wales, for Ray's home was at Neath, only six miles from Tonypandy where Farr lives

---

Week - end weather— showers, bright periods, cool.

Candy girl who has become a film star in only one year . . . glamorous Ellen Drew, who arrived in England from Hollywood yesterday.

You see her at Waterloo in the picture below, with Ray Milland, British screen star, with whom she will act in the screen version of "French Without Tears."

Miss Drew is partly British, too—her grandparents came from Dublin.

B.B.C. and Govt. Control

BY A SPECIAL CORRESPONDENT

Reports in London last night that the Government would take over control of broadcasting on June 7 came as a complete surprise to B.B.C. chiefs.

The reports suggested that the B.B.C. would become a Government news service —to a great extent a propaganda machine, except that the entertainment side would not be touched.

An important B.B.C. executive said to the "Daily Mirror" early to-day:—

"If this is true, I am certain it will be news even to the Director-General himself.

"But we cannot deny it. We are not in a position to conceive any move that the Government may be planning to make."

The B.B.C. Charter enables the Government to take control whenever the Postmaster-General decides that an emergency justifies it.

ALLIED FRONT GROWS

BRITAIN and France have made vital progress in strengthening the front against aggression. The partners' talks with Turkey, reported Reuter from Paris early to-day, are on the point of being successfully concluded.

This will establish a system of security in the Eastern Mediterranean, an area of paramount strategic importance.

Britain's talks with Russia are also going well.

And this good news last night was strengthened by M. Bonnet, France's Foreign Minister, who said he hoped his own country's conversations with the Soviet would soon be successfully completed.

As her diplomats worked for international strength, France showed the world last night how much she is in earnest about the part she herself will play in deterring aggression.

M. Reynaud, Minister of Finance, told the nation over the radio of new defence measures which will cost 17,000,000,000 francs (about £97,000,000).

In eight months France has budgeted
(Continued on back page)

DAILY MIRROR, Tuesday, April 25, 1939.

Daily Mirror

No. 11,039.   ONE PENNY

Registered at the G.P.O. as a Newspaper.
Geraldine House, Fetter-lane, E.C.4.
HOLBORN 4321.

JAPS STORM HOSPITAL, ATTACK BRITON

★ While flames leapt from a Manchester store, this girl, nineteen-year-old Sheila Carney, stuck to her job of lift-girl and carried fifty girls to safety. Twice she made the journey to the top floor and back and while other girls fainted, she remained calm until every assistant was safe. Then she collapsed. See story on page 5.

Saved 50 in Her Lift

TWENTY-FIVE JAPANESE SAILORS, LED BY AN OFFICER, STORMED THEIR WAY INTO A SHANGHAI HOSPITAL YESTERDAY, DEMANDED TO SEE THE BODY OF A BRITISH DOCTOR KILLED IN A ROAD CRASH AND HIS SERIOUSLY INJURED WIDOW. LATER THEIR COMMANDING OFFICER FORCED HIMSELF INTO THE ROOM WHERE THE ENGLISHWOMAN HAD JUST BEEN OPERATED ON.

During a dispute with the British hospital authorities, the Japanese officer slapped the face of the English Assistant Police Commissioner, Mr. A. H. Samson.

The crash victim, Dr. Bertram Lillie, aged thirty-eight, of London, had just returned from leave in England to his post as President of the Lester Institute of Technical Education in Shanghai.

He was driving his wife and Police Sergeant Wimsett, an Englishman, through the Japanese-occupied district of Hongkew when Japanese bluejackets jumped on to the running board.

Dr. Lillie refused to stop. His car swerved and crashed into a bus.

One Japanese sailor was seriously wounded. Dr. Lillie and his two passengers were taken to the Hongkew General Hospital, where the doctor was found to be dead. His wife was seriously injured and had to be operated on.

Then twenty-five uniformed Japanese sailors arrived at the hospital, demanded to see Dr. and Mrs. Lillie.

The English superintendent, Dr. Couper Patrick, refused.

He told them that Dr. Lillie was dead and after some dispute showed them his body. They then ordered him to show them Mrs. Lillie. Dr. Patrick explained that she was on the operating table.

In the argument that followed, the English Police Assistant Commissioner's face was slapped.

"Take Care" To Hitler

THE British Government, anxious that Hitler in his speech next Friday should not commit himself to statements which he might find impossible to withdraw, have sent Sir Nevile Henderson back to Berlin to make Britain's position clear.

Sir Nevile, says the Daily Mirror Diplomatic Correspondent, will seek an immediate interview with Hitler.

He will tell him that Britain fully supports President Roosevelt's plan, that a British pact with Russia is nearing completion, and that this country will impose conscription if the crisis continues.

This information, it is believed, will warn Hitler not to announce that an Anglo-Russian pact would be considered by Germany an act of war.

In Berlin last night, it was officially announced that the Reichstag meeting, at which Hitler will speak, will be held at twelve o'clock, noon, on Friday, in the Kroll Opera House.

The conscription question will be considered by the Cabinet to-morrow.

It is believed that, to overcome Labour opposition to a compulsory scheme, the Government

(Continued on back page)

ANOTHER FRENCH SHIP BURNED

FIRE destroyed the 9,847 tons steamship Angers near La Seyne shipyard, Toulon, France, last night, shortly before midnight.

A military powder depot and petrol stocks nearby were not menaced, authorities said as they ordered an investigation to learn whether sabotage was responsible for the fire.—Associated Press.

The Angers, formerly the Capacorna, built in 1907 at Hamburg, was being broken up.

The ship was owned by a subsidiary of the Messageries Maritime, a French company.

Authorities still are investigating the burning of the liner Paris at Le Havre last Tuesday on the theory that it was committed by foreign agents.

HELD BREATH FIVE MINUTES

HOW long can you hold your breath? A minute, a minute and a half, perhaps, or even two at the most?

Mr. A. J. Sheffield, of Fleeman-grove, West Bridgford, Nottingham, has astonished doctors by holding his breath for five minutes forty seconds.

Mr. Sheffield was having a medical test when applying for admission to the Observation Section of the R.A.F. Volunteer Reserve.

BUDGET BLOW TO DRIVERS EXPECTED

BY OUR POLITICAL CORRESPONDENT

MEMBERS of Parliament fear a Budget surprise this afternoon—increases in the motor horse power and petrol taxes.

In the Lobbies last night M.P.s were saying that Sir John Simon, Chancellor of the Exchequer, would raise the horse power tax from 15s. to £1 per unit.

The petrol tax, now 9d. a gallon, would be increased by one penny.

If the horse power tax were raised not only the manufacturers but private motorists would suffer.

DAILY MIRROR, Wednesday, April 26, 1939.

Daily Mirror

No. 11,040.   ONE PENNY.
Registered at the G.P.O. as a Newspaper.
Geraldine House, Fetter-lane, E.C.4.
HOLBORN 4321.

CONSCRIPTION— MEN OF 18-21 MUST BE SOLDIERS

ALL PAY BUDGET

Sir JOHN SIMON'S peace-time war Budget of £942,600,000 was favourably received in the House of Commons, the City and throughout the country last night.

Chief points the Chancellor announced are:—

There is no increase in income tax.

Tax on private cars is raised from 15s. to 25s. per horse-power as from next January 1. Motorcycle taxes will be raised correspondingly.

Sugar duty raised by ¼d. per lb. from five o'clock last night.

Tobacco duty up by 2s. per lb. This increase will be passed on to smokers. It is approximately 1½d. an ounce, and cigarette smokers will probably pay the same price for a packet of fewer cigarettes.

This arrangement would not interfere with the automatic machine trade.

Imperial Tobacco Company have not yet authorised any increase in prices.

Surtax is increased. Incomes from £2,000 to £8,000 will be taxed a further 5 per cent., and incomes above £8,000 a further 10 per cent.

Death duties go up. Estates of over £50,000 will pay an additional 10 per cent. There is no tax increase on agricultural property.

Photographic films and plates will be taxed The rate is to be about 2d. on the popular sizes of roll films

Theatres Gain

And Sir John Simon announced two concessions to the taxpayer.

Entertainments tax on the "living theatre" is reduced so as to cut prices by 1d. This will operate from September 3 next.

Medicine stamp duties are repealed. The duties were, said Sir John, "a troublesome question which I propose to settle once and for all." The medicine tax had brought in a revenue of £590,000.

A new drive is to be launched on the taxdodger. It will be directed, the Chancellor declared, "against the ingenious use of the one-man company."

The Budget has been framed, Sir John stressed, to meet the "cruel necessity" of leaping defence costs.

In the coming year £630,000,000 will be needed for defence instead of the £580,000,000 he estimated only two months ago.

"And," Sir John Simon added ominously, "it may well be more."

The Chancellor in a broadcast speech last night said:—

"No one will escape.

"The five tax increases—motor-cars, surtax, estate duty, tobacco and sugar—have been arranged to call for a contribution from all kinds of citizens.

"Our defence expenditure this year— £630,000,000 was not far short of £2,000,000 a day. It was £13 per head of the population of the United Kingdom. It was more than three times the total public expenditure for all purposes before the war.

"Though these burdens are hard to bear," Sir John added, "remember that in these difficult days Britain's best contribution to the peace of the world is that she herself should be strong."

Budget Speech—Page 24.
W. M. on the Budget—Page 13.

30 FEET

A baby fell 30ft. from the open window you see in this picture . . . he was caught by the shop sun blind and suffered nothing worse than a bruised nose.

You'll find his picture — and the full story—on page 3.

34 Millions a Year More

Total estimated effect of the alterations proposed in the Budget are £24,270,000 increase this year and £53,945,000 in a full year.

The principal receipts are estimated at:
Income tax, £327,000,000.
Surtax, £70,000,000.
Estate duties, £80,000,000.
Stamp , £21,000,000.
National Defence Contribution, £25,000,000.
Other inland revenue duties, £1,250,000.
Total inland revenue, £524,250,000.
Customs and Excise, £349,020,000.
Motor vehicle duties, £43,450,000.
Total receipts from taxes, £916,720,000.
Total revenue, £942,600,000.

After a dramatic Cabinet meeting last night —the first ever known to be called immediately after a Budget speech — the Government decided to introduce a scheme of compulsory military training.

Mr. Chamberlain later paid a surprise visit to the King at Buckingham Palace, and informed him of the vital decision taken. He remained with the King for nearly an hour.

In the House of Commons to-day the Premier will announce the Cabinet's plan, and a Bill will later be introduced to make the scheme law.

The Government have decided, says the "Daily Mirror" Political Correspondent, to conscript men between the ages of eighteen and twenty-one—it may be raised to twenty-three—for a short period of military training.

Soldiers thus enrolled will follow their compulsory service with a short period in the Territorial Army.

Details are still being worked out. It is believed that recruits will serve four months in the Army and four years in the Territorials.

There are available over a million men between the ages of eighteen and twenty-one. Many are in reserved occupations and the reserved list is likely to be drastically revised to free the greatest possible number of men.

If the age limit is raised to twenty-five over 3,000,000 men would be available—too many for the Army to train in the immediate future.

Two main reasons have influenced the Government in coming to a conscription decision:

(1) Pressure from France, Poland, Rumania and Greece for a sign of Britain's capacity to fulfil her pledges.

(2) Representations from the Army Council, who consider that conscription is imperative if full advantage is to be taken of our defence resources.

By Age Classes

The Government will not attempt to force the Conscription Bill through the House. They will welcome long debates in the knowledge that in view of facts regarding the international situation the country will realise the need for immediate conscription.

The scheme will be so arranged as to provide the maximum number of instructors for the period of service.

It is proposed to conscript men by age classes. The Government are prepared to make concessions to the Labour and Trade Union movements in order to remove their opposition.

Mr. Chamberlain will see Labour and Trade Union delegates this morning before he makes his statement in the House of Commons.

A special Cabinet committee will consider Trade Union objections to compulsion.

In order to placate the Labour movement,
(Continued on back page)

DAILY MIRROR, Friday, April 28, 1939.

Daily Mirror

No. 11,042　　ONE PENNY
Registered at the G.P.O. as a Newspaper.
Geraldine House, Fetter-lane, E.C.4.
HOLBORN 4321.

Two Seasons in One Day

Many parts of Britain had two seasons in a few hours yesterday. Ipswich saw hailstones, marbles size, sleet, rain, then brilliant sun and blue sky—all in fifteen minutes. London had sleet storms, too, and more hail is predicted for to-day—with warmer weather in a day or two.

Farmers and fruit growers report heavy losses, blossom having been ruined by overnight frost.

BIG 'YES' TO YOUTH ARMY AS HITLER PONDERS

THE HOUSE OF COMMONS LAST NIGHT APPROVED BY 376 VOTES TO 145 THE GOVERNMENT'S PLAN TO CONSCRIPT THE YOUTH OF BRITAIN. THE LABOUR AMENDMENT WAS DEFEATED BY 380 VOTES TO 143—A MAJORITY OF 237.

IN THE HOUSE OF LORDS THE GOVERMENT PLAN WAS APPROVED WITHOUT A DIVISION.

HITLER, angered by the swift events of the past twenty-four hours, hurriedly rewrote last night parts of the speech he will make to-day to the Reichstag.

The tactical advantage has suddenly swung in favour of Hitler's opponents.

Britain is conscripting an army. Russia has indicated her readiness to help the Democracies. Japan has told Germany she will not fight with the Axis.

M. Maisky, Russia's Ambassador in London, who arrived in Paris yesterday on his way back from Moscow, said:

"I return very content.

"Russia's position in a possible conflict is perfectly clear. We are going to assist Europe in case of aggression."

The Anglo-Russian talks, held up while Britain examines Russia's proposal for an all-in collective security pact, are still going on in Moscow.

"I am satisfied," M. Maisky commented, "that our negotiations have reached a point where both parties will have to wait."

The important Russian proposals submitted

(Continued on back page)

It'll Be the FRONT Door To-Morrow

Leaving Westminster Abbey yesterday by a side door in this picture is Lady Diana Percy, sister of the Duke of Northumberland. She'd been at a rehearsal of her wedding there to-morrow—to Viscount Brackley, son of the Earl and Countess of Ellesmere.

Peers and millionaires will be among the guests . . . and with them will be twelve girls from arms works and factories on Tyneside and from Post Office and shipping concerns, chosen by ballot among their workmates.

CIGS 6½D. FOR TEN TO-DAY

TO-DAY you will pay 6½d. for ten cigarettes of the "sixpenny" brands.

The increase in price was announced yesterday by the Imperial Tobacco Company, the combine that controls most of the cigarette firms, and by Carreras.

"Popular" brands of tobacco will cost three-halfpence an ounce more.

Largest manufacturers of the "ten for sixpence" cigarettes are John Player and Sons, and W. D. and H. O. Wills (branches of the Imperial Tobacco Company), and Carreras.

Some of the most popular makes are Player's Navy Cut, Goldflake, Craven A and Bachelor's.

Now, special packets of cigarettes made for automatic machines may be introduced by the Imperial Tobacco Company.

There are 350,000 cigarette machines in the country. Their owners wait to hear whether the special packets will contain—

cigarettes thinner in diameter, by about a millimetre;

or one cigarette fewer (nine instead of ten).

In favour of nine-for-sixpence is Mr. P. Harper, director of a Croydon, Surrey, automatic machine company.

He said: "It is technically impossible, without altering the whole machine, to provide for the extra halfpenny. However, most machines are built to take the special packets.

"If these special packets are not provided," Mr. Harper added, "the machines would be useless."

MR. EDEN JOINS UP

Mr. Anthony Eden, ex-Foreign Secretary and ex-captain in the King's Royal Rifle Corps, has accepted a commission in the Rangers, crack Territorial regiment.

He is now undergoing a refresher course at Tidworth, on Salisbury Plain, and will be gazetted as major shortly. He was asked to accept the rank of lieutenant-colonel, but declined.

GERMANS FIGHT SOLDIERS

UNREST in Germany is indicated by two reports last night.

Travellers arriving at Metz, France, from the Saar said German troops had been sent there to reinforce police unable to cope with rioting workmen.

Disorders broke out at Burbach, where miners refused to work more than sixty hours a week, and also protested against the quality of food.

The troops are said to have charged the rioters, and some miners were killed.

The travellers also report that the Saarbruecken police had to intervene in a large cafe on Hitler's birthday when Nazis and anti-Nazis clashed. About twenty arrests were made, they added.

Unrest in the middle classes has forced the Government to modify the tax law introduced last month. This law, providing for a thirty per cent. tax on increases of income, has now been limited to incomes of £600.

British United Press and Exchange messages.

On Other Pages

WHICH IS CORRECT?

Two Guinness

or

Two Guinnesses

Some people call for "Two Guinnesses" and others for "Two Guinness." Now which is correct? The answer is each — or either—or both.' It just doesn't matter so long as you get your Guinness(es).

But if there is any doubt about the *plural*, there is none about Guinness itself. Just taste that clean, bracing flavour, with its fresh invigoration. It's unmistakable. It's the flavour of Guinness and nothing else. It comes from a special roasting of barley, a special method of brewing the malt and hops. Just look at the delicious creamy head. That comes from the special Guinness yeast. And, of course, the most distinctive thing of all about a Guinness is its *goodness*.

Does your wife also like Guinness? Then take two Guinness — or two Guinnesses-home tonight.

G.E.570.

DAILY MIRROR, Tuesday, May 2, 1939.

Daily Mirror

No. 11,945   ONE PENNY

Registered at the G.P.O. as a Newspaper.
Geraldine House, Fetter-lane, E.C.4.
HOLBORN 4321.

FIRST 50,000 OF NEW ARMY AT ONCE: JOBS KEPT OPEN

OI!
Shouts The King

Laughing happily, swaying from side to side to the music's rhythm, the King and Queen shouted enthusiastic "Oi's" as they sang the "Lambeth Walk" at the Victoria Palace, London, last night.

ON the eve of their visit to the United States, they had made last-minute arrangements to see "Me and My Girl."

It was not until someone at the back of the gallery shouted: "Isn't that the King and Queen?" that the audience knew that their Majesties were in the theatre.

When it came to the famous song the audience took their cue for the "Ois" from the King and Queen, and when it was over audience and cast joined in giving their Majesties a great ovation.

At each "Oi!" the Queen flicked her thumb back in the approved Lambeth fashion.

Rocked with Laughter

The Queen, dressed all in white, with a fox fur cape over a white satin gown, and with diamond earrings and two white flowers in her hair, acknowledged the rousing cheers which filled the theatre.

During the interval the King—who had rocked with laughter right from the time when the curtain went up—requested that Lupino Lane be presented to him.

"It is the most enjoyable evening I have ever spent," he said, "but you don't do the Lambeth Walk the same way that the Queen and I do it. We do it the ballroom style," added the King, smiling. "We shall have to do it your way now."

The Queen, who had danced the Lambeth Walk at a ball at Balmoral Castle last October, said: "It is certainly wonderful the way you do it." She asked Mr. Lane where he had received a little monkey that she had sent him years ago when she was the Duchess of York.

Saw Him Dancing

"I told the Queen I had," Mr. Lane told the *Daily Mirror*.

"They saw me dancing at the London Hippodrome a few years ago in a show called 'Brighter London.' That was when they were the Duke and Duchess of York. The Queen sent me a little monkey—I had played the part of Jacko in the show."

By a coincidence, the B.B.C. had chosen to televise last night's performance. But television audiences did not see their Majesties, as their visit was unofficial.

Arms Before the Man

Because they did not want to interrupt work and handicap the progress of national defence, French workers—including Socialists and Communists—yesterday abandoned the traditional May 1 demonstrations for the first time in twenty years.

Conscription —The Terms

All men of twenty will be called up in batches of 50,000, beginning this month, for six months' service. Ten days' notice will be given every man.

✦ ✦ ✦

Employers who refuse to reinstate soldiers after their service in jobs "no less favourable" than they had can be fined £50 and will be ordered to compensate the men—probably with four weeks' wages.

✦ ✦ ✦

Every man of twenty must register. Those who do not will be fined £5 and will still be required to serve their training period at whatever age they are enrolled.

✦ ✦ ✦

Special allowances will be paid in case of need to wives and dependants.

✦ ✦ ✦

A new naval reserve is to be set up —the Royal Naval Special Reserve. Conscripts will have the right to ask to serve in the new naval force or in the R.A.F., but only a small percentage will be needed in these services.

SIMON DENIES BUDGET LEAK

WHEN an M.P. last night demanded an investigation into a story that tobacco movements involving a tax saving of £150,000 to £200,000 took place because of Budget "leakages," Sir John Simon, Chancellor of the Exchequer, said:

"I hope that is not so and I do not think it is so."

In the debate on the Budget in Committee of Ways and Means, Mr. E. Dunn (Soc. Rother Valley) said some of his constituents were seriously disturbed as to whether or not there had been "leakages" before the Chancellor made his statement in the House.

"I am informed," said Mr. Dunn, "that between Manchester Docks and Nottingham from April 17 to 25, there were taken full train loads of forty to fifty wagons, approximately eight to nine tons each, of tobacco; that, in addition, the sidings at Nottingham were full to capacity, and that the sidings outside Woodhead Tunnel on the L.N.E.R. were also packed with wagons containing tobacco.

Sir John Simon replied: "I think the explanation was quite straightforward and innocent.

"I have no doubt the tobacco trade did take out of bond as much as they were allowed to take merely as a precaution, but I think the movement which Mr. Dunn referred to at Manchester Docks and Nottingham was nothing more than that.

"I think there is a big factory there and a bonded warehouse. It might very well be what was being moved was not being moved out of bond but from one place to another.

"I am glad to say for the trade generally, as far as I know, we may take it that this year there has been no breach of confidence and the usual secrecy has been observed which we are all pleased to secure."

BY OUR POLITICAL CORRESPONDENT

BRITAIN'S YOUTH ARMY IS TO BE CONSCRIPTED IN BATCHES OF 50,000, BEGINNING THIS MONTH; EVERY MAN WILL HAVE TEN DAYS' NOTICE. FINES UP TO £50 WILL BE IMPOSED ON EMPLOYERS WHO REFUSE TO REINSTATE MEN AFTER SERVICE.

Details of the new Army Bill—the Military Training Bill— were published late last night after long Ministerial talks and consultations with the Army chiefs.

It provides that "every male British subject" who is twenty must register for six months' military service unless he is medically unfit, or is a conscientious objector whose position has been modified by a tribunal.

After his six months' service he must serve three and a half years in the Territorials or Army Reserve.

The new soldiers will be enrolled by the Ministry of Labour and will be registered on a Military Training Register.

Recruits will first be called to undergo a medical inspection.

Lower Medical Standard

Then they will receive a calling up paper, giving them ten days' notice and telling them when and where they must report.

A man will be regarded as "duly enlisted as a militia man," the Bill says, on the day he is notified to present himself.

THE MEDICAL STANDARD WILL BE LOWER THAN THAT OF THE REGULAR ARMY. THE PLAN IS TO BUILD UP THE PHYSIQUE OF THE YOUNG SOLDIERS.

Conscientious objectors must enrol on a special register, must go before special "Hardship Tribunals," where they may be legally represented, and must then perform either non-combatant duties with the Army or work of national importance.

Those of the required age who do not register will be subject to a fine of £5 and must do their six months' service whatever their ages.

Men will have the right to ask to go into the Navy or the R.A.F., but only a few thousand will be needed for these Services.

Ireland has provided a difficult problem. The Military Training Bill says "His Majesty may by Order in Council direct that this Act shall extend to Northern Ireland and to the Isle of Man, subject to such modifications and adaptations as may be specified in the order."

New Naval Reserve

Only a few thousand men are involved in Northern Ireland, and from a military point of view this is not a matter of importance.

As every British subject who is resident in this country is embraced in the Bill, it presumably includes Southern Irishmen who are working in England.

They would not be excused by claiming to be citizens of Eire.

If a Southern Irishman joined one of the Eire forces he would be automatically excluded from the present Bill.

It would be no use for a Southern Irishman to return to Ireland until he was over twenty-one, as provisions in the Bill would make him

(Continued on back page)

DAILY MIRROR, Wednesday, May 3, 1939.

Daily Mirror

No. 11,046   ONE PENNY
Registered at the G.P.O. as a Newspaper.
Geraldine House, Fetter-lane, E.C.4.
HOLBORN 4321.

Dolly Shares Her Joy

★ 4,000-HOME KILLER PROBE

CRIPPLE GIRL OF 9 GETS £2,082

A GIRL of nine was awarded £2,082 damages at Liverpool Assizes yesterday for injuries in an accident.

The child—Emily Kathleen Smith, of Manor-road, Hoylake, Cheshire — is a cripple, unlikely ever to marry.

When told of the award yesterday she clapped hands for joy.

But this is what her counsel, Mr. E. G. Hemmerde, K.C., told the Court:—

By the time Emily was thirty, there would be such a condition of quite unbearable pain that a hip joint would have to be fused or pinned.

This was so severe that it could not be done in less than two operations, and thereafter her leg would be completely stiff.

There were risks that she could not undertake maternity without great difficulties, dangers and serious operations.

In his summing up to the jury, Mr. Justice Stable said it was not certain that the girl would ever marry or have any children, but the difficulty of her childbearing was one of the facts on which the jury had to make up their minds.

They must bear in mind that in those days she would no longer be a child but a grown-up woman.

"I'd Like To Be Girl Guide"

"Daddy teaches me sums at night when he comes home from work," said the child.

"I will put the money away, because when I am old, no one will be able to look after me and I shall have to be pushed about in a chair.

"Daddy is a dairyman. I always wanted to be a dairymaid, but owing to my injuries, I don't think I shall ever be one. I would like to be a Girl Guide and go to school like other little girls."

Meanwhile she comforts herself with her favourite doll—Rose.

Emily was knocked down nearly three years ago while riding her toy cycle. She was pinned under a lorry wheel.

For two and a half years she lought for life in hospital.

A year ago, while exercising in her attempt for a cure, she fell and broke her left leg. But she struggled on.

Her left hip had been completely dislocated, she had six fractures of the pelvis, and she was kept in a frame for nine months.

HITLER'S LATEST PLAN

Germany, according to the Danish newspaper *Politiken*, has proposed mutual guarantee treaties to Denmark, Sweden, Norway and Finland.

The Danish Foreign Minister refuses to deny the report. In Sweden it is admitted that the Government has been sounded as to its attitude to such a treaty.—Exchange.

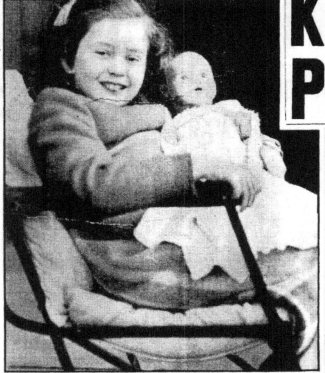

Happily clasping her favourite doll Rose . . . nine-year-old Emily Kathleen Smith, of Manor-road, Hoylake (Cheshire), in a wheel-chair after she had been awarded £2,082 damages at Liverpool yesterday. Emily clapped her hands for joy when she learned of the award.

POLES ANGER NAZIS

A FURIOUS campaign against Poland is rising to a new intensity in the German Press.

The suggestion that Colonel Beck, the Polish Foreign Minister, might, in self-defence, proclaim a Polish Protectorate over Danzig, has produced angry comments and headlines.

"This is grotesque," says one Berlin paper, "because of the important fact that the Fuehrer has proclaimed the German nature of Danzig. Has Poland lost all reason?"

And the *Angriff* comments: With an audacity that is as astounding as it is dangerous, a large section of the Polish Press has begun spreading the most ridiculous political statements.

When the Polish Parliament meets on Friday Colonel Beck will make his important statement on foreign policy.

Adopting Hitler's Tactics

Poland is to adopt the same tactics as Herr Hitler. The official Polish reply will be handed to the German Government by the Polish Charge d'Affaires in Berlin exactly five minutes before Colonel Beck's speech.

Sir Nevile Henderson, British Ambassador in Berlin, saw von Ribbentrop yesterday and had a twenty minutes talk with him on the international situation.

Travellers returning to Berlin from the Polish frontier area report that the big towns are full of troops.

Poles are angry at anti-Polish incidents in German areas in Pomorze. Insults to Polish officials and the Catholic religion are reported daily.

Herr Hitler returned to his mountain retreat above Berchtesgaden yesterday. He will remain there, it is believed, for several days.

Press Must Be Free

"The Press of Britain must continue in time of war. It must be free to publish 'undoctored' news," said Sir Samuel Hoare, Home Secretary, in a speech to the Newspaper Society in London last night.

"Nothing," he added, "had so alarmed the public during the General Strike as the absence of news." Steps would be taken to protect newspapers from too great a withdrawal of trained workers.

If war should come, Sir Samuel said, a censorship would be necessary.

"But the best way to avoid errors is to take the leaders of the Press into your confidence, to appeal to their sense of patriotic responsibility. That is the British way."

Sir Samuel's speech is on page 4.

A THOUSAND houses an hour were being visited last night by Manchester police hunting for the murderer of Patricia Carney, aged five.

A hundred police are being used in the house-to-house search on the new housing estate at Wythenshawe, where there are 4,000 homes.

"We are convinced," Detective Superintendent Page told the "Daily Mirror," "that the killer is a madman, responsible for other attacks on children here. Someone must be shielding him."

Patricia's body was found yesterday in a lonely country lane at Ringway, three miles from her home in Askern-avenue, Northenden. She had been outraged and strangled.

A man with a bicycle is stated to have been seen with a little girl on the handlebars

(Continued on back page)

DAILY MIRROR, Saturday, May 6, 1939.

Daily Mirror

No. 11,049   ONE PENNY
Registered at the G.P.O. as a Newspaper.
Geraldine House, Fetter-lane, E.C.4.
HOLBORN 4321.

GOD SPEED

Last Night in Europe

Britain last night sent a Note to Moscow rejecting, for the time being, the proposed alliance between Britain, France and the Soviet.

Declarations of willingness to defend threatened countries were suggested instead.

Germany has rejected Colonel Beck's speech as a basis of negotiation. (See page 3.)

BODY FIND IN CELLAR

FROM OUR OWN CORRESPONDENT

NOTTINGHAM, Friday.

HACKING into the wall of a cellar of a house in Rose-street, here, to-day, a squad of police found the remains of a woman who has been missing for five years.

The body, fully clothed, is believed to be that of a Mrs. Beatrice May Gamble, aged forty-two, who formerly lived in the house. She had four children—three boys and a girl—one of whom is married.

Her husband, Harry Gamble, an unemployed stage hand, was interviewed in London last night by a Nottingham police superintendent and a sergeant.

Shortly before midnight he left St. Pancras to return to Nottingham with them and help them in their inquiries.

Mr. Gamble had left Nottingham eighteen months ago.

Nottingham police decided to try digging as a "last hope" when the case of Mrs. Gamble came up for periodical review.

Records showed that while many avenues had been explored according to routine, no attempt had been made at digging.

Accordingly permission of the present tenants was sought to allow digging

The police noticed that some bricks in the cellar wall were not firmly embedded. They removed a ton of coal, hacked at the wall and found the body bricked in.

Radio S O S

Since Mrs. Gamble's disappearance, descriptions and inquiries, including wireless broadcasts, have been made from time to time.

Professor H. S. Holden, Director of Nottingham Forensic Science Laboratory, was called and after he had examined the remains they were taken to the mortuary in a coffin which had been made by police in the yard of the house.

Some time after Mrs. Gamble disappeared, an S O S was broadcast asking her to go to the bedside of her dying mother.

Mrs. Gamble's married daughter, Mrs. Daisy Smith, of Broad Oak-terrace, Nottingham, lives a few yards away from the house where her mother's body was found.

"I was seventeen when mother disappeared," Mrs. Smith told the *Daily Mirror* last night.

(Continued on back page)

The King and Queen, who leave England to-day in the liner Empress of Australia (above) for Canada.

The Princess Elizabeth and Princess Margaret will travel to Portsmouth on the royal train to say good-bye

BRITAIN'S SALUTE TO THE KING

BY A SPECIAL CORRESPONDENT

"GOD SPEED." To-day the nation gives this salute to the King and Queen, who this afternoon sail from Portsmouth in the Empress of Australia for their tour of Canada and their visit to the United States.

Their departure is historic as the first occasion on which a reigning monarch of this country has crossed the Atlantic.

With them will go the Empire's good wishes —for their own happiness during their six weeks' absence from these shores and for the forging of a still more intimate tie with the New World.

The King last night appointed the Council of State which will act for him in his absence.

Although the Queen is going with him she is one of the Council of State. Her appointment was necessary under the Regency Act of 1937, which says that the Sovereign's Consort must be one of the Counsellors.

The other Counsellors, who must be the four persons next in succession to the Throne (minors excepted), are the Duke of Gloucester, the Duke of Kent, the Princess Royal and Princess Arthur of Connaught.

Liner Booked For Return

It was officially announced last night that the King and Queen will return from their tour in the Empress of Britain (42,000 tons).

The ship will be specially chartered, as the Empress of Australia has been for the outgoing voyage.

The Empress of Britain is even more magnificently suited than the Empress of Australia, and only very slight alterations will be needed. She is now on a world cruise, and is due home about May 21.

The King and Queen will travel as public figures. Yesterday, although State affairs could not be entirely excluded, they sought to be private people, surrounded only by their family and their closest friends.

Family Farewell Dinner

The King and Queen had a family farewell dinner party at Buckingham Palace last night. Queen Mary, the Duke and Duchess of Gloucester and the Duke and Duchess of Kent were present.

Princess Elizabeth, who had received special permission to stay up, was with the King and Queen when they greeted their relatives and guests. Princess Margaret had by that time gone to bed.

In the morning the King had spent busy hours on State business.

After working in his study, he held a Privy Council at Buckingham Palace.

Next Sir John Gilmour was received on his reappointment as Lord High Commissioner of the Church of Scotland.

The Prime Minister then had audience for more than thirty minutes and afterwards the King received the Lord Chamberlain, Lord Clarendon.

But during the afternoon and evening the
(Continued on back page.)

'DEATH DIVE' —HURT ANKLE

A YOUNG naval officer, driving from Portsmouth to London yesterday, skidded in his car.

Plunged 100ft. in what seemed a certain death dive over the Devil's Punch Bowl—"black spot" near Hindhead, Surrey;
Turned four somersaults;
Crashed into bushes below.

Climbing out of the car, the driver brushed the dust from his clothes, crawled up the 100ft. slope to the main road.

His only injury was a sprained ankle.

Trembling a little from shock, he stopped a passing car. "I've just been over the top," he explained, and asked for a lift to the nearest garage.

An employee at the garage told the *Daily Mirror*:—

"I was amazed when the driver told me he had crashed into the 'Bowl.' He limped into the garage and asked if his car could be brought up.

The Devil's Punch Bowl, famed beauty spot, has claimed many victims. Five years ago a motor-coach with six passengers crashed over the side. One man was killed, the rest seriously injured.

DAILY MIRROR, Tuesday, May 9, 1939

Daily Mirror

No. 11,951.   ONE PENNY.

Registered at the G.P.O. as a Newspaper

Geraldine House, Fetter-lane, E.C.4

HOLBORN 4321

He Sat at His Wedding

Leaning on the arm of his bride, Miss Madge Tuffin, as they leave St. Nicholas Church, Sevenoaks (Kent), in the picture below is Detective Vincent Jackson, of Rochester Police Force. He's got his right arm in a sling and he limped as he walked . . . because last week he fell 15ft. through a roof while watching for burglars, fractured a wrist and tore leg ligaments.

He was able yesterday to limp to the altar . . . and there he was given a chair to sit on while his bride knelt.

DUKE'S BANNED SPEECH

" I break my self-imposed silence now only because of the manifest danger that we may all be drawing nearer to a repetition of the grim events that happened a quarter of a century ago. . . . Peace is a matter far too vital for our happiness to be treated as a political question."

SO declared the Duke of Windsor in making a plea for peace in the name of the world's peoples in his broadcast to the United States from historic Verdun, France, yesterday.

The B.B.C. refused, without giving any reason, to relay his words, although Eire stations did so.

About 50,000,000 American people tuned in, and relays in Europe and Africa brought his total audience to 400,000,000.

And in England the Duke's mother, Queen Mary, listened as her son, alone but for radio engineers, sat before a microphone in the sitting-room of his suite in the Hotel Coq Hardir, Verdun, to address the world.

The Duke made it plain that he had not consulted the British Government, but according to British United Press it is understood that he obtained the King's permission, by wireless from the liner Empress of Australia, to deliver the speech.

He told his radio audience last night:—

" I speak simply as a soldier of the last war whose most earnest prayer it is that such cruel and destructive madness shall never again overtake mankind."

" For two and a half years I have deliberately kept out of public affairs, and I still propose to do so. I speak for no one but myself, without the previous knowledge of any Government."

"No People Want War"

His travels, his study of human nature, had left him with the profound conviction that there was no land in which the people wanted war.

" International understanding does not always spring up spontaneously of itself. There are times when it has to be deliberately sought and negotiated, and political tension is what weaken that spirit of mutual concession in which conflicting claims can be best adjusted."

For the first time his voice betrayed the emotion he felt when, after denouncing "poisonous propaganda," he said:

" I personally deplore, for example, the use of such terms as 'encirclement' and 'aggression.' They can only arouse just those dangerous passions that it should be the aim of us all to subdue.

" Somehow I feel that my words to-night will find a sincere echo in all who hear them. It is not for me to put forward concrete proposals —that must be left to those who have the power to guide the nations towards closer understanding.

" God grant that they may accomplish that great task before it is too late."

In America the speech was received with enthusiasm.

The Duke said last night that the Duchess and himself had no intention of going to America in the near future.

Daily Mirror, British United Press, Associated Press.

One-legged pilot Paddy Flynn, who continued to fly after a crash in which he fractured his spine and lost a leg, is dead. He and a nineteen-year-old girl were killed yesterday when their 'plane collided with an R.A.F. machine over Horne (Surrey) last night. The story is on page 3.

One of the pioneer pilots of Imperial Airways, Paddy lay for four and a half years on his back after the accident that robbed him of a leg. He thought his flying days were over. They weren't—until yesterday.

RUSSIA OFFERS NEW PACTS

SOVIET Russia is offering all the smaller States in her western neighbourhood defensive guarantees on the lines of those given by Britain and France to Rumania and Greece, says a Reuter message from Bukarest last night.

Countries such as Turkey, Bulgaria, Rumania and Finland might be glad to accept the guarantees.

M. Potemkin, the Russian envoy, will arrive in Warsaw to-day, where a Soviet-Polish pact is likely to be discussed.

Meanwhile, the delay in reaching agreement with Russia causes growing dismay in Britain. Mr. Chamberlain faced a storm of questions in the House of Commons yesterday, but said only this:

" It is our purpose to obtain the fullest co-operation with Russia in a policy which we are pursuing."

The British proposals—a guarantee for Poland from Russia and an assurance that Britain would help Russia if she were attacked when making good that guarantee—were handed to M. Molotoff, Russian Premier, by Sir William Seeds, the British Ambassador in Moscow, yesterday.

An Anglo-Turkish alliance, writes the "Daily Mirror" Political Correspondent, will be announced within the next twenty-four hours, and it is believed that it will hasten Russia's acceptance of the British terms.

In Tokio, the Japanese War Minister, General Itagaki, announced that he favoured a military pact with Germany and Italy.

Mussolini met his army chiefs in Rome last night, told them to have the army "entirely ready."

BY 387 VOTES TO 145 THE CONSCRIPTION BILL WAS GIVEN ITS SECOND READING IN THE HOUSE OF COMMONS LAST NIGHT. — SEE PAGE 2.

GUN PROOF CAR FOR KING

THE KING AND QUEEN, WHEN THEY REACH U.S.A. FROM CANADA, WILL TRAVEL IN A BULLET-PROOF CAR FROM WASHINGTON RAILWAY STATION TO THE PRESIDENT'S HOME, WHITE HOUSE.

The streets will be guarded by 11,000 troops, all with loaded rifles and facing the crowds of sightseers.

These elaborate precautions are part of the plans devised for the safety of the royal visitors.

For the first time the preparations have not been left entirely to the G-men and the Secret Service.

The U.S. Army and Navy have

(Continued on back page)

50

DAILY MIRROR, Monday, May 15, 1939

Daily Mirror

No. 11,056   ONE PENNY
Registered at the G.P.O. as a Newspaper
Geraldine House, Fetter-lane, E.C.4.
HOLBORN 4321.

ROBERT TAYLOR ELOPES

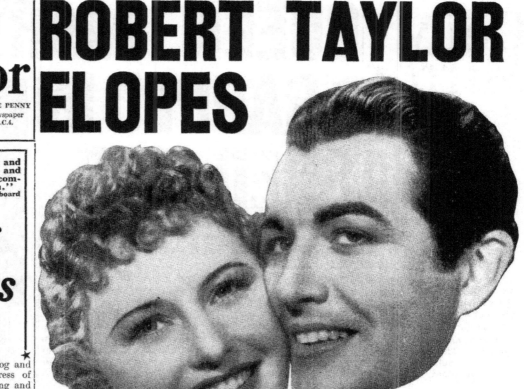

Film stars Robert Taylor and Barbara Stanwyck "eloped" to San Diego and were married there yesterday. (See back page.)

"Conduct us speedily and safely on our voyage and bring us in peace and comfort to our desired haven."
Prayer at divine service on board the royal liner yesterday.

King 2 Days Late

AFTER eighty hours in fog and ice, the liner Empress of Australia, carrying the King and Queen to Canada, was last night steaming at full speed ahead.

But three days of crawling past icebergs and ice fields has put the royal tour out of gear, and it is stated that the liner will not be able to reach Quebec to-morrow as had been hoped. This further delay will disarrange the latest plans for the visit.

Hundreds of French Canadians, too excited to go to bed, last night knelt in Quebec churches and prayed that the King and Queen would soon arrive safely.

Ice Scrapes Sides

From the liner, Reuter's correspondent on board radioed yesterday:—

"We ploughed through ice at four knots for some time, the icefloes bumping and scraping our sides, some carrying away our paint and leaving behind us a track of black sea which looked like an arterial road through the white ice."

"To avoid running into still thicker ice, Captain Meikle changed the course southward, but to our great disappointment we ran into fog again, though we were still able to proceed fitfully.

"While everybody aboard is making the best of a bad job, the King and Queen are concerned for those in Canada who are inconvenienced by the change in arrangements.

"As she leant on the rail of the promenade deck, gazing forward, the Queen exclaimed, 'It's the people I am sorry for—all those who have been making plans to see us in Canada and have perhaps travelled miles to do so.'"

As the ship ploughed through the ice, the Queen went up to the bridge and stood by Captain Meikle's side, while the King, seizing his cine-camera, ran to the bows of the ship by the look-out man.

Filmed the Cruisers

Here he filmed the prow of the great liner as it crashed through the ice, and then hurried to the stern. Climbing the companion way to the top of the deck house the King then filmed the cruisers following the liner.

Quebec officials last night expressed the opinion that it would be impossible for the liner to arrive in Quebec before Wednesday morning, even if the weather improved immediately.

They added that there would be no further changes in the arrangements for the royal welcome in Quebec until the time of arrival was known for certain.

The Canadian Government decided yesterday to petition the King to extend his stay two or three days. The decision was reached when the entire Dominion was thrown into (Continued on back page)

The Quins in Tears

The only people in Canada who do not think much of present arrangements for the royal visit are the Dionne Quins.

There was a stormy scene, which led to tears, in the Callander nursery yesterday, when the Quins learned that Princesses Elizabeth and Margaret Rose were not coming with the King and Queen.

Marie, the philosopher of the five sisters, saved the situation by consoling herself and the others with the remark: "Maybe Grandmother Queen would be lonely if the Princesses did not stay at home."

✦ ✦ ✦

U.S.A. officials supervising arrangements for the royal party's stay in Washington in June say they have received a request from the British authorities that hot water be provided in all bedrooms for filling the visitors' hot water bottles, cables the "Daily Mirror" New York correspondent.

The average Washington June temperature is ninety degrees!

MINER SAVES FRIEND AS HE FALLS TO DEATH

FROM OUR OWN CORRESPONDENT

GARW VALLEY (Glam.), Sunday.

TWO men fought a fire on a colliery refuse tip. Suddenly one of them felt himself pushed violently forward; he fell sprawling half a dozen yards away.

He picked himself up, turned angrily to storm at his companion —found he had disappeared.

He was buried beneath a fall of shifting refuse.

And Yorweth Williams, of Pontycymmer, realised that his friend had pushed him to safety as he himself was engulfed.

Soon relays of miners were working to free Alfred Griffiths. Foremost among them was Williams.

He refused to take his spell of rest, but went on digging feverishly although at the point of exhaustion.

At last the rescuers reached Griffiths and carried him to safety.

For two hours doctors, police and ambulance men worked to restore life.

For a moment life returned. Griffiths smiled up into the face of the man who held his head—the face of Yorweth Williams, whose life he had saved. Then he died.

"He was my friend and neighbour," Williams said to me.

"He saved my life in that split-second as the ground gave way . . . he could see death in front of him.

"This was a friend."

DAILY MIRROR, Wednesday, May 24, 1939.

Daily Mirror

No. 11,064   ONE PENNY
Registered at the G.P.O. as a newspaper.
Geraldine House, Fetter-lane, E.C.4.
HOLBORN 4321.

QUEEN MARY IS TRAPPED IN SMASHED CAR

QUEEN MARY—she will be 72 on Friday—was trapped in her overturned car at Putney yesterday. After her return to Marlborough House she was examined by Sir Stanley Hewett and Lord Dawson of Penn, who later issued this bulletin:—

"Her Majesty Queen Mary is suffering from bruising and shock as the result of an accident this afternoon in which her Majesty's car was overturned. Though the bruising is considerable and will need some days' complete rest, her Majesty's general condition is this evening satisfactory."

News of Queen Mary's accident was flashed to the King and Queen in Canada, and the message was handed to them when the royal train reached Jackfish, Ontario. The remainder of the Royal Family were also informed. The Duke of Windsor received the news by telephone at his home in Paris within half an hour of the accident. The King sent a cable to his mother.

FULL STORY OF THE CRASH BEGINS ON BACK PAGE

The driver of the lorry which came into collision with the royal car photographed at the scene of the accident.

Queen Mary's car after the collision. It had run on from the point of impact, the chauffeur desperately trying to correct the skid into which it had been forced. At the kerbside it turned over, throwing Queen Mary, Lord Claud Hamilton and Lady Constance Milnes-Gaskell in a heap.

DAILY MIRROR, Thursday, May 25, 1939.

Daily Mirror

No. 11,065   ONE PENNY
Registered at the G.P.O. as a Newspaper.
Geraldine House, Fetter-lane, E.C.4.
HOLBORN 4321.

25 LOST SAFE

The rescue, the most amazing in naval history, still goes on. Fifty-nine men were on board when the Squalus submerged and stuck fast on the sea bottom.

Twenty-six of them died at once as the whirling water flooded their quarters.

At dawn to-day the first diver was lowered from the salvage ship Falcon. Thirty-nine other divers stood ready to follow.

Contact was made by messages rapped out in Morse code on the steel sides of Squalus. The answer came back: "Conditions satisfactory."

Miss Hilda Dinnivan, aged eighteen, photographed yesterday, when she told at the inquest of her discovery of her grandfather, Mr. Walter Dinnivan, murdered in their home in Poole-road, Dorset. See story on back page.

MEN

FROM OUR OWN CORRESPONDENT

NEW YORK, Wednesday.

TWENTY-FIVE men were rescued to-night from the U.S. submarine Squalus, sunk in 240ft. of water off the New Hampshire coast, U.S.A.

Then Falcon lowered the diving bell —a huge rubber, bell-shaped watertight hood, made to slip over the submarine's hatch as a man puts on his hat.

The bell is the real hero of the rescue. It is being used to save life for the first time.

The bell fell. A message was tapped out. The submarine crew opened the hatch.

Six men and one officer stepped out of a living tomb and were slowly hauled to the surface.

As the bell appeared the crew of the Falcon broke into a great cheer. Seven men were back to life.

On shore fifty women watch and wait. None of them knows which is a widow for their men were all aboard that steel trap.

They are brave. They do not weep. But they cannot turn their eyes from the sea.

On the Falcon the rescued men stepped from the diving bell into a decompression chamber which they dare not leave until they have been acclimatised to normal air pressure.

And as the bell descends again the divers get a new message from the Squalus "Hurry, hurry."

Stepped Out—to Life

Inside the bell are two men. They have electric light and telephone, and as the submarine hatch is covered again the rescuers release a powerful suction hood that seals the hatch.

The Falcon's phone rings—nine more men coming up. The bell is raised and nine who hardly hoped to live another day step out.

Again the bell went down. Just after midnight it brought nine men up.

At Portsmouth, U.S.A., where women and children waited at the pierhead for news there was a sudden emotional outburst to-night. Crowds of relatives besieged naval officers, demanded to know if their men were among the living or the dead.

And, below the sea, more men stepped up to take their places in the rescuing bell. One man stands back—the Commander. True to the sea's tradition he will be the last to leave.

Rescue work will go on far into the night. When all the living have been rescued twenty-five picked divers will descend in relays to search the flooded compartments in case one or two of the trapped may be clinging feebly to life.

Squalus survivors landed at Portsmouth to-
(Continued on back page)

Life Is a Great Adventure

—The King

THE KING ENDED HIS EMPIRE DAY BROADCAST FROM WINNIPEG LAST NIGHT WITH A CALL TO YOUTH— "A SPECIAL WORD OF GREETING," HE CALLED IT, "TO THOSE OF MY LISTENERS WHO ARE YOUNG." THE KING WENT ON:—

"It is true—and I deplore it deeply—that the skies are overcast in more than one quarter at the present time.

"**Do not on that account lose heart. Life is a great adventure, and every one of you can be a pioneer, blazing by thought and service a trail to better things.**

"Hold fast to all that is just and of good report in the heritage which your fathers left you, but strive also to improve and equalise that heritage for all men and women in the years to come.

◆ ◆ ◆

"Remember, too, that the key to all true progress lies in faith, hope and love.

"May God give you their support, and may God help them to prevail."

Speech in full—page 5.
Scenes in Winnipeg—Page 2.

QUEEN MARY'S BOUQUET

From "The Lorry Driver"

BY A SPECIAL CORRESPONDENT

THE driver of the lorry which was in collision with Queen Mary's car, Albert Cooper, of Hammersmith, W., sent a friend with a bunch of irises to Marlborough House yesterday. He was too upset to take them himself.

"Queen Mary will want to keep these in her room," a police officer on duty at Marlborough House told me.

After an X-ray examination the following bulletin was issued last night:

"Her Majesty Queen Mary's progress is taking a satisfactory course, though stiffness and pain are troublesome. X-ray examination excludes any damage to the bones. The condition of the eye is improving."

An earlier bulletin announced that she had passed a restless night, partly due to an eye injury which was painful, though it gave no cause for anxiety. It is understood that it is her left eye which is affected.

The lorry-driver spent a sleepless night on Tuesday wondering how Queen Mary was progressing. Not until he had heard the late wireless bulletin "Queen Mary's condition is satisfactory" did he go to bed.

Still pale and worried, he was late for work yesterday for the first time in his life.

He was worried because he feared that the
(Continued on back page)

Albert Cooper.

GOVERNMENT LOSE SEAT

THE Labour Party have won Kennington from the Government.

Result of the by-election caused by the death of Sir George Harvey was:—

L. Wilmot (Lab.), 10,715.
Major Angus Kennedy (Con.), 7,119.
Majority, 3,596.

Conservative majority at the last election was 545.

Mr. Wilmot's victory is Labour's twelfth gain from Government parties since the General Election in 1935 and the sixth in London.

DAILY MIRROR, Friday, May 26, 1939.

Daily Mirror

No. 11,966 ONE PENNY
Registered at the G.P.O. as a Newspaper.
Geraldine House, Fetter-lane, E.C.4.
HOLBORN 4321.

"I want my wife above everything else in the world. I need her at my side"... pleaded the Rev. John Kyrle Chatfield (below) as he sat alone in his study. A picture of Mrs. Chatfield is on right.

NAZIS BACK JAPAN'S BLOCKADE

JAPAN FLUNG DOWN A NEW CHALLENGE TO THE WESTERN POWERS YESTERDAY WHEN SHE ANNOUNCED A NAVAL BLOCKADE OF THE COAST OF CHINA.

The blockade is a violation of international law, since Japan, after two years of fighting, has not yet declared war on China.

If British, French and American ships are halted on the high seas by Japanese destroyers, joint action will have to be taken.

It is believed that the Japanese move has been engineered by Germany and Italy in the hope that British and French warships will be sent from the Mediterranean to the Far East.

Japan believes that U.S.A. would not join in any attempt to end the blockade.

A Japanese naval spokesman in Tokio yesterday declared:—

"Japan demands the right to stop any ship to see if she is carrying war material to the Chinese."

He declared the blockade would extend 200 miles from the coast, and added that soon he would reveal sensational instances of foreign ships helping the Chinese leader Chiang Kai-Shek.

Two Liners Stopped

When the Japanese spokesman was asked what would happen if other nations fought the blockade by sending escort ships with their merchant vessels, he replied, "It probably would not be necessary in the case of the United States."

Already Japan has shown how far she will go to stop trade with China.

The French liner Aramis and the British P. and O. liner Ranpura were this week stopped by Japanese destroyers.

When Mr. Arthur Henderson, M.P., asks in the House of Commons to-day what steps are to be taken following the Ranpura incident, Sir John Simon, in the Premier's absence, will probably say that a firm note of protest has already been sent.

But M.P.s will insist that firmer action is necessary to stop repeated acts of aggression against British ships.

The Japanese yesterday threatened to land more marines in Amoy, the International Settlement, where British, French and American marines arrived following a landing from Japanese warships.

Britain's Ambassador to China, Sir Archibald Clark Kerr, left Hong Kong yesterday on board the cruiser Cornwall. He will inspect the island of Amoy before going on to Shanghai.

—Foreign messages from Reuter British United Press and Associated Press.

RECTOR'S WIFE VANISHES

BY A SPECIAL CORRESPONDENT

RETURNING from a holiday, the Rev. John Kyrle Chatfield, sixty-five, of Langar-cum-Barnstone, Notts, hurried into his rectory, eager to greet his twenty-four-year-old wife again.

The rectory was deserted. He shouted, "Selina, Selina"—the name of his wife—but only the echoes of his voice answered.

Then the rector's eye fell on a note. It was from his wife. It told him she had gone away.

Mr. Chatfield's voice broke as yesterday he told me of that dark day in his life in February last. Since then he has not heard of his wife or his nineteen-year-old maid, Maud Browne, who disappeared with her.

"I beg of you to find Selina for me," the rector whispered. "I want my wife above everything else in the world I need her at my side."

Went on Cycle

The rector's wife and maid were last seen leaving the rectory on their bicycles.

Despite his anxiety, the rector has carried on with his routine work in the parish.

As he preaches in his church he looks down at two empty seats in the choir stalls—the seats which his wife and maid used to occupy. At times there is a weariness in his voice, and he sighs.

"I cannot understand it," the rector told me. "Miss Browne came to the house last autumn. My wife and she became firm friends.

"While on holiday my wife wrote to me several times. It is strange, so strange."

The rector, whose first wife died in 1933, has two daughters, aged twenty-six and twenty-

(Continued on back page)

"CHILDREN"—BY DUKE OF KENT

"OF course, children can be annoying and troublesome," owned the Duke of Kent, himself the father of two youngsters, yesterday.

"Parents with quick tempers are apt to go too far at times," he added, "although a scolding, or even punishment, does not do any child much harm, but there is a world of difference between a scolding and a cruel assault on a child."

The Duke was speaking at the annual meeting of the National Society for the Prevention of Cruelty to Children. There was still, he said, an appalling number of cases of ill-treatment of children.

Chestnut Corner

DAILY MIRROR, Monday, May 29, 1939.

Daily Mirror

No. 11,068   ONE PENNY

Registered at the G.P.O. as a Newspaper.
Geraldine House, Fetter-lane, E.C.4.
HOLBORN 4321.

OUTLOOK FOR TO-DAY
FAIR AND WARMER

THEIR outlook is through a telescope on Hastings (Sussex) sea-front. But WE think this is the most charming view in sight.

13 HAD NIGHT OF SEA TERROR

FROM OUR OWN CORRESPONDENT

CLACTON, Sunday.

THIRTEEN people, including four women and a boy aged nine, spent a night of terror, buffeted and drenched by the sea, in a ketch stranded on the Gun Fleet Sands, off Walton-on-Naze.

They could not sleep. Heavy waves, pounding the boat incessantly, made that impossible.

Yet they laughed and joked when they were rescued to-day by Walton lifeboat.

The ketch, Our Laddie, of Lowestoft, which had set off from Dagenham on Friday night for a holiday trip on the coast, was driven ashore by the high wind last night.

For eight hours the boat was stranded. It sprang a leak, and flares were lit. These brought the lifeboat to the rescue.

Taken to a Walton hotel were: Mr. and Mrs. R. Gerrans, of Station-road, Harold Wood, Essex, and Mr. A. G. Burton, the owners of the ketch, Mr. B. D. Gerrans, Mr. John Smyrke, Miss Doreen Edgar, Miss Deidrie Williamson, Miss Mavis Gibb, all Londoners, and the nine-year-old son of Mr. and Mrs. Gerrans.

"Didn't Care—Fiance Near"

The skipper of the ketch and his mate, and two friends, Mr. Pat Finlayson and Mr. P. Cousins, refused to leave the boat and were towed to Harwich. Also aboard was Snap, the ship's dog.

Before he turned in to-night to make up for three nights' lost sleep, the sturdy son of Mr. and Mrs. Gerrans told me: "Sailors don't care, anyhow. Pity we were taken off so soon."

But lifeboat Coxswain Tom Bloom, who was feted by the party, said: "They're lucky to be alive."

"It was terrifying," twenty-year-old Miss Edgar told me, "but I didn't care so much because I was with my fiance, Mr. Burton. We hope to be married soon.

"We were in darkness. All we could hear was the howling of the wind.

"Some one started community singing to keep the party's spirits up. We had had no sleep for two nights."

(Picture on back page)

Cops Feel the Pinch

Two plain clothes detectives who kept watch at the rear of an Orpington, Kent, cinema following a number of cycle thefts in the district are now looking for someone who stole the lamps and pumps from their own bicycles which were parked round the corner.

IN NIGHTIE, CHASES BULL

WEARING only her nightdress, a girl, aged nineteen, chased a bull round the garden of her home last night.

Eventually she lassooed it with a clothes line, tied it up to the garden fence and ran for help.

The bull was taken to a nearby farm, from which it had escaped. The girl was Miss Tranquil Thwaites, of Crampshaw-lane, Ashtead, Surrey.

She told the Daily Mirror last night:

"I was in bed when I heard my mother shouting from the garden.

"I looked out of the window and saw her standing in the doorway. The bull was a few yards away ploughing up the garden. It had already done considerable damage.

"Running downstairs, I dashed into the garden and fetched a clothes line from the potting shed.

"I then went after the bull. I managed to get the rope over its head and then through the ring in its nose.

"I led it by the rope up to the fence and tied it up. Then I sent for help to the farm.

"I was not too sure of the bull when I first saw it, but I was frightened of what it might have done had it been left in the garden.

"Anyway, I shall sleep much better now that I know it's not there.

"I am going to Paris in the morning. I work there as a teacher of English, and have been home on holiday for a few weeks."

POLICE CHIEF'S HOME RAIDED

WHILE Sir Hugh Turnbull, Commissioner of Police for the City of London, was away last night, thieves broke into his home at Regent's Park, bound and gagged a manservant and raided every room.

Other members of the staff made the discovery late last night.

They 'phoned the City Police, Scotland Yard were told, and police cars were rushed to the house.

All the Fun of Whitsun

If you're basking in the Whit sun, playing, bathing, lazing . . . here's the best of all holiday reading :—

A page of Popeye—Page 16.

A page of Live Letter Box—Page 10.

And three features every girl must read :—

1. How to go on a cruise and bring back a husband — your own, not somebody else's—Page 8.

2. How to be a real sea nymph—the graceful diver—Page 12.

3. Take a wardrobe census for the summer. What to wear and what to shed—Page 23.

And

All the news and pictures

DAILY MIRROR, Tuesday, May 30, 1939.

Daily Mirror

No. 11,969   ONE PENNY

Registered at the G.P.O. as a Newspaper.

Geraldine House, Fetter-lane, E.C.4.

HOLBORN 4321.

Masks Burn in Streets

Gas masks were burned in streets in Nationalist areas of Belfast last night following a broadcast by the Irish Republican Army from a pirate short-wave station.

Police chased a man who was calling at houses collecting the masks. They fired several shots at the man, but he eluded them.

✦ ✦ ✦

The broadcast described gas masks as British propaganda to enlist the sympathies of the people on Britain's side in a conflict.

The demonstration was a result of a co-ordinated movement throughout the Nationalist districts.

MOTHER DIVES TO SAVE 3

Seeing that her husband was being dragged under water by two girls of thirteen he was trying to rescue a mother last night dived in the river and saved all three.

SHE managed to pull her husband to a boat, then helped him to pull in the two girls.

The husband was Mr. Albert E. Richardson, of Pitfield-street, Hoxton.

He was out for an evening on the River Lea at Clapton with his wife and two-year-old daughter, Patricia, and four young friends, when a small rowing boat was in collision with his and overturned.

The occupants of the boat, Lola Harris, of Homeleigh-road, Stamford Hill, and Mildred Gellman, of Amhurst-road, Stoke Newington, were thrown in the water.

Mr. Richardson immediately dived in and

(Continued on back page)

He's a tough baby! Still in the car when his parents found it—and him—after a thief had taken him for a three-mile ride. Ralph Plotnek, aged thirteen months, chuckles happily despite his "kid-napping" adventure.

But his mother, reduced to a state of collapse when his absence was discovered, says, "I hope I never have another shock like that." It was two hours before she learned that her baby was safe.

Russia Decides

Molotoff, the Soviet Foreign Affairs Commissar, is to speak on foreign policy to-morrow at the session of the Supreme Soviet.

This was announced last night, and it indicates that Russia has reached a decision on the latest Anglo-French proposals for a military pact with the Soviet.

And were the agreement not near—or on the other hand, definitely eliminated—the speech would have been delayed.

Turkish President Ismet Ineunu last night announced "agreement in principle" in the Franco-Turkish negotiations for a mutual aid pact in line with that with Britain.

BOY STOLEN WITH CAR

FROM OUR SPECIAL CORRESPONDENT

BIRMINGHAM, Monday.

WHEN thieves stole a motor car parked outside an hotel near Stourbridge, Worcestershire, they did not know about Ralph.

But Ralph—aged thirteen months—was in the car, sound asleep on the back seat.

When they had travelled three miles the thieves must have found the baby, for they abandoned the car in a lonely lane.

And in Stourbridge, Ralph's father and mother, Mr. and Mrs. Plotnek, of Newport-road, Sparkbrook, Birmingham, came out of the hotel to find the car had disappeared.

"The baby," Mrs. Plotnek cried. The alarm was given. Police cars searched the roads. Motorists were stopped and questioned.

The father went in one police car, his wife in another.

Then after an hour's searching, Mr. Plotnek saw his stolen car. He ran towards it, pulled open the rear door—found Ralph still sleeping in his cot.

"We had taken him to Dudley Zoo," Mrs. Plotnek said to me, "and stopped at the hotel to meet some friends.

"We both got out, leaving Ralph asleep in his carrier cot in the back seat. We were back within two minutes, but the car had gone."

I interviewed Ralph. He said, "Pom, pom"—that means motor-car.

Ralph had enjoyed his day.

FEARS FOR CRAZY FLYER

THOUSANDS of people waited for a tiny monoplane to wing over Croydon Airport last night and write the last chapter to the crazy Atlantic adventure of Thomas (Screwy) Smith.

Drawn there by rumours of Smith's arrival they heard pilots and officials express conviction that Smith could not possibly make it.

Well Overdue

At 2 a.m. he was well overdue and fears were felt for his safety.

Earlier reports had come in that his 'plane had been seen—first passing over Londonderry, then over Wigtownshire, and later over St. Bees, Cumberland.

The twenty-five-year-old Los Angeles airman set off in his baby 'plane on a transatlantic flight from Old Orchard Maine at 9.47 a.m. on Sunday (British Summer Time).

He is flying a 'plane driven by only a four-cylinder sixty-five horse-power engine.

250 FIREMEN FIGHT BLAZE

FIRE brigades from all over London this morning fought a fire at the premises of Thomas P. Cook and Co., hardware cabinet manufacturers, of Tabernacle-street, Finsbury.

The flames cou'd be seen from as far away as Alexandra Palace, Crouch End and Hampstead Heath.

More than 250 firemen, including steel-helmeted members of the Auxiliary Fire Service, fought the fire, and police reserves had to be called out to control the crowds.

Horses are kept in a stable separated from the burning building by only a narrow passage. Stablemen were summoned to pacify them, and water was played on the side of the building nearest the stables.

The roof of the factory, which employs about fifty men, fell in, and the flames threatened a neighbouring tobacco warehouse.

56

DAILY MIRROR, Thursday, June 1, 1939.

Daily Mirror

No. 11,071   ONE PENNY
Registered at the G.P.O. as a Newspaper.
Geraldine House, Fetter-lane, E.C.4.
HOLBORN 4321.

STILL POLES APART

The Anglo - French proposals contain reservations which may make agreement ineffective.—M. Molotoff.

RUSSIA SHOCK FOR BRITAIN: PACT STILL TOO WEAK

M. MOLOTOFF, RUSSIA'S FOREIGN COMMISSAR, WARNED BRITAIN AND FRANCE, IN A SPEECH TO THE RUSSIAN PARLIAMENT LAST NIGHT, THAT THEIR PEACE PROPOSALS DO NOT YET GO FAR ENOUGH TO SATISFY THE SOVIET.

A wealthy seventy-three-year-old man is looking for her . . . Miss Joan McGlynn-Nash, who has vanished from the Ramsgate home of Mr. Arthur Peel Nash, who adopted her. See story on page 19.

LOST HIS LEG—WED IN BED

BY A SPECIAL CORRESPONDENT

A YOUNG bride speeded up her wedding to cheer her fiance, a pilot officer in the R.A.F., who had been badly injured in a crash. She married him secretly in a military hospital the day after he had had a leg amputated.

Their wedding breakfast was a sixpenny fruit loaf and a bottle of champagne. But after the ceremony the bride, Kathleen Hewitt, slim, blonde, clasped the hand of her husband, Leonard Hinks Edwards, twenty-four, of Leuchars Aerodrome, and said:

"I would not have had it different for worlds.

"It was not our plan to wed in hospital, but we are together now and that is what matters."

A hospital sister and an R.A.F. officer were the witnesses at the wedding which took place in a ward of the Edinburgh Castle Military Hospital.

When she was told of the crash Kathleen hurried 200 miles from her home in Mold, North Wales, to Edinburgh, to be by his side. She visited him every day.

At her home in Pontymwyn, Mold, I spoke to Mrs. Edwards by telephone last night.

"We had planned to marry this year," she said, "and when I heard that Len had crashed I knew that my place was in Edinburgh.

"I left my home and hurried there. We de-
(Continued on back page.)

Hitler's Hands Off Denmark

Germany, in a treaty signed yesterday, promised not to attack Denmark. The treaty was a mutual non-aggression pact, signed at the German Foreign Office.

Hitler's Foreign Minister, von Ribbentrop, and M. Herluf Zahle, Danish Minister in Berlin, were the signatories, says the Associated Press.

This is one of the treaties suggested to the Scandinavian and Baltic countries by Hitler, Denmark, Latvia and Estonia agreed to treaties, but Norway, Sweden and Finland preferred complete neutrality.

Similar pacts are being negotiated with Latvia and Estonia, Baltic neighbours of Russia.

GAS BOMBS IN LONDON CINEMAS

G AS bombs were found last night in two London cinemas.

One, unexploded, was found under a seat in the auditorium at the Empire, Leicester-square, by a fireman after the audience had gone.

The other exploded in a lavatory during the performance at the New Victoria, near Victoria Station, but none of the audience was aware of it.

One man was taken from the lavatory where the bomb exploded, suffering from burns on the hand, and was treated in hospital.

Gas seeping under the door was first noticed by the foreman at the cinema. He rushed to the manager, Mr. Geoffrey Cohen.

"I opened the door," Mr. Cohen said to the "Daily Mirror," "and found the lavatory full of thick white gas. I have been to A.R.P. classes, but was unable to recognise it by the smell or taste.

"It made my eyes smart and affected my throat."

A sergeant and three constables who went into the cloakroom without respirators were affected by the fumes. After being seen by the divisional surgeon they were placed on the sick list.

He announced that the negotiations with Britain were still going on, and added:

"But we insist on our own point of view, concerning which we do not need to consult anyone."

He laid down three conditions on which Russia will insist before entering a pact. They are:—

1. The pact must be exclusively of a defensive character.

2. The pact must guarantee all the countries without exception on the western borders of the Soviet Union.

3. It must be a concrete agreement for assistance in the event of future attacks.

The second of these conditions is the critical one. It means that the Soviet Government has not moved from the position it took up weeks ago.

M. Molotoff declared that the recent German-Italian alliance was definitely aggressive.

"The Soviet Union stands for the union of all peace-loving powers to curb aggression, but we must be careful to remember Stalin's warning not to pull other people's chestnuts out of the fire."

Step Forward

He agreed that the latest British proposals admitted reciprocity, and therefore were a step forward, but added there were "several reservations which may render agreement ineffective."

The democratic countries had hitherto under-estimated the changes in the world situation, he added, and while abandoning collective security, had tried a policy of appeasement.

"The Soviet Government opposes both these views," he said.

M. Molotoff said that the Munich defeat was the culminating point of non-intervention. The collapse of that policy was inevitable. Yet aggressors continued to adhere to their policy.

He declared that Russia never feels any sympathy for aggression, and does not approve efforts to conceal the true facts of the situation from the public.

"Are there," he asked, "any signs that the democratic Powers want to make a real effort to check aggression? They may merely want to secure it by other channels.

"We stand for peace, but we must be care-
(Continued on back page.)

DAILY MIRROR, Friday, June 2, 1939.

Daily Mirror

No. 11,072   ONE PENNY
Registered at the G.P.O. as a Newspaper.
Geraldine House, Fetter-lane, E.C.4.
HOLBORN 4321.

84 TRAPPED AS NEW SUBMARINE FAILS TO RISE

The new British submarine Thetis, missing yesterday on her trials—a picture taken at her launching eleven months ago.

WOMEN WEEP AT GATE

FROM OUR SPECIAL CORRESPONDENT

BIRKENHEAD, Friday morning.

MOTHERS and sweethearts surged round the little office at the gates of Cammell Laird's yard at Birkenhead this morning, earnestly seeking news of their men.

They had heard by radio of the submarine's disappearance.

Relatives comforted each other with encouraging words, and some leaned quietly crying, against the wall of the yard.

Many women carried children in their arms. Frequently they started to go home, but always they returned to gaze anxiously at the only lighted window of the huge offices

Report Cheered

There was a sudden cheer when Mr. Woodward, secretary of the company, came out to tell the crowd the report, later denied by the Admiralty, that the ship had been found.

One woman said: "Thank goodness at least that is something."

Mr. Woodward said: "I can only tell you the submarine has been located by means of a marker buoy dropped from an aeroplane. I cannot tell you the position of the vessel."

Her face tear-stained the mother-in-law of an engine-room hand, Walter Arnold, said to me:—

"I have been waiting here since I heard the news on the wireless.

"Walter and my daughter were only married a short time ago. His wife was with me when we heard the news and she collapsed.

"She cries repeatedly for him and although she was too ill for me to leave her she made me come down to get any news that I could.

"She could not bear to come down herself."

AT least 84 men, probably more, are trapped on board the new British submarine Thetis which failed to reappear after diving yesterday in 22 fathoms of water in Liverpool Bay at the mouth of the Mersey.

There are nine naval officers, 48 sailors and an unknown number of technicians from Cammell Laird's yard in the submerged ship.

The Thetis left the builder's yard at 10 o'clock yesterday morning. At 1.40 p.m. she dived. She has not been seen since.

SHE HAS SUFFICIENT AIR TO REMAIN UNDER WATER FOR 36 HOURS—UNTIL 1.30 TO-MORROW MORNING.

A launch accompanying the Thetis watched her dive. She was due to stay down for three hours. When she did not appear the launch sent out rapid warnings to the Admiralty and to Cammell Laird's, the builders.

The Navy responded at once. A broadcast message sent all warships near at hand to the scene. A rescue fleet was organised. Eight R.A.F. 'planes patrolled the area until dusk.

At Portland, where the Home Fleet is stationed, there was an instant call for action.

All liberty men from the sixth destroyer flotilla and the first minesweeper flotilla were ordered to return. An S O S was flashed on cinema screens. Theatre and cinema managers at Portland and Weymouth stopped sailors at the pay boxes.

And, quickly, one cruiser, ten destroyers, seven minesweepers and two submarines were speeding to the spot.

The Brazen, a destroyer, was soon where the Thetis was last seen.

This morning news was flashed that the marked buoys of the Thetis had been found by rescue ships. It was the last of a series of conflicting reports.

Just before midnight it was reported that she had been found by aircraft off Great Orme's Head, Llandudno.

In 30 Fathoms

But the Admiralty then stated "the submarine has not yet been located.

"An unconfirmed report was received by us from an aircraft that a buoy had been sighted just as darkness was falling thirteen or fourteen miles off Orme's Head and it was suggested that it might be the submarine's buoy.

"There is no confirmation of that report from any surface craft which are now searching the area."

(Continued on back page.)

★ Fitted with Two Escape Hatches ★

Every submarine in the British Navy has, since the Poisedon disaster in Chinese waters, been fitted with two specially constructed escape hatches, by which in an emergency the crew may escape through air locks.

Sufficient sets of Davis submerged escape apparatus, supplying oxygen, are provided in every submarine for every member of the crew. Every submarine is also fitted with two special indicator buoys which can be released from inside and come to the surface to show its position to surface craft.

The method of escape is:—

A man enters a chamber under the escape hatch through the bottom door, which is then closed, having put on his apparatus before. He floods the chamber, in which an air lock is formed, and when the internal and external pressures have equalised the escape hatch is opened, and he passes through and to the surface in the bubble formed by the air lock.

Immediately he has gone the escape hatch is closed, and the process quickly repeated until all have escaped.

Two men can be sent to the surface every five minutes by each escape hatch.

In a Nutshell

DAILY MIRROR, Saturday, June 3, 1939.

Daily Mirror

No. 1. 173   ONE PENNY
Registered at the G.P.O. as a Newspaper.
Geraldine House, Fetter-lane, E.C.4.
HOLBORN 4321.

HOPE ABANDONED —CABLE BREAKS ON SUBMARINE

Heroine of the ordeal in the homes . . . Mrs. Bolus, in light frock with a flower pinned on the front, speaking words of comfort and courage to the women whose anxiety she shared.

All hope of saving the 90 men trapped in the British submarine, Thetis, was abandoned at midnight.

The rescue had failed late yesterday afternoon when a cable attached to the jutting stern of the Thetis parted, and the stricken ship sank into the mud to become the tomb of the men who built and served her.

Work went on, but hope faded as the hours passed ; and at ten o'clock the Admiralty announced that they "regret to state that hope of saving any further lives is now diminishing."

And, a minute after midnight the secretary of Cammell Laird's shipbuilding yard at Birkenhead came to the throng of anxious men and women relatives.

In a low voice he said, " There is no longer any hope of anyone being alive."

And to the crowd who surged round the gates he repeated his news and added: " It is best for you now to disperse quietly, and ease the pain of these poor people inside."

Through the gates passed a car with nurses to tend the heartbroken mothers, wives and sweethearts.

A petty officer in uniform hand-in-hand with a girl of sixteen came out of the wooden hut at the entrance. The girl's brother was in the submarine.

Women Weep with
Bowed Heads

" It is flooded," the young sailor said to the crowd, and brushed away a tear. The girl wept.

The crowd remained for a time at the yard entrance. The gates opened and a line of cars streamed out.

They carried the women who had waited all day with courage in their eyes and fear at their hearts.

Now that the need for courage was gone they wept without control. Their heads were bowed.

It was the climax of the worst disaster

Continued on Back Page

THE SMILE OF A HEROINE

FROM OUR SPECIAL CORRESPONDENT
BIRKENHEAD, Friday.

A WOMAN, weighted down with her own grief, to-day revealed herself as a heroine.

For of all the valour wrought of this grim drama on the submarine Thetis none shines so radiantly as that of the wife of her commander, Lieutenant-Commander G. H. Bolus.

With the ever-present knowledge that the commander must be the last to leave his crippled ship, Mrs. Bolus has thrust aside her own burden of anxiety to bring comfort to the fear-racked women and relatives of her husband's crew.

A flaxen-haired woman with an expression of utter serenity, she has moved among these suffering women ever since the first alarm was given.

A gentle smile, a touch on the shoulder, a soft word of encouragement—with these she has forged courage in the hearts of distraught women.

Hear this tribute paid to her by one of these women — the mother of Leading Seaman Walter Luck, of Warwick-road, Upton.

" That woman is OUR commander," Mrs. Luck said, a tremor in her voice.

" We feel the respect for her that a ship's crew has for its senior officer.

" We are her crew and she gives us the encouragement a crew seeks from its commander.

" Never have I known anyone who could so hearten one in misfortune.

" She is a very great and noble lady."

The Commander Calls
a Conference

Snatching only the briefest rest, Mrs. Bolus has been on duty now for hours, her post the sorrow-laden little hut at the entrance to the Cammell Laird works.

Until far into the early hours of this morning she was there, reviving flagging hopes, running all over Birkenhead in her car to take home the tired womenfolk of the crew, urging them to seek the sleep which came to so few of them last night.

This morning she was there again, this afternoon the same.

No trace of despondency was there in her

Continued on Page 5

STOKER DIED IN BID TO ESCAPE

ON the eve of her first wedding anniversary, Mrs. Caroline Hole was last night keeping vigil in her home at Avon-dale-terrace, Devonport, for her stoker husband, on board the Thetis.

As she saw a telegraph boy coming, she went to the door, her face alight with hope. But the telegram read:

" Regret to inform you that Stoker Hole is believed to have died while endeavouring to escape from Submarine Thetis. This will be confirmed when definite news is received."

The telegram, handed in at Gosport, is signed: " Submarines, Gosport."

Just a year ago to-day, Mrs. Hole was married to her stoker husband, Wilfred Hole, aged twenty-six.

They have a month-old baby whom her husband has seen only once—three weeks ago.

DAILY MIRROR, Tuesday, June 6, 1939.

Daily Mirror

No. 11,075 ✦ ✦ ✦ ONE PENNY
Registered at the G.P.O. as a Newspaper
Geraldine House, Fetter-lane, E.C.4.
HOLBORN 4321.

PREMIER SOBS AS HE TELLS OF THE THETIS

BY OUR POLITICAL CORRESPONDENT

MR. NEVILLE CHAMBERLAIN was in tears when he made his statement on the disaster of the Thetis in the House of Commons yesterday

The Premier was so overcome when he reached the concluding paragraphs of his manuscript that his words became quite inaudible and his shoulders shook with emotion.

The House was hushed throughout the statement except when the Premier announced that a public inquiry would be held. At that point a subdued cheer broke out from all sides of the House.

Afterwards Mr. A. V. Alexander, who had put a private notice question regarding the disaster, congratulated the Government on deciding to hold a public inquiry.

He expressed the hope, however, that to allay public anxiety, the public inquiry would precede the formal naval investigation.

"No Hushing-Up of Facts"

The Premier made it clear that although there would be no hushing up of facts, it would be necessary to hold a private naval inquiry as soon as the submarine had been salvaged.

In view of the announcement about the public inquiry, M.P.s who had come prepared to demand this very thing were silenced.

I am told that the public investigation will probably be held under the Tribunals of Inquiry (Evidence) Act. Evidence will be on oath and a prominent High Court Judge with knowledge of Admiralty procedure is likely to preside.

Many M.P.s hope that at least two Members of Parliament will be included on the inquiry.

FULL PUBLIC INQUIRY

WHEN Mr. A. V. Alexander asked the Prime Minister if he would make a statement on the disaster, Mr. Chamberlain replied: "The following is a full account, so far as the facts are yet known, of this lamentable disaster.

"On June 1 H.M. Submarine Thetis, a vessel built by Cammell Laird, Ltd., was carrying out acceptance trials in Liverpool Bay.

"She was accompanied by a tug belonging to the firm, carrying a naval submarine officer on board.

"There were on board a full complement of naval personnel. In command was Lieutenant-Commander Bolus. Captain Oram, commanding officer of the flotilla, and Engineer Captain Jackson, on the staff of Admiralty submarines, were also on board together with a party of Admiralty officers and certain contractor's personnel, normally carried in such acceptance trials.

"Four other naval officers were on board to gain experience in handling submarines of similar class, now building.

"The presence of these additional personnel in no way contributed to the sinking of the submarine.

"At 1.40 p.m. she dived for three hours. She failed to reappear at the appointed time.

"Torpedo Tube Door Open"

"It is evident that the accident occurred while the vessel was submerged.

"So far as can be ascertained, the sinking of the Thetis was caused by the flooding of the two forward compartments through one of the bow torpedo tubes.

"The rear door of one of these tubes came open or was open through reasons which cannot be fully explained.

"The men in escaping from the compartment were unable in the time available to close the watertight doors behind them.

"The flooding was restricted to the second compartment.

"Main ballast tanks were emptied by compressed air with the intention of bringing the submarine to the surface, but she continued to dive and hit the bottom at an angle of 35 degrees.

"She hit the bottom at 130 feet.

"The Thetis came to rest on the bottom on an even keel. The impact on the bottom destroyed the vessel's signalling apparatus and she was unable to communicate with surface vessels.

"Marker buoys were released from the vessel and smoke floats sent up, but these were not observed by the escorting tug which had followed the expected course of the submarine.

"With a view to facilitating the escape of the personnel, all possible measures were taken by the crew to lighten the submarine, and the stern came to the surface at daylight on June 2.

"The Thetis had been due to surface at 4.40 p.m. on Thursday, June 1.

Sighted by 'Planes

"The Rear-Admiral of Submarines, Portsmouth, asked the Admiralty for news at a quarter past five, and a negative reply was given.

"The Commander-in-Chief, Plymouth, under whose command the subsequent operations fell, was informed that the Thetis had failed to surface at 6.50 p.m.

"According to pre-arranged procedure to deal with such an emergency, the following vessels were dispatched and proceeded at maximum speed to the scene of the accident:—

"H.M.S. Brazen, Plymouth Command, eight destroyers of the Sixth Destroyer Flotilla, six

(Continued on back page.)

GANG HELPED BY WOMAN

DETECTIVES are seeking a woman accomplice of thieves who, wearing drill smocks usually worn by employees, calmly loaded a van and made off with £600 worth of cigarettes and tobacco at a Weston-super-Mare, Somerset, store, while passers-by looked on.

A woman looked over an empty house in Union-street, Weston, and it is thought that she left the door unlocked.

The thieves entered the empty building, knocked a hole in the wall and crawled into the wholesale tobacco store of Councillor Louis Brown.

GIRL DIVES UNDER YOUTH, SAVES LIFE

PROMPTITUDE of a Birkenhead girl saved the life of Joseph William Leonard Palmer, aged twenty-one, of Church-street, Chesterton, Staffs, at Prestatyn, Flintshire, yesterday.

Palmer, who is staying at the Bastion-road Camp, Prestatyn, went for a sea bathe and got into difficulties. Hearing his cries his brother, John, swam out to him, but found he could render little assistance and he, too, was obliged to shout for help.

Miss Audrey Mavis Hancock, aged twenty, of Prenton-road, West Birkenhead, who was bathing nearby, swam towards the brothers, and by diving under Leonard Palmer managed to keep him afloat.

He was in a semi-conscious condition, but recovered.

★ THE WOMAN WHO KNOWS ALL ABOUT WOMEN

In London to-day is Miss Clare Boothe . . . the woman who knows all about women . . . wrote all she knows, put it on the stage in the play "Women" . . .

And . . . HAS GOT AWAY WITH IT.

That's the most surprising thing about Clare Boothe—the getting away with it. Because, she has taken Man into the "women only" domain, the beauty parlour, the bridge clubs, the hen parties.

And has shown Woman, the Cat, the fury, the get-anybody's man so long as you get a man.

AND WOMEN HAVE TAKEN IT!

Here are some of Clare Boothe's women: "This is the last time I go through this lousy baby business for any man. If men had babies . . .

"There would never be more than one child in the family."

Well, here on the left is the woman who has debunked women. Incidentally, she's Mrs. Henry Luce.

DAILY MIRROR, Wednesday, June 7, 1939.

Daily Mirror

No. 11,076. ONE PENNY.

Registered at the G.P.O. as a Newspaper.
Geraldine House, Fetter-lane, E.C.4.
HOLBORN 4221.

CANADA IS INVADED— HI YA KING

ON GUN CHARGE

On a firearm charge in connection with an incident near the Duchess of Kent's house in Belgrave-square, S.W.

Ledwedge Vincent Lawlor on his way to Westminster Police Court yesterday. He was remanded for a week, after a police-constable described how, after he had heard a shot fired near the Duchess's car, he gave chase and caught a cyclist. See story on page 24.

★

FROM OUR OWN CORRESPONDENT

NIAGARA, Canada, Tuesday.

AT THE RATE OF 30,000 AN HOUR AMERICANS ARE POURING INTO CANADA TO-NIGHT TO GIVE THEIR FIRST SALUTE TO THE KING AND QUEEN WHO ARRIVE IN AMERICA TO-MORROW.

The border is in turmoil. Men, women, youths and small children, shouting with excitement, crowded over Peace Bridge, Niagara. Flags were waved. Songs were sung.

The greatest republic was enjoying its first sight of the greatest monarchy.

Celebrations will go on in Niagara all night. The town is jammed with American cars.

I travelled by train to-day from America into Canada. Every coach was packed.

Boy and Girl Students with Cheer Leader

Boy and girl students from New York, commanded by a cheer leader, rehearsed again and again their welcome roar, that runs:—

Ra Ra Ra, Welcome King and Queen, Ra Ra Ra, you're the swellest folks we've seen.

The train carried dozens of sacks full of parcels and letters which the King's secretaries will never find time to o pen.

As the train swayed girls stumbled in the middle of curtsies they constantly rehearse—" just in case we meet the King."

At Windsor, Ontario, where the royal train is due to-night, thousands of people came from Detroit, only a few hundred yards across the river

And it was near Windsor to-day that the King heard his first real American welcome

As the train stopped for a few moments at Washago, the King appeared, and a voice shouted, " Hi ya King ! "

The King grinned and shouted back " Im fine. How are you ? "

The crowd cheered.

A negro with a Union Jack pinned to his white trilby told me that Father Devine—the leader of his religious sect—is sending their Majesties a basket of flowers labelled " Peace you're both wonderful'

Round-up of Suspects

As the Border rang with celebrations and Canadian champagne flowed almost like Niagara Falls, hundreds of detectives and Mounties took up their position along to-morrow's Royal route into U.S.A.

There has been a round-up of suspects. At Hamilton, Ontario, gaols are full of men whom the police think safer behind bars until the great day is over.

In New York fresh orders for the protection of the King and Queen were issued to-day by the city's Police Commissioner. He announced that spectators along the route must stand to attention while they are actually passing. All windows along the route must be closed, and police will be stationed on the roofs of all high buildings to keep watch on the crowds.

Strong forces of police will also be posted along the west side of the elevated highway for high speed traffic by which their majesties will travel to the world's fair.

"Wear White Suits"

The Royal garden party at the British Embassy in Washington to-morrow may not be an affair of toppers after all.

For Lady Lindsay, wife of the British ambassador, to-day explained that hot weather may spare American men the duty of wearing morning dress. She urged women who are invited to the party to " permit " their husbands to wear their summer white suits if the weather is unduly hot.

She added that it might add to comfort if the guests brought shooting-sticks, because there will be only 300 chairs available for 1,400 guests.

In printing this news American newspapers explain to their readers that shooting-sticks are " ground spears with folding seats attached."

FELL, WEDGED IN BUS SEAT

A HEAVILY built woman who collapsed through the heat in a bus at Gravesend, Kent, yesterday, fell between the seats and was wedged.

Although the conductor and passengers tried to free her, they could not move her.

All the passengers got out and the bus was driven to the local hospital.

There the woman, Mrs. H. G. Schwiso, fifty-five, of Arcadia-road, Northfleet, was freed and detained in the hospital.

Her condition was at first serious, but late last night she was improving.

To-day Very warm, but there are thunderstorms on the way.

Yesterday June's heat made Britain gasp—Back Page.

61

DAILY MIRROR, Friday, June 9, 1939.

Daily Mirror

No. 11,078   ONE PENNY
Registered at the G.P.O. as a Newspaper.
Geraldine House, Fetter-lane, E.C.4.
HOLBORN 4321.

FIRST LADIES

U.S. O.K.s KING

FROM OUR SPECIAL CORRESPONDENT

WASHINGTON, Thursday.

THE land of amazing parades saw its most astounding ever when the King and Queen drove through 600,000 whooping and cheering Americans to the White House, in Washington, the U.S. capital, to-day.

The King, dressed in the uniform of Admiral of the Fleet, rode in the first car of the procession with President Roosevelt. They chatted happily like old friends.

In the second car were the Queen and Mrs. Roosevelt, both dressed in blue wool frocks—and taking turns to hold the Queen's white parasol as protection against the brilliant sun.

America's royal visitors smiled and waved to a crowd which roared greetings of a kind new to their ears.

"Attaboy, King! Attaboy, Queen!" roared men, women and children.

They Went "Haywire"

The women said: "She's lovely. Pretty as a picture." The men said: "He's swell. I like them. They're just folks."

And those who thought "Attaboy" didn't make enough noise just screamed "Whee!" which is American for "Hurrah."

Overhead glittering pursuit 'planes roared. The King and Queen saw dignified American citizens go haywire with admiration, fling their hats into the air.

One American occupying a £20 vantage point on a hotel balcony actually held up his top hat with one hand and hammered it into

Continued on Back Page

'Common Basis of Humanity'

Lord Halifax spoke of the possibility of meeting the dictators "on the common basis of humanity." Meanwhile——

Germany is building aerodromes and arms works in Spain—page 2.

Italy, who signed the Nyon anti-piracy pact, boasts her submarines sank merchant ships trading with Spain—page 2.

Germans disarm police, depose council of Czech town of Klavno after alleged murder of Nazi. Schools, theatres shut and public warned shots will be fired into any windows left open at night—page 2.

Caption: Sharing a parasol in the brilliant sunshine . . . the Queen and Mrs. Roosevelt driving together from the station at Washington to the White House.

Nazis —New Colony Offer

By OUR POLITICAL CORRESPONDENT

LORD HALIFAX, the Foreign Secretary, created a sensation last night when, in the House of Lords, he made a new peace offer to Germany—an offer interpreted as a return to the policy of appeasement.

He said Britain and France did not wish to embarrass Germany in the economic field; indeed, a really prosperous Germany would be good for all Europe.

"Our one aim," Lord Halifax added, "is to throw the whole of our weight in the scale of a peaceful settlement."

He expressed doubts about the usefulness of a conference, but continued:—

"I can say, however, that if there seems to be a real attempt to reach a settlement and a conference is suggested, we should be prepared to make the best contribution we could to bring it to a successful result."

He drew attention to the prompt messages of sympathy from Hitler and Mussolini over the loss of the Thetis and suggested that it might be possible to set aside political differences and meet.

"The way is open," Lord Halifax said, "to new opportunities by which all may benefit."

In the Lobbies of the House of Commons M.P.s read the speech with rising excitement. This, it was thought, was a plain indication that Britain is prepared to discuss handing back the ex-German colonies.

It was regarded, too, as an invitation to Hitler to state on what terms he will participate in a world conference.

Opposition M.P.s were bitterly hostile. This speech, they said, at the very moment when an attempt is being made to conclude a pact with an already suspicious Russia, is a grave diplomatic blunder.

The Russians are not pleased that Mr Wil-

Continued on Back Page

JUST MAKING THINGS HUM

HOT and perspiring sailors went round the decks of H.M.S. Newcastle, lying at anchor in Portland Harbour, at top speed last night—chased by a swarm of angry bees.

They'd been found in a sailing cutter stowed amidships.

A few of the braver spirits tried to entice the bees into pans of grease.

But it was no go; the bees wouldn't be enticed. So a worried Lieutenant-Commander and the Captain of Marines had "distress" signals sent to the shore.

Out sped a high-speed naval launch, carrying a plain-clothes constable and a beekeeper, Mr. C. Hawkins, armed with a skep.

Mr. Hawkins scooped up the bees, now swarming, with his bare hands, bundled them in the skep, and sailed away.

DAILY MIRROR, Friday, June 16, 1939.

Daily Mirror

No. 11,084   ONE PENNY
Registered at the G.P.O. as a Newspaper.
Geraldine House, Fetter-lane, E.C.4.
HOLBORN 4321.

BABY SWALLOWS PIN : SAVED BY AIR RACE

Japs Shift Troops

AS British troops with fixed bayonets guarded the entrances to the British Concession in Tientsin last night, Mr. Neville Chamberlain, the Premier, told Parliament that Britain had warned Japan of the danger of provocative action.

"The situation is obviously a grave one," the Premier said.

Just after this announcement the news was flashed from Tientsin that British and Japanese troops guarding the principal entrance to the British Concession had been suddenly withdrawn.

It also followed the sending of a Note by the British Consul-General to the Japanese Consul-General lodging "a most vigorous protest" against the searching of British subjects entering and leaving the British and French Concessions.

Japan's "Inner Cabinet" will meet in Tokio to-day to discuss the situation.

The United States Government has expressed concern to Japan over the blockade of Tientsin.

Reuter, Exchange, British United Press and Associated Press.

ARMY WIDOWS TO GET MORE

INCREASE in pensions drawn by widows of soldiers, airmen and sailors who died as the result of service will be paid as from June 1 last, it was announced last night.

Only widows of Army, Navy and Air Force men who have been killed as a result of their service since the Great War will benefit.

Widows of men killed in the war of 1914-1918 will not be covered by the new scheme, nor will widows of men who died as a result of war wounds.

Sir Kingsley Wood, Secretary for Air, said in the House of Commons that pensions for widows not above the age of forty and without children will now range from 15s. 6d. to 23s. a week, and for widows above the age of forty or not above that age but with children, from 22s. 6d. to 30s. In addition, allowance will be granted for children.

Thetis Victims

Sir V. Warrender, Financial Secretary to the War Office, said that under the new scale the minimum pension for a soldier's widow under forty without children will be 15s. 6d. a week, as against 10s. 6d. at present, and for a widow over forty or under that age with children 22s. 6d. a week, as against the present rates of 17s. 6d. or 20s. In the case of a widow over sixty, there would be the usual additions for rank and children.

Widows of seamen who died in the submarine Thetis will benefit by an Admiralty Fleet order issued yesterday.

A widow not over forty years of age, if without a child eligible for an allowance, will in future receive 15s. 6d. a week, instead of 10s. 6d. Other widows will have their pensions increased from 17s. 6d. to 22s. 6d.

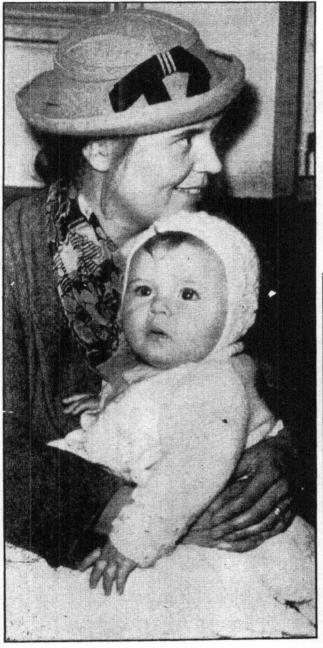

End of the first stage of the dash to save a child's life . . . Mrs. Le Gallez and her baby—quite unperturbed despite the pin in her throat—at Great Ormond-street Hospital.

BY A SPECIAL CORRESPONDENT

"RESERVE TWO SEATS IN YOUR 'PLANE—IT'S A MATTER OF LIFE OR DEATH."

That message, telephoned to the Guernsey depot of Jersey Airways yesterday began a baby's 200-mile race for life, with an open safety pin in her throat.

The baby, Olive Le Gallez, aged eight

Continued on Back Page

DAILY MIRROR, Friday, June 23, 1939.

Daily Mirror

No. 11,090   ONE PENNY
Registered at the G.P.O. as a Newspaper.
Geraldine House, Fetter-lane, E.C.4.
HOLBORN 4321.

HOME SWEET HOME

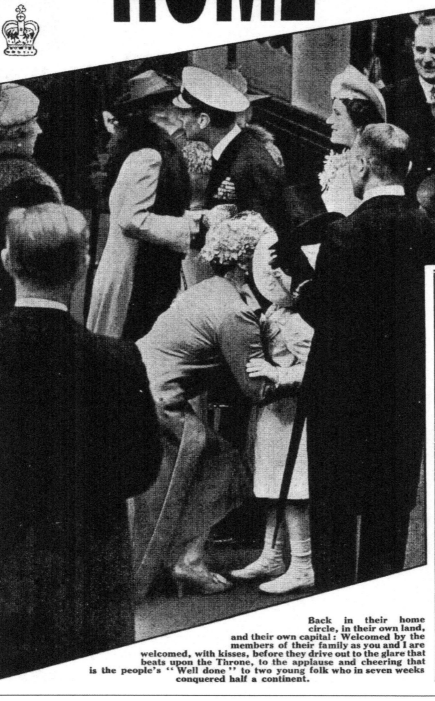

Back in their home circle, in their own land, and their own capital: Welcomed by the members of their family as you and I are welcomed, with kisses, before they drive out to the glare that beats upon the Throne, to the applause and cheering that is the people's "Well done" to two young folk who in seven weeks conquered half a continent.

Daily Mirror

No. 11,093   ONE PENNY
Registered at the G.P.O. as a Newspaper.
Geraldine House, Fetter-lane, E.C.4.
HOLBORN 4321.

M.P., RICH WIFE, IN AIR CRASH

Mrs. J. R. Robinson with her baby daughter . . . a picture taken at the christening in the crypt of the House of Commons just over a fortnight ago.

Wife Cites Mother

Citing her mother as co-respondent, Mrs. Mary Gladys Smith (picture right), of Hounslow, Middlesex, yesterday sued her husband, William Henry Smith (below) for divorce.

She alleged that at a dance her husband danced with his mother-in-law, then drove her to her flat and stayed the night.

Mrs. Smith was granted a decree nisi with costs and was granted the custody of the one child of the marriage.

"Not a very satisfactory case, but I must accept the evidence," said Mr. Justice Bucknill.

See story on page 2.

A BRITISH M.P. sat at the bedside of his wife, an American heiress, in a nursing home at Boulogne, last night, anxiously awaiting the doctors' report on an operation performed on her after she had been injured in an air crash near Le Touquet.

To his joy Mr. John Roland Robinson, thirty-two, barrister, M.P. for Blackpool, was told that his wife, formerly Miss Maysie Gasque, whose father had large interests in F. W. Woolworth and Co., of New York, was "in no danger."

Mr. and Mrs. Robinson were on their way to Blackpool, where she was due to keep her first public engagement to-day since the birth of her baby daughter two months ago.

Mr. Robinson, telephoning his father, Mr. R. W. Robinson, a Blackpool solicitor, said:

"Only a miracle of divine providence saved our lives, but we are still smiling."

Mr. Robinson stated that just after taking off at Le Touquet, the engine "cut out," the machine crashed and overturned.

They were thrown out. Mrs. Robinson fell near the plane and Mr. Robinson, although scarcely conscious, lifted her away in case it caught fire.

French fishermen and officials carried Mrs. Robinson and the pilot, Mr. Robert D. Morrison, on stretchers.

Mayor Performs Operation

Mrs. Robinson had a wound across her forehead and cuts on her head and neck. Her left leg was broken in two places.

There the Mayor of Le Touquet, Dr. Puget, and a Dr. Leroy operated on her leg and X-rayed the head injury.

Dr. Leroy told the Daily Mirror last night:—"It was a delicate operation, but it was perfectly satisfactory and Mrs. Robinson will make a quick recovery."

Mr. Robinson had a black eye and cuts about the head and body. The pilot was cut about head and legs.

Mr. and Mrs. Robinson had been spending the week-end at Lady Dudley's villa.

They live at Hampstead, N.W. He was M.P. for Widnes from 1931 to 1935.

Mrs. Robinson is a niece of Mr. Hubert Templeton Parson, president of F. W. Woolworth and Co., of New York.

Her father, who also had large interests in Woolworth's, died in London last October.

When Mr. and Mrs. Robinson were married in 1934 they flew to the Continent on the first part of their honeymoon. Their other child, a boy, was born in 1935.

"Daily Mirror," Associated Press, Reuter and British United Press messages

WIVES SPEAK OUT TO DUKE OF KENT

WOMEN spoke out to the Duke of Kent when he visited the land settlement at Snaith, Yorkshire, yesterday, in his tour of social centres.

"It is all poverty and hard work here," explained Mrs. Mary Sutton, thirty-nine, who comes from Sunderland.

"Aren't you happy here?" asked the Duke. "Unless they alter things it is impossible to make it pay," replied Mrs. Sutton.

Then Mr. R. Purdie, another tenant, called out: "It's impossible to make it pay."

The Duke appeared interested, but made no comments, although he talked earnestly with land settlement officials.

Mrs. Sutton and Mr. and Mrs Purdie said to the Daily Mirror that they are "fed-up" and going back to Durham.

NAVY'S AUGUST LEAVE OFF

THE Admiralty made the following announcement last night:

"It has been decided to advance the normal summer leave period of ships of the Home Fleet to July, to enable dockings and refits to be completed during that month preparatory to the carrying out of exercises in August.

"This decision will necessarily involve the cancellation of visits to certain seaside resorts during July; and Navy Week, normally held in the first week of August, will have to be abandoned this year."

Big Show Was Planned

Navy Week was to have been held this year at Portsmouth, Plymouth and Chatham on Saturday, August 5, and from August 7 to 12 inclusive.

Battleships, battle cruisers, aircraft carriers and other naval craft were to have been inspected by the public, and demonstrations and displays by officers and men of life in the Royal Navy were to have been given.

Greater prominence was to have been given this year to the work of the Fleet Air Arm, and a new feature for the Week—air attacks on warships—had been planned.

A large number of new warships, including the aircraft carrier Ark Royal, would also have been open to visitors.

Mrs. E. Boulan, aged fifty . . . three times married, now cited as co-respondent by her daughter.

DAILY MIRROR, Friday, June 30, 1939.

Daily Mirror

No. 11,096   ONE PENNY
Registered at the G.P.O. as a Newspaper.
Geraldine House, Fetter-lane, E.C.4.
HOLBORN 4321.

IF YOU MARCH BRITAIN WILL FIGHT

—Halifax Tells Hitler

Phyllis Brooks.

PUTS WORK BEFORE CARY

BY A SPECIAL CORRESPONDENT

ALTHOUGH film star Cary Grant came to London to talk about wedding bells with Phyllis Brooks, the young Hollywood actress, there is to be no marriage for them just yet.

"There will be definitely no London marriage for us," Miss Brooks told me last night. "We have talked it over, and decided that if we got married soon it would not be convenient for my work.

"I shall not see Cary any more while he is in England. We shall both be too busy. But I've arranged to see him next in New York, where we shall have another talk about things.

"At the moment we have no marriage plans. But in the distant future, perhaps, we shall decide to get married, but the wedding will not take place in England."

Phyllis Brooks, who is twenty, is now making a film at Elstree. She met Cary Grant, who is English-born, at his ranch in California. Recently she announced that she expected to marry him here.

BRITAIN WILL RESIST. LORD HALIFAX MADE THAT CLEAR TO HITLER AND THE WORLD IN A STRIKING SPEECH IN LONDON LAST NIGHT.

"LET ME EMPHASISE IT SO THAT NOBODY MAY MISUNDERSTAND IT," HE SAID. "THE THREAT OF MILITARY FORCE IS HOLDING THE WORLD TO RANSOM AND OUR IMMEDIATE TASK IS TO RESIST AGGRESSION."

He ridiculed the German talk of encirclement, told the Germans that if they were being isolated "it was the fault of the German Government alone," declared that if the Reich dropped its menaces Britain would be the first to co-operate.

Lord Halifax touched on Britain's strength; our unchallengeable Navy; our Air Force which now " has nothing to fear from any other," and our Army, once derided now a powerful weapon of defence.

And he emphasised how these forces will be used.

"It is now understood in this country, although it may not be so well understood elsewhere, that in the event of further aggression, we are resolved to use the whole of our strength to resist it."

We Must Preserve Law and Order

Loud applause punctuated the speech, and the loudest of all greeted the sentence: "We know that if international law and order is to be preserved we must be prepared to fight in its defence."

Mr. A. V. Alexander, the Labour leader, who followed Lord Halifax, said:—

"I must say and I believe I shall be speaking the thoughts of at least a large number present to-night when I say I was most surprised at the power and the strength and the firmness of the great utterance to which we have just listened."

And Mr. Arthur Greenwood, deputy leader of the Labour Party, speaking at Caxton Hall, declared: "I hear rumours to-day about a war breaking out to-morrow. I do not know. All I know is this: That British Labour, ever ready to try and understand the problems of other peoples, to understand the problems of the German people, would, if the challenge came, stand and fight."

Tell Germany Where We Stand

Lord Halifax's speech, the Daily Mirror Political Correspondent writes, is the first of a British drive to tell Germany exactly where Britain stands.

Peers, M.P.s, industrialists and trade unionists are pledged to see that Hitler is told the truth about Britain's determination to fight for democracy.

It is known in London that Hitler and von Ribbentrop are convinced that Mr. Chamberlain will not allow this country to become involved in a war against Germany.

The Fuehrer is prepared to carry out his plans for the absorption of Danzig without taking Britain into consideration—thus repeating Germany's tragic mistake of 1914.

Britons hope that in his broadcast on Sunday the Premier will cut out diplomatic language and tell Germany frankly that Britain will fight if necessary.

Lord Halifax's speech—page 8.

★ The Queen Goes to the Ballet

Wearing a gown of rose pink with a feather cape dyed to match. . . . The Queen leaving the Royal Opera House, Covent Garden, last night, after she and the King had seen the Russian Ballet.

It was their first evening out since their return from Canada and the United States.

The Duke and Duchess of Kent were also at the performance.

DUKE'S VICAR ASKS FOR AID

FROM OUR OWN CORRESPONDENT
NEW YORK, Thursday.

DECLARING he is penniless and threatened by starvation, the Rev. Anderson Jardine, who officiated at the wedding of the Duke and Duchess of Windsor, is planning to appeal to them for aid.

Mr. Jardine, who defied the Church of England authorities when he was vicar of St. Paul's, Darlington, to marry the Duke, is now living with his wife in Hollywood.

"Three weeks ago," said Mr. Jardine, "we were turned out of our flat because we could not pay the rent.

"I decided we'd live in an old motor-car, but a friend said we'd do nothing of the sort, and took us in as his guest.

"In such straits I plan to ask the Duke for help. I remember at his wedding he drew me aside and told me if ever I was in trouble he'd help me.

"Last winter, when I was down on my uck, I tried to reach the Duke by telephone, but failed to get a reply. Now I'll try again."

★ Poland's Oath

"We swear to defend the eternal right of Poland to the Baltic and to protect the maritime future of our country.

"To maintain an invincible guard at the mouth of the Vistula. Continually to increase our achievements on sea and ashore, and to protect our brothers across the frontier, who form an integral part of our nation.

"So help us God."

This solemn oath was taken yesterday by 80,000 Poles gathered at Gdynia for the climax of the country's Naval Week.

Poland warns Nazis: Page 2.

DAILY MIRROR, Saturday, July 1, 1939.

Daily Mirror

No. 11,097   ONE PENNY

Registered at the G.P.O. as a Newspaper

Geraldine House, Fetter-lane, E.C.4.
HOLBORN 4321.

Boy, 19 Haunted by Love

A BOY widower mourned for nine weeks the wife who died of a broken heart after the death of their baby son.

Then they found him, shot through the head, sprawled over the grave of his wife and child. He died in hospital yesterday.

Kenneth Stockdale, of Bawtry, Doncaster, was nineteen years old. When he was seventeen he married Connie Hayes. She was seventeen, too.

Their boy and girl romance bloomed into the perfect marriage. Their son was born and their happiness was complete.

Bryan, the baby, was a strong, healthy child, but when he was eight months old he fell ill and died.

To Forget . . .

His young mother could not recover from the shock of that tragedy. For a month she wept. Then she died.

And Kenneth Stockdale, so early a widower, declared that he would seek a new life—to forget.

He was a miner, but he refused to descend the pit again.

"It's no good," he told a friend, "I know I shall see their faces, smiling at me in the darkness. I am haunted by the happiness I have lost."

He joined the Territorials. A few days ago he returned, bronzed and fit from camp.

"The day he came back he insisted on taking me to the pictures," his mother-in-law, Mrs. Hilda Hayes, of Bawtry, said last night. "He seemed gay for the first time since Connie died.

"But when we were returning he told me that he could not go on with the old life. He was trying to join the Navy."

Three days later he left his lodgings, telling his landlady that he would be home for supper.

In hospital yesterday he was able to speak for a moment to his father.

"I couldn't live without them, Dad," he said.

(Pictures on back page.)

58 DINED—AND ALL WERE ROYAL

THE Duke and Duchess of Kent were among fifty-eight royal personages dining in the historic Pitti Palace, Florence, last night in honour of the Duke of Spoleto and Princess Irene of Greece, who will be married to-day.

No one except royalty was present.

Of the three Kings and three Queens present, one of each was throneless.

Guests included the King and Queen of Italy, King George of Greece, Queen Giovanna of Bulgaria, ex-King Alfonso of Spain, and former Queen Helen of Rumania.

Princess Irene of Greece, to-day's bride, is a cousin of the Duchess of Kent. The Duke of Spoleto is a nephew of the King of Italy.—Associated Press.

Inskipped His Lessons

'oys at Clifton College, Bristol, roared with laughter last night when the new headmaster, Mr. D. L. Hallward, read extracts from some school reports of Sir Thomas Inskip, Secretary for the Dominions, and an old Cliftonian, who was presenting the prizes.

Sir Thomas joined in the laughter.

An extract from the reports of 1891 to 1893 read: "He has no sense of responsibility in the house."

Another extract from an 1888 report read: "He still takes things too easily," and one from an 1886 report was: "Might do better yet."

Sir Thomas, in his speech, said:

"Notwithstanding the grave events about us, your future can be as bright and happy as that of other generations of schoolboys."

RODE CYCLE THROUGH HOUSE

HOLIDAYMAKERS ran for cover as a cyclist sped down Adam's Hill, a Worcestershire beauty spot, his brakes useless and his machine out of control.

Mr. Alfred Darby, whose house lies at the bottom of the hill, watched in amazement as the cyclist dashed through his gate at 30 m.p.h. and shot across the yard into the house.

Inside, the runaway machine upset a heavy table, at which the family had been having tea a few minutes before, smashed two chairs and ended up by crashing into the front door.

Only then did the cyclist fall off. He was not hurt, and all he said was: "Cor blimey!"

This story was told at Stourbridge yesterday when the cyclist, Norman Crumpton, of Gerrard-street, Lozells, Birmingham, was fined £1 with 10s. costs for riding his bicycle to the common danger.

CHURCHILL, EDEN TO ENTER CABINET

BY OUR POLITICAL CORRESPONDENT

MR. CHAMBERLAIN, UNDER PRESSURE OF HIS MINISTERS AND AS A GESTURE OF THE STRENGTH OF THE BRITISH OPPOSITION TO AGGRESSION, WILL SHORTLY BRING MR. WINSTON CHURCHILL AND MR. EDEN INTO THE CABINET.

The Government is determined, at all costs, to demonstrate to Germany that any military seizure of Danzig will force Britain into the fight.

It is expected that Mr. Chamberlain will emphasise that point when he broadcasts to-morrow.

The Prime Minister will make his Cabinet decision within the next few days, after he has consulted with the British Ambassadors from Warsaw and Bukarest, who have flown to England to report to Lord Halifax and to attend a big Foreign Office conference which will be held to-morrow.

Continued on Back Page

★ Dempsey's Wife Keeps Bedside Vigil

Fighting the greatest battle of his career—a fight for life—Jack Dempsey, former world's boxing champion, lies in a New York hospital.

Keeping constant watch at his bedside is his lovely wife—actress Hannah Williams, whose picture you see here.

The forty-four-year-old boxer was rushed to hospital and operated on for appendicitis. Then doctors announced grave complications. Dempsey now lies in a darkened room with a fifty-fifty chance of living.

◆ ◆ ◆

Outside the hospital wait scores of friends anxious for better news. Pugnosed pugilists, whom the big-hearted ex-champion befriended in the past, call at the hospital with bunches of flowers. Hundreds of telephone calls come from all parts of the country to ask "How's Jack?"

◆ ◆ ◆

When Mrs. Dempsey tip-toed to her husband's bedside after the operation she tried in vain to fight back her tears. Jack forgot his own pain to whisper: "Keep your chin up, darling; I'm all right."

Daily Mirror

No. 11,098   ONE PENNY

Registered at the G.P.O. as a Newspaper
Geraldine House, Fetter-lane, E.C.4.
HOLBORN 4321.

RICH MAN SHOT IN FLAT

A MAN and a woman were found dead yesterday in a block of luxury flats in Piccadilly. The tragedies were not in any way connected.

The man, Captain Edmund B. Charteris, aged sixty-eight, was found shot through the head in his flat on the ground floor of Arlington House. A Service revolver was at his side. He was in pyjamas.

During the night he had risen and told his wife he was going for a glass of water. A maid found him in the morning.

Captain Charteris was married for the second time only two months ago. He was a rich man, a grandson of the Earl of Glengall, an Irish title now extinct.

He had served in the Royal Horse Guards (The Blues), and for many years, until his death, was an unpaid private secretary in the War Office.

His first marriage was dissovled in 1921 and last May he married at Caxton Hall Mrs. Dorothy Alice Sheldon of Mount-street. W

His bride's marriage to Mr. J. S. Sheldon—she had married him when she was seventeen—was dissolved two years ago.

Beauty Queen Dead

Later yesterday, on the fifth floor of Arlington House, Miss Marcia Franklin, a beauty queen, aged thirty, was found dead in her flat. A post-mortem examination will be made to-day.

She was the daughter of a wealthy Grimsby trawler owner. She was a handsome brunette.

Five years ago she won the title "Miss Grimsby" in a beauty contest, and almost won the title "Miss England."

She was chosen "Miss Nottingham," and in 1934 won the beauty contest organised

(Continued on back page)

TRIP GIRLS "SLUDGE," SAYS VICAR

"EVERY Sunday evening there is dumped into our village a herd of unwanted, undesirable females from neighbouring towns. Many of them, because of their conduct, can only be described as human sludge."

Speaking from the pulpit of the parish church of Mottram, in Longdendale, Cheshire, yesterday, the vicar and Rural Dean, Canon Michael Power, launched this attack on week-end trippers.

Three hundred hands were raised when he asked for approval of a campaign to stop music and singing in public-houses on Sunday.

"Our Village a By-Word"

"Sunday night in Mottram stinks in the nostrils of all godly people," he told his congregation.

"Our fair village has become a by-word. Its behaviour has never been such as it is at present.

"I make bold to say that many of these women who invade our village on Sunday evenings come for other purposes than for refreshment.

"I used to be told that the face was a true index to the mind. I have looked at these women who have come into the village, and they are the sort I would not describe as paragons of virtue."

At Your Service

THIS girl, one of 20,000 National Service volunteers who marched past the King and Queen in Hyde Park yesterday, was wearing for the first time in public the uniform of the Women's Air Force.

"We are resolved," said the King, as he thanked the volunteers, "to leave nothing undone to maintain our country's security."

Facts confirm his words. Since the call for volunteers went out 2,350,000 men and women have joined the fighting forces and the defence services.

More are still needed. The Auxiliary Fire Service has vacancies for 100,000, the Civil Nursing Reserve for 50,000.

Britain's Strength Halted

a Hitler March

Already Britain's strength has proved its power. It is now known that only the strong warnings issued by Britain and France averted this week-end a Nazi invasion of Danzig; an invasion that would have led to war

Now Hitler, baulked of his plan to seize Danzig, is expected to meet Mussolini this month, probably in Venice, to discuss the European situation.

In Berlin it is reported that only two things will convince Hitler that Britain will fight if provoked—the signing of the Russian pact, and the coming inclusion of Mr. Churchill in the Cabinet.

Mr. Chamberlain, in a broadcast message to the nation last night [reported on page five] said: "Let no one make the mistake of supposing that we are not ready to throw our whole strength into the scale, if need be, to resist aggression."

Europe yesterday: back page. Hyde Park Rally: page 14.

SIX CHOSE CRIME

FROM OUR SPECIAL CORRESPONDENT
NEW YORK, Sunday.

SIX brothers, "dead-end kids," children of a Philadelphian slum, decided to become gangsters. For them crime was going to pay.

The Lanzetti boys were handsome, clever, with the sharpness of the slum boy. Their parents, of Italian descent, were devout, honest and very poor. So the brothers decided, twenty years ago, that they would shoot their way out of poverty.

They succeeded. They became big shots in America's underworld. They terrorised Philadelphia.

Every crime was in their calendar. They were accused of kidnapping, blackmail, coining, murder. The white slave traffic of the city was a racket they controlled.

The six Lanzetti boys had "made good." They were rich. They wielded power with their guns. Now in gangster words, they're all washed up.

Brother Teo was the first casualty. As he swaggered out of an expensive restaurant, in 1925, he was shot down by rival gunmen.

Brother Pius was sipping a drink in a bar when three gunmen pulled out their guns riddled him with bullets.

Brother Benito is in prison serving a sentence for dope carrying. Brother Ignatius was recently released from gaol after a long sentence. Brother Lucien is at liberty, a desperate man hiding from his enemies, who have sworn to shoot him.

To-day a body was thrown from a car that speeded along a Philadelphia street. It was the last brother, Willie Lanzetti.

There were ten bullets in him. He had been savagely beaten before he died.

The underworld had dethroned the Lanzettis, self-boosted as "America's First Criminal Family," the vice kings from the dead-end.

DAILY MIRROR, Tuesday, July 4, 1939.

Daily Mirror

No. 11,099 ONE PENNY
Registered at the G.P.O. as a Newspaper.
Geraldine House, Fetter-lane, E.C.4.
HOLBORN 4321.

More

The workless total last month (1,349,579) was 142,703 fewer than May's, and 453,333 fewer than that of June last year. The new total is, except for September, 1937 (1,339,204), the lowest for ten years.

The number of insured people working on June 12 was about 12,810,000. That is 143,000 more than the May total and an increase of about 600,000 on June of last year.

at

Work

The total of 1,349,579 unemployed is made up of 1,098,793 wholly unemployed; 195,625 temporarily stopped and 55,161 normally in casual work.

Applicants for benefit totalled 1,231,559, 22 per cent. of whom had been unemployed for a year or more.

The improvement extended to all but a few industries, says the Ministry of Labour, but there was a slight decline in employment in the coal-mining industry.

TAKE AWAY YOUR GUNS
—Poles Tell
Danzig

POLAND IS ABOUT TO FORCE A SHOW-DOWN OVER DANZIG. A NOTE TO BE SENT FROM WARSAW TO THE DANZIG SENATE WILL DEMAND THAT THE FREE CITY SHOULD BE DE-MILITARISED.

For days German guns have been landing in Danzig; German troops in civilian clothes arrived to form a Free Corps; fortifications have been strengthened.

"Intensive measures of a military character are being carried out in Danzig," Mr. Chamberlain told the House of Commons yesterday, "and an increasing number of German nationals have arrived, ostensibly as tourists."

Danzig and Berlin deny these reports, and Poland may demand that the credentials of the tourists should be examined by a neutral commission.

In Danzig yesterday a conscription decree was issued, enforcing all men and women to perform when needed "tasks of special importance to the State."

And a Nazi leader declared that if this decree leads Poland to take action "adequate aid will arrive from Germany within two hours."

More consignments of arms reached Danzig yesterday from Germany, including two tanks, six guns and a large amount of ammunition.

Flying to Warsaw

Count Racaynskt, the Polish Ambassador in London, will fly to Warsaw this morning for an important conference with Colonel Beck, the Foreign Minister. He returns to London on Friday.

Sir Nevile Henderson, our Berlin Ambassador, who arrived in London yesterday, will see Lord Halifax this morning says the Daily Mirror political correspondent. Later in the day there will be an important meeting of the Cabinet Foreign Affairs Committee.

Mr. Chamberlain saw the King at Buckingham Palace last night.

In Paris, says British United Press, it is reported that Hitler may address a note to the British and French Governments before he takes any action regarding Danzig.

It is suggested that Berlin would try to convince Britain and France of her peaceful intentions and of her desire for an agreement on all questions — once the Danzig problem was settled.

Berlin Angry

As this tactic is the one he successfully adopted before Munich, it is not likely to deceive Britain or France.

Berlin is displeased with Britain's new propaganda drive.

The Voelkischer Beobachter, in an article promoted by the unprinted British Labour Party appeal, says these "back-door" methods are a "too grotesque speculation on German forgetfulness and stupidity."

"Old soldiers remember still those pretty leaflets with the black-red-yellow edge which rained down on us from Flanders skies"

"Lord Perth and Sir Robert Vansittart can save themselves the cost of postage. Such simpletons may perhaps exert some influence on the old maids of the western suburbs of London, but German people only laugh at them"

GANG-SMASHER RETIRING

Superintendent George Yandell "the man-who-never-forgets," of Scotland Yard, the man who smashed Leopold Harris's firebug gang, retires in a month.

The mouse

... and the boy who hid it in his pyjama pocket when he was wheeled to the operating theatre ...

See Page 14

STAGE STAR AWAITS BABY

FLORENCE DESMOND, the stage, screen and radio comedienne, is expecting her first baby.

"I don't mind a bit whether it's a boy or a girl," she told the "Daily Mirror" last night.

"I'm tremendously pleased about it and now I'm going to spend all my time 'joking after myself."

Miss Desmond, in private life Mrs. Charles F. Hughesdon, wife of the airman and insurance broker, did not appear in "Band Waggon" at the London Palladium last night. Her part was taken by Miss Beryl Orde.

"The doctor has warned me that I must get all the rest I can," said Miss Desmond.

"I hope to appear in another show next spring, for I love the stage, and I see no reason why I shouldn't combine motherhood and my career."

Miss Desmond was formerly the wife of Captain Campbell Black, the airman, who was killed in an air crash in 1936. She married Mr. Hughesdon a year later.

Salute To Heroes

ALL night the 103 men on board the trapped submarine Thetis had waited for a signal that they had been found. None came.

A conference was called while the ship lay with her bow in the mud and her stern jutting out of the water. For an hour these doomed men calmly made their plans to guide their rescuers.

They decided to wait until daylight. Then Captain Oram and Lieutenant Woods climbed into the escape chambers.

There was a strong tide running. It was unlikely that they would be picked up. Strapped to Captain Oram's arm, in a water-tight envelope, were simple directions to the salvage men.

In the escape chamber the water rose. And, just as it reached his ears Captain Oram heard the boom of a depth charge. They had been found.

♦ ♦ ♦

Captain Oram, still suffering from the strain of that experience, told quietly the facts of the disaster when the official inquiry opened yesterday in the Law Courts, London.

The tragic story was lit with the bravery of gallant men. Sir Donald Somervell, K.C., the Attorney-General, who represented the Admiralty, paid tribute to the morale and heroism of those on board.

"Those in control sought the best thing to do. Those under their orders carried them out in acute physical distress with an increasing realisation that their position might become, as it did, a hopeless one."

♦ ♦ ♦

And Captain Oram showed the first sign of emotion as he spoke of his lost companions.

"That last conference; the quiet decisions and expert advice of men fighting for breath. The crew jesting until speech became impossible.

In the flooded forward torpedo tubes Lieutenant Woods twice fought oxygen poisoning and dizziness to close the door through which water was pouring.

"He was cold and shivering," said Captain Oram, "and he showed great gallantry in offering to go a second time into the chamber when he had seen two other men unable to withstand the pressure."

"There was no panic. They showed a quiet bravery of which the memory will live with me for ever," said Captain Oram.

The inquiry evidence begins on page 8.

BRIDAL SUITES FOR AIRLINERS

HONEYMOON couples going from London to Paris will soon be able to book special private suites on the new 21-ton Ensign air-liners being introduced on this route.

Imperial Airways are completing these suites as an addition to the present saloon accommodation.

Built as a state-room for four, each suite has two specially designed settees, its own separate entrance from the airport, and its own promenade deck in miniature.

Light-weight aircraft fabrics, designed by Imperial Airways' own staff, are used for the decorations, which tone with the general interior of the air-liner.

DAILY MIRROR, Monday, July 10, 1939.

Daily Mirror

No. 11,104 ◆ ONE PENNY
Registered at the G.P.O. as a Newspaper.
Geraldine House, Fetter-lane, E.C.4.
HOLBORN 4321.

OCEAN FLIGHT TO SON

Mr. Guido Coen

A YOUNG New York lawyer, making a 4,000-mile "mercy flight," arrived in Southampton last night on Yankee Clipper, the Pan-American Airways flying-boat, on the first regular air passenger service to England.

His son, aged six, is seriously ill with infantile paralysis in hospital at Livorno, Italy.

Mr. Guido Coen left Port Washington on Saturday, and twenty-seven and a half hours later was in Southampton, 3,100 miles away. He is flying 900 miles from Croydon to Florence, via Paris. He expects to see his son to-day.

Hatless and looking worried, Mr. Coen asked an airport official at Southampton: "Is there a cable from my wife for me?"

He was very disappointed when the official said there was not.

"I pray I'm not too late," he said as he entered a special train for London.

"Desperately Ill"

American consulate officers met Mr. Coen at Victoria with visas for France and Italy which they had rushed through for him.

Before hurrying to Croydon to fly to Paris he told the *Daily Mirror*:—

"I received a cable from my wife on Thursday night with the news that Luciano, our son, was ill.

"I was just able to get a place in the Yankee Clipper. Pan-American Airways made a place for me.

"I am very grateful.

"I have not seen my son for seven months. I don't know if I shall ever see him again alive. He is desperately ill.

"The last message I had was on Friday night, and then there was no change in my son's condition.

"I was not able to give details of where I would be available, but if there is a possibility my wife will try to get through to the American Consulate authorities in London and Paris.

"I am going right on to Paris to-night. If there is no machine available on a service to Italy I will charter a special 'plane.

"I Pray—"

"I hope when I get to Paris there will be a message for me letting me know how Luciano is.

"I can't bear to think of his suffering. I pray that I may not be too late."

Other passengers in the Yankee Clipper said that Mr. Coen was too worried to be thrilled by the 3,500-mile flight.

Passages for eighteen people had been booked for many months, but the company decided to make room in the 'plane for Mr. Coen.

Wading out into the Thames in this picture at Laleham (Middlesex), in a diving helmet built from scraps, is seventeen-year-old Joyce Golding, of Oberstein-road, Battersea.

Ten minutes later, when she was walking on the river bed, about 10ft. below the surface, a valve failed on the air supply—pumped by a cycle inflator through a length of garden hose.

Bathers went to the rescue and Joyce, fighting for breath, was dragged up to safety. (See story on back page.)

HE GOT HIS 5s. WORTH

Oh! Mr. Pilot
Whatever shall I do?
I wanted a flip at Birmingham,
But I queued up in the wrong queue.

MR. Nicholas, of Small Heath, Birmingham, went to Birmingham airport on Saturday, and stood in the queue to take a 5s. flight in an air liner.

He got his ticket, got into another queue and then into a 'plane. He went up, and was up for so long that he thought he was having a remarkably full 5s. worth.

At last he inquired why the flight was so long. He was then told that he was on his way to Weston-super-Mare. He had got into the wrong 'plane, one taking a party of councillors and others.

At Weston he was put up at an hotel for the night, and yesterday the air company flew him back to Birmingham. For his 5s. he had had 47s. worth of air travel as well as hotel accommodation.

CURATES HOAX BEAUTIES

PRETTY girls in their smartest frocks faced rain and wind at the week-end to reach Willesden Parish Church fete in time to enter a beauty contest which it was announced four curates would judge.

They arrived to find the entry list closed—and the joke on them.

But the girls, curious to see the competitors who might have been their rivals, concealed their disappointment as they waited for the parade.

When the entrants took a bow the watching girls gasped.

The aspiring "beauties" were all men dressed as women.

While the audience laughed the four curates unsmilingly judged them and awarded the winner—a chorister—with a bouquet of onions.

Shoes the Problem

The perpetrator of the hoax, the Rev. J. H. Pickerill, was not the least apologetic about it yesterday.

"If women regard beauty as their preserve, that is their affair," he laughed. "I said nothing about the sex of the entrants.

Mr. Pickerill's fellow-judges were: The Rev. Norman S. Pollock, of St. Gabriel's, Cricklewood, Rev. C. W. Banner, of Christ Church, Willesden, and Rev. R. F. Thorne, of All Souls, Harlesden.

"Some of the competitors made a remarkably good effort." Mr. Pickerill told the *Daily Mirror.*

"Shoes were a problem, but we made a very passable pair of sandals for one competitor from a pair of white canvas shoes cut to the necessary shape and coloured blue."

Women Scrub a Street

FORTY mothers have turned a poor street into the cleanest strip of pavement in the world, just to keep clean little Tommy's trousers and little Winnie's frocks.

In Vernon-street, Barrow-in-Furness, Lancs—a dreary street in the town rich in broad tree-planted highways—money is scarce and children plentiful.

To the children the street is a playground, but their mothers found that constant washing soon wore out the clothes soiled in play.

So they took to their buckets and brushes. Every day they scrub the pavements until they are as white as their scrubbed kitchen tables.

Even the walls of the houses are douched down to keep them free from dust and dirt.

Vernon-street has become the healthiest of playgrounds and the mothers enjoy the fun.

As Mrs. Briton, who has lived in the street for thirty years, explained: "It's good sport showing that you keep your pavement as white as anyone else.

"We are each responsible for the bit of pavement outside our house, and there's quite a rivalry to see whose is the cleanest. I reckon we're as particular as we would be about our front parlours."

One mother said: "There's a park about ten minutes away, but most of the children seem to prefer to stop near home.

"It may seem queer to you, scrubbing pavements. But it keeps our spirits up, and the friendly competition, chat and gossip as we scrub away with brushes and buckets make quite a game of it."

THANK GOODNESS, MINER'S LIQUID MAKE-UP GIVES A MATT FINISH ALL OVER!

RUSSIA: NO ADVANCE

AN official bulletin broadcast in Moscow late last night, said that the resumed Anglo-Russian talks had not produced any definite result.

The discussions yesterday between Sir William Seeds, Mr. Strang, of the Foreign Office, and M. Molotoff, the Foreign Commissar, had lasted for three hours, the longest session the talks have so far produced.

The English representatives refused to say more than that the pact had not been signed and that the conversations would be continued.

In Moscow, says Exchange, the official statement was regarded as an indication the latest proposals from London had failed to remove Soviet objections.

The source of this latest Russian dissatisfaction is so far unknown.

DAILY MIRROR, Wednesday, July 12, 1939.

Daily Mirror

No. 11,106 ✦ ONE PENNY
Registered at the G.P.O. as a Newspaper.
Geraldine House, Fetter-lane, E.C.4.
HOLBORN 4321.

SHE IS MODEST ASLEEP

A GIRL, an only child, is so modest that she goes to bed wearing:—

> A vest;
> Pyjamas;
> Trousers;
> Night-dress and
> A woollen coat.

This is revealed in a report made to Kent Education Committee by Dr. G. Stableforth, who has completed investigations into nightclothes worn by schoolchildren in Kent.

One Sleep Suit Each

He says that in the poorer districts he found quite a number of children had only one sleeping suit.

When that was being washed they slept in their day clothes.

"One little girl told me that of the nine children in her family only the two youngest had any night clothes," he writes.

"In one road where there were to be found some of the worst cases, I was told that there was only one tap to serve six houses, and in one of these houses were nine children and their father and mother. Four girls slept in one bed and none of them had anything but day clothes."

Dr. Stableforth also investigated washing of children, and he found that while mothers washed their babies at least once a day, or every other day, up to two years of age, after they were two the washing became far less frequent.

BOY FINDS £131 IN OLD CHAIR

PLAYING in a deserted house near his home last night a boy found a bundle of £1 notes, 131 of them, in the lining of an old arm chair.

This was a few hours after the tenant, Mrs. Flood, had vacated the house, telling the neighbours, "You can have the furniture."

Mrs. Flood, who is aged seventy, has lived in the house for thirty years. Her husband died last year.

The boy, Derek Cassidy, aged ten, of Harford-street, Liverpool, whose mother is a flower seller, told the Daily Mirror:

"I was playing in the house and came across an old chair. I could see something peeping through the lining. It was a bundle of notes. I rushed out into the street, and a neighbour took me to the police station."

Many of the notes were brown Bradburys.

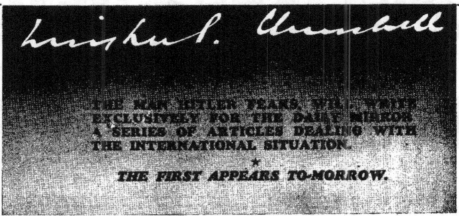
Almost Perfect Crime

Victim of what the police call 'an almost perfect crime" . . . Mrs. Margaret Jackson, of Sholden, near Deal (Kent), whose husband found her body on the bed in the front room of their home.

✦ ✦ ✦

C.I.D. men are convinced that Mrs. Jackson knew her murderer and admitted him to the house, the front and rear doors of which were locked. See story on page 5.

TURKISH WOMEN FLYERS FOR EUROPE

A SQUADRON of 'planes piloted by Turkey's five "Flying Amazons" will leave Ankara for Europe early next week. They are expected to visit Paris and London.

At the head of the five beautiful girls will be Mlle. Lieutenant Fabia Gueuckchen, favourite adopted daughter of the late Kemel Ataturk and the only commissioned woman officer in the Turkish Flying Force.

TWINS TOSS TO SAVE HER

BY A SPECIAL CORRESPONDENT

THE toss of a penny decided which of twin brothers, aged sixteen, was to give a blood transfusion to their mother in a London hospital yesterday.

"Heads," called Basil, as a house surgeon spun the coin in the air.

Heads it was.

Turning to his brother David, Basil patted him on the shoulder.

"Bad luck, old man," he said. "I'll tell ma you volunteered, anyway."

The twins' father—Mr. Lewis Bresh, of Wayland-avenue, Dalston, E.—rushed to St. Mark's Hospital, Islington, N.1, as soon as he heard that his wife needed a blood transfusion.

A test was made, but it was found that his blood fell into a different group. So Mr. Bresh telephoned his twin sons.

David and Basil hurried to the hospital, each determined to be the donor.

"Let's Share This"

They were given a test. Then they were told that their blood was in the right group. But it did not end there.

"Well, that settles it," said David. "It'll have to be me."

"Whatever gave you that idea?" asked Basil, hotly. "If mum's getting any blood it's going to be mine."

Then David hit on an idea.

"Listen," he said, "we've shared most things. Let's share this. We'll give half a pint each."

But, although that would have settled it for the twins—it couldn't be done. At last the house surgeon intervened.

"I'll toss up for it," he said.

Basil could hardly conceal his excitement when he saw that he had won.

"But David was very disappointed," Mr. Bresh told me last night. "It's a pity they both couldn't have given a transfusion.

"I have not yet been able to see my wife, but I know it will cheer her immensely when I tell her the whole story. Basil is very proud."

DAILY MIRROR, Friday, July 14, 1939.

Daily Mirror

No. 11,168.   ONE PENNY

Registered at the G.P.O. as a Newspaper.
Geraldine House, Fetter-lane, E.C.4.
HOLBORN 4321.

IT'S OUT

The rabbit Bobbie swallowed (actual size).

THE three year-old boy who swallowed his toy metal rabbit went home from hospital last night . . . with his rabbit inside an envelope.

For six days Bobbie Crichton, of Exeter-road, Southgate, N., could not play with his favourite toy. He did not know where it was, but doctors at the Royal Northern Hospital, Holloway, found out.

Yesterday the surgeon at the hospital thought an operation to remove the toy rabbit might be necessary.

Later, however, they decided to let nature take its course.

Bobbie's parents cancelled the holiday, on which they were about to leave when the accident happened.

His father, Mr. John Crichton, a draughtsman, has gone back to work.

His firm suggested that he should come back now and take his holiday later.

"It's been a terribly worrying time this week," Mrs. Crichton told the *Daily Mirror* last night.

"I'm relieved beyond words that everything has ended well, but I shouldn't like to live through the worry again for all the money in the world."

Bobbie Crichton

NAZIS' SOVIET TRADE BAIT

WHILE the British Government was sending another "communication" yesterday in its international negotiations for a Soviet Pact, it was reported that Germany is to offer £75,000,000 trade credits to Russia.

A delegation, representing Germany's heavy industries, is leaving for Moscow in about two weeks to start negotiations which have already been the subject of conversations between the Soviet authorities and the German Ambassador.

General Colson, Chief of the French General Staff, may shortly be sent to Moscow, says Reuter.

The trade talks between Britain, France and Poland end to-day, and Mr. Chamberlain is expected to announce the terms of the agreement in the House of Commons on Monday. Britain will advance £25,000,000 to Poland and France £3,500,000. In addition both countries will extend credit facilities totalling £15,000,000 to enable the Poles to buy arms and supplies.

VAST NEW LOAN TO BUY ARMS

NEW MEASURES TO STRENGTHEN BRITAIN'S ALREADY MIGHTY DEFENCES WERE REVEALED YESTERDAY.

1. The Prime Minister announced that the Reserve Fleet will be called up on July 31 for two months and the King will hold a great review of 130 ships of the Reserve Fleet in Weymouth Bay on August 9.

2. Sir John Simon, Chancellor of the Exchequer, revealed that a vast new defence loan of over £300,000,000 will be raised by public subscription. Small and large investors will be given the chance to arm Britain.

3. Sales of British ships to foreigners are forbidden in the new Shipping Assistance Bill, which authorises financial help up to £10,000,000 to liner services fighting subsidised foreign competition.

This week-end Britain's new Army musters. The first 30,000 militiamen report to their regimental depots to-morrow to begin their six months service.

UP TO YOU!

BY OUR POLITICAL CORRESPONDENT

SIR JOHN SIMON, Chancellor of the Exchequer, announcing in the House of Commons last night the great new loan for defence said:

"It will be necessary to ask the generous investor, great and small, to contribute on the most generous scale out of his savings and resources to a new Defence Loan. I have no doubt that appeal will be answered."

He had told the House the colossal figure involved—a figure no Continental Power could raise. The money will be readily forthcoming.

The small investor will be asked to play a big part in raising the loan.

Sir John explained how the original estimate of £630,000,000 for defence had leapt to £730,000,000 and that nearly £500,000,000 will be met by borrowing.

Of that sum, £150,000,000 will be raised by Treasury Bills and over £300,000,000 by an issue to the public.

It was the second announcement in the House of Commons of Britain's increasing preparations.

Earlier, the Premier had intimated that on July 31 12,000 more reservists will be called up for two months to serve with the Home Fleet during summer manoeuvres.

This is the first time since the Great War —apart from the last September crisis—that the Reserve Fleet has taken part in exercises.

Mr. Chamberlain added:—

"It is anticipated that the exercises will last until approximately the third week of September, and that the Reservists will be free to return to their homes after the ships have been reduced to reserve at the end of that month."

Sir Archibald Southby (Con., Epsom): Can

Continued on Back Page

Continued on Back Page

★ Lady Sarah Spencer-Churchill — whose coming-out party at Blenheim Palace, Oxfordshire, seat of her parents, the Duke and Duchess of Marlborough, was followed by a "fur theft" scare—leaving her London home in Kensington Palace-gardens to be presented at last night's Court.

ANTI-GAS DRILL FOR MOTHERS

WELFARE clinics will be used in the next three months for teaching mothers in big population centres of Britain how to protect their young children from the effects of gas in an air-raid.

Anti-gas cradles and hoods for infants are now being mass-produced in several factories.

The Home Office plan to have equipment available for 1,300,000 babies.

Trained in Groups

By the autumn local authorities will have received their first supplies, and a start will be made by training groups of mothers.

They will then be asked to pass on their knowledge to others in the area.

The cradles and hoods were finally approved by the Home Office after months of experiment and research and will provide complete protection from gas for little children.

They will not be issued to mothers until an emergency arises, but will be stored by local authorities.

MURDERER, YET SHE LOVES HIM

FROM OUR OWN CORRESPONDENT

NEW YORK, Thursday.

A BEAUTIFUL red-haired authoress staying near Weathersfield Prison, Connecticut, is pleading with the authorities to pardon a "cold-blooded murderer" serving a life sentence there.

The authoress, Miss Ruby Lawrence, of St. Catherine's, Canada, does not deny a romantic attachment for the murderer, Luman Beckett. But, when asked whether she plans to marry him, she replies with a smile. "He hasn't asked me—yet."

Prison Warden Walker says: "Miss Lawrence and Beckett want to pool their resources to buy a ranch in Canada."

Seventeen years ago, Beckett, now forty-one, was sent to prison for murdering a taxi driver. There he has remained, forgotten by the world, although under another name he has sold fiction.

DAILY MIRROR, Wednesday, July 19, 1939.

Daily Mirror

No. 11,112 **ONE PENNY**

Registered at the G.P.O. as a Newspaper
Geraldine House, Fetter-lane, E.C.4.
HOLBORN 4321.

Why He Looked Round

A MOTOR-CYCLIST turned round to admire a girl on a bicycle, crashed into a car, and spent nine months in hospital.

"It's a wonder there aren't more accidents," the girl said yesterday. "Drivers and motor-cyclists often stare at girls cycling along the road."

The injured man, Mr. Robert Godwin, of Burgoyne-road, Sunbury, Middlesex, appeared on crutches at Feltham yesterday to plead guilty to careless driving. The summons was dismissed.

"The suffering you have caused yourself is more than any fine," the magistrate said.

And the girl, pretty, brunette Rosina Deal, aged seventeen, of Fulmer-road, Fulham, who had given "sympathetic" evidence, explained later how she felt when the crash occurred.

As she spoke to me last night, says a *Daily Mirror* representative, Rosina wore grey corduroy shorts and a blue shirt—the same costume she was wearing on the day of the accident.

"No, I did not mind him looking at me in the least," she said. "Why should I? After all, there was no harm in it, and I am just terribly sorry he was so badly injured.

"We Took No Notice"

"My girl friend and I were riding along the Sunbury road when the motor-cyclist passed us, and both the rider and his pillion passenger looked round and smiled.

"We did not take any notice. That sort of thing happens too often for us to be surprised, but I had seen the car coming.

"There was a collision. My friend and I jumped off our machines and ran to the two men who were sprawled in the road.

"Godwin had a fractured leg, and was groaning. I held his head in my lap and made him as comfortable as I could until the ambulance arrived."

Robert, who is eighteen and an only son, was looking wistfully at snapshots of his motorcycle, now lying neglected and unused in the back garden, when a *Daily Mirror* reporter saw him at his home last night.

"It will be months before he can think of riding it," his mother said. "If I had my way, he would never ride again. I thought, and still think, he didn't notice this girl and does not pay particular attention to girls. Why, he's nothing but a schoolboy.

"He has never had a girl and is far too young for that sort of thing."

But Robert blushed as his mother spoke

Continued on Back Page

Soviet Pact Halts

Negotiations between Britain and Russia have come to a standstill (says the "Daily Mirror" Political Correspondent).

In a long cipher message from Moscow to Whitehall yesterday, Sir William Seeds, British Ambassador, indicated that there could be no early agreement regarding Britain's proposal for an anti-aggression pact.

In fact, new points raised make it difficult to see any end to these negotiations.

The Cabinet will to-day decide whether fresh instructions shall be sent to Moscow. The view in Whitehall is that "ultimately" an agreement between Britain, France and Russia will be reached —but without any guarantees to other States.

AIR DASH TO PALACE BALL

Jack Jackson, the band leader, will fly from Southport to London to-night—at the command of the King and Queen.

He is to play at the Court ball at Buckingham Palace. He is on tour with one of his bands and is appearing at the Garrick Theatre, Southport.

Asked by a Court official to grant Jack Jackson "special facilities" for the 200-mile night journey, the management of the theatre will have a car waiting to take him to Southport sands at the end of his second-house performance. There a special 'plane will be waiting, chartered on behalf of the King and Queen. As soon as he lands at a London airport another car will be waiting to rush him to the Palace.

"I'm getting a big kick out of this," Jack told the "Daily Mirror" last night. "I've played before royalty on other occasions, but I have never been asked to play specially for the King and Queen.

"My second band will go to Buckingham Palace and will carry on there until I arrive. I'll be leaving the theatre about 9.30 p.m. and if all goes according to plan, I should be at Buckingham Palace by midnight."

Here's what made Robert Godwin turn round . . . Rosina Deal on her bicycle.

£2,000 GEM SWITCH

BECAUSE he looked away for a moment from diamonds lying on the counter in his office a Hatton-garden merchant lost £2,000 yesterday.

He was discussing a deal with two "clients" with whom he had been negotiating for a week. While his back was turned for a few seconds the men swiftly substituted paste imitations for the gems.

It was not until they had left that the merchant, Mr. Eyna Podolski, of the British Watch Case Co., discovered the change-over.

Mr. Podolsky, who lives at Dartmouth-road, Cricklewood, N.W., said last night: "The paste gems were so cleverly made that I did not suspect anything till the men had gone."

WEALTH WITH £2 START

BY A SPECIAL CORRESPONDENT

A former country chemist who started a company on an idea and £2 capital thirteen years ago, yesterday sold the company for £600,000.

HE is Mr. Wilfrid Hill, aged seventy-one, City magnate and manufacturer of Brylcream, the hair preparation. The business has been bought by the Beecham-Maclean drug combine.

In 1896, Mr. Hill ran a small chemist's shop in Coleshill, near Birmingham.

He started a company to produce carbide and lubricating oil for bicycles. As a sideline, he

Continued on Back Page

DAILY MIRROR, Saturday, July 22, 1939.

Daily Mirror

No. 11,115   ONE PENNY

Registered at the G.P.O. as a Newspaper.
Geraldine House, Fetter-lane, E.C.4.
HOLBORN 4321.

GIVE US LOAN FOR PEACE

—Say Nazis

BY OUR POLITICAL CORRESPONDENT

THE GOVERNMENT IS TO BE ASKED IN PARLIAMENT NEXT WEEK TO SAY WHAT DOCTOR WOHLTHAT, GERMANY'S TRADE AMBASSADOR, HAS BEEN DOING IN LONDON.

Mr. Arthur Henderson will press the President of the Board of Trade to answer, for the Doctor, here ostensibly to attend the International Whaling Conference, is believed to have brought a plan to London.

That plan is an offer from Hitler to promise peace to Europe on condition that he gets a huge loan to solve his economic difficulties.

The price is believed to be £500,000,000 in the form of a loan backed by all the democratic Powers.

Flew to Berlin

Dr. Wohlthat is Field Marshal Goering's right-hand man. And Goering is responsible for the great plan to avert the collapse of the Nazi regime.

Dr. Wohlthat arrived here with his secretary last Sunday and booked a suite at the Hotel Victoria.

Yesterday afternoon he packed his bags and signed the alien departure papers. He went by car to Croydon Airport, accompanied by an official of the German Embassy, and boarded a 'plane for Berlin.

During his stay he saw Cabinet Ministers and industrialists.

The Nazis proposal is that Germany shall switch over from war to peace production. All arms industries will cease to turn out munitions, aeroplanes and guns, and will concentrate on peace products.

The only difficulty is money. The request for a loan would be countered by the suggestion that before any money is granted to Germany for any such scheme a neutral commission must investigate Germany's arms resources.

And Hitler will not accept that.

Dr. Wohlthat.

"Doesn't Want a War"

Hitler, now on holiday in Bavaria, is 100 per cent. determined to get Danzig, a Berlin spokesman said yesterday, but he is equally anxious to get it without war.

He is willing to wait. It is added, not years but possibly months for the knot to be unravelled without being cut by a sword.

A uniformed Danziger named Lipski was arrested yesterday in Poland and charged with espionage, says Reuter.

He is alleged to have been discovered by Polish frontier guards at two o'clock yesterday morning near Latin, a village 500 yards over the frontier, in Polish territory.

Mrs. J. B. S. Coats, wife of a member of the millionaire Paisley cotton family, to whom a son has been born. With Mrs. Coats in this picture are her daughter, Mary Manuela, and her son Christopher, who, at the age of four, was found dead in the bottom of a lift last December. He had entered the lift alone, became frightened when it moved, and was crushed as the momentum carried him past the landing when he opened the inner door to get out.

"Mother and son are doing famously. He's the grandest little chap," Mr. Coats told the "Daily Mirror." "Both my wife and I were overjoyed at the arrival of another son.

"Although nothing will ever really be the same as Christopher, we love our new baby deeply and I'm sure he will help to fill the gap which has been in our lives since last December.

"My wife has been wonderfully brave since the dreadful accident and this will help to make her forget."

The new baby will be given the Scottish name of Calium.

"It's 'not a family name, but just one my wife and I hit on."

New Baby Will Help Her to Forget Lost Son

SCHOONER GIRL WEDS

AS the schooner glided past the red Devon cliffs to her anchorage the girl in the wheelhouse gazed out at the tiny church, lapped by the waters of the Dart.

"Some day," she said, "I shall be married in that church."

To-day the girl, Miss Marguerite Alice Davis, daughter of Mr. T. B. Davis, Britain's shyest millionaire, will step ashore from her father's racing schooner Westward to be married in the church of St. Petrox, Dartmouth, the church by the river.

Her bridegroom is Mr. Alexander Simpson-Smith, the Harley-street specialist. He is thirty-nine, she is twenty-five.

A few weeks ago Mr. Simpson-Smith was called from dinner to operate on a baby, aged eight months, who had been flown from Guernsey to London with a safety-pin in her throat.

He arrived at the Great Ormond-street hospital in evening clothes. The operation was successful.

The bride lives afloat all summer, for her father, once a ship's boy at 3s. a week, has

Continued on Back Page

150-Seater Air Liner Takes Wing

Golden Hind, the biggest flying-boat ever built in Britain, rose gracefully in the air for the first time over the sunlit Medway last night.

This giant flying-boat, built so that she could carry in freight and passengers the equivalent of 150 people at a cruising speed of 185 m.p.h., was watched admiringly by hundreds of workmen on the river bank as she circled overhead for sixteen minutes.

The Golden Hind will go into Imperial Airways trans-ocean services—possibly on the North Atlantic route.

"She's a beauty," said Mr. J. Lankester Parker, the test pilot. "I am entirely satisfied with her."

One million rivets have gone into her huge glistening hull, and she is capable of flying 6,000 miles without a stop.

(Picture on page 19.)

THETIS LIFTED —1 A.M. DRAMA

"Thetis has been lifted."

THIS dramatic message was wirelessed at 1 a.m. to-day to Liverpool by the Zelo, salvage vessel which has been carrying out salvage work in Liverpool Bay since the submarine failed to rise after a trial dive two months ago, becoming the tomb of ninety-nine men.

Mr. G. R. Critchley, manager of the Liverpool and Glasgow Salvage Company, told the *Daily Mirror* this morning:

"The first lift has been satisfactory up to now. The Thetis is clear of the sea-bed and is right under the Zelo, suspended by eight lifting wires.

"Weather conditions are ideal, and at 2.30 a.m. the Zelo will start to move, and we hope she will be able to travel with the Thetis for four miles toward Anglesey before the submarine gradually touches the sea-bed again on the early morning tide about 9 a.m.

In Searchlights' Glare

"The wires will then be tightened and we will wait for the next lift as the tide starts to rise again."

The Thetis will have to be moved sixteen miles before she is beached on Anglesey.

The eight hawsers—four forward and four aft—which are cradling Thetis were in place last night, and the Zelo awaited the tide for the first lift.

Throughout the night, searchlights from two mine-sweepers which are standing by the Zelo were played on the scene of the operations.

The Admiralty vessels are H.M.S. Hebe, on board which is Captain Fitzroy, who is in charge of the salvage work, and H.M.S. Speedy.

Shipping is restricted to within five miles of the Zelo.

70, SWAM OUT OF HIS HOUSE

WATER from a flooded stream during yesterday's storm rushed through the village of North Cheriton, Yeovil, and swept four feet deep into some of the cottages.

It broke the windows of a room where Mr. George Serrell, aged seventy, sat writing.

"Before I knew where I was," he said, "I was up to my chest in water, and swept off my feet. I had to swim to safety."

A boy was washed more than fifty yards down a flooded drain and drowned during a cloudburst in Glasgow last night.

The boy, Duncan Frazer, aged eight, of Carsaig-drive, was playing with two children near the railway line at Craigton, on a low-lying piece of waste land.

As the children ran towards home, through a torrential downpour which flooded the ground 3ft. deep within a few minutes, Duncan disappeared.

Some time later a woman found him at the exit of a drain, 2ft. wide, on the other side of the railway line.

Other storm news—page 2.

DAILY MIRROR, Tuesday, July 25, 1939.

Daily Mirror

No. 11,117   ONE PENNY
Registered at the G.P.O. as a Newspaper.
Geraldine House, Fetter-lane, E.C.4.
HOLBORN 4321.

YARD FOIL BOMB PLOT ON M.P.s

THE 8,000,000 TO 1 CHANCE

Church Guide to Love

The Methodist Conference at Liverpool yesterday approved by a large majority a "frank and comprehensive" declaration on trial marriages and birth control.

Trial marrage was condemned—"It is folly to incur the obligations of marriage while there is doubt about the reality of love."

But birth control was approved.

"The careless, improvident and undesigned begetting of children," said the declaration, "is entirely to be deprecated.

"No explicit command of Scripture can be cited either for or against contraception. Conception control commends itself more to the Christian judgment when it is associated not with refusal of parenthood but in the positive aim of producing the healthiest family in the healthiest way."

The Rev. E. Clifford Urwin, of London, who presented the declaraton to the Conference, said: "Young people are thinking about this question and will be grateful for wise guidance."

SOMEBODY'S HOLIDAY FIND IS LIVE SHELL

BY A SPECIAL CORRESPONDENT

SOMEWHERE in England, possibly standing on the mantelpiece of a suburban home, is a live 18-pounder shell, which the War Office describe as "definitely dangerous."

The shell disappeared from War Department land at Lydd Ranges, Kent. Police have failed to locate it, and last night a warning was broadcast by radio.

Major John Harvey, range commandant at Lydd Camp, told the *Daily Mirror*:

"We believe that some person—probably a holidaymaker—roamed on to the War Department land, saw the shell, and carried it off as a souvenir.

"It may be in somebody's house, and we fear that a ghastly accident might happen."

War-Time Type

He explained that the shell was a war-time type, believed to have been used for practice purposes. "It buried itself in the shingle on the beach without exploding," he said. "It was exposed by the tide, and a red flag was put by it. Then it was left to await destruction."

The B.B.C. message last night said the shell was found to be missing between the first and eighteenth of this month from a spot a mile on the Dungeness side of Jury's Gap, 800 yards from the sea.

Anyone finding the shell was asked to tell the Kent County Police at Ashford, who late last night were still searching for it.

OPERATED ON, PRINCE NEVER KNEW

BY A SPECIAL CORRESPONDENT

"COME along and drink your orange juice."

Prince Edward, three-year-old son of the Duke and Duchess of Kent, obediently left his toys and ran across the room at his home in Belgrave-square, London, to where his nurse was standing with his morning drink.

"Down it goes," said the nurse as the little boy drained the glass and went back to play.

Soon afterwards Prince Edward became sleepy. His nurse watched him closely. He sat on the floor playing more and more slowly. Suddenly he was asleep. This was the signal for immediate activity.

The nurse picked him up and carried him into his night nursery. Doctors came with their surgical instruments already sterilised.

A few minutes later the doctors had completed an operation for the removal of Prince Edward's adenoids.

He slept on. Unknown to him his orange juice had been drugged sufficiently to keep him unconscious while the doctors performed their task.

"Don't You Worry"

When he awoke he still had no idea that an operation had been performed. He opened his eyes, yawned stretched and remarked: "I have got a sore throat, nurse."

"Don't you worry. Go to sleep again. You'll soon be all right," said the nurse, reassuringly.

She was right. Prince Edward, a healthy youngster full of energy, was quite himself again a few days later.

"He is perfectly fit now and looking forward to his holiday," I was told last night.

The holiday will be to some extent a reward

Continued on Back Page

DETAILS OF THE GREAT I.R.A. PLOT TO BLOW UP THE HOUSES OF PARLIAMENT BECAME KNOWN LAST NIGHT AFTER SIR SAMUEL HOARE'S SENSATIONAL REVELATION IN THE HOUSE OF COMMONS.

The plot was discovered when Scotland Yard officers raided a house in North London during their search for explosives.

There, in notes written by a "staff officer" of the I.R.A., the police found detailed instructions to bomb-throwers.

The final plans provided for a series of gelignite explosions—at least half a dozen—in different parts of the House of Commons and the House of Lords early in the morning.

Maps were found with each entrance clearly marked and with accompanying notes showing when tradesmen's carts visited the kitchen entrances and when the terraces were comparatively unguarded.

"More Ruthless"

Sir Samuel Hoare, revealing the plot to bomb Parliament, in the House of Commons yesterday added:

"We have reliable information that the I.R.A. campaign is being closely watched and actively stimulated by foreign organisations."

He could have been more precise. The facts are that financial support and technical advice on the making of explosives have for the past five months been given to the I.R.A. by German agents.

Sir Samuel Hoare, introducing yesterday his new Bill to stamp out the terror, warned the House of Commons that "the I.R.A. campaign henceforth is to be more ruthless. Human life will not be spared."

He showed a photograph of a famous plan—Plan S—which sets out the methods to be employed by the I.R.A. men.

"Time after time in recent weeks," he said, "the police have been baulked by the absence of powers to search and control suspects who, they were convinced, were terrorist leaders. That was so in the case of the Piccadilly outrage.

"The police were convinced that they had arrested some of the perpetrators, but they had not evidence sufficient to take action in a court of law and the result was that these suspected persons, after a day or two were released."

The House gave the Bill a second reading with an overwhelming majority.

Reunited with her mother in this picture is Gwyneth West, aged sixteen, of Chalvey (Bucks). Gwyneth disappeared . . her mother got a clue that the girl had gone to London.

She took the first train she could . . . WITHIN AN HOUR SHE MET HER DAUGHTER. And in London there are eight million people.

See story on page 2.

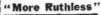

HAIL
IN JULY

You've all heard of Goodwood, in Sussex, in the Sunny South of England. Glorious Goodwood, they call it.

Well, this was Goodwood yesterday, July 24 . . . with traffic ploughing along a road inches deep in hail!

Other places also experienced weather freaks. See story on page 3.

DAILY MIRROR, Wednesday, July 26, 1939.

Daily Mirror

No. 11,118   ONE PENNY

Registered at the G.P.O. as a Newspaper.
Geraldine House, Fetter-lane, E.C.4.
HOLBORN 4321.

British, French Air Lines Pool

Imperial Airways and Air France have signed an agreement to increase services between Great Britain and France, and to pool receipts and resources, it was revealed last night.

Under this plan there will be twenty services each way between London and Paris every day in summer, as compared with fourteen at present.

In winter there will be fourteen services each way every day instead of nine services which were run last year. All machines will do the journey in about an hour and a quarter.

Tickets will be interchangeable, but there will be no change in the fares.

The new scheme will come into operation at the beginning of the winter season.

Air France is one of the largest combines in Europe.

RETURNED LOST £100, HURT

A WOMAN who dropped a roll of Treasury notes yesterday —more than £100—swerved her car to fling off a girl who jumped on to the running-board to return the money.

THE GIRL'S LEG WAS CUT AS SHE TRIED TO HOLD ON. WHEN SHE SHOUTED THE WOMAN STOPPED, ACCEPTED THE MONEY, COUNTED IT, AND DROVE OFF.

The girl, Beryl Manning, of Cardiff-road, Newport, Mon, had seen the roll of notes, about two inches thick, drop at her feet as she stood on the sea wall at Weston-super-Mare.

"The woman dropped the notes out of her handbag as she climbed the sea wall," Miss Manning told the *Daily Mirror*.

"As I was picking them up she started off in her car. I rushed after her and jumped on to the running board, grabbing the door handle.

"I don't know whether she imagined I was going to attack her, but she suddenly swerved and I cut my leg as I was flung against the door hinges.

"I shouted and then she stopped. When I gave her the notes she counted them as I stood there.

"THEN SHE SAID, 'WELL, WHAT ARE YOU WAITING FOR? THEY ARE ALL HERE.'

"With that she slammed the door and drove off."

Ace Pilot Crashes

BY A SPECIAL CORRESPONDENT

GRAVELY injured when a warplane he was testing crashed at the Austin aero shadow factory near Birmingham last night, Captain Thomas Neville Stack, famous air ace, regained consciousness as he lay in Selly Oak Hospital.

Turning his head he saw his wife and nineteen-year-old son Anthony sitting by his bed. " I'm O.K., so don't worry," he whispered with a wan smile.

Captain Stack suffered terrible leg injuries. His mechanic, Mr. Harold Crawford, was also injured, and early to-day both were critically ill.

Pulled from Wreck

Workmen saw the Fairey Battle Bomber, which Captain Stack was testing, crash on to the private aerodrome.

The machine did not catch fire and they ran to the wreckage and pulled pilot and mechanic clear.

While Captain Stack was on his way to hospital, a works official telephoned to his King's Norton home and broke the news to Mrs. Stack. She and her college-boy son, Anthony, rushed to his bedside.

Captain Stack's elder son is a cadet at Cranwell.

WAR CHIEFS FOR MOSCOW

BY OUR POLITICAL CORRESPONDENT

MR. NEVILLE CHAMBERLAIN will announce in the House of Commons this week that substantial progress has been made in the Anglo-Russian talks.

The full terms of the Pact will be published before the House rises on August 4, and within three weeks a Naval and Air Mission will go to Moscow to arrange for a hard-and-fast military agreement. A French General has been detailed to co-operate with the British Mission.

Most Points Met

The military pact is closely linked with the political agreement.

Most of the points raised by the Soviet Government in regard to indirect aggression have been met.

Whitehall believes that there is little difference between the British and Russian points of view, and any obstacles now remaining will be quickly overcome.

It is anticipated that the agreement will be signed in Moscow shortly after the military mission has started its negotiations.

Winston Churchill Writes for Us Again To-morrow

While a little girl in HER party frock looks on enraptured . . . the Queen, wearing an ostrich feather boa with a dress of pale mauve and hat embroidered to match, at a garden party yesterday at Grove House, Regent's Park, London.

DAILY MIRROR, Tuesday, August 8, 1939.

Daily Mirror

No. 11,129 ONE PENNY
Registered at the G.P.O. as a Newspaper.
Geraldine House, Fetter-lane, E.C.4.
HOLBORN 4321.

"We Are Not GERMAN Propagandists!" BUT—

200 LOSE CLOTHES ON RAIL

BY A SPECIAL CORRESPONDENT

SOMEWHERE in England is a railway van, with the number 8,883 on its side. In it are suitcases containing the clothes of about 200 holidaymakers.

It should have arrived at Scarborough on Saturday; but it didn't; and the L.N.E.R. can't find it anywhere.

So yesterday holiday girls from Leicester, Manchester and Coventry stood outside Scarborough railway station screaming in chorus:

"We want our luggage . . . We want our luggage."

But all the railway officials could do was make promises. For they had to admit that they hadn't the faintest idea where van No. 8,883 was.

An official said last night : "Every available man at all stations is searching for the van."

In it are hundreds of pounds worth of beach wear, evening gowns, cosmetics and pyjamas, which the passengers had sent in advance.

Continued on Back Page

In his own home at Roehampton (London), this picture of Sir Barry Domvile, The Link chairman, was taken yesterday.

It shows Sir Barry and his wife looking at the invitation (lovingly framed!) to the Salzburg Festival (in Germany). There is a picture on the table of Hitler; a statuette of a dachshund (German) dog; another of a German storm trooper.

But no John Bull . . . not even a picture of Mr. Chamberlain!

"The Link is not an instrument for German propaganda," says the Admiral. "It's a damn lie."

Last night members of The Link Council met in London. One of them revealed he had been paid £150 for a book in praise of the Nazi regime.
(See story on back page.)

BOMBER KILLS GIRL ON CLIFF

TERRIFIED holidaymakers ran for their lives yesterday when a twin-engined R.A.F. bomber appeared suddenly from a bank of mist crashing down towards them on Beachy Head, Eastbourne.

All got clear except one woman who was walking alone. The plane struck her, killing her instantly.

Then, spinning and turning, it careered a hundred yards to the cliff edge and toppled 500 feet into the sea below, splintering as it fell.

Police-Sergeant Siggs was in a car park about a quarter of a mile away when the accident happened.

He and others who heard the crash, ran to the spot and found the trail of wreckage leading to the cliff edge. They were horrified to find the body of the woman.

The crash occurred a few hundred yards from the coastguard station, and the wreckage of the 'plane fell close to the lighthouse.

Mr. Leslie Saywood, of the Beachy Head Hotel, told the *Daily Mirror*:

"It is fortunate that there has been a thick mist hanging over the Head all day. Usually on a Bank Holiday there are thousands of people walking along the top.

Police Race to Spot

"As it was, several people had narrow escapes as the 'plane crashed."

It was impossible to reach the spot where the 'plane fell except by sea, and immediately a motor-boat was launched at Eastbourne and a party of police raced to the spot.

It was not until late that the bodies of the crew were recovered.

They were Sergeant Harry Donald Terry Farrow (pilot), Acting-Sergeant Alfred John William Sargent and Aircraftman Second Class Leslie Phillips. The machine belonged to No. 107 Squadron.

The body of one man could not be recovered until the tide receded, and it was then carried along the beach for some miles.

TWO DIRECTORS SHOT AT MEETING

AFTER a shot had been heard two men attending a directors' meeting at Peterhead, Aberdeenshire, yesterday, were taken to Aberdeen Royal Infirmary.

They were Mr. William Mackintosh, fifty-five, of Balmoral-terrace, Peterhead, a director of the firm of James Sutherland (Peterhead), Ltd., haulage contractors and bus proprietors, severe head injuries;

Bailie William MacDougal Gordon, senior magistrate of Peterhead, leg injury.

The meeting of directors was in progress at the company's headquarters at Victoria Stables, Peterhead, when a shot was heard.

A revolver was found in the directors' room by the police.

Later George Birnie Anderson, aged fifty-six, of St. Mary-street, Peterhead, was detained and charged. He will appear at Aberdeen Sheriff's Court to-day.

DAILY MIRROR, Friday, August 11, 1939.

Daily Mirror

No. 11,133   ONE PENNY
Registered at the G.P.O. as a Newspaper.
Geraldine House, Fetter-lane, E.C.4.
HOLBORN 4321.

All About the

See Page 2

Danzig "Hour Nears"

"THE hour of liberation is at hand!" Albert Foerster, the Danzig Nazi leader, screamed to a crowd of 100,000 last night.

His phrase was word for word that used by Henlein, the Sudeten Nazis' chief last September, as the Czech crisis neared its climax.

"Home to the Reich!" chanted the well-drilled Danzig crowds, as the Sudetens chanted it a year ago.

Foerster, in a broadcast of whose speech Hitler was listening, accused the Poles of threatening to attack Danzig.

"It must be clear to us and to the whole German people, as well as sensible foreigners, that such constantly repeated Polish expressions cannot continue," he said.

"In recent weeks we have done everything in Danzig to defend ourselves and answer attacks of whatever kind.

"Fifth Column" Appeal

One passage in Foerster's speech appealed directly to "Fifth Column" sympathisers with Hitler in other countries. He said:

"Many persons unknown to us in foreign countries, especially in France and England, agree with us," and cited Winston Churchill—"one of the greatest German haters"—as one of many leaders favouring revision of the Danzig and the Polish Corridor questions.

Foerster said that the demonstration was not held merely to stage a "sensation."

"The situation is much too grave for us to make sensations, but we are forced finally and absolutely clearly to express our meaning," he cried.

"The people of Danzig to-day are absolutely clear and firm in their conviction that the hour of liberation is at hand, and Danzig will again return to the Reich.

"In this hour we can do nothing better than to swear we will hold together—come what may—and resist every attack on this holy German soil with all the means at our disposal, and that we will carry out every order that our Fuehrer gives us.

"May the day be not distant on which we come together here again, not in a protest

Continued on Back Page

HEIR WED IN IRON LUNG

FROM OUR OWN CORRESPONDENT
CHICAGO, Thursday.

MILLIONAIRE'S son, Fred Snite, twenty-nine, who for three years has lain in an iron lung, was married at his home in Chicago to-day to the girl who has never given up hope of his recovery.

His bride, Teresa Larkin, twenty-five, was his sweetheart before he was stricken with infantile paralysis in Shanghai.

Her nursing and loyalty gave him the will to face life in a cumbersome breathing apparatus probably for the rest of his days. Now she is to devote her life to caring for him.

Their honeymoon will be spent in a trailer specially built to carry the iron lung.

Fred remained in the iron lung throughout the ceremony which took place a few hours after the marriage licence was issued.

Teresa stood behind the apparatus where Fred lay smiling happily into a mirror at her.

By them stood a surpliced priest, the Rev. John Morrison, who pronounced them husband and wife.

"He's the most wonderful man in the world," said the bride after the ceremony.

"We'll go to Niagara Falls for our honeymoon," said Fred.

"We want to find out if the water's still running."

School Romance

Teresa is an old friend of the Snite family. She is the daughter of Mr. and Mrs. Thomas Larkin, of Dayton, Ohio, and she will inherit part of their substantial fortune.

Her romance with Fred began years ago when she was a pupil with his sister at a New Jersey school.

When Fred was stricken and the iron lung became his home, she hid her sorrow and constantly urged him never to give up hope.

For a long time she lived in Fred's Chicago home, reading to him for hours daily and acting as hostess at his parties.

Her faith worked wonders.

Fred's courage astounded the doctors and nurses.

He grew strong enough to travel thousands of miles in the iron lung.

Recently he returned to Chicago from Lourdes, where he made a pilgrimage to the Grotto of Miracles.

Teresa secretly accompanied him. She shunned the limelight and kept her name off the sailing list. Many thought she was one of Fred's nurses.

To-day after the wedding friends paid tribute to the bride's courage.

"It set the seal on Fred's love for her," a friend of the family told me.

"She still hopes that one day Fred will once again become the healthy, athletic, young man he was before his illness."

WIFE SAYS ACTOR BEAT, SLAPPED HER

FROM OUR OWN CORRESPONDENT
NEW YORK, Thursday.

Allegations that the English actor Pat Somerset stayed intoxicated for two or three days at a time and sometimes removed his clothes in the presence of others were made against him in a divorce suit brought in Hollywood by his fourth wife, Mrs. Barbara Somerset.

Mrs. Somerset also complained that he beat and slapped her, was sarcastic, critical and called her objectionable names.

The Man in the Iron Lung, Fred Snite, junr., with his bride, Miss Teresa Larkin.

King Asked to Knight "Hot Dog"

Five million signatures to a resolution petitioning King George to knight the hot dog are being sought by the Retail Meat Dealers' Association of the United States, says Associated Press.

During their tour of America the King and Queen ate hot dogs—sausages plastered with mustard in a sliced roll—at President Roosevelt's picnic.

Passing the resolution yesterday, the Association pointed out that in 1609 James I knighted sirloin.

So they are petitioning King George VI to create the title "Sir Hot Dog."

40 MILES TO GET THE KING A BATH

THE King made both train and car journeys yesterday to rejoin his family at Balmoral after reviewing the Reserve Fleet at Weymouth.

And while he was still on the train, hot-water boilers were carried forty miles so that he could have his morning bath in comfort.

The boilers were brought on railway wagons from Perth when it was known that the King would stop for three hours at Larbert, Stirlingshire.

Carried in Buckets

Fire was kindled beneath them, and the hot water for the King's bath was carried in buckets to the tanks of the train.

After a three-hour halt at Larbert—where the people were unaware of its presence—the train went on to Perth.

There the King left it, and within three minutes had started an eighty miles car drive to his family on Deeside, by way of the famous Devil's Elbow.

Police cars escorted him.

He was home in time for lunch with the Queen and the Princesses.

DAILY MIRROR, Wednesday, August 16, 1939.

Daily Mirror

No. 11,136   ONE PENNY
Registered at the G.P.O. as a Newspaper.
Geraldine House, Fetter-lane. E.C.4
HOLBORN 4321.

FANS MOB STAR: 18 HURT

Shrieking, "Isn't he one big heart-throb," hundreds of girls stormed the Tivoli Cinema (London) last night in a frantic effort to tear buttons from film star Tyrone Power's clothes and snatch flowers from his button-hole. Eighteen casualties were treated in the cinema lounge. See story on back page.

NUN Whips BOY

FROM OUR SPECIAL CORRESPONDENT

BRISTOL, Tuesday.

A NUN, dressed in her robes and hood, sat in Bristol Police Court dock to-day while a boy of sixteen told the magistrates that she had beaten him with a stick and plunged him in a bath of cold water because he was " constantly after the girls."

She was Mary Cecilia Quinn, a sister at Nazareth House. Stoke Bishop, Bristol, and she pleaded guilty to assaulting the boy in a manner likely to cause him unnecessary suffering or injury to his health.

The boy, whose mother is dead, was described as timid and physically below the average. It was stated that a doctor found a total of twenty-nine weals on his body.

Quinn, in a statement to the police, said "It is very rare for a child to be placed in a cold bath, and when I order such punishment I am very careful.

"When I punish a boy I usually have another sister with me who usually tells me when she thinks I have punished him enough.

"On this occasion I had no one with me, as the sister who generally accompanies me is away ill."

She was bound over for twelve months.

"Threw Water Over Me"

The boy told the magistrates:
"I was in the kitchen, and she asked me what I was doing there. She came through the kitchen and caught hold of me and knocked my head against the door.

"She told me to go down to the bathroom. I went in front of her and then I was told to undress and get into a bath of cold water.

"I was hit with a stick on the back as I was getting into the water, and then when I was in the bath she threw about five buckets of water over me."

The boy admitted that he had been in trouble on many occasions for various offences.

Mr. H. S. Cox, for the N.S.P.C.C., said that Sister Quinn told a police officer: "I did hit him. He is a very difficult child. He is not a bad boy and I have a certain regard for him.

"He is constantly after the girls in the house. I punished him because I had found him in the

Continued on Back Page

Found Body: Claimed 5s.

A farm labourer spoke up at the end of an inquest at the village of Horndean, Hants, yesterday, to ask the coroner:

"Don't I get 5s. for finding the body?"

The coroner (Major G. H. Warner) wasn't sure. He consulted a reference book. The labourer—Thomas Wendys, one of the villagers—was right. And he got the 5s.

PACT SAVES WIFE OF M.P.

BY A SPECIAL CORRESPONDENT

FEARING that if they journeyed together an accident might orphan their three children, Mr. Anthony C. Crossley, M.P., and his wife resolved always to travel apart.

The accident they guarded against happened yesterday

Mr. Crossley was one of the five people killed when a British Airways 'plane burst into flames and crashed into the sea near Vordinborg, Denmark.

At the time, his wife was packing at their home in Mallord-street, Chelsea, London, preparing to go by boat.

"For years we have both flown to our annual fishing holiday in Sweden," Mrs. Crossley told the Daily Mirror last night. "But then we promised each other we would always travel separately. There were our three children to consider

"Now I am thankful that we kept our promise, and I am spared to bring up the children."

Mrs. Crossley has cancelled her plans to go to the Continent.

Her father-in-law—Sir Kenneth Crossley, Bart., head of Crossley Motors—is overcome with grief at the loss of his only son, who until a few years ago disliked flying.

Sir Kenneth's woman secretary said at his Cheshire home "Although he is keen on flying—he keeps a 'plane—I doubt if he will ever fly again."

There were six people in the machine which left Heston for Stockholm. The survivor is the pilot Captain C. F. C. Wright, who escaped with cuts as the air-liner sank.

In addition to Mr. Crossley, the victims were:

Mr. S. J. Simonton (American), Mr. C. A. Castello (Mexican), Herr Beuss (German) (passengers) and Mr. A. S. M. Leigh, radio officer of the 'plane, of Rye Hill Park, Peckham, S.E.

Captain Wright, who is married and lives at Feltham, Middlesex, said in hospital:—

"I broke the window before me with my hands because the flames blocked the door. I escaped. Outside I tried to open the cabin door, but it was impossible.

"I swam and was picked up by fishermen."

Three months ago Captain Wright flew over the same route with his young wife on the first day of their honeymoon.

Mrs. Wright said "My husband took a busman's holiday and flew as a passenger.

Mr. Simonton, one of the victims, leaves a wife and child, who live in London.

Mr. Crossley, who was thirty-six on Sunday, had been Conservative M.P. for the Stretford Division of Manchester since 1935.

Pictures on back page.

EGYPT FORCE STRONGER

Six thousand troops arrived at Suez from India yesterday to strengthen the British defence forces in Egypt. They will camp near the pyramids at Cairo.

DAILY MIRROR, Friday, August 18, 1939.

Daily Mirror

No. 11,138   ONE PENNY

Registered at the G.P.O. as a Newspaper.
Geraldine House, Fetter-lane, E.C.4.
HOLBORN 4321

BOY SUCKS OUT SNAKE POISON

USING a bottle of home-made lemonade to rinse out their mouths, a mother and her ten-year-old son yesterday took turns to suck snake poison from the ankle of a sixteen-year-old youth bitten by an adder on Hove Downs, near Brighton.

Jack Gladwell, of North-street, Portslade, had gone with his mother, his sister Barbara, aged thirteen, and his two brothers, Raymond, aged ten, and Christopher, aged eight, on a picnic.

While the others went blackberrying, Jack sat on the grass to mind the picnic basket.

Tired of waiting for his tea he jumped up and walked through the blackberry bushes to tell his mother to hurry up.

In the bushes the snake was basking.

Accidentally he trod on it, and it sank its fangs into his ankle.

The youth shouted for help, and Mrs. Gladwell and the three children rushed to his aid.

Raymond, who got there first, flung himself on the

Continued on Back Page

Friend to Wed, She Dies

BY A SPECIAL CORRESPONDENT

HEARTBROKEN because the man she loved was to marry someone else, a girl aged eighteen yesterday fell 80ft. from the roof of the Office of Works, on the edge of St. James's Park, London, and was killed.

She was Miss Doreen Goodfellow, of Sevenoaks-road, Brockley, S.E., employed in the duplicating department of the Air Ministry's building in King Charles-street, adjoining the Office of Works.

Last night Doreen's mother, Mrs. Frederick Goodfellow, told the *Daily Mirror*: "I knew there was something the matter with Doreen yesterday. She was very sad, and I asked her what it was. She told me that nobody could help her.

"Then she told me that the man she loved—she called him Leslie—was going to marry another girl this Saturday It was cruel to see her.

"He Meant so Much"

"He meant so much to her. Doreen never said a lot about him He is about twenty-five.

"I know that they have known each other for some months She used to tell me every time he took her to the pictures or out to lunch, which he did frequently.

"I often asked her to bring him home to meet us, but he would never come.

"Doreen always used to say that he had been kept late at his office in Whitehall.

"Last week-end Doreen came home and said that her friend was going to be married next Saturday. At that time I did not even know the man's full name.

"I think Doreen was heartbroken.

"After the news of my daughter's death I went to this man's office and spoke to him. He told me that he had arranged his wedding plans only a few days ago."

Doreen, known as Robin to her friends, was the youngest of three children.

Doreen Goodfellow (right), the dead girl. Broken line in picture above shows her 80ft. fall from the roof of the building.

ARMY SECRETS IN HAREWOOD NEWS

IMPORTANT military secrets which in the opinion of War Office officials should never have been published, appeared in the "Harewood News," a typewritten "newspaper" published by the two sons of the Princess Royal and the Earl of Harewood.

Army officers and War Office officials held a conference at the War Office yesterday after their attention had been drawn to the article.

Newspapers have been specially asked by the War Office not to reproduce the article concerned.

The "Harewood News," which has a circulation of 200, is produced three or four times a year, but reaches a far greater number of people, particularly in Yorkshire, because it passes from hand to hand and is valued for its inside racing information.

The two sons of the Earl of Harewood are Viscount Lascelles, aged sixteen, and the Hon. Gerald Lascelles, aged fifteen.

SUBMARINE DID NOT RISE

When a submarine failed to surface off Portland last night, slides were shown on Weymouth and Portland cinema screens recalling naval ratings of H.M.S. Walker and Walpole, torpedo boat destroyers, and of the anti-submarine vessel H.M.S. Bittern, to their ships.

But while sailors were being rushed back and the ships were being prepared, the submarine reappeared and the order was cancelled.

The submarine was exercising with the patrol vessel H.M.S. Kittiwake when she failed to surface and the Kittiwake's commander radioed to the naval base.

HITLER GIVES HIS ORDERS TO HUNGARY

A PERSISTENT report from many European news centres last night suggested that Hitler's surrender-or-be-wiped-out tactics, so successful in Austria and Czechoslovakia, were being applied to Hungary.

The report, received from sources in Berlin, Munich and Salzburg, was that Count Csaky, Hungarian Foreign Minister, was "received" in a long interview by Hitler at Berchtesgaden yesterday afternoon and evening.

A denial issued at Berchtesgaden only gave a greater air of mystery to the meeting: not one observer doubted last night that it had taken place.

Csaky left Fuschl Castle, Salzburg (where he had been staying with von Ribbentrop), and, says Reuter, drove by unfrequented roads to Berchtesgaden.

The talks are believed to have extended well into the evening. Count Csaky had to hurry back to Salzburg, where Dr. Frick, German Minister of Interior, gave a dinner in the Count's honour.

Csaky, who, so far, is "in favour" with the

Nazis, was given an ominous title last night: "the Guido Schmidt of Hungary."

Schmidt, Austrian Foreign Minister under Schuschnigg (now the Nazis' prisoner), made frequent visits to Germany before Hitler grabbed Austria. He is said to have prepared the way for Austria's surrender.

The main points of the Hitler-Csaky conversation were thought last night to be a Nazi demand to occupy Ruthenia (taken from the Czechs by Hungary after the Munich agreement) and a demand that Hungary place herself unconditionally under Hitler's orders

Troops Digging In

Occupation of Ruthenia and Hungary would give the Germans tremendous strategic advantages in a war against Poland and Rumania.

In Upper Silesia German troops have "dug in" within 300 feet of Poland's border.

A forty-mile drive along the German-Polish Border showed me (writes an Associated Press correspondent from Gleiwitz) that the closing of "a section of the Polish Border" has increased the speed with which German en-

Continued on Back Page

To all who have SHORT holidays

READ WHAT THIS DOCTOR SAYS:

"After nearly nine months' hard work I became thoroughly run down. During my holiday I had a glass of Guinness each night before going to bed. At the end of my ten days' vacation I felt ready for duty again." M.B.

That settles it. Let's all have a Guinness a day during our holidays. Partly because Guinness is so obviously right for hot or strenuous days—so clean and refreshing with its pleasing tang of hops. Partly because Guinness gives you strength, so that the refreshment does not vanish in a few minutes. And finally because all the time it's toning you up for the year to come. Treat yourself to a Guinness daily. Guinness is good for you.

The above doctor's letter is quoted with special permission. G.E.189.C.

DAILY MIRROR, Tuesday, August 22, 1939

Daily Mirror

No. 11,141   ONE PENNY
Registered at the G.P.O. as a Newspaper.
Geraldine House, Fetter-lane, E.C.4.
HOLBORN 4321.

SKY BLAST KILLS 7, INJURES 22 IN PARK HUT

John Ridgewell (left) and Leslie Walker.

In this little shed—in Valentine Park, Ilford (Essex)—the lightning's victims were killed and injured. Strewn with pathetic relics of their dash to it for shelter, it is itself undamaged.

More storm pictures are on pages 3, 14 and 15.

A flash of lightning swept through a packed park shelter yesterday, killed seven people and injured twenty-two, three seriously.

YET the little wooden shelter—in Valentine Park, Ilford, Essex—was hardly touched. It had one slight burn.

A rainstorm sent about thirty people, including women and children and electric cable workmen, crowding into the hut.

One man propped up his bicycle outside. And it is thought that this acted as a conductor.

There was a roar like artillery, and a forked flash struck out of the gloom of the storm.

The people were packed close, and apparently the shock was transmitted from one to the other. In a second they were flung down and scattered.

The screams of injured women and children could be heard a quarter of a mile away. Among the dead lay two little boys.

In a few minutes six ambulances raced to the spot, but even then a motor wagon had to be commandeered to help take away the dead and hurt.

Park-Keeper Frank Crisp told the *Daily Mirror*:—

"It was like a battle-field. Men and women were strewn all over the place. Some of them had their clothing burnt nearly off them.

Screamed as "Dad" Dies

"A dead man was lying over the cross-bar of a bicycle. On the saddle sat his son, a boy of about nine, screaming 'Dad!'

"In the corner a young woman was lying dead. She had hardly a stitch of clothing on her. Her body was terribly injured.

"A little boy was running round on the grass outside the shelter. As I got there he ran inside and went from one body to another. He was trying to find his mother."

The boy was Tony Ruane. His parents, Mr. and Mrs. Alice Ruane, had taken him to the park for a picnic.

It was the first day of Mr. Ruane's holiday.

Mrs. Ruane was killed instantly. Flames enveloped her. Her husband tried to beat out the flames with his hands. He was badly burned about the hands.

Late last night Tony, in hospital with leg injuries, was fretting for his mother. He had not been told that she was dead.

One of the victims, Mrs. Caroline Cribett, a teacher at Salisbury Intermediate School, had

Continued on back page

Nazi Pact with Soviet

THE official Nazi news agency announced last night that Germany and Soviet Russia have agreed to conclude a non-aggression pact.

Herr von Ribbentrop, the German Foreign Minister, will arrive in Moscow tomorrow to complete the negotiations.

The announcement is made while a British military mission is in Moscow. It went to discuss with the Russian war chiefs resistance to the menace of Germany.

The Berlin statement followed rumours of a mysterious aeroplane flight by Ribbentrop—already thought to be on his way to Russia.

On Sunday Germany and Russia signed a trade pact.—*Reuter and British United Press.*

Parliament may be recalled.—See back page.

CURATE WEDS A MANNEQUIN

AFTER announcing his marriage to a West End mannequin whose marriage had been dissolved, a young curate, the Rev. O. T. Jehu, has resigned from his post at Holy Innocents' Church, Hornsey, London, N.

His bride is Mrs. Muriel (Jay) Martin, a fashion shop model.

They have taken a small flat in Hornsey.

Mr. Jehu told the *Daily Mirror* yesterday:—

"Mrs. Jehu has also given up her job. It would have been incompatible with her position as a wife for her to have carried on.

"At the moment I have made no plans for the future.

"Our Lives Before Us"

"I may take a curateship somewhere else. I have two or three things under consideration.

"Both my wife and I are young—not yet thirty—and we have our lives before us.

"I am really sorry to leave the church here, but I feel it is the only thing to do."

One woman member of the congregation sent a congratulatory telegram and a silver horseshoe for luck from her baby son on hearing that Mr. Jehu was to marry.

She told the *Daily Mirror*:—

"All of us are sorry that he has left us.

"He was one of the most popular curates in North London."

Mr. Jehu was curate of Minster-in-Thanet from 1933 to 1936. His father is the Rev. Timothy Bright Jehu, former rector of Hinton Blewett, who came to London to take a curateship at St. George's, Hanover - square, London, W.

DAILY MIRROR, Thursday, August 24, 1939

Daily Mirror

No. 11,143   ONE PENNY
Registered at the G.P.O. as a Newspaper.
Geraldine House, Fetter-lane, E.C.4.
HOLBORN 4321.

3 a.m. EDITION

Nazis, Soviet Sign

THE German-Soviet non-aggression pact was signed in Moscow this morning by Molotov, Soviet Premier, and Von Ribbentrop, Hitler's Foreign Minister, in the presence of Stalin.

According to a Reuter message from Berlin, the text of the agreement, issued by the official German News Agency, reads:

"Guided by the desire to strengthen the cause of peace between Germany and the Soviet Republics, and based on the fundamental stipulations of the neutrality agreement concluded in April, 1926, the German Government and Soviet have come to the following agreement:—

Article 1: The two contracting Powers undertake to refrain from any act of force, any aggressive act and any attacks against each other or in conjunction with any other Powers.

"Third Power" Clause

Article 2: If one of the contracting Powers should become the object of warlike action on the part of a third Power, the other contracting Power will in no way support the third Power.

Article 3: The Governments of the two consulting Powers will in future remain in consultation with one another in order to inform themselves about questions which touch their common interests.

Article 4: Neither of the two contracting Powers will join any other group of Powers which directly or indirectly is directed against one of the two.

Article 5: In case differences or conflict should arise between the two contracting Powers on questions of any kind, the two partners will solve these disputes or conflicts exclusively by friendly exchange of views or, if necessary, by arbitration commissions.

For Ten Years

Article 6: The Agreement is concluded for the duration of ten years with the stipulation that unless one of the contracting partners gives notice to terminate it one year before its expiration it will automatically be prolonged by five years.

Article 7: The present agreement shall be ratified in the shortest possible time. The ratification documents are to be exchanged in Berlin. The treaty comes into force immediately after it has been signed.

✦ ✦ ✦

Colonel F. H. N. Davidson, second military officer of the British Mission in Moscow, and Group Captain A. C. Collier, second air officer, are returning to London by air to report.

Commandant Pichon, a member of the French Military Mission, is leaving Moscow by air for Paris to-day, the Moscow correspondent of the Havas Agency telegraphs.

Messages: Reuter, Associated Press, British United Press.

Mr. Winston Churchill — back from his visit to France, where he visited the Maginot Line—at Croydon last night.

A magnificent article by him is on page 14 and 15.

HITLER REPLIES: WILL NOT TURN ASIDE

BY A SPECIAL CORRESPONDENT

'The Fuehrer left the British Ambassador in no doubt that the obligations undertaken by the British Government could not cause Germany to renounce the pursuance of her national, vital interests.'

THIS STATEMENT, ISSUED BY THE OFFICIAL GERMAN NEWS AGENCY, WAS HITLER'S REPLY TO THE BRITISH GOVERNMENT MESSAGE TAKEN TO HIM AT BERCHTESGADEN YESTERDAY BY SIR NEVILE HENDERSON, AMBASSADOR IN BERLIN.

THE MESSAGE EMPHASISED BRITAIN'S RESOLVE TO SUPPORT POLAND

LATE LAST NIGHT SIR NEVILE HANDED HITLER A PERSONAL MESSAGE FROM MR. CHAMBERLAIN EMPHASISING EVERY POINT IN THE OFFICIAL DECLARATION WHICH THE AMBASSADOR GAVE THE FUEHRER EARLIER IN THE DAY.

IN EFFECT, THE PRIVATE NOTE REPEATED THAT BRITAIN HOPES FOR A PEACEFUL SOLUTION OVER THE DANZIG PROBLEM, BUT IN THE EVENT OF POLAND'S INDEPENDENCE BEING MENACED, BRITAIN WILL FIGHT.

To-day the British Parliament meets in special session to rush through emergency powers which will enable the Government immediately to take any necessary measures.

The King travelled overnight from Scotland to London. Early to-day he holds a meeting of the Privy Council at Buckingham Palace, and he will give an audience to the Prime Minister to hear the latest developments in the situation.

Halifax on Radio

LORD HALIFAX WILL BROADCAST TO THE NATION FROM No. 10, DOWNING-STREET, AT 9.30 TO-NIGHT IN THE NATIONAL PROGRAMME. HIS SPEECH WILL BE RELAYED TO AMERICA AND OTHER COUNTRIES.

These, according to Associated Press, are the demands Hitler is insisting on:—

1. The unconditional return of Danzig to the Reich.

2. The return of those sections of Poland which were once German, namely, Pommerellen, Pomorze and Polish Upper Silesia.

3. A re-arrangement of Polish-German relations much along the lines of the Protectorate of Bohemia and Moravia.

Arms Export Ban

Berlin says that Germany has communicated her views by special couriers to the British Government and most of the other European Powers.

Britain has prohibited the export of arms, and also a number of materials—including scrap steel, other vital metals, cotton, rubber, oil and petrol—which would be useful in war.

In France a general military requisition order was issued early to-day by the Government, giving the military authorities power to commandeer anything they may require.

Foreign messages: British United Press, Associated Press, Reuter, Exchange.

Lights Out For All

EVERYONE must prepare fully NOW to comply with lighting restrictions which will be enforced at short notice, says a Government official statement issued last night.

Restrictions will demand effective screening or extinction of all lights—in houses and other buildings, vehicles and streets.

Air raid precaution plans are being speedily completed down to the last detail. All telephones in the air raid warning system are being manned night and day.

✦ ✦ ✦

All householders are warned to complete the building of their air raid shelters now and to study Public Information Leaflet No. 2, relating to the masking of windows, and to have ready now the necessary curtains or other material for screening windows, skylights, glazed doors, etc. Shopkeepers are asked to make similar preparations.

Owners of illuminated signs and advertisements should ensure that the signs can be extinguished rapidly at short notice.

The statement concludes with a warning that should an emergency arise a complete black-out will be immediately enforced, and that all necessary preparations must therefore be made at once.

✦ ✦ ✦

Owners of vehicles are advised to obtain details of road lighting restrictions, obtainable from any police station.

A police notice states that side and rear lamps must be retained, but electric bulbs must not exceed seven watts, acetylene lamps must not consume more than half-cubic foot an hour, and in oil lamps only one burner, not exceeding three-quarters of an inch in width, will be allowed.

Glasses on all lamps must be masked with at least two thicknesses of white tissue paper.

Traffic-direction indicators, stop lights, reversing lights and head lamps may be used if properly masked.

WEST END DIMS—SEE BACK PAGE.

DAILY MIRROR, Friday, August 25, 1939.

Daily Mirror

No. 11,144   ONE PENNY
Registered at the G.P.O. as a Newspaper.
Geraldine House, Fetter-lane, E.C.4.
HOLBORN 4321.

BRITAIN READY —CRISIS BILL IS LAW

The Emergency Powers (Defence) Bill became law at 10.15 last night, only seven-and-a-half hours after Parliament had assembled.

The British Government is thus armed to-day with the power to take any step the crisis demands.

IN BERLIN, FROM 7 O'CLOCK LAST NIGHT UNTIL 12.40 THIS MORNING, HITLER WAS IN CONFERENCE WITH HIS NAVY, ARMY AND AIR CHIEFS.

He had flown back from Berchtesgaden and he called the meeting in the German Chancellery.

Himmler, the police chief, who played one of the principal parts in the occupation of Austria and Czechoslovakia, left the conference at 10 o'clock.

As he left, General Von Brauchitsch, Chief of the German General Staff, arrived.

Others present at the conference were Marshal Goering, Von Ribbentrop (back from Moscow), General Von Keitel, Chief of Staff of the High Command, and Admiral Raeder, Chief of Staff of the Navy.

No Going Back

EARLIER LAST NIGHT LORD HALIFAX, THE FOREIGN SECRETARY, TOLD THE WORLD IN A BROADCAST : "IT IS NOT THE BRITISH WAY TO GO BACK ON OBLIGATIONS."

In giving this affirmation of Britain's pledges to aid Poland, he declared it had been often said that there would have been no Great War had the British Government made clear where it stood in 1914.

In 1939, faced with the possibility of conflict, the Government had stated its attitude to the world—and in special messages to Hitler himself.

In a grave statement which opened the Commons debate, Mr. Chamberlain declared, "We shall fight as a united nation." He said Britain was confronted with imminent peril of war. Germany was in complete readiness.

Vital Speed

And during the debate he intervened with a dramatic appeal for speed in giving the Government emergency powers.

"Let us get on to the action which we are going to take, and which will give to the world notice of our unity," he said.

The House responded. By the huge majority of 457 votes to four, it agreed that the Emergency Powers (Defence) Bill should be rushed through all its stages that night.

The four members who voted against the motion were Mr. Edmund Harvey (Ind., Com-

Continued on Back Page

RAIL STRIKE DEFINITELY OFF—LEADER

"THE strike is definitely off."

This statement was made by Mr. W. J. R. Squance, general secretary of the Associated Society of Locomotive Engineers and Firemen, last night, after a three-hour conference between Mr. Ernest Brown, Minister of Labour, and the Executive Committee of the society.

The conference discussed the strike of "loco" men called for Saturday midnight.

The union leaders are to meet the general managers of the railways to-day.

In Face of Danger

An official statement issued after the conference, said:

"The Minister of Labour referred to the grave international situation and to the statements testifying to national unity and determination in the face of danger which had just been made in Parliament.

"He stressed that all that might be made on the railways, in particular those for the evacuation of women, children and aged persons from London and other large towns.

"The executive committee informed the Minister that the decision to call for the withdrawal of the labour of their members would be suspended contingent upon a meeting being arranged between this executive and the general managers during to-morrow for the purpose of renewed examination of the issues between the parties.

OTHER CRISIS NEWS

School Teachers Told to Report

Teachers from schools in the evacuating areas must report at their schools to-morrow morning.

The announcement by the Ministry of Health, issued last night, adds : " The Government wish to emphasise that this is not a notification that evacuation is to take place. If evacuation should become necessary full notice will be given and everyone concerned will be told what to do.

The announcement applies to teachers serving in schools in the following areas :—

London, Acton, Edmonton, Hornsey, Tottenham, Willesden, East Ham, West Ham, Barking, Ilford, Leyton, Walthamstow, Rochester, Chatham, Gillingham, Southampton, Portsmouth, Gosport, Liverpool, Bootle, Crosby, Birkenhead, Wallasey, Manchester, Salford, Stretford, Newcastle-on-Tyne, Gateshead, Birmingham, Smethwick, Hull, Bradford, Leeds, Sheffield, and in Scotland : Edinburgh, Glasgow, Dundee, Clydebank, Rosyth.

" The possibility of putting an evacuation scheme for children into operation depends on organisation by school units under the charge of the teachers" it is added.

Allied Mission Still in Moscow

WITHOUT EXPLANATION, THE BRITISH AND FRENCH MILITARY MISSIONS, WHO WERE TO HAVE LEFT MOSCOW AT 12.30 THIS MORNING, DECIDED NOT TO GO.

Places had been reserved for them on the crack Soviet train the Red Arrow for Leningrad, en route for Finland.

All that officials would say, says Reuter, was : "The Missions may or may not leave to-morrow."

Members of the Missions refused to comment on unofficial reports that military staff talks between Britain, France and Russia might be resumed.

Diplomatic circles doubted these reports.

Colonel F. H. N. Davidson, second military officer of the British Mission, and Group Captain A. C. Collier, second air officer, arrived by 'plane at Croydon at 11.10 p.m. last night "to report."

FRANCE TAKES OVER INDUSTRY

THE French Government last night took over all factories working for national defence.

Premier Daladier issued an order to these industries cancelling all holidays and "inviting" these industries to recall their workers who are now on holiday.

General mobilisation is not expected to be long delayed in France if the crisis continues. Frontier reservists have been called up.

Daladier, who is to address the nation by radio to-night, is planning a National Government.

His Cabinet met for two and a half hours yesterday and will sit every day from now on. President Lebrun, presiding, said France would not flinch from her duty.

Lines to Poland Cut

About 700 buses have been requisitioned in Paris alone. They are being held in readiness to rush troops from the capital to important points.

Six hundred thousand more Polish reservists have manned their stations in the last twenty-four hours.

Diplomatic circles in Paris reported last night that all communication between France and Poland—all telegraph and telephone lines pass through Germany—had been disrupted since 5 p.m.

Reuter, Exchange, British United Press and Associated Press.

DAILY MIRROR, Monday, August 28, 1939.

Daily Mirror

No. 11,146   ONE PENNY

Registered at the G.P.O. as a Newspaper.

.... there is our sure faith that, through endurance and courage, we can save the world from one of the most ruthless and desperate tyrannies that have ever threatened mankind.—See W.M. on page 11.

HITLER REFUSES TALK: DEMANDS DANZIG

WHILE THE BRITISH REPLY TO HITLER WAS BEING DRAFTED YESTERDAY THE GERMAN CHANCELLOR WAS FLATLY REFUSING TO ENTER NEGOTIATIONS WITH POLAND FOR A PEACEFUL SOLUTION TO THE CRISIS.

HITLER'S REFUSAL WAS CONTAINED IN A MESSAGE FLOWN TO M. DALADIER IN PARIS LAST NIGHT. IT WAS HANDED TO HIM BY A GERMAN ENVOY. THE INTERVIEW LASTED TWO MINUTES.

THEN AN OFFICIAL STATEMENT WAS ISSUED. IT ANNOUNCED THAT DALADIER HAD IMMEDIATELY ANSWERED HITLER'S STATEMENT TO THE AMBASSADORS LAST FRIDAY WITH A PROPOSAL THAT GERMANY AND POLAND SHOULD NEGOTIATE.

HITLER REFUSED. AND THE REFUSAL WAS CONFIRMED IN LAST NIGHT'S MESSAGE.

At 12.15 this morning a Press conference was hurriedly called in Berlin. The German journalists were handed copies of a long letter which Hitler has sent to Daladier.

Hitler declared that he has frequently shown his sympathy towards France.

But, the Fuehrer wrote, Danzig and the Corridor must return to the Reich.

"Corridor Must Return"

"I make a clear demand. Danzig and the Corridor must be returned.

"If fate should force us to fight again, I should be fighting to right a wrong.

"I am aware of the consequences, the heaviest of which would fall on Poland, because, however, the fight ended, Poland would not exist as the same State."

France has been answered. The fate of Europe now rests on the German reply to the British message approved by the Cabinet yesterday.

That note will be flown back to Berlin to-day by Sir Nevile Henderson.

Hitler's answer is expected in London to-morrow, and Parliament will probably meet on Wednesday to consider the situation.

The British Note was drafted at a lengthy conference of Ministers, and the Cabinet meeting, which had been planned for 10.30 a.m., did not take place until 3 o'clock.

It lasted for an hour and three-quarters. When it ended an official statement was issued announcing to-day's meeting of the Cabinet and Sir Nevile Henderson's journey to Berlin. The statement added:

"The reports which have appeared as to the contents of Herr Hitler's communication to the British Government are entirely unauthorised and quite inaccurate."

Premier Sees the King

The British Note, writes the Daily Mirror Diplomatic Correspondent, will be a firm refusal to withdraw from her obligations to Poland. It will answer every point raised by Hitler.

Whitehall continues to admire Poland's calm handling of the situation. The Poles are confident they can match and their 'planes are in readiness to bomb Berlin.

When the Cabinet had dispersed amid the cheers of the waiting crowd, the Prime

Continued on Back Page

Continued on Back Page

MYSTERY MAN AT EMBASSY

A MYSTERY man who arrived in England by air yesterday spent three hours at the German Embassy in Carlton House-terrace, London.— and is thought to have flown to Germany last night.

He arrived at the Embassy in a Diplomatic Corps car. All he would say when he left after three hours was: "I don't know who I am."

He said it rather sadly and shook his head. He spoke in good English, with the trace of a foreign accent. Then he was driven away.

An hour later three men arrived in a car at Heston Airport. One was seen off in a German 'plane understood to be bound for Amsterdam and Berlin. The airport officials would not say who he was.

The visitor to the Embassy was a tall, sunburned man, in a grey striped suit and black Homburg hat, carrying gloves and an umbrella.

He jumped out of the Diplomatic Corps car shortly before 3 p.m.

He did not appear to know by which door to enter the Embassy.

After his three hours' visit, he left by the car in which he had arrived.

Having refused to tell his name, he was pressed to say if he had arrived by air from Croydon or elsewhere. He waved his hand in a gesture that might have meant agreement or denial, and the car sped away.

He Watched Crowds

The car was driven into Belgravia by a roundabout route which included Pall Mall, The Mall, Horse Guards-parade (where there were crowds of sightseers), Birdcage-walk, and past Buckingham Palace, where there were also a number of spectators.

The car slowed down near the Horse Guards-parade, as if the passengers wished to look at the crowds by the Foreign Office and in Downing-street, but did not stop.

Information about the identity of the caller was not available at the Embassy.

Heston Airport officials received the three men who arrived at the port.

One man, who had a small travelling case, was taken to a German three-engine air liner, the Gustav Boelcke.

Five minutes later the 'plane set off.

Airport officials refused to answer any questions about the traveller.

The two men who had arrived with him were driven away immediately.

Duchess of Kent Flies Home

The Duchess of Kent returned to London yesterday by air from France. She flew in the King's private 'plane, piloted by Wing-Commander E. H. Fielden, Captain of the King's Flight.

The Duchess, who has been on holiday with the Duke of Kent, remained behind in Yugoslavia when the Duke returned to London earlier in the week.

Her sister is the wife of Prince Regent Paul of Yugoslavia.

Navy Controls All Ships

All British merchant ships are now under Admiralty control.

From midnight on Saturday every British ship afloat came under Admiralty direction.

Merchant ships must now obey any instructions given them, including any change of course found necessary by the Navy authorities.

DAILY MIRROR, Tuesday, August 29, 1939.

Daily Mirror

No. 11,147   ONE PENNY
Registered at the G.P.O. as a Newspaper.

We have survived the war of nerves. We mean to survive any greater test of our endurance. For we know what the alternative is.

It is submission to the gangster's commands. It is the loss of all that we value in life.

We have made every conceivable effort to save peace. If war comes we shall be ready to face it bravely. See W.M. on page 11.

BRITISH ENVOY HANDS NOTE TO HITLER

BRITAIN'S REPLY TO GERMANY WAS HANDED TO HITLER BY SIR NEVILE HENDERSON IN THE CHANCELLERY IN BERLIN AT 10.25 LAST NIGHT.

SIR NEVILE HAD ARRIVED AT THE TEMPLEHOF AERODROME AT HALF-PAST EIGHT. HE WENT AT ONCE TO THE BRITISH EMBASSY.

THEN, AT 10.15, HIS SHINING BLACK LIMOUSINE, FLYING A UNION JACK, LEFT FOR THE CHANCELLERY.

At 10.23 the great bronze doors opened and the Ambassador's car passed into the Courtyard of Honour.

Sir Nevile stepped out. A roll of drums sounded, a guard of honour presented arms.

Hitler's chief adjutant, Herr Brueckner and Dr. Meissner, Secretary of State in the Foreign Office, met Sir Nevile and conducted him at once to Hitler's private study.

Von Ribbentrop, the German Foreign Secretary, was with Hitler and the whole Nazi Cabinet, including Goering and Hess had assembled in the Chancellery.

Sir Nevile remained at the Chancellery for an hour and twenty minutes. At 11.44 the great gates opened, the drums sounded again and the black car moved out.

In the street a crowd of a few hundred people, tense and silent, had watched Sir Nevile's car arrive and depart.

Sir Nevile drove back to the Embassy. At one o'clock this morning he had a long telephone talk to London.

The contents of the British Note and the original message from Hitler will be announced by the Premier to-day when Parliament, specially recalled, meets at 2.45 p.m.

'Plane Kept Ready

It is possible, too, that Hitler's answer may by that time be in the Premier's hands.

When Sir Nevile's 'plane reached Berlin last night he said he might be flying back to-day. He asked attendants to keep his 'plane ready for an instant-take-off.

Meanwhile, the Admiralty has closed the Mediterranean to British ships. In addition, all British ships in Baltic ports have been ordered to leave as soon as possible.

The Queen left Balmoral yesterday to join the King. She drove to Perth, where she boarded the night train to London. She arrives at Euston at eight o'clock this morning. The Princesses are remaining at Balmoral.

Trains Stopped

All direct train communication between Germany and France is now at an end. French and Belgian trains for Germany and German trains for France were stopped yesterday on the German-Belgian frontier.

Queen Wilhelmina broadcast to the people of Holland last night after proclaiming a general mobilisation of the Army and the Navy.

Mechanised divisions of the German Army occupied every strategic point along the 250-mile Slovak-Polish frontier last night.

In Moscow the discussion of the Soviet-German pact in the Soviet parliament has been adjourned.

POWERS for the defence of the nation are given in the first list of regulations under the Emergency Powers (Defence) Act, issued yesterday.

BILLETING BY ORDER

Evacuation and the provision of billets can be made compulsory.

The occupier of a house can be ordered to provide food or lodgings, or both, to a specified number of persons.

Any suitable property can be earmarked as a temporary refuge for people caught in the streets during a raid.

The Government can take over the railways, take possession of land, preserve agricultural acres for the growth of food, control all merchant shipping.—Full regulations: Page 4

U.S. TO SEND US HER 'PLANES

FROM OUR OWN CORRESPONDENT
NEW YORK, Monday.

INFLUENTIAL Congressmen who in the past have bitterly opposed the Roosevelt foreign policy, to-day assured the President that they would not oppose his plan to revoke the Neutrality Act.

This means that Britain and France will be assured of huge supplies of arms and aeroplanes from America should war break out.

President Roosevelt will call Congress immediately a war begins, and his first step will be to end the Neutrality Act which forbids the sending of supplies to nations at war.

300 a Month—Now

In Washington to-night it was stated that American manufacturers estimate they can at once ship abroad 300 aeroplanes a month.

By next spring they will be able to export 1,000 'planes a month.

Mr. Louis Johnson, U.S. Assistant Secretary for War, addressing veterans of foreign wars at Boston, Massachusetts, yesterday, said:—
"U.S.A. is approaching an international peril in which appeals to remain neutral will be meaningless and absurd."

Inside News

What you can draw from the bank; Britain lays in meat store; liner Bremen ordered home; Holland mobilises: Page 2.

Home front, Gas masks for all: Page 4.

SCHOOLS URGED TO STAY OPEN

ALL schools in evacuation areas should continue in session for the present, even if their scheduled holidays are not over, said the Board of Education last night.

Children still away from home on holiday need not be brought back.

The Ministry of Health is pleased with the results of yesterday's evacuation rehearsal in an area containing eleven million people, with a school population of more than a million.

In London the Under-Secretaries for Health, Education and Transport—Miss Florence Horsbrugh, Mr. Kenneth Lindsay and Mr. Robert Bernays—visited schools to report to the Government.

They said that they had been greatly impressed

Continued on Back Page

Daily Mirror

No. 11,148.　　ONE PENNY
Registered at the G.P.O. as a Newspaper.

★ READY

We have said our last word. We are ready. There is nothing more to be done for the salvation of peace. War, if it has to come, will not be our responsibility. We wait for the decision: It is with Hitler.—See W.M. on page 11.

MIDNIGHT TALKS ON HITLER'S ANSWER

NAZI ARMY IS WARNED

DETAINED IN NEW YORK

German's giant liner Bremen, held at New York yesterday while U.S. officials searched her. Then authorities declared she must undergo safety tests. See story on back page.

MR. CHAMBERLAIN AND LORD HALIFAX SAT TOGETHER UNTIL AFTER MIDNIGHT STUDYING HITLER'S REPLY TO THE BRITISH NOTE.

At 12.45 this morning Lord Halifax, accompanied by Mr. R. A. Butler, the Under-Secretary for Foreign Affairs, left 10, Downing-street, for the Foreign Office. They had been with the Premier for almost two hours.

Hitler had handed his reply to Sir Nevile Henderson in the Berlin Chancellery at 7.15 last night.

Sir Nevile remained in Hitler's private study for twenty-five minutes. Hitler and von Ribbentrop gave him verbal explanations of the German point of view.

It had been thought that the reply would be flown at once to London, but when no aeroplane left the Templehof Aerodrome, it was realised that the message was being sent in cipher.

Text of the note remains a close secret, but in Berlin it is believed, says British United Press, that the Nazis are showing more inclination to negotiate.

Immediately Sir Nevile left, Hitler received Baron Attolico, the Italian Ambassador. The interview lasted fifteen minutes. At 10.30 the Baron called at the Chancellery again.

King Leopold of the Belgians and Queen Wilhelmina of Holland made a joint offer of their services to solve the crisis yesterday.

When the House of Commons met yesterday for only fifty-five minutes Mr. Chamberlain declared: "I cannot say that the danger of war has in any way receded . . . our obligations to Poland will be carried out."

He announced that all Britain's defences are ready to resist attack. The Fleet is prepared, anti-aircraft defences have been deployed, the R.A.F. is at war strength.

"We Shall Hold Fast"

"We will not abate any jot of our resolution," the Premier added, "to hold fast to the lines which we have laid down for ourselves." His speech begins on page 4.

The House adjourned until next Tuesday. It will almost certainly be recalled before that day; probably to-morrow.

The aeroplane in which Sir Nevile Henderson flew to Berlin returned to Heston yesterday. It carried three passengers.

Luggage unloaded bore the name of Sir George Ogilvie-Forbes, Counsellor at the British Embassy in Berlin. But Sir George was still in Berlin.

One of the passengers was Sir Paul Dukes, famous figure in the British Intelligence Service. The others were a tall, fair-haired man who drove away with Sir Paul and a military-looking man who refused to let his luggage out of his sight.

AN official statement issued in Warsaw last night declares that the occupation of Slovakia by German troops is a German act of aggression.

The occupation, the statement adds, is a threat to Polish security.

A spokesman of the Polish Foreign Office declared that Poland has been informed that German mobilisation is complete and that the German troops in Slovakia are now ready to march into Poland.

He added that in the face of the threatened situation the Polish Government saw itself compelled to take important military measures.

As a result of the occupation additional classes of Polish reserves have been mobilised.

Guard for Consuls

Colonel Beck, the Polish Foreign Minister, summoned Dr. Schatmany, the Slovak Minister to Poland, and protested against Slovakia's admission of German troops, says British United Press.

And Poland has replied, too, to the arrest of their Consul at Marienweider, in East Prussia.

The Polish Government has now isolated the German Consulates at Lvov and Teschen.

Police guards have been placed round the German Consulates and the Consuls are not allowed to leave.

"Must Supply Food"

German martial law was proclaimed in "independent" Slovakia yesterday by Premier Josef Tiso, says Associated Press.

Notices signed by him appeared in the streets, declaring—

"All difficulties between Slovak citizens and German troops are to be tried in German military courts.

"Slovaks must furnish the food supply of the German Army, here to protect our young State against the threatening Polish danger."

A Moscow broadcast last night revealed that Soviet troops are being moved to the western frontier "in view of the serious international situation."

RUSSIA HOLDS UP PACT

The Soviet Parliament will not ratify the pact with Germany this month, it was announced in Moscow last night, says Reuter.

This delay is believed to be a deliberate attempt to restrain Hitler until a Danzig settlement has been worked out.

OUR MIND IS MADE UP: EDEN

MR. ANTHONY EDEN, broadcasting to the U.S.A. this morning, said if any of his listeners were to visit Britain now, the impression would be one of surprise at Britain's normality and calm.

"There is no excitement, no hysteria, no demonstration; the national spirit is essentially one of sober resolution," said Mr. Eden.

"This even temper is due neither to fatalism nor to any lack of imagination, but to a much simpler reason: the British people has made up its mind.

"The days of false optimism or of wishful thinking are gone.

"Whatever the differences in the past," Mr. Eden added, "the Prime Minister and the Foreign Secretary have the support of the whole country in their determination to fulfil our engagements and in their desire to build a constructive peace, if once the method and menace of force is removed.

"We are all of us convinced that the issues by which we are confronted can admit of no patch-work compromise. We pray that the victory will be peaceful, but whether peaceful or not, the challenge will be met.

"The British people could not accept a compromise solution which merely postponed until six months hence another world crisis.

"In the meanwhile, it becomes daily more evident that in his negotiation of the German-Soviet pact the German Government has been guilty of an extraordinary psychological error.

"Those who have been thunderstruck have not been the Powers of the Peace Front, but the friends and political allies of the Nazi Government, whose whole political philosophy has thus been thrown into confusion."

Mr. Eden concluded: "We cannot live for ever at the pistol point."

DAILY MIRROR, Monday, September 4, 1939

Daily Mirror

No. 11,152   ♦   ONE PENNY
Registered at the G.P.O. as a Newspaper.

POLES ATTACK

POLISH troops are fighting on German territory, according to a Warsaw message.

A Polish counter-attack pushed back the Germans and penetrated East Prussia near Deutsch Eylau, it was claimed.

The Polish Embassy in London described a Nazi report that troops had cut the Corridor as "entirely false."

Later (according to the Havas Agency) the Polish Radio announced that Poland had retaken the frontier station of Zbaszyn.

The German News Agency claimed that Nazi troops operating on the Southern front had taken the town of Radomsko.

Radomsko, north of the industrial region round Kattowitz, is about forty miles from the Polish frontier.

1,500 Raid Casualties

The Poles' latest estimate of casualties in German air raids was issued last night in Warsaw

It is alleged that 1,500 people were killed or injured in German air bombardment of open towns and villages during Friday and Saturday. A considerable proportion of the victims were women and children.

[The German Government had secured from

Contd. on Bk. Page, Col. 1

BRITAIN'S FIRST DAY OF WAR: CHURCHILL IS NEW NAVY CHIEF

BRITAIN AND GERMANY HAVE BEEN AT WAR SINCE ELEVEN O'CLOCK YESTERDAY MORNING.   FRANCE AND GERMANY HAVE BEEN AT WAR SINCE YESTERDAY AT 5 P.M.

A British War Cabinet of nine members was set up last night. Mr. Winston Churchill, who was First Lord of the Admiralty when Britain last went to war, returns to that post.

Full list of the War Cabinet is:—

PRIME MINISTER: Mr. Neville Chamberlain.
CHANCELLOR OF THE EXCHEQUER:
  Sir John Simon.
FOREIGN SECRETARY: Viscount Halifax.
DEFENCE MINISTER: Lord Chatfield.
FIRST LORD: Mr. Winston Churchill.

SECRETARY FOR WAR:
  Mr. Leslie Hore-Belisha.
SECRETARY FOR AIR: Sir Kingsley Wood.
LORD PRIVY SEAL: Sir Samuel Hoare.
MINISTER WITHOUT PORTFOLIO:
  Lord Hankey.

There are other Ministerial changes. Mr. Eden becomes Dominions Secretary, Sir Thomas Inskip goes to the House of Lords as Lord Chancellor, Lord Stanhope, ex-First Lord, becomes Lord President of the Council, Sir John Anderson is the Home Secretary and Minister of Home Security—a new title.

None of these is in the Cabinet, which is restricted to the Big Nine. These are the men who will be responsible for carrying on the war.

But Mr. Eden is to have special access to the Cabinet.

The Liberal Party explained last night that although Sir Archibald Sinclair had been offered a ministerial post, the Party had decided at this moment not to enter the Government.

Petrol Will Be Rationed

The first meeting of the new war Cabinet took place last night. Mr. Churchill was the first to leave and the crowd broke into a cheer as he walked out. Mr. Hore-Belisha was driven away by a woman chauffeur in uniform.

The Premier went from Downing-street to Buckingham Palace where he stayed with the King for three-quarters of an hour.

It was announced last night that as from September 16 all petrol will be rationed. In the meantime all car owners are asked not to use their cars more than is vitally necessary.

To-day all banks throughout Britain will be closed.

Australia yesterday declared war on Germany. "Where Britain stands, stand the people of the Empire and the British world," said Prime Minister Menzies in a broadcast message last night.

New Zealand has cabled her full support to Britain. There is a rush of recruits in Canada. At Toronto a queue of 2,000 men lined outside the Recruiting Office.

Japan has assured Britain of her neutrality in the present war.

Britain's last two-hour ultimatum to Germany was revealed to the people of Britain in a memorable broadcast from Downing-street by Mr. Chamberlain at 11.15 yesterday morning. By that time

cont'd in Col. 4, Back Page

"BREMEN IS CAPTURED"

—French Report

The £4,000,000 German liner Bremen was reported to have been captured yesterday and taken to a British port.

A report from a high French source stated that the Bremen was captured at 4 p.m., but the area in which the liner was captured was not mentioned.

A French Government radio station broadcast the report which was picked up by the Mutual Broadcasting System of America.—Associated Press and British United Press.

The King to His People

"The task will be hard. There may be dark days ahead. . . . But we can only do the right as we see the right, and reverently commit our cause to God. If one and all we keep resolutely faithful to it, ready for whatever service or sacrifice it may demand, then, with God's help, we shall prevail."

These words were broadcast by the King last night. And to every household in the country a copy of his message, bearing his own signature facsimile, will be sent as a permanent record. The full speech is on page 3.

DAILY MIRROR, Thursday, September 7, 1939

Daily Mirror

No. 11,155 ♦ ONE PENNY
Registered at the G.P.O. as a Newspaper.

FRENCH BREAK THROUGH—CROSS NAZI FRONTIER

FRENCH TROOPS, SUPPORTED BY TANKS, HAVE BROKEN THROUGH THE GERMAN LINES IN THE DIRECTION OF SAARBRUECKEN, AND ARE THREATENING INVASION OF THE SAAR BASIN, A RICH INDUSTRIAL AREA WHICH SUPPORTS NEARLY A MILLION PEOPLE.

An official communique issued in Paris last night said:—

"Our first-line troops progressed beyond the German frontier, with an advance varying according to the different parts of the front."

The French met and pushed back fully mechanised Nazi troops.

Aircraft were active in co-operation with the land forces, and the supply services were in excellent working order.

"Our troops' morale is excellent," adds the communique.

100 Miles Front

The communique stated that French troops on the northern flank had made "local advances," adding that they were in contact with the enemy all the way from the beginning of the Franco-German frontier where the Moselle river flows, to the Rhine, 100 miles to the south-east.

Advance units thrust at strongly emplaced German machine-gun nests among the hills between Moselle and the Rhine, supported by the strongly growing momentum of the main line of troops from the Maginot fortifications.

A heavy artillery bombardment, meanwhile, had weakened Germany's line along the Rhine frontier to the Swiss frontier, the communique continued.

The German area which has borne the brunt of Anglo-French aerial attacks lies opposite Belgium. The raids most successful were in the triangle formed by Aachen (Aix-la-Chapelle), Eschweller and Stolberg.

To the north-west of the Saar area lies the independent Duchy of Luxemburg.

Town Evacuated

The French have behind them the impregnable Maginot Line. The Nazi's western wall, the Siegfried Line, runs behind the Saar territory, so that the break-through is not a penetration of the Siegfried Line.

The Germans had already evacuated women and children from Saarbruecken. A correspondent of the Danish newspaper, "Berlingske Tidende," who is in the town, describes it as "completely lifeless."

All trains in the Saar area, adds the correspondent, are crammed with as many as thirty people to each compartment. Journeys that usually take one hour now take seven or eight.

On the French right hand is a wooded, wild and deserted region ranging in height from 400ft. to 1,500ft. above sea level.

In the centre is the Saar area, on the left Luxembourg—and at their backs the French have their own plains of Lorraine.

Advance Posts Crushed

It is towards the north, in the pocket between Haguenau and Luxembourg that the French are attacking.

Local gains have been achieved, positions straightened and German advance posts crushed.

On the Eastern Front, the Poles were fighting desperately last night to stem the Nazi advance.

According to a Swedish Foreign Office source in Copenhagen, the Swedish Minister in Warsaw has reported that the Polish Government moved from Warsaw to Lublin, thirty miles south-east of the capital.

The Germans claimed that they had occu—

Cont. on Back Page, Col. 1

First Air Raid Facts

FIFTEEN HOURS LATE

HERE is the truth about the great "air raid" on England —the first of the war—which yesterday caused rumours of the most fantastic nature to shoot all through the Home Counties.

Not until some fifteen hours afterwards did officialdom allow the country to know the truth.

In the meantime, stories of a wildly exaggerated kind had been allowed to circulate, and no effort made to check them.

It was not until 10.18 last night that those in authority decided that, at last, the public might know the truth. This is it, issued from the Ministry of Information:—

The enemy air reconnaissance off the East Coast, referred to in this morning's bulletin issued by the Ministry of Information led to the dispatch of fighter aircraft.

Contact was not made with the enemy, who turned back before reaching the coast.

On returning, some of our aircraft were mistaken for enemy aircraft, which caused certain coastal batteries to open fire. This accounts for the rumours of a heavy aerial engagement.

This, then, was the climax to an extraordinary day of which the following is the diary:—

EARLY MORNING. — Air-raid warning sounded. Workers on way to office take shelter.

TWO HOURS LATER.—All clear sounded. London goes to work unperturbed. In the City and West End not even the sound of a shot had been heard.

NOON.—Still no official announcement. Wild and fantastic rumours begin to circulate. Staries of great damage outside London spread with amazing rapidity. Press appeal in vain for news.

SEVEN HOURS AFTER FIRST WARNING.—The following statement is issued:

"We are officially informed that enemy aircraft were reported near East Coast of England early this morning. So far as is known they did not penetrate our defences at any point, and no damage has been reported."

This stilled the rumours. Nothing, it ap—

Cont. on Back Page, Col. 4

Larder Is Well Filled

BRITAIN'S huge purchases of food and raw materials in preparation for war smashed all imports records during July.

During the month, according to figures issued last night, Britain's imports totalled 8,253,000 tons.

This was an increase of 617,000 tons, or 8 per cent., on the previous July.

Continued increase in grain imports from the Argentine was shown by an 80 per cent. rise in tonnage from the Atlantic coast.

Two-thirds of the total increase in imports was from countries in northern and western Europe.

Three-quarters of the increase was in British tonnage, which rose by 446,000 tons or 10 per cent.

Norwegian was higher by 96,000 tons; Dutch by 54,000 tons; and Danish showed a big increase.

There was a drop of 102,000 tons (26 per cent.) in German tonnage. The British shipping represented 61 per cent. of the total tonnage that arrived with cargo.

Increased coal exports to Italy contributed to an increase in tonnage sailing to central and eastern Mediterranean.

S. AFRICA "AT WAR"

SOUTH Africa is at war with Germany.

This information was given by Mr. R. W. Close, South African Minister in Washington, to Mr. Cordell Hull, U.S. Secretary of State (Foreign Minister) yesterday, according to a Reuter message.

A new government under General Smuts was formed in South Africa yesterday, after the Union of South Africa House of Assembly had rejected a motion by General Hertzog, the former Prime Minister, that relations with the belligerent countries should "continue as if no war was being waged."

The House passed a motion submitted by General Smuts, calling for severance of relations with Germany and continued co-operation with the British Commonwealth.

U.S. SPEEDS 'PLANE ORDER

U.S. AIRCRAFT factories yesterday continued to speed up work on 600 'planes ordered by Britain, France and Australia, despite the fact that the Neutrality Act, invoked by President Roosevelt on Tuesday night, forbids delivery of them.

It was understood, says a Washington message, that the factories were working on the assumption that an amendment of the Neutrality Act might be passed to permit the shipment.

Washington political experts yesterday forecast the repeal of the Act.

It was suggested that, despite the Act, the 'planes could be sent via Canada, which is technically neutral because she has not yet declared war. But Mr. Cordell Hull, the Secretary of State, declared last night that transhipment was specifically forbidden by Statute.

President Roosevelt yesterday ordered a patrol by destroyers, coastguard cutters and 'planes for several hundred miles off the American coast to gather information about the activities of ships belonging to the nations at war.

This is to protect the neutrality of the United States.

Messages from Daily Mirror correspondents, Associated Press, British United Press and Reuter.

DAILY MIRROR, Tuesday, September 12, 1939.

Daily Mirror

No. 11,159   ONE PENNY
Registered at the G.P.O. as a Newspaper.

OUR ARMY IN FRANCE FOR BIG BATTLE

BRITAIN'S EXPEDITIONARY FORCE HAS LANDED IN FRANCE. SOON AFTER BRITAIN DECLARED WAR TRANSPORTS LEFT ENGLAND CARRYING THE FINEST MECHANISED ARMY IN EUROPE—THE FIRST TROOPS OF THE BRITISH ARMY.

This force, comprising thousands of tanks and motorised units, is now in position in France. It will support the great drive against the Siegfried Line.

The departure of the British Expeditionary Force was veiled in secrecy. All that some members of the public knew was that endless columns of motorised units passed through certain towns and villages in southern England at night.

BROADCASTING LAST NIGHT ROLAND DORGELES, FRENCH WAR AUTHOR, SAID : " BRITISH TROOPS, THIS TIME WONDERFULLY PREPARED, ARE ALREADY FIGHTING IN LARGE NUMBERS BY OUR SIDE, AND THEIR NUMBERS WILL INCREASE CONTINUALLY."

But already two great armies—the German and the French—face each other for the first great battle of the war, the Battle of the Saar. French and Germans attacked yesterday along a 100-mile front. Both sides were throwing heavier reinforcements into the fighting. The preliminary phase of the operations with which France opened the campaign to relieve the pressure on her Polish ally has already ended, and Army headquarters on the northern flank yesterday sent units as large as a division into the fight.

The French war communique issued last night, states:

"Despite the resistance of the enemy, our attacks have continued to make substantial progress on a front of about twenty kilometres east of the Saar."

The troops yesterday were moving up to the front in a steady stream. French air scouts reported that roads in north-eastern Germany were congested with troops and convoys, and that the railways were almost a continuous line of troop trains.

Observers reported that their attacks against the German concentration centres and communication lines were hampering the movement of the Nazi troops.

And in the vineyards of the Moselle the first bayonet charges on the Western Front since 1918 took place yesterday.

They occurred during a second German counter-attack against the French left-wing. This attack in the Saar, stretching to the Luxembourg frontier, was entirely halted after fighting which extended along the German side of the frontier as far as Buschsdorf.

At the other end of the Saar front the French continued local operations. It is here that intense shelling by the French guns has been taking place, to cut railways, main roads and other important communications.

French bombers have also been active on this front and have carried out heavy bombing attacks on German concentration points in the Saar valley behind the Siegfried Line. These raids have hampered German action, and have contributed to the dis-organisation of the German supply system.

Monks' A.R.P. Shave

Monks at St. Bernard's Monastery, Charnwood Forest Leicestershire, were proud of their beards.

That was before the crisis. Now they are clean-shaven.

They found that beards and gas masks didn't go well together. The masks didn't fit very well.

And the whiskers tickled. So they shaved.

He May be Our First War Casualty

An airman, reported missing, may be one of the first British casualties in the war.

He is R.A.F. Sergeant Leslie Robert Ward, twenty-six. His wife, who lives in St. James-road, Emsworth (Hants), has received official notification that he is missing. She is expecting a baby.

Sergeant Ward, a good footballer and a pianist, was a very popular N.C.O.

Poles Stand Firm

The Poles fight on. For twelve days now they have resisted the might of the three German armies advancing on Warsaw from the north, the south and the east.

Official German statements last night admitted that the heroic defence of the Poles had slowed down the German offensive.

The Polish Army have now formed a new line along the banks of three rivers, the Vistula, the Bug and the San.

And there they stand and fight. "The

Continued on Back Page

The Smile

Her gracious smile has always been infectious.
Always spontaneous.
To-day it's an EXAMPLE to us all.
Now turn to pages 8 and 9.
AND SMILE WITH THEM.

Rail Jam —a Joke

PASSENGERS joked and laughed as they pushed their way into crowded carriages yesterday — first day of train rationing. Services were cut by half.

When it was a case of an hour to wait after missing a train by minutes, travellers just sat down on platform seats—if they could find room—and watched the wartime world go by.

"Go to Work Earlier"

" The public have taken it wonderfully well," a Southern Railway official told me. " We've had hardly any complaints.

" We have tried to keep as many rush-hour trains on as possible.

" It is hoped that some of the public will ' stagger ' the rush hours by going to work a little earlier."

The Two-Train Dodge

Observers were on duty at some stations to watch the effect of the new train timings. Where possible, additional trains may be run to relieve the worst congestions.

The morning rush to London was the worst period of the day. Many trains were packed long before they reached their termini. Crowds waiting at stations near London were unable to get on them.

Some people took trains going in the opposite direction and went lower down the line to be sure of a place on the next train.

Most trains were running to time, but there was a delay of forty-five minutes in the arrival of a West Country train at Waterloo in the afternoon.

£7,000 IS ROYAL GIFT

THE King has given £5,000 and the Queen £2,000 to aid war wounded.

Their donations head a Mansion House fund opened by the Lord Mayor of London in response to the Duke of Gloucester's appeal for the Red Cross and St. John Emergency Committee.

Other royal donations are:— Queen Mary, £1,800; the Duke and Duchess of Gloucester, £1,000; the Duke and Duchess of Kent, £750; the Princess Royal and the Earl of Harewood, £500; the Duke of Connaught, £500.

The King and Queen will not stay at the Palace of Holyroodhouse, Edinburgh, during October. It was announced yesterday.

SEALED ENGLISH TRAIN FOR NAZIS

BY arrangement between the British and Eire Governments fifty members of the German colony in Dublin left last night en route for Holland and Germany.

The party will be conducted through England in a train with sealed compartments and a military guard.

They will embark on a Dutch steamer for Holland. Some of the party have been called up for service in Germany.

PROFITEERS ARE WARNED

A warning to profiteers was issued last night. Sir Warren Fisher, north-western Regional Commissioner, asked the Town Clerk of Manchester (Mr. R. H. Adcock) to warn firms suspected of profiteering in the Manchester area.

Mr. Adcock stated last night that there had been cases reported of people trying to make an unreasonable profit.

" Sir Warren has asked me to warn such persons that in no circumstances will firms be allowed to act in that way," he added.

" He will take the appropriate action to prevent it where firms have not got a satisfactory explanation for the increased charges of the commodities in which they are trading."

DAILY MIRROR, Saturday, Sept. 16, 1939.

Daily Mirror

No. 11,163   ONE PENNY
Registered at the G.P.O. as a Newspaper.

THE NAVY SINKS U-BOATS, SEIZES WAR CARGOES

Duke Talks to Premier for an Hour

The Duke of Windsor visited No. 10, Downing-street yesterday afternoon and met the Prime Minister.

The Duke, who was alone, had a private talk with Mr. Chamberlain lasting just over an hour.

Hardly anyone recognised him when he arrived, but a small crowd gathered around the door of No. 10 by the time he left.

No other Cabinet Ministers were present and the visit was officially described as "a purely informal meeting between the Duke of Windsor and the Premier."

Nazis Retreat in West

HITLER'S TROOPS WERE REPORTED LAST NIGHT TO BE RETREATING FROM THEIR ADVANCE POSITIONS ALL ALONG THE NORTHERN FLANK OF THE WESTERN FRONT. THE FRENCH, DIRECTED BY GENERAL GAMELIN, BATTLED THROUGH A SHELL SCREEN LAID DOWN BY THE GERMANS OVER A FORTY-MILE SECTOR.

This extends from the Moselle River, where the front touches the Luxembourg border, south-east to a point two miles beyond Saarbruecken.

French troops are now in direct contact with the German fortification troops just in front of the Siegfried Line.

French troops attacking in the Moselle region captured the village of Perl, just inside the German frontier, and are advancing along the road to Saarburg, about nine miles to the north.

As French tanks and motorised units moved slowly forward the Germans were compelled to evacuate the railway station at Perl. They had no time to blow up the bridge over the lines.

In the face of machine-gun fire the French gained a foothold in the first houses of the village. Latest reports were that Perl had been completely occupied.

Saarbruecken itself was reported in an Associated Press message from Basle (Switzerland) to have been "reduced to ruins" by bombardment from the Maginot forts."

'Planes Dive at Lines

Earlier the capture of four German villages —two near the Moselle and two east of Saarbruecken—was reported. The French attack regained much of the ground lost when the Germans counter-attacked last Sunday and fought for a time on French soil.

German troops and civilians have been evacuated from towns in the hills east of Saarbruecken.

The Germans are reported to have lost control of some Saar mines.

Many German 'planes from the Polish front are now appearing in the West. Both the German air force and the German guns are reported to be contesting every French advance more and more hotly.

France's War Communique No. 24, issued last night, tells of the battle:

"We have strengthened the positions taken during previous days and repelled a counter-attack, inflicting losses on the enemy.

"There has been strong reaction on the enemy's aircraft and artillery on part of the front. Our pursuit 'planes have repulsed

Continued on Back Page

PENSIONS FOR RAID VICTIMS

PENSIONS similar to those for private soldiers will be paid to the dependants of civilians killed and injured in air raids or other warlike operations.

Provision for this is included in a scheme the Minister of Pensions has laid before Parliament.

Rates of pension will vary according to the degree of physical disablement, with a maximum of 32s. 6d. a week for a single man or 22s. 6d. for a single woman.

Married men will receive additional allowances for wife and children.

Pension for the widow of a man fatally injured will also be at the service rate fixed for the widow of a private soldier—15s. 6d. a week for a childless widow under forty, and 22s. 6d. a week for others, with an allowance of 5s. for each child up to the age of fifteen.

Injury allowances will be paid at a weekly rate without regard to means and needs.

They will vary only with the size of the family, and according as the injured person is treated at home or in hospital.

For example, a man with a wife and two children will receive 28s. 6d. a week if he is treated in hospital, while a single man will receive 18s. if treated at home.

Health Insurance benefit will not be claimable while these allowances are in issue.

THE BRITISH NAVY IS ALREADY DRIVING THE U-BOATS OFF THE SEAS. AN ADMIRALTY COMMUNIQUE, ISSUED LAST NIGHT, ANNOUNCED FOR THE FIRST TIME THAT GERMAN SUBMARINES HAD BEEN FOUND AND SUNK. THE MESSAGE SAYS:

"His Majesty's destroyers, patrol vessels and aircraft have been carrying out constant patrols over wide areas in search of enemy U-boats.

"Many attacks have been made and a number of U-boats have been destroyed.

"Survivors have been rescued and captured when possible."

The submarine hunt is up. Allied cruisers and destroyers are intensifying their search. Every mile of sea is patrolled.

A special watch is being kept for German ships masquerading as neutrals which are believed to be acting as mother-ships or the U-boats. They wait at secret rendezvous in the Atlantic.

A second wave of submarines is believed to have left German bases to relieve those operating on the high seas during the first fortnight of the war.

U-Boats Short of Fuel

Many U-boats now at sea have run short of fuel and have fired their last torpedo. Their radio messages have been intercepted, says a Paris report.

In the first week of war the Navy captured valuable prizes on the way to Germany. The war contraband already seized includes:—

28,500 tons of petroleum,	3,400 tons of haematite ore,
26,350 tons of iron ore,	7,300 tons of wood-pulp,
4,600 tons of manganese ore —of great value in munitions manufacture.	6,000 tons of pebble phosphate, and many mixed cargoes.

Thirty-one seamen and a canary, survivors of the British steamer Vancouver City, which was sunk by a U-boat on its way to England with a cargo of 8,500 tons of sugar, were brought into Liverpool yesterday.

Put Canary First

The second mate, George Harvey, of Dublin, risked his life to save his canary.

"We never saw the submarine," Eric Bristard, the ship's carpenter, of Newport, Mon., said to the Daily Mirror. "The torpedo hit us in number four hold, and we sank in twelve minutes. Three men were killed by the explosion and one lifeboat was damaged."

John Taylor, the deck boy, who comes from Belfast, was hurt when the other lifeboat was being lowered. After hours in the water, he said, we were picked up by a Dutch tanker.

"Everything went down with the ship except George's canary, which he went back to save.

"The canary chirped cheerfully all the time we were in the open boat."

The bos'n, Michael Conway, of Bristol, said: We had sailed round the world and we were forty-one days out at sea with a cargo of sugar. There was no warning whatever. There was a terrific explosion and the boat sank quickly, stern first."

U.S. ORDERS— QUIT RUSSIA

THE United States Embassy in Moscow has advised American citizens to leave the U.S.S.R. in accordance with usual instructions in times of threatened danger.

Soviet recruits called up yesterday under the regular draft number approximately 1,000,000, according to a Moscow estimate.

This is the first class to be called up under the recently adopted military service law.

The reason for the call up, as stressed in an editorial in the official Kremlin organ Pravda, is that "Many capitalist countries are enveloped by the flames of war, and the Soviet Union must not be caught unawares."

A Berlin report says that Germany and the Soviet Union have agreed to form a buffer Polish State between them after the Germans have crushed Polish resistance. They will not establish a common frontier.

The Poles, according to this message, may be allowed to retain from one-third to one-half their present territory, and the Southern area around Cracow is to remain Polish.

Reuter, British United Press and Exchange.

Petrol Rationing Off for a Week; No Bus Cuts: Page 3

Daily Mirror

No. 11,164   ♦   ONE PENNY
Registered at the G.P.O. as a Newspaper.

SOVIET TROOPS INVADE POLAND: GOVT. FLEES

RUSSIAN AND GERMAN TROOPS WILL MEET TO-DAY IN THE POLAND THEY HAVE BOTH INVADED. THE SOVIET STRUCK AT DAWN YESTERDAY. THEIR ARMIES MARCHED ACROSS THE WHOLE LENGTH OF THE POLISH FRONTIER.

" The Red Army was ordered this morning to cross the frontier of Poland," announced M. Molotov, the Russian Premier, " to take under its protection the lives and property of the peoples of western White Russia, and the western Ukraine."

In Warsaw it was reported that Polish frontier guards had resisted the Russian advance and that " heavy fighting " was going on in the north-east.

The Polish Embassy in Paris announced that the Russian Army invaded Poland "as far as Molodeczno, where the Polish Army is resisting the Russian aggression."

But from Riga it is reported that the Russians have advanced fifty miles into Poland. To-day they expect to meet the German troops at Brest Litovsk and at Lwow (Lemberg).

Polish Government officials and some members of the Government have left the country. Some of them drove out from Kutz, close to the Rumanian frontier, in buses, motor-cars and lorries. They had only just enough petrol to take them the few miles across the frontier.

Leaders Reach Rumania

President Moscicki and Colonel Beck, the Foreign Minister, have reached Cernauti, in Rumania. The Polish State archives have arrived in Rumania.

The Poles deny that their Government has fled the country.

Russia last night formally announced to Britain, France, Germany, Italy and Japan that her policy towards them would be that of neutrality.

The announcement followed the dramatic statement by M. Molotov that Russia had marched across the border.

"The internal bankruptcy and patent incapacity of the Polish State," he said on the radio, " has been demonstrated by the events of the past fortnight. Our duty now is to extend the fraternal hand of assistance to the Ukrainian and White Russian peoples."

The Poles learned of the invasion in dramatic fashion. At 4 o'clock yesterday morning the Polish Ambassador in Moscow was handed a note announcing that the Red Army was about to march. He declined to accept it.

Two hours later the Soviet Army marched in.

"Self-Condemned"

The Polish Embassy in London issued a statement denying that the Government was in flight.

"The Soviet Government," the statement added, " stands self-condemned as a violator of its international obligations, thus contradicting all the moral principles upon which Soviet Russia pretended to base her foreign policy since her admittance into the League of Nations."

Eye-witnesses of the Russian invasion of Poland say that monster tanks formed the spearhead of a swift Russian advance close to the Polish-Rumanian border. With the tanks came infantry forces. The Russians advanced at some points as much as thirty-seven miles into Southern Poland without resistance.

And as Poland turned to fight the invader from the East, the Germans claimed new successes.

The German High Command sent an ulti-

Continued on Back Page

What It All Means

BY OUR DIPLOMATIC CORRESPONDENT

OFFICIAL circles in London are not inclined to take a pessimistic view of the situation created by Russia's invasion of Poland.

It is pointed out that such a situation might conceivably have arisen even if Russia had been our ally.

By international law, and taking the view that Poland is in a state of disintegration, the Soviet would feel compelled to protect the White Russians in Poland.

Therefore there is so far no reason, it is held, why Britain should regard the invasion as an act leading to any breach with Russia.

No Surprise

POLAND WILL NOT, IT IS FELT, DECLARE WAR ON RUSSIA. IF SHE DID SO THE WHOLE POSITION WOULD BE CHANGED

Russia's move came as no surprise to well-informed circles in London, and there is nothing in it to suggest that it means a closer political and military understanding between Russia and Germany.

One point is clear—that the Polish Government will be unable to function from, or even remain, in Rumania.

This would mean a new powder magazine in Europe giving Germany reason to quarrel with Rumania.

NAZIS 'WARN' BRITAIN

ACCUSING Britain of waging war on women and children by blockade, Germany last night threatened to hit back with "any weapons."

Official circles in London replied that if this meant air bombing by the Nazis they must be prepared for retaliation.

The Ministry of Information says that an official statement issued in Berlin threatened that the Reich will use any means at its disposal:—

"To demonstrate realistically to enemies of Germany the horrors of the methods they themselves have chosen."

London view is that the economic pressure used by Britain, which has for its aim the early termination of hostilities with the minimum of violence, is recognised by all civilised nations as a perfectly legitimate and proper weapon to be used during hostilities.

The German Government, the Ministry statement recalls, recently gave the solemn undertaking in response to President Roosevelt's appeal with regard to aerial bombardment.

The German Government might do well to recall that the undertakings given to President Roosevelt by other Powers to whom his appeal was addressed, "can only be effective so long as they all of them keep to the word they have given."

The Ministry of Information last night described as being "devoid of all foundation" statements made in a recent German broadcast relating to Britain's war aims.

These were stated to be:—
(1) Complete restoration of Poland and annexation of Danzig by Poland.
(2) Complete restoration of Czechoslovakia, minimum area on the basis of the Munich agreement and rectification of frontiers.
(3) Restoration of Austria under the rule of the Emperor Otto of Hapsburg, to include the Catholic provinces of Germany, Bavaria, Palatinate and the Rhine Province.

RUSSIA TO RESPECT NEUTRAL STATES

M. MOLOTOV, the Soviet Prime Minister, has given assurances to the Finnish and other Scandinavian countries that Russia would respect their neutrality, says a report from Helsingfors, Finland.

The Prime Ministers and Foreign Ministers of Sweden, Norway, Denmark and Finland meet at the Danish Foreign Office at Copenhagen to-day to discuss their positions.

The position of these States, already made precarious by the British and German naval blockades, has been further complicated by Russia's invasion of Poland.—Associated Press.

Poland Fights on

The Polish Telegraph Agency, which is with the Government at Kuty on the Polish side of the Polish-Rumanian frontier last night issued the following statement:—

"The Polish Government is functioning on Polish territory at Kuty, which is its temporary headquarters. The fight of the Polish Army against the German aggressor is continuing in spite of the numerical superiority of seventy divisions, an air superiority of ten to one, and a colossal superiority in mechanised troops.

"The Polish Army resists and is fighting a battle, and will go on resisting."—Reuter.

BOMB HITS NAZI AIR H.Q.

THE entrance to the German Air Ministry, Goering's headquarters in Leipzigerstrasse, Berlin, was wrecked by a bomb placed by an anti-Nazi.

And, declared a speaker broadcasting yesterday from a secret German transmitter, " this bomb is only the signal of things which will happen shortly

" We shall use more effective bombs next time They shall not miss their mark."

An account of the wrecking of the entrance to the German Air Ministry was wired to the Copenhagen newspaper Politiken by its Berlin correspondent.

All the windows on the side of the building facing Leipzigerstrasse the correspondent says, were smashed.

The explosion also damaged the windows of Wertheim's, a big departmental store opposite the Air Ministry and other shops in the vicinity

"Hitler—Criminal Lunatic"

The secret broadcaster said he spoke from the "German Freedom Sender within the Reich," as a representative of the "Association of German Officers."

He warned Hitler that all Nazi chiefs will be regarded as outlawed.

This, the speaker added, was the first time he had broadcast from the station. In future he would speak to the German people four times a day

Already hordes of secret police are searching for the station

"Must we risk the liberty of Germany for the ambition of a madman who wants to become the Kaiser of Europe?" asked another broadcaster

"We will not be willing tools in the hands of a criminal lunatic.

"Down with the murderer of innocent women and children, down with Adolf Hitler and his helpers. Long live the honour of the German Army, long live the free Germany!"

DAILY MIRROR, Wednesday, Sept. 20, 1939.

Daily Mirror

No. 11,166 ✦ ✦ ONE PENNY
Registered at the G.P.O. as a Newspaper.

LIFT YOUR BLOCKADE OR—NAZI THREAT

HITLER, BOASTING OVER HIS TEMPORARY CONQUEST OF DANZIG, IN A SPEECH LAST NIGHT IN THE ONCE FREE CITY, TURNED THE STREAM OF HIS HATE TO THE NATION HE FEARS—ENGLAND.

In his frenzy he revealed his fear of the naval blockade, declaring almost hysterically that Britain was waging war on women and children.

"**England will know,**" he shouted, "**that we ourselves are in possession of a weapon which can't be matched by our enemies—our mighty air force.**"

Dealing with the length of the war, he said: "When England says that it will last three years, then I can only say that I am sorry for France.

"If it lasts three years the word capitulation will not arise on our side, nor in the fourth, fifth, sixth and seventh years."

Hitler began in a low, hoarse voice. He said:

"**I am treading for the first time on soil which has been settled by German people for half a millennium.**

"For half a millennium this soil has been German and has remained German; and everybody must be convinced by now that it will continue German.

"This land here was a victim of the madness of that time and the Polish State so-called was a project of this stupidity.

"What Germany had to sacrifice for this State of Poland is not known to the world. Only one thing I must say here. All this territory which was then incorporated in Poland is exclusively the product of German industry and German activity.

"Nevertheless, I have always made the attempt to find a tolerable solution which might lead to an acceptable arrangement.

"I have striven to shape definitive frontiers in the west and in the south of Germany in order to safeguard the future of peace. I made the same attempt in the east.

"Especially Intolerable"

"Especially intolerable were two circumstances.

"Here, first, a city whose German character cannot be doubted, was not only prevented from joining the German Reich, but attempts were also made through the years to colonise it for Poland.

"Secondly, a German province was cut off from the Reich and allowed only one means of communication with it in a way that permitted all kinds of trickery.

"No other country in the world would have borne this state of affairs as long as Germany has. I do not know what England would have said to such a peaceful solution at her cost, or what would have been done by France or America.

"I tried to find a solution. I submitted proposals orally to those in power in Poland at that time. They knew these proposals—they were more than moderate.

"What I did I did to save the German people and the Polish people from other sufferings.

"Wild Terror"

"I do know, however, that countless Germans gave a sigh of relief when that happened for they believed it had gone too far to meet the Poles.

"Poland's answer was first mobilisation, and then wild terror began. My request to the Polish Foreign Minister to visit me in Berlin was rejected.

"The martyrdom of our countrymen began. I have put to myself this question: Who could have blinded Poland thus?

"It is that same place in which the universal warmongers have sat and are still sitting, not only for the last ten years, but for centuries.

"It was there that the Poles were persuaded to resist Germany. There a guarantee was given to Poland. There the Poles were given the opportunity to begin war.

"For these men Poland was only a pawn in the game. To-day these men are calmly saying that it is no longer a question of Poland, but of the German Government. I have con-

Continued on Page 5

Adolf Plays the Bogy-Man

Hitler hinted at a secret weapon in the hands of the Nazis when he said:

"England has already started war on women and children.

"But the moment may come when we use a weapon which is not yet known and with which we could not ourselves be attacked.

"It is to be hoped that no one will then complain in the name of humanity."

WAR'S FIRST CASUALTY LIST

THE first R.A.F. casualties of the war were announced by the Air Ministry last night:—

Missing (believed killed):
549741, Aircraftman Second Class, K. G. Day.
Missing (believed prisoner of war):
561012, Sergeant G. F. Booth.
36187, Pilot-Officer L. H. Edwards.
548555, Aircraftman, Second Class, L. J. Slattery.
Missing:
34213, Flight-Lieutenant W. F. Barton.
546065, Aircraftman, First Class, G. T. Brocking.
531493, Leading Aircraftman H. Dore.
36138, Flying-Officer H. L. Emden.
537187, Aircraftman, First Class, R. Evans.
565602, Sergeant D. E. Jarvis.
546679, Aircraftman, First Class, E. W. Lyon.
540695, Sergeant A. S. Prince.
524808, Leading Aircraftman J. Quilter.
519859, Corporal J. L. Ricketts.
39340, Flying-Officer J. F. Ross.
552231, Aircraftman, First Class, G. Sheffield.
550292, Acting-Sergeant B. G. Walton.

KING'S SURPRISE

THE King paid a surprise visit to troops who are in training in the west of England yesterday.

Accompanied by two generals and a party of A.D.Cs. he visited in turn all the units which make up a modern infantry division.

Many of the soldiers were sleeping soundly when the King arrived.

The King ate his lunch sheltered in a corner of a field sitting on a rug behind a haystack.

681 COURAGEOUS MEN ESCAPED

KNOWN survivors of the torpedoed aircraft-carrier Courageous were officially stated yesterday to number 681.

An Admiralty statement said:

The following are approximate figures of the complement of H.M.S. Courageous, and of the survivors of the disaster, up to 1 p.m. to-day, September 19:

Complement: Officers 90; ratings 1,170; total 1,260.

Survivors: Lists already published—Officers 45; ratings 381; total 426.

Approximate number of additional survivors, lists to be published as soon as names are available: Officers 25; ratings 230; total 255.

Approximate total of known survivors: Officers 70; ratings 611; total 681.

Navy "Saw Red," Sank U-boat: pages 8 and 9.

ENGINEER BEATS U-BOAT

A BRITISH engineer has saved his ship, after it had been torpedoed and left in a sinking condition.

His ship, the City of Paris, was the leading vessel of a convoy when, in the twilight, she was struck.

The captain of the ship, in a vivid report of the sea drama, says:

"We suddenly experienced a terrific explosion which seemed to be right under the bridge on the port side.

"Sandbags arranged round the wheelhouse for protection collapsed and we shipped sea water over the bridge. It was dusk and we could see no sign of a submarine."

The explosion had a strange effect. It released the brake of the starboard windlass and the anchor chain ran out. The ship came to anchor.

The chief engineer, Mr. Edward Harrower, of Liverpool, acted at once. He stopped his engines as soon as the explosion rocked the ship. The captain's report goes on:

"The crew behaved admirably, and all boats were safely lowered—a tricky business.

"Fifteen or twenty minutes after the explosion only the chief and second officers, the chief engineer, second, fifth and sixth engineer officers, the wireless operator, purser and myself were left on board.

"We decided to leave the ship and were all picked up and taken to port by a British destroyer."

Next morning the captain and his officers decided to go back. The chief engineer at once set to work. He found that the condenser was leaking and the turbines out of action.

For two hours the engineer and his staff worked while water rose in the hold.

Then he reported to the captain. He could give him enough power to steam at six and a half knots.

The captain took the wheel himself.

"Next morning," his report adds, "with the help of tugs we safely reached dock." The City of Paris will sail again.

The 1st Bomb

HONOUR of being the first man to drop a bomb on Germany in the present war belongs to a nineteen-year-old aircraftman flying observer, John Oscar Smith.

In a letter to his parents, Mr. John Smith, once of the Durham Light Infantry, and Mrs. Smith, of The Bungalow, Furlong-walk, Lower Gornal, he describes his exploit in the Kiel Canal raid.

"I was in the leading machine of ten which flew over the Kiel Canal," he wrote. "We had a rare scrap and I quite enjoyed it. We put a bomb clean through the middle of the Admiral Graf Spee, Germany's pocket battleship.

"I am sorry to say we spoiled all the sailors' underpants which were hanging out on the deck. I was the first to bomb Germany in this war—when we returned we got a rousing reception when they heard we were the 'Kiel boys.'"

✦

"Oscar has always been like that," said his mother, commenting on the letter.

"Always, in no matter what he undertakes, he has supreme confidence, and somehow he instils that confidence into us. I am never afraid for Oscar."

✦

While Mrs. Smith was talking, her daughter, Karin, was busy preparing to go on A.R.P. work—night duty at the telephone exchange. Her father was already out on decontamination work, while weary, but proud, Mrs. Smith, who did nursing service throughout the whole of the last war, had just returned from duty at the Birmingham Hospital.

"Oscar," she continued, "is an old Wolverhampton Grammar schoolboy. His whole heart was in the Services, and he went straight from school into the Air Force.

When it was suggested that the men who carried out the raid might receive some decorations, she smiled proudly and her eyes sparkled. "Well, Oscar" she said, as if speaking to herself, "you dropped the first bomb, oh son, pray God you live to see the last."

Germany has three "pocket" battleships, the Deutschland, Admiral Scheer, and Admiral Graf Spee, the latter being the last to be completed—in 1934.

DAILY MIRROR, Saturday, Sept. 23, 1939.

Daily Mirror

No. 11,169
ONE PENNY
Registered at the G.P.O. as a Newspaper.

Return to France

The Duke of Windsor flew to France in an R.A.F. 'plane yesterday to take up his duties as a Major-General in the British Army. He will serve in the field with the troops.

Shortly before he left he called—wearing his new uniform, but with khaki slacks and suede shoes—at the War Office and had a brief interview with an official.

His brother, Major-General the Duke of Gloucester, Chief Liaison Officer of the Forces, has also taken up his appointment with the British Expeditionary Force in France.

The King last night left London for the first time since the outbreak of war to spend the week-end at Windsor.

GET THE MEN OF BRITAIN BACK TO WORK

WAR HAS BEEN ALLOWED TO PLAY TOO MUCH HAVOC WITH BRITAIN'S BUSINESS AND INDUSTRIAL LIFE.

Ministry of Labour figures issued last night showed that up to 11th September, 76,000 men had found jobs and 175,000 women had lost work.

The figures tell only a small chapter of the story.

They ignore the thousands of black-coated workers suddenly unemployed, of one-man businesses closed down, of the hundreds of people idle in the entertainment and kindred industries.

The authorities are to blame. Wise planning and wise decisions could have averted this temporary slowing of Britain's machine.

Sir Samuel Hoare, speaking as a member of the War Cabinet, broadcast a belated appeal to employers last night to restore men and women they had discharged.

"Get back your workers," he said, "you will want many of them before the world is much older."

No Room Soon for Idle Hands

"At this moment of transition there is bound to be dislocation," he added. "You cannot move a million and a quarter women and children from the towns to the country without dislocation. You cannot pass from peace industry into war production without dislocation."

He spoke truly. But the country now feels that the dislocation has gone too far; that official instructions must be reversed, that the Government must act quickly to keep Britain marching to victory.

Sir Samuel declared that the Government is doing its utmost to mitigate the dislocation.

"Soon there will be no room for idle hands. Gigantic programmes are every day gathering momentum.

"I am certain that at no distant date there is scarcely an able-bodied man or woman whose services the country will not need.

"Be patient, therefore, if you have sought war work and have not yet found it. The war work will soon be seeking you."

There are thousands of people in Britain who hope that Sir Samuel is right.

But he threatened no penalties for employers who recklessly discharge their workers. Instead he appealed.

"Be courageous, also, you employers. Stick to your workers, and keep them fit and ready

Continued on Back Page

Germany has lost 150,000 men and 600 'planes in the conquest of Poland.

+ + +

Warsaw will be cut in two by the dividing line between the Russian and Nazi halves of Poland.

(SEE PAGE 2.)

"Beautiful" Bombing

"The whole town of Lwow was enveloped in fire and smoke. This, indeed, was a picture more beautiful than I was ever capable of imagining."

This description of the bombing of the town was given over the radio by one of the German pilots who took part in it. "I had the good luck," he said, "to see the railway station and the numerous trains there blown up and scattered in all directions."—Reuter.

TWO MORE U-BOATS SUNK

TWO more U-boats will trouble British shipping no longer.

A destroyer found one disguised with rigging to resemble a fishing-boat, apparently unable to submerge. The tell-tale periscope betrayed her, and she was sent to her doom.

Another U-boat, lurking ready to strike was rammed "by accident" by a British trawler.

The destroyer sank the first U-boat after a ten-minute battle, Captain Frederick Pickering, master of the Steel Mariner, said when he arrived at New York yesterday. He and his crew saw the battle off Avonmouth.

"The destroyer appeared soon after we had sighted the U-boat," added the captain, "and for the space of ten minutes heavy firing took place. Finally the submarine sank."

Rammed by Trawler

Arthur Darwood, skipper of the British trawler told how his boat rammed the submarine, when he returned to Grimsby yesterday.

He said he sighted two British warships and an aeroplane circling overhead. The warships were making a signal that there was a submarine in the vicinity, and the trawler continued on her course at full speed.

Suddenly there was a crash and the trawler's bows rose in the air.

As the crew looked astern, they saw the water boiling with air bubbles.

President Roosevelt, during a Press conference at the White House yesterday, revealed that two foreign submarines had been sighted off Alaska and Nova Scotia, says Exchange.

Major-General the Duke of Windsor acknowledging with a salute the greeting of the crowd which watched him leave the War Office yesterday, the first time he has worn uniform for three years.

WAR COUNCIL 'IN SUSSEX'

THE Supreme War Council met in England yesterday — in the committee - room adjoining the council chamber of a Sussex town.

France's representatives, flying in a French civil 'plane, arrived at an aerodrome a few miles from the meeting place. Police cars waited to take them to the meeting. M. Daladier and others wore leather flying kit.

Their return journey was made from a different aerodrome.

The council was timed for 11.30 a.m., but the French representatives were half an hour late.

Talked to Mayor

Meanwhile, Mr. Chamberlain and Lord Halifax, who had travelled by train, chatted with the local Mayor.

Britain's representatives were Mr. Chamberlain, Lord Halifax, Viscount Gort and Lord Chatfield, Minister for Co-ordination of Defence. France was represented by M. Dala-dier, the Premier; General Gamelin, Commander-in-Chief of the French Armed Forces; Admiral Darlan, Chief of the Naval Staff, and M. Dautry, Minister of Armaments.

M. Dautry, a brilliant railway engineer, is one of the newcomers to the French Cabinet. His great aim in life is to see the building of the Channel tunnel.

There were two sessions of the Council, morning and afternoon, with an interval for lunch.

Developments since the meeting of September 12 were reviewed, and their effect on the future course of events estimated.

There was complete agreement on the course to be followed both to meet these developments and to give effect to the Allied plans.

Munitions and supplies were discussed and agreement was reached on procedure for co-ordination.

The council ended as the clock was striking 4 p.m., and the crowd, which had now grown to several thousands, cheered the departure.

DAILY MIRROR, Monday, Sept. 25, 1939.

Daily Mirror

No. 11,170   ONE PENNY

Registered at the G.P.O. as a Newspaper.

I See Hitler's New Line

A new frontier is menaced. Here is the first story of what is happening on the border of Holland.

DUTCH ARM AS TROOPS LABOUR

BY OUR SPECIAL CORRESPONDENT

AMSTERDAM, Sunday.

WHILE THE DUTCH TROOPS LOOK ON, THE NAZIS ARE FEVERISHLY WORKING TO PREPARE A NEW LINE, A LINE ALONG THE FRONTIER OF HOLLAND.

The Dutch know that the new fortifications cannot be a line of defence for Britain and France will certainly not violate Holland's neutrality and throw troops through their territory to the German border.

The line is a base for attack. It completes the Siegfried Line which now ends at Gelsenkirchen, twenty miles from Holland.

And now, day and night, German labour battalions are at work mixing concrete and laying barbed wire.

In a tour of the frontier district to-day I saw in the distance uniformed men working with haste to unload lorries and distribute materials.

The Dutch Army is ready. The frontier force has been mobilised to full strength. Constant watch is kept on the Nazi activities.

And Germany's other neutral neighbours are ready, too. Switzerland is mobilised. The Belgians have manned their line of forts.

And in Luxembourg watchers on the German frontier realise that all is not well in the Siegfried Line.

To-day a mystery explosion rocked workings at Minden, near here.

A dynamite charge went off without the customary warning of whistles and flags, blocking two entrances leading to the subterranean passages of the Line.

Fortifications Delayed

The explosion may mean serious delay in the completion of the fortifications. German engineers, who were driving workmen day and night to reinforce the Line, had to stop their operations.

Villagers and visitors on the Luxembourg banks of the River Moselle at Steinheim have been able to see hundreds of workmen, stripped to the waist, labouring on excavations for the Siegfried Line.

But for the moment the German plan remains a mystery. Dare they strike west through Holland and Belgium to attack France? That manoeuvre is fraught with peril.

There is an alternative: to attack eastwards through Hungary to the coveted oil wells of Rumania. That move would bring in Turkey, would force Germany again into a war on two fronts.

U.S. Hunt Mystery Ship

FROM OUR OWN CORRESPONDENT

New York, Sun.

Scores of United States coastguard cutters and aeroplanes are to-day searching for a German submarine refuelling ship off Boston.

The patrol boats have orders to halt any ship carrying supplies to German submarines, even outside the three-mile limit.

The battleship Wyoming has left Boston under sealed orders, and it is reported that search is being made for a mysterious grey-painted vessel.

The instructions to act outside the three-mile limit is emphasised in a dispatch to the Chilian Foreign Office stating that the United States will propose to the Pan-American Neutrality Congress an extension of jurisdiction over territorial waters of the American continent to as much as 300 miles.

—and now read of this drama 350 miles out at sea

Bomber Sinks U-Boat

SWOOPING from the clouds 350 miles from the nearest land, an R.A.F. 'plane bombed and sank a U-boat while the crews of two ships looked on in amazement.

The crews who saw this drama were those of the British steamer Kafiristan, who had taken to the lifeboats after their boat had been sunk by the submarine, and of the U.S. liner American Farmer, which was speeding to their rescue.

The American Farmer brought the twenty-nine surviving members of the crew of the Kafiristan into New York yesterday.

Mr. Armistead Lee, of Chatham, Virginia, passenger, told how, as they sighted the life boats belonging to the Kafiristan, they saw a British bomber swoop down "from nowhere as if by magic."

"The bomber," he said, "swooped on the submarine and apparently destroyed it with a bomb. There were nine men on the deck of the submarine, but no one appeared to see the bomber coming.

"It sprayed the deck with machine-gun fire and the crew rushed to the conning tower hatch. The submarine submerged so fast that some of us who were watching thought that the hatch was not even fastened down."

Hit Conning Tower

"Then the 'plane circled and dropped a bomb. It re-circled, dived within 15ft. of the water and dropped another bomb. We saw the bow of the submarine lift; then the whole ship slid backwards into the water.

"The bomber next flew over us. One of the fliers waved triumphantly and pointed down as if signalling that the submarine was destroyed."

Captain Pederson, master of the American Farmer, said that one bomb struck the conning tower squarely. "As the 'plane passed us we could see two empty bomb racks."

Captain John Busby, master of the Kafiristan, said that the submarine fired a warning shot. Six out of thirty-four of his crew were drowned in launching the first lifeboat while the Kafiristan was still moving.

British seamen of another ship sunk by a U-

Continued on Back Page

RUSSIANS HELD IN WARSAW

MORE than sixty members of the Soviet Embassy in Warsaw, including twenty-two women and twenty-three children, are held prisoner by armed men in the cellars of the battered Embassy building.

This was revealed last night when the German Army broadcast an offer of a safe conduct through the German lines to members of the Soviet Embassy and any other foreign diplomats left in Warsaw.

The message was broadcast on the wave-length of Warsaw No. 1 station in Polish, French and Russian.

It stated that the diplomats will be awaited on the Praga-Radzymin road to-day at noon.

Only the Soviet Ambassador himself and the military attache are safe on Russian territory.

Warsaw is holding out against the Nazi invaders despite the most devastating artillery bombardment the shattered capital has yet suffered.

The defiant Warsaw radio calmly reported that "terrific shelling" had killed more than 1,000 civilians in the last twenty-four hours. (See page 3.)

KNEW HITLER AS COWARD

HITLER may be a hero to the Nazi Party, but he was no hero to his dentist.

In fact the dentist, Dr. Martin Buechler, who died at the week-end, declared that the Fuehrer was the most cowardly patient he had ever treated.

He revealed that on one occasion Hitler actually fainted with fear.

Dr. Buechler, once a well-known member of the Nazi party, left Germany soon after Hitler came to power. He went to live in Buenos Aires.

"There are courageous people who do not behave like heroes when facing the dentist's forceps, but Hitler was perhaps my most cowardly patient," Buechler said.

"He literally trembled when I had to use the syringe. This vigorous man behaved like a nervous wreck when sitting in the chair and asked to open his mouth."

Man Nazis Banned

World-famous creator of psycho-analysis—who described National Socialism as an illustration of the thirst for power of the lower instincts—Professor Sigmund Freud, has died in London.

Although he did not mention Hitler's name, everybody knew who was meant when Freud spoke of "the danger which might arise when the lowest instincts of the unconscious come to power in a political system."

His books were burnt by the Nazis and his teachings are banned in Germany.

IT'S AN ARMY SECRET

And as it's highly confidential we'll have to censor it — picture taken as troops left for the Front.

DAILY MIRROR, Tuesday, Sept. 26, 1939.

Daily Mirror

No. 11,171 ♦ ONE PENNY
Registered at the G.P.O. as a Newspaper

CAPTAIN SAVES CREW, DIES WITH HIS SHIP

AT THE CANTEEN DOOR

Look up, Sir Kingsley, you're missing something. . . .

Canteen girls waving to the King and his Majesty smiling back as with Air Marshal Sir Frederick Bowhill and the Air Minister he visited the headquarters of the R.A.F. Coastal Command yesterday.

THE HAZELSIDE, A BRITISH FREIGHTER, HAD BEEN TORPEDOED. SHE WAS SINKING. EIGHTEEN MEN SURVIVED THE SHELLING. THEY CROWDED INTO THE ONLY BOAT LEFT, A JOLLY-BOAT BUILT TO CARRY EIGHT.

The master of the ship, Captain Joseph Davies, ordered his wounded radio operator into the jollyboat.

"Jump in yourself, sir," shouted the bos'n.

Captain Davies shook his head, gave the order that was his own death warrant.

"Pull away," he shouted, "there are enough of you in that boat already!"

The jollyboat pushed off. The Hazelside, her decks a shambles, tilted stern up and disappeared.

Captain Davies was seen for a moment swimming in the heavy swell. Then he vanished

Attacked Without Warning

The Hazelside had been attacked without warning, in sight of land. Watchers on shore saw the water spout high as the shells struck.

As the first German shell screeched over his decks, Captain Davies decided to race to safety.

But the next shell struck his ship amidships, wrecked two of his lifeboats and killed three of his crew.

The radio operator, Wilfred Birkett, bleeding from a wound, repeated again and again a call for help.

And help arrived from the skies. Just as the Hazelside sank a British 'plane appeared.

A bomb was dropped on the spot where the U-boat had quickly submerged. Signal flares from the 'plane directed a rescue boat.

The jollyboat was picked up. Beside it a raft bobbed on the water.

It held three men and two boys. The boys are brothers, James and Brian McGannon, of Belfast.

Brian, aged fifteen, was making his first sea trip. When the order was given to abandon ship, James lashed a lifebelt round Brian, threw him into the water and dived in after him.

Saved by Raft

They were in the sea for twenty minutes when James found floating timber and a loose rope. He bound the wood together into a rough raft that saved their lives.

Eleven men died in the Hazelside. Three were killed by the shell fire. The others, including the captain, the first and third officers and the second engineer, were drowned.

In her home in Whitchurch, Glamorgan, Mrs. George Alden had been packing her bags to set off to meet her husband, due home after seven months at sea in the Hazelside.

She scarcely noticed that the radio music had ceased until she heard the name of her

Continued on Back Page

Slovak Appeal to Britain

Germany, which at the outbreak of war disarmed the Slovak forces, has now marched in and taken over the whole of Slovakia.

The Slovak Consul in London (M. Milan Harmine) handed a declaration to the British Foreign Office yesterday. It read:—

"The whole of Slovakia i: occupied by Nazi armed forces.

"The voice of the Slovak people has been temporarily silenced by the ruthless abrogation of all treaties and agreements.

"In the name of Slovakia I solemnly protest against this shameful betrayal and declare that the aim and ideals of Great Britain and France are identical to those of my sorely-tried people."

FRENCH ARMY ATTACK AGAIN

FRANCE'S big guns began to pound the main fortifications of the Siegfried Line for the first time yesterday. Heavy artillery was in new advance positions for which the French Army's gains had cleared the way.

The reception given to German counter-attacks in the past two days appears to have discouraged the Nazi troops. They are now restricting themselves to artillery fire in the areas south-east of Zweibruecken.

For the first time the stretch along the Rhine between Strasbourg and the Swiss frontier near Basle has shown a certain liveliness.

Hitherto there had been nothing more than occasional bursts of artillery fire, but yesterday prolonged and violent cannonades were exchanged over the grey waters of the Rhine.

Nazi 'Planes Down

French air reconnaissance has established that the Germans are concentrating south of the Black Forest.

French official Communique No. 44, issued last night, states: "Activity of our advance infantry elements to the east of the Sarre. Strong enemy artillery action in the same region."

The French Army announced last night that "many" German 'planes were shot down by the French over the Western Front yesterday.

They said that two German chaser 'planes fell behind the French lines and the General Staff communique indicated that the French victories had been won against superior German squadrons.—Reuter and Associated Press.

A false German claim that eight French 'planes were shot down on Sunday is denied in a Paris semi-official statement last night.

The French communique on the operations of 'ptember 25," it says, "mentions aerial co. ats on the previous day, concerning which a German communique has given incorrect details by announcing that eight French machines were brought down. Actually our losses were only two machines."—Reuter and Associated Press.

CIPHER GIRLS PUZZLE KING

HALF a dozen girls busily decoding secret messages in a country house "somewhere near London" yesterday looked up in amazement to find the King in the room.

The King was visiting the secret headquarters of the R.A.F. Coastal Command. He picked up one message in code and looked at it in bewilderment.

"What exactly do you do when a message comes in?" he asked the girls, and they explained to him part of the system of deciphering.

"It is very intricate," he remarked. "I couldn't learn it in a day's march."

'We are getting rather good at arithmetic,' said the head of the section.

"You certainly should know your multiplication tables," replied the King.

Some of the girls are always : duty—day and night—and form the vital link between the defenders of Britain. Every message of importance goes through them in code.

He left the house to inspect trenches and shelters which are being dug, said a word to the canteen girls who blushed delightedly among their piles of chocolate and buns, glanced in at the sergeants' mess and asked about the comforts of the men in one of the dormitory huts.

On his way to the canteen the King

stopped and chatted to a workman wearing the war medals of 1914-18.

The man was piling sandbags around reserve electrical equipment, and the King asked if the sandbags would stand up against the winter rains and frost. The workman answered, "Oh, they will last two or three years."

Sir Kingsley Wood, the Air Minister, who was standing nearby, at once said with a smile: "Just about the length of the war."

In the officers' mess the King heard stories of encounters between U-boats and R.A.F. patrols.

The King was taken into the warren of corridors, lined heavily with cables and wires, and the honeycomb of small active rooms into which a once spacious house has been transformed.

DAILY MIRROR, Thursday, Sept. 28, 1939.

Daily Mirror

No. 11,173 ◆ ONE PENNY
Registered at the G.P.O. as a Newspaper.

Poland —the End

WARSAW has surrendered to the Germans for the second time within twenty-four years.

For twelve days the capital of Poland has been shelled by the encircling guns, bombed night and day from the air, cut off from food and supplies.

Last night, after a heroic defence that thrilled the world, the defenders asked for a twenty-four-hour armistice.

And just before midnight Warsaw Radio No. 1, now in German hands, announced that the city had at last capitulated.

The announcer said that the city will be formally handed over to the German military authorities to-morrow.

"According to the latest reports," he added, "the Polish forces in the city number 100,000 men."

"City Entirely in Ruins"

The defenders had earlier broadcast their last message, the news that the men and women of Warsaw could no longer withstand the rain of steel. Their announcement said:

"The city is entirely in ruins. The reservoirs and water-filters were destroyed days ago."

"It is extremely difficult to help civilians because of fire and the lack of water."

"Nine hospitals filled with wounded have been destroyed."

"Smoke and dust make breathing nearly impossible."

"Modlin (the great fortress to the northwest of Warsaw) continues its defence."

"Thirteen German 'planes were shot down on Tuesday, bringing the total of enemy 'planes brought down to 106."

"Our armistice proposal has so far brought no answer."

So Warsaw went down with its streets littered with unburied dead, and with the wounded untended amid the ruins of its roads.

It last fell to the invading Germans in 1915, when it was part of the Tsar's Russian Empire.

Its fate in a new war is not yet decided. Certain it is that Hitler's power will pass.

Before the Polish rifles were silenced a radio message was received from their friends abroad.

Martial Law Ordered

The leader of the Polish Community in France broadcast:

"We are proud to be citizens of the Polish State, which will rise again, stronger and greater than ever.

"We are organising a great Polish Army on the soil of France, an army that will avenge the injuries done by our barbaric enemies.

"Your heroic battle against overwhelming odds will be an example to us all."

Meanwhile Hitler has ordered the establishment of martial law in the German-occupied territories of Poland.

It is claimed that the Russians are taking extremely good care of the large Jewish population in the White Russian part of Poland. Their civic rights have been restored to them, with full representation on the local Soviets.—Reuter, British United Press and Associated Press.

NOW YOU KNOW THERE'S A WAR

★ **INCOME TAX** is up 2'- to 7'6. You pay 1'6 extra this year, the other 6d. afterwards. Allowance for wife and children is down £10. Earned income allowance now £250.

BEER will cost you 1d. a pint more.

WHISKY will be increased 1'3 a bottle more at once.

TOBACCO will be 1½d. an ounce more than yesterday.

SURTAX is raised to a maximum of 9'6 in the £ making 17'- in £ on top-scale incomes.

SUGAR is up 1d. a pound "to get at the non-smokers and non-drinkers."

DEATH DUTIES are increased at a rate which makes those at top of the scale contribute 60 per cent. to Exchequer.

EXCESS PROFITS of firms will be taxed at 60 per cent.

PROFITEERS will be taxed later.

What Chancellor said : See page 6

Do Your Bit and SMILE

Smiler here is West End showgirl Judy McCrea in her off-stage role of Air Raid Warden in Paddington.

'MOSCOW ORDERS'

RIBBENTROP, Hitler's Foreign Minister, opened his talks with Molotov, Soviet Premier, in Moscow last night.

Count von der Schulenberg, German Ambassador, was present.

According to the Berlin radio, Forster, the Danzig Nazi leader, accompanied Ribbentrop to Moscow.

As Ribbentrop arrived in the Soviet capital, the German Freedom station, which is operated inside the Reich by Hitler's German opponents, declared:

"Germany is in the same situation to-day as Austria was when Schuschnigg was called to Berchtesgaden. Von Ribbentrop has been summoned to Moscow.

"The Poles will fight on, as the Czechs are now fighting. It will need an army corps to watch them and the Red Army in the East. Who can say whether the Red Army will not one day be thrown against you?"

The Germans fear Soviet domination of the Baltic Sea and it is believed that a subject discussed by Ribbentrop and Molotov was possible Soviet action in connection with the sinking of

Continued on Back Page

NO "POOLS" THIS WINTER

THERE will be no more football pools for the present. They may be banned for the duration of the war.

Government have taken this decision because the pressure on the Post Office is already so great that they feel they are not justified in increasing it.

Decision means about 10,000 women and girls will be out of jobs. See page 3.

FIVE B.B.C. CHIEFS RESIGN

B.B.C. programmes are now to come under the control of the Ministry of Information.

This was announced last night when it was stated that Sir Allan Powell, chairman, and Mr. C. H. G. Millis, vice-chairman, now constitute the entire Board of Government. The appointment of the five other members has been terminated.

The B.B.C.'s charter remains in full force apart from this change.

Certain powers vested in the Postmaster-General have been transferred to the Minister of Information, including programme matters, hours of working, and the possible control of the service in emergency.

Contact between the Ministry and the B.B.C. has been provided for by the appointment of Sir Kenneth Lee as director of the Radio Relations and Communications Division in the Ministry of Information, with the assistance of certain members of the B.B.C.'s staff who are accommodated in the Ministry.

DAILY MIRROR, Monday, Oct. 2, 1939.

Daily Mirror

No. 11,176 ✦ ONE PENNY
Registered at the G.P.O. as a Newspaper.

HITLER'S PEACE TRICK: I'LL GO

I R.A.F. 'PLANE BEAT 15

IN a desperate running battle with fifteen German fighters over the Siegfried Line, four out of five R.A.F. reconnaisance machines were brought down, but the fifth, left alone, accounted for two of the Nazi machines and fought off the pursuit.

Then with eighty bullet holes in the fabric, ailerons and rudder damaged, both petrol tanks burst, and the navigator wounded in the forehead, the 'plane recrossed the frontier.

As it did so the engine failed as petrol poured from the tank. The pilot stopped the hole with his handkerchief and saved enough gas to bring his 'plane home.

The landing had to be faced with the retractable undercarriage jammed half-way open and the off-side tyre shot away. As the machine touched down it spun in a circle, cartwheeling over on one wing and caught fire.

Three Shot Down

The navigator was flung out on his head with his clothes on fire. The gunner was jammed inside, but without a thought for his own safety the navigator hauled him out and smothered his blazing coat with bare hands.

The British 'planes were well over the German frontier when the Nazi planes swooped down.

The reconnaissance was the work to be done. Nothing must stop it. The formation flew on.

Intense fighting lasted for thirty-five minutes. Three of our machines were shot down, another made a forced landing, but out of the twelve men forming the crews, eight were seen to escape by parachute.

The squadron-leader alone was left, but he flew on just the same to finish his job.

A stream of bullets hit the engine of the leading Messerschmidt. The enemy machine swerved and in a second burst into flames and plunged to earth. Keeping up his fire the gunner landed further bursts into a second fighter.

Biggest Air Battle

Biggest air battle since the beginning of the war took place over the Siegfried line on Saturday night, it was learned yesterday.

Two or three British and French squadrons took part.

Apart from air action the front has been "straightened" along nearly a mile to the south-west of Saarlouis, in the lower valley of the Nied.

Yesterday's official French war communique merely announced an "improvement" in French positions. It may be stated, however, that this improvement was substantial.

The importance of the sector lies in the fact that it is situated in the angle formed by the rivers Sarre and Nied, which joins the Sarre about five miles north-west of Saarbruecken.

The ground between the two valleys forms a rugged plateau, ending a sort of balcony which dominates the valley of the Sarre and the important town of Saarlouis.

Foreign messages from Reuter, Exchange, British United Press and Associated Press.

Reply—in Advance

Millions last night heard a phrase in Mr. Winston Churchill's broadcast speech which puzzled them. He referred to "Hitler or his successors."

The "or his successors" was taken in well-informed circles to be a reference to the belief that Hitler may offer to abdicate.

Mr. Churchill's speech was Britain's reply in advance. Hitler must now think up another plan.

Mr. Churchill's speech made a tremendous impression through America. It was heard in Washington by Senators gathered for to-morrow's debate. Comments included "Hitler is now getting plenty of his own medicine"

Political experts say the speech will have the effect of swinging plenty of millions more Americans towards the Allies.

"The War Goes On" MR. CHURCHILL

BRITAIN'S answer to the "blackmail" peace threat came from Mr. Winston Churchill, First Lord of the Admiralty, in his broadcast speech last night.

"It was," he declared, "for Hitler to say when the war would begin, but it is not for him or his successors to say when it will end. It began when he wanted it, and it will end only when we are convinced that he has had enough.

"Now we have begun; now we are going on; now, with the help of God, and all that is meant thereby, and with the conviction that we are the defenders of civilisation and freedom, we are going on to the end."

He made clear the plight into which Hitler has now brought his country through his alliance with Stalin. Germany dare not now attack either the Baltic or Balkan States. Stalin bars the way.

"Russia has pursued a cold policy of self-interest. We could have wished that the Russian armies should be standing on their present line as the friends and allies of Poland, instead of as invaders," he declared.

But that the Russian armies should stand on this line, was clearly necessary for the safety of Russia against the Nazi menace. At any rate the line is there, and an Eastern Front has been created which Nazi Germany does not dare assail.

When Herr von Ribbentrop was summoned to Moscow last week, it was to learn the fact, and to accept the fact, that the Nazi designs upon the Baltic States and upon the Ukraine must come to a dead stop.

"I cannot forecast to you the action of Russia. It is a riddle wrapped in mystery in-

Continued on Page Two

BY A POLITICAL CORRESPONDENT

HITLER, CHECKMATED IN THE EAST AND ATTACKED IN THE WEST BY THE MIGHT OF BRITAIN AND FRANCE, IS BELIEVED TO BE PREPARING WHAT HE CONSIDERS TO BE HIS CLEVEREST DIPLOMATIC TRICK—AN OFFER TO ABDICATE.

He knows he cannot win. He knows he cannot last. His only hope is a new manœuvre which he trusts, with a pathetic belief in his own cunning, will persuade Britain and France to call off the war.

In neutral countries it is realised that Hitler's position, desperate as it was before, has become worse since the threat of German-Soviet action has failed to impress the Allies.

And neutral observers in Berlin anticipate that he will go a step further in his attempt to end the war.

When he meets the Reichstag this week it is believed that he will offer to create an independent Poland—a buffer State; that he will suggest a token disarmament, a Five-Power Conference on economic and colonial claims and concessions to the Czechs.

Then, last surprise of all, he will play his trump card. "They say they are fighting Hitlerism," he will declare. "Then I am prepared to go. I have created the Greater Germany. Now I am ready to hand over my burden to Marshal Goering.

"IF BRITAIN AND FRANCE ACCEPT MY OFFER, MY TASK IS DONE. I SHALL RETIRE TO DEVOTE MY LIFE TO ART AND LITERATURE."

The trick if Hitler does decide to try it—and no one really knows yet what his "peace" plans are—will avail him nothing.

Britain and France will not be moved from their purpose because one gangster has been substituted for another

Ciano in Berlin

Both Governments are on their guard against Hitler's next attempt to drive a wedge between the Allies. Such an attempt is fore-doomed.

Meanwhile, Count Ciano, Italy's Foreign Minister, arrived in Berlin last night and saw Hitler in his study. Ribbentrop was present during the interview.

In Moscow, M. Sarajoglu, the Turkish Foreign Minister, met M. Molotov, the Soviet Premier, last night. For three days the Turkish Envoy has been kicking his heels in Moscow while Ribbentrop and Stalin reached agreement.

Now it is revealed that before Ribbentrop's arrival, Sarajoglu had proposed that Russia and Turkey should make a new pact consistent with Turkey's obligations to Britain and France.

Latvia, Finland Next?

He will get his answer this week-end.

In Ankara it is pointed out that the British-Turkish agreement contained a clause safeguarding Turkey against becoming entangled in any dispute between Britain and Russia.

The Rome radio last night, broadcasting in English, declared that Latvia and Finland will shortly make agreements with Russia similar to that made by Estonia.

The Latvian Foreign Minister is leaving for Moscow to-day.

So events shape in Europe for the most vital political week of the war.

When the House of Commons meets to-day Mr. Chamberlain is expected to make a short statement on the Hitler-Stalin "peace" offer.

But it is probable that he will defer his full speech until Hitler makes his latest offer before the Reichstag.

Whatever Hitler says, the decision of the Commons is clear. They will not tolerate aggression. Britain will fight until tyranny is overthrown.

MORE MEN

THE twenty—twenty-one years Army Class is now liable to be called to the colours. A Royal Proclamation to this effect was issued last night.

The men will register at labour exchanges on a date to be announced, but calling-up notices may wait until November.

Provisional date for registration is October 21. Details are on page 2.

Men who reached the age of twenty-two yesterday will not register.

Ministry of Information Sacks 127: See Back Page

DAILY MIRROR, Wednesday, October 4, 1939.

Daily Mirror

No. 11,178   ONE PENNY
Registered at the G.P.O. as a Newspaper.

Men Over 41 Will March Again For Britain

Imperial War Cabinet

Dominion Governments are to be invited shortly to send envoys to London to form an Imperial War Cabinet.

Members of this Cabinet would be in the closest touch with the Supreme War Council

NAZI WARSHIP IS AT LARGE IN ATLANTIC

A 10,000-TON GERMAN POCKET-BATTLESHIP, THE ADMIRAL SCHEER, IS AT LARGE IN THE GREAT WATERS OF THE SOUTH ATLANTIC OCEAN.

She has already sunk one ship, the British steamer Clement, whose crew, landed at Rio de Janeiro, Brazil, yesterday, told this story of their meeting with the sea raider.

"At eleven o'clock on Sunday morning a German 'plane suddenly appeared in the sky. It dived down towards us, firing a machine gun across our bows.

"We hove to and abandoned the ship. When we were in the lifeboats a German battleship—we took her for the Admiral Scheer—steamed up, fired a score of shells at the Clement, then finished her off with a torpedo."

The Clement sank in forty-five minutes.

Three lifeboats reached shore. A fourth was picked up by the Brazilian steamer Itatinga and the men taken to Bahia.

The crew also reported that the master of the Clement, Captain F. C. P. Harris, of Liverpool, and the chief engineer, Mr. W. Bryant, of Wallasey, were taken captive by the Germans.

Photographers on the German warship took pictures of the Clement as she sank.

Twenty-five years ago they marched to do "their bit" in the front line, now they will volunteer just as readily to defend the home front.

VETERANS of the last war, the "over forty-ones," whom in the old days the Germans learned to respect and fear, will soon march again to defend Britain.

For Sir Victor Warrender said in the Commons yesterday:

"Opportunities for taking in men who present themselves as volunteers, though over conscription age for the Army will very soon occur."

But their job this time will not be over in Flanders, but on the Home Front.

The duty of many of them will be to train young soldiers destined for service overseas—to teach them all "the tricks" they learned in warfare twenty-five years ago.

Others will take over duties at home now being performed by younger men.

They will guard bridges, power stations and other important points by night and day.

Half a Million of Them

The British Legion has half a million of these men, all of whom have been intensively trained and have been on active service. Sixty per cent. are capable of carrying on under this new scheme.

The veterans are eager to answer the call for Britain. In factories, workshops and British Legion clubs throughout Britain they were last night excitedly discussing the plan. For it means that ex-officers and men now too old for a field force or anti-aircraft unit all have the chance to "do their bit."

"The Army Council will decide how exactly the veterans will be used, and then recruiting will begin," an official at the War Office told the Daily Mirror yesterday.

BELGIANS ARREST GERMAN SOLDIERS

A GERMAN Army lorry containing twelve soldiers and a machine-gun and coming from Aix-la-Chapelle (Aachen) crossed the Belgian frontier yesterday.

They were held up by barbed wire placed across the road and the soldiers were arrested by the gendarmes guarding the frontier.

The driver of the lorry had mistaken the road.—Exchange.

Hitler Plan To-day?

HITLER may make his speech in the Reichstag to-morrow, but in the meantime the terms of his "blackmail peace" offer to Britain and France are likely to be sent through diplomatic channels to-day.

This was the report from Rome last night, following the speech in the House of Commons by Mr. Chamberlain in which he made it clear that no threats will now deter Britain and France. We fight on till rule by violence is crushed. (See page 2.)

Hitler, it is believed, is anxious to get in his answer to this as quickly as possible.

Rome radio, says the British United Press, quotes the German newspaper Angriff as saying that this will prove a historic week, and that the peace proposals will be made in the form of a demarche to all interested Governments.

The newspaper is quoted as saying that Italy will support the peace move.

After quoting this the announcer stated that Britain and France had left no room for doubt as to their attitude towards such a peace. Signor Mussolini is likely to assist Hitler with an ultimatum.

The Italian newspaper, Popolo d'Italia, says that the new demarcation line by which the Russians withdraw east from the Vistula to the Bug, shows that Germany is in a position to create a new Polish state.

POLES TO JOIN R.A.F.

POLISH and other Allied pilots or mechanics may join the British forces soon under an Order in Council announced last night.

During the continuance in force of the Defence (Armed Forces) Regulations, an alien may hold a commission or may be entered or enlisted in any of his Majesty's forces as if he were a British subject.

There will be no limit to the number of aliens who may serve together at any one time in any corps or unit.

But there is no present intention of forming a foreign legion.

Neither is it intended to commission or enlist aliens on a large scale.

Individuals of foreign nationality who want to join up can register at the nearest employment exchange.

Carries Two 'Planes

The Admiral Scheer is one of three Nazi pocket battleships. Her tonnage is 10,000; she carries six 11in. and eight 5.9 guns. She is fast and can steam for 10,000 miles without refuelling.

She carries two aeroplanes, which are released from her deck by catapult.

Somewhere in the South Atlantic too is the Columbus, Germany's third largest liner. She slipped out from Vera Cruz, Mexico, yesterday, and is reported to be planning a dash across the ocean.

Mr. Chamberlain, announcing the Admiral Scheer's activities, said in the House of Commons yesterday: "She will be dealt with according to pre-arranged plan."

The United States is strengthening its neutrality patrol. Forty de-commissioned destroyers are being modernised and refitted to join it.

In Copenhagen yesterday the captain of the Danish steamer Vendia, sunk by a U-boat, told a court of inquiry that his ship, clearly marked with Danish flags, drifted broadside on towards the submarine.

The Danish captain called out in German: "Shall I come over with a boat?"

The U-boat's reply was a torpedo fired from 200 yards' range.

The explosion killed eleven men.

Sweden Acts

The U-boat campaign against neutral shipping has forced Sweden to take action.

In future all Swedish ships will leave port under convoy of Swedish warships.

The Commander-in-Chief of the Swedish

Continued on Back Page

The German pocket battleship, Admiral Scheer, armed with six 11in. and eight 5.9 guns, which is at large in the South Atlantic.

Daily Mirror

No. 11,179   ✦   ONE PENNY
Registered at the G.P.O. as a Newspaper.

HITLER JITTERS

AS MUSSO. SAYS 'NO'

MUSSOLINI'S REFUSAL TO IDENTIFY ITALY WITH THE GERMAN " PEACE " PLAN HAS FORCED HITLER TO REALISE HOW DESPERATE IS HIS POSITION.

When it became clear that Italy would not help, Hitler summoned a meeting of his war council.

Goering, Ribbentrop and Hess took part. General von Brauchitsch flew from the Western Front to attend.

And, as the diplomatic war turned against Germany, neutral observers in Berlin reported a new wave of nervousness in the Wilhelmstrasse. Hitler has the jitters.

Turkey's continued loyalty to her friendship with Britain and France, the refusal of Russia to go beyond her neutrality attitude, and the final blow of Mussolini's refusal have made it clear to Hitler how rapidly his position has worsened.

Reichstag To-morrow

Now, it is believed, Hitler will use his peace plan for home consumption; a propaganda instrument to persuade the German people that the war goes on because the democracies have refused his offer of a " reasonable and just peace."

Hitler will address the Reichstag at noon to-morrow, the German official news agency announced last night.

Meanwhile Ribbentrop, accepting defeat on the diplomatic front, is believed to be urging Hitler to strike a lightning blow in the west with a manœuvre that would throw German troops across Holland and Belgium.

The official Italian news agency, confirming Mussolini's rejection of the German advance, announced:

"In the present state of affairs Italy will take no initiative of that kind. Reports that the Duce is considering calling a peace conference are without foundation."

In Berlin, Hitler's plans are being kept secret. It is thought that he will fly to-day to Warsaw to watch the triumphal entry of his troops into the capital, whose ruins are a monument to its heroic defenders.

In Belgium, a report that the German plan might be dispatched through Brussels was denied.

The Belgians, their normal trade upset by the war, now seek a commercial alliance with Britain, says the *Daily Mirror* Brussels correspondent.

Bosses Showed the Way

Three German Communists and two Nazis, who were imprisoned in Haarlem (Holland) for minor offences, emulated Stalin and Hitler and joined forces.

Together they overpowered their gaoler and escaped.

Prison warders immediately organised a hunt, but the five fugitives got clean away.

They have not been traced, says British United Press.

JAPS BREAK WITH NAZIS

THE Rome and Paris radios reported last night that Admiral Nomura, the Japanese Premier and Foreign Minister, has denounced the Anti-Comintern Pact between Germany, Japan and Italy, says British United Press.

Ever since the Germans concluded a non-aggression pact with Russia, Japan has been denouncing Germany for secretly negotiating with the common enemy.

GOERING
said, "Tighten your belts," grew fatter on butter from England.

Goering Got His Butter in England

BUTTER MAKES YOU FAT. THE PEOPLE OF GERMANY ARE BETTER WITHOUT TOO MUCH OF IT.

—MARSHAL GOERING.

FOR months before the war Goering, the apostle of " Guns before Butter," has been receiving regular supplies of butter, forwarded to him from Bradford, in Yorkshire.

At weekly intervals, in the period when Goering was exhorting the German people to tighten their belts, parcels of butter, varying in weight from two to four pounds, were dispatched to Goering and other Nazi chiefs.

A dozen parcels went every week. Some were the size of a small hat-box. All were sent by the principal of a large export wool firm in Bradford.

Goebbels in It, Too

In the week before war broke out, no less than nine such parcels were sent, three addressed to General Goering, Dr. Goebbels and Dr. Bergmann, the remainder going to wives of other prominent members of the Nazi Party.

At that time the butter ration in Germany was a quarter of a pound per head. Now it is even less.

But Goering and Goebbels were getting guns AND butter.

✦ ✦ ✦

The facts of Goering's butter consignment were revealed to the Government by a private individual, and the story was issued last night through the Ministry of Information.

In the household of the man said to have sent the butter it was said: "The report is untrue, laughable. He is a strong anti-Nazi."

The Ministry of Information, told of the denial, declared that the story was true and that they vouched for its truth.

✦ ✦ ✦

TAILPIECE: The German newspaper *Voelkischer Beobachter* announces: It is a hostile act for a German to say " I am hungry." People who say so are the inner enemy. They will be dealt with by the police.

'WORK TO WIN' LINE-UP

BRITAIN'S employers and Labour combined all their forces last night in the fight against Hitlerism. Their leaders reached complete agreement to co-operate in securing the maximum production of arms and munitions.

This will shorten the war. All the difficulties which cropped up during 1914-1918 will be avoided. Britain's war production will be in top gear all the time.

Political circles regard the agreement as a vitally important factor toward victory. It represents on the industrial front the complete determination of the forces on the battlefront.

It was made at a meeting at which Mr. Ernest Brown, Minister of Labour and National Service, met the full General Council of the T.U.C. and representatives of the Employers' Confederation.

Leading the trade union representatives in talks which were described as " historic " was Mr. W. Holmes, the recently-appointed T.U.C. chairman.

The employers and the T.U.C. General Council agreed to set up a central advisory committee to consult with the Government.

This close contact will mean that all problems affecting industry's war effort will be solved with the utmost speed.

New Call

The war-winning pact arranges for the mobilisation and allocation of labour.

Another step toward unity in the war effort will be taken in the Premier's Room at the House of Commons to-day. Mr. Chamberlain will hear Labour's demand for representation on the Ministry of Supply Council and on the Food and Fuel Councils.

Agreement on principle is expected.

It is also probable that Mr. Chamberlain will emphasise that if Labour is on these councils they should also be on all other councils of war.

The suggestion that Labour should come into the Government during the present emergency period will again be put forward. So far, Labour has declined to join the Cabinet failing a place in the War Cabinet.

But as the war develops a Cabinet reconstruction is expected.

Labour may then be included.

ZEPP CAPTAIN GETS BIG JOB

CAPTAIN ALBERT SAMMT, commander of the Graf Zeppelin, which " visited " the Scottish coast several times last August, during a North Sea cruise, has been appointed technical adviser of the German Air Ministry.

Reports that he had flown over Scotland were denied in official quarters in Berlin, but admitted by Captain Sammt himself.

He said he went up the Scottish coast towards the Shetlands.

Experts of the Nazi Air Ministry and officers were in the Zeppelin during the flight.

DAILY MIRROR, Saturday, October 7, 1939.

Daily Mirror

No. 11,181
ONE PENNY
Registered at the G.P.O. as a Newspaper.

WORLD'S SNUB FOR THE HITLER PLAN

BRITAIN: "No peace proposals are acceptable which do not free Europe from the menace of aggression. Something more than words will be required from Hitler to establish confidence."

FRANCE: "We must wage the war imposed on us until the victory which alone will permit the establishment in Europe of a regime of real justice and lasting peace."

UNITED STATES: "The peace offered was one of conquest... Hitler's speech was the plea of a guilty soul that recognises its own crime. Britain will go on."

THESE WERE THE ANSWERS THE GREAT DEMOCRACIES GAVE TO HITLER'S "PEACE" SPEECH. AND LAST NIGHT, ANGERED AT THE FAILURE TO IMPRESS THE WORLD, BERLIN OFFICIALS THREATENED: "THE FUEHRER HAS FOR THE LAST TIME ANNOUNCED READINESS TO TALK PEACE. IN LESS THAN A WEEK HE EXPECTS TO KNOW DEFINITELY WHAT HIS ADVERSARIES THINK ABOUT IT."

A statement on the authority of the Government gave Britain's first reaction. And for France, Premier Daladier declared his country's determination to fight for a genuine peace, free from the menace of aggression.

In Moscow, the fact that Hitler made no reference to the possibility of Soviet aid in the European war was taken by observers as another indication of Russia's determination to remain neutral. It is understood that the Soviet Government was satisfied with the speech.

Early today, an Associated Press message from Berlin said that Hitler would accept an armistice if it were proposed by President Roosevelt or the head of any important neutral State, with a view to a European settlement.

'Peace Proposals Vague and Obscure'

Said the British reply: "The speech abounds in perversions of the truth which will be readily recognised by the people of this country, and indeed of the whole world.

"Herr Hitler's statement that he had never broken his promise only shows that words have for him a meaning totally different from that commonly attached to them.

"If there has been misapprehension about German foreign policy, it can only be attributed to Herr Hitler's open aspirations for world domination in 'Mein Kampf,' to his utterances since he came into power, and still more to his acts.

"His proposals for peace are in many respects vague and obscure, but it is noted that they contain no suggestion of reparation for the wrongs done by Germany to other peoples.

"Nevertheless, they will, as has been declared by the Prime Minister and the Foreign Secretary, be subjected to careful examination in consultation with the Governments of the Dominions and the French Republic.

"But it is necessary to remember two things: First, that no peace proposals are likely to be found acceptable which do not effectively free Europe from the menace of aggression; and, second, that assurances given by the German Government in the past have on so many occasions proved worthless, that something more than words will be required today to establish the confidence which must be the essential basis of peace."

The Fuehrer's speech (reported in full on page 2) was rambling and obscure. He made a general demand for a conference on economics and disarmament, a specific demand for colonies. The "Poland of Versailles" would never rise again, he de-

Continued on Back Page

Finland Says No

FINLAND is standing firm against the demands of Russia.

Her President, M. Kallto (Rome Radio reports) has refused to follow the examples of Estonia and Latvia and negotiate a trade agreement.

Russia has replied that now she reserves the right to take "appropriate action."

Estonian Ports

From Estonia, Russia may get the mainland ports of Virtsu and Rohurulo, as well as the port of Baltiski for naval bases.

Nearly 25,000 Russian soldiers are expected soon on the islands of Saare Maa and Hiiu Maa, on which naval bases have been granted already.

British United Press and Associated Press.

May Wed and Keep Jobs

Women Civil Servants need no longer fear that they will lose their jobs if they marry. Those who become brides may keep their jobs for the duration of the war, if their departments wish to retain their services.

The Civil Service Clerical Association has been advised that women will have to resign formally on marriage, but will be re-engaged for the war period.

German Troops Mass

GERMANY is continuing to mass troops along the Belgian frontier, according to reports reaching Brussels. The Brussels newspaper, *Le Soir*, reports that 1,200 fresh German troops have arrived in the village of Roetgen, near the border, although this village has only a normal population of 2,000.

The same situation, says the newspaper, prevails at other villages near the frontier, and at Aix-la-Chapelle.

Meanwhile German newspapers reaching Brussels report that the first trains bringing Polish prisoners to Western Germany are arriving. Some are already at Cologne.

These Poles will be sent to various camps in the Rhineland and near the Belgian frontier.

French war communique No. 66 says: "There was activity by light units which made contact with the enemy at numerous points on the front. An attack upon one of our posts west of Wissembourg was repulsed."

Sir Edmund Ironside, Chief of the Imperial General Staff, and Air-Chief Marshal Sir Cyril Newall yesterday met General Gamelin, General Vuillemin and General Georges.—*Exchange and British United Press.*

AFTER TODAY

WAR'S WAR, AND, WHILE GIVING ALL THE NEWS AND PICTURES, WE MUST DO OUR BEST TO CONSERVE PAPER. THAT'S OUR JOB.

YOU, A READER OF THE "DAILY MIRROR," CAN HELP US.

Restrictions have been placed on all Newsagents. They cannot order more copies of a paper than they are sure of selling.

That means unless you order your copy of the "Daily Mirror" you may find one day that you cannot get it.

YOU HAVE SHOWN THAT YOU APPRECIATE OUR WAR NEWS SERVICE, THAT THE "MIRROR" IS YOUR PAPER, SO MAKE SURE OF IT BY GIVING YOUR NEWSAGENT AN ORDER

TODAY

DAILY MIRROR, Thursday, Oct. 12, 1939.

Daily Mirror

No. 11,185 ✦ ✦ ONE PENNY
Registered at the G.P.O. as a newspaper.

BRITAIN SIGNS A NEW TRADE PACT WITH RUSSIA

WILL LEAD OUR ARMY

BRITAIN has appointed leaders of two Army corps to take the field in France. They are General Sir John Dill, D.S.O., and General Alan F. Brooke, D.S.O., both Ulstermen. Dill will be fifty-five on Christmas Day; Brooke, a gunnery expert, is fifty-six.

Dill has been described as the best general Britain has had since Marlborough.

When he commanded in Palestine an Arab chief offered a reward of £500 to anyone who would bring Dill to him "dead or alive."

During the last two years he has been General Officer Commanding at Aldershot.

At the beginning of the last war Dill was a captain, but by 1918 he was a Brigadier-General, General Staff for Operations at General Headquarters.

He took the leading part on the British side in Anglo-French Staff talks in 1936, and he has visited and studied the Maginot Line.

Brooke since his has been G.O.C. Southern Command. Previously he was G.O.C. Anti-Aircraft Command. Territorial Army, which was formed last year.

Throughout the last war he was an artillery staff officer. Afterwards he was commandant of the School of Artillery, Inspector of Artillery, Director of Military Training and Divisional Commander in the Southern Command.

War Minister's statement on "Our Hidden Army"—page 3.

General Dill (above) and General Brooke (below), our Corps Commanders.

MAYORS BACK UP BUTCHERS

SEVENTY Hastings butchers attended an emergency meeting yesterday and protested against what they described as unfair distribution of meat.

A deputation was sent to the Mayor (Councillor E. M. Ford), who then went to the meeting himself and said he would approach the Ministry of Food, and promised to mobilise the whole of the Sussex Mayors to support his action.

Many of the butchers stated that their customers were forced to go to shops owned by large companies in order to get supplies. They feared that as a result customers would register with the companies' shops, and the small traders would be ruined.

Some of the butchers said that they had been unable to provide for the needs of evacuated children.

The Ministry of Food had been approached and had said there was no meat shortage.

Germans Get Out

THE Germans are clearing out of Eastern Europe. In Berlin secret plans are being made for the greatest migration in history.

It is proposed to transfer—

750,000 Germans from Rumania;
600,000 from Yugoslavia;
480,000 from Hungary; and
120,000 from Latvia, Lithuania and Estonia.

German settlers are in despair. For years they have believed that Hitler would march east and make them masters of the lands in which they are now minorities.

Stalin has ended these hopes. Now the Germans are being bundled back home or into the newly won territory in Poland.

Already 6,000 Germans, says Exchange, have been removed from Latvia into the Polish Corridor.

For German ships are waiting to take more away. The settlers must not take gold or jewels with them. If they refuse to leave they lose their German nationality.

Meanwhile Germans awaiting evacuation from the Baltic States, crowd Tallinn and other cities to such an extent that the Estonian Government sent orders to the provincial authorities yesterday to prevent the flow to the ports.

In Finland, where a nation waits to hear Russia's terms, the Government are preparing plans to evacuate Helsinki, the capital.

Throughout the country hope is felt that America will yet intervene to persuade Moscow to modify her demands.

But as Dr. Paasikivi, the Finn envoy, arrived in Moscow—where every Scandinavian Minister turned out to meet him in a gesture of their sympathy and support—all Finland prepared to defend the State.

M. Kekkonen, the Home Secretary, broadcast a message: "There is no immediate dan-

Continued on Back Page

BY OUR POLITICAL CORRESPONDENT

A COMMERCIAL AGREEMENT FOR THE EXCHANGE OF RUSSIAN TIMBER FOR BRITISH RUBBER AND TIN WAS CONCLUDED AND SIGNED LAST NIGHT BY THE BRITISH AND RUSSIAN GOVERNMENTS.

This surprise trade development means that normal trade in timber between the White Sea and Britain will be resumed.

The trade was seriously interrupted at the outbreak of war. Some of the tin will come from Cornwall, and both this commodity and the rubber will be safeguarded by the Ministry of Economic Warfare.

There is little possibility of consignments passing into German hands.

The Ministry of Supply which has brought off the deal is satisfied that the Russian timber is the best possible quality. It will be used for pit props and building.

It is emphasised in London and Moscow that the deal is of a commercial character.

It has no political implications. Nevertheless, the fact that normal trade is being resumed will come as a rude shock to the Nazis.

It is known in neutral countries that Germany took pride in having interrupted the supplies of pit props which are vital to our coal industry.

As the Russian ports are icebound from November, the cargoes will have to be rushed to and from Britain within the next few weeks.

The speed is the essence of the contract. The Soviet Government will put colossal ice-breakers at the disposal of the shipping interests.

This pact is only the beginning of a series. The next barter deal will be an exchange of British machinery for Russian wheat.

SHIPS CHASE NAZI BOMBER

A GERMAN bomber, shot down by British destroyers, lay at the mercy of our warships between Egersund and Flekkefjord, at the south-west of Norway.

The destroyers bore down on the crippled plane. But when capture seemed certain, the pilot of the bomber, by coaxing the engines, managed to taxi to within the three-mile limit of Norwegian waters.

The British destroyers turned back.

A German officer then tried to blow the plane up by firing a pistol into the petrol tank.

Further efforts to destroy the machine were prevented by a Norwegian torpedo boat which appeared suddenly.

The airmen were interned, says British United Press.

NAVY "SILENCES" NORTH ATLANTIC

"**T**HE Silent Navy has made it a Silent North Atlantic."

This was how an officer of the American liner Manhattan summed up his impression of the effectiveness of the Fleet's Atlantic "sweeps" when the liner reached this country yesterday from New York.

"Not only did we not see any German craft," said the officer, "but our radio did not pick up even one S O S throughout the voyage."

The Gracie Tonic

Britain got a tonic last night— AND WHAT A TONIC!

It came over the air from Gracie Fields—the woman who only a few weeks ago was almost at the door of death.

Yet last night she made millions forget that there is a war on. Only Gracie could have done it. Only Gracie could have put it over.

Men have got peerages for doing less than that for their country.

She was at the microphone for half an hour. And there wasn't a single war song in her list. "I want to take people out of the war," she said. And, inspired artist that she is, she did it—triumphantly.

Try to imagine the scene of Gracie's broadcast. It was a little parish hall "somewhere in England," which could only hold 120 people. Yet for half an hour that hall became the centre of England.

It was not the usual B.B.C. audience, but bulky sergeant-majors side by side with girls in khaki and auxiliary firemen. This was a war occasion to make you forget the war.

The Last Chorus

Who among the millions of listeners could have remembered anything else while Gracie sang "The Wizard of Oz"? Who could have kept a laugh from his lips while Gracie sang "The Biggest Aspidistra in the World"? True, she did bring Hitler and Goebbels into the latter part, but that was the nearest she got to the war.

As Louis Levy, conductor of the B.B.C. variety orchestra, in his shirt sleeves and braces swung into the last chorus, "Wish me luck as you wave me good-bye," the audience broke the bonds of restraint and began to shout and cheer as they joined in the song.

As Gracie left the hall hundreds of people lining the railings outside suddenly flashed on torches which lit up her figure as she emerged into the darkness.

Extra police drafted to the scene tried in vain to make the people douse the lights, but there was a surge forward through the gates as she clambered into her car. "God bless

Continued on Back Page

DAILY MIRROR, Saturday, Oct. 14, 1939.

Daily Mirror

No. 11,187   ONE PENNY
Registered at the G.P.O. as a Newspaper.

FRIDAY 13th WAS BAD FOR NAZIS

FIRST AIR RAID ON BRITAIN DRIVEN OFF

Navy Sink 3 U-Boats

THE British Navy sank three more U-boats yesterday. Where and how they were caught and destroyed is still a Navy secret.

The new blow to Germany's now dwindling submarine fleet was disclosed in two Admiralty statements last night. The first said:—

"The Admiralty announce that Friday, October 13, has proved an unlucky day for the U-boats, two having been destroyed. The hunting craft were able to rescue some survivors."

Later the Admiralty flashed:—

"A third U-boat has been sunk. A few survivors have been picked up by hunting craft."

This is the highest number of U-boat sinkings in any one day. Friday, 13!

And as the Navy recorded three more victories over the submarines details were announced of the capture of the German liner Cap Norte (13,615 tons).

When British warships found her she was in disguise. She had been repainted. Her funnel was yellow instead of black, the Swedish flag was painted on her side, she bore the name Ancona.

Her cargo included tobacco, cocoa honey, coffee, wheat, wool and skins.

Poles with British Fleet

Three Polish destroyers, the Blyskawica, Grom and Burza are now working with the British Fleet.

Some British sailors are on board. They have been impressed by the fighting spirit of the Poles.

An attempt was made to remove a gun from each ship so as to make them more stable in heavier weather. But the Poles refused to surrender their guns.

Every man in the ships' companies was horrified at the suggestion that they should have fewer guns to fight the enemy.

VON SCHUSCHNIGG TORTURED BY NAZIS

BECAUSE he refused to sign an appeal calling on the Austrians to support the war, Kurt von Schuschnigg, former Austrian Chancellor, is being kept naked and slowly beaten to death by the Nazis.

When the war began he was confronted with the alternatives—sign or be tortured. Unhesitatingly he chose torture.

Each day he is asked afresh to sign the proclamation, says a Paris dispatch from Edgar Mowrer in the Chicago Daily News, states the Daily Mirror New York correspondent.

Knowing what awaits him he steadily refuses, and is then clubbed into unconsciousness.

He is a prisoner in Vienna.

4 ARMY SHIRTS A MINUTE

"Somewhere in London" army shirts are being produced at the rate of one every fifteen seconds.

A Daily Mirror representative visited three London factories yesterday and saw uniforms being made at the weekly rate of: 3,000 greatcoats, 7,000 battle dress suits, 10,000 shorts, 6,000 caps and 2,500 ordinary service dress and warrant officers' uniforms.

EXPRESS SMASH IN BLACK-OUT

BY A SPECIAL CORRESPONDENT

POWERFUL acetylene flares broke the black-out last night at Bletchley Railway Station, Bucks, as soldiers on leave, women A.R.P. workers and railway officials dug amid the wreckage of the Scots express to save trapped passengers. The search was abandoned because of the danger that the station roof would fall if the engine were moved.

At least three people were killed and many were injured when the first and second parts of the express were in collision.

The three dead were the driver of a shunting engine, an R.A.F. man on leave and a relief postman who was loading mails.

The first part of the train was standing at the platform while a light engine was shunting a coach on to the rear of the train. The second section of the express crashed into it.

The shunting engine was forced upon the platform, and smashed into a waiting room and a refreshment buffet.

People who rushed to help those in the wrecked room found that the driver of the light engine and another man were dead. The driver's name is believed to be Butler and his address Manorroad, Bletchley.

As the injured people were lifted from the wreckage in the darkness, railway officials gave the word, "Ignore the black-out," and then the powerful lights were switched on.

There was heavy rain, mist limiting visibility to twenty yards.

Shook Building Down

The fireman of the light engine is thought to be killed. A shunter and a waitress, who was serving in the buffet, are injured. The waitress was flung against a tea urn and scalded.

Buried in the wreckage were thought to be the driver and fireman of the second portion of the express and some passengers.

Mr. G. Jarvis, of the Park Hotel, Bletchley, said, "The engines did not mount the platform. It was the terrific concussion that brought the waiting room and buffet down."

The express was running in three portions. The third portion was stopped further down the line.

Bletchley School Clinic was converted into a casualty clearing station and ambulances from all over the district took seven more seriously injured twenty miles to Northampton Hospital.

The black-out restrictions were withdrawn in the neighbourhood of the clinic.

B.B.C. Will Broadcast Battles

The B.B.C. is planning eventually to broadcast battles on the Western Front, says a British United Press message from France.

A mobile broadcasting unit has already reached G.H.Q. It is equipped to give direct broadcasts but first relays will be on gramophone records, flown to London.

A GERMAN AIR RAID ON ENGLAND HAS BEEN BEATEN OFF BY R.A.F. PLANES. NO ENEMY MACHINES REACHED OUR SHORES.

Facts of the raid that failed were revealed by four German flyers, picked up in the North Sea, when they were landed yesterday in Denmark.

They said they formed part of a squadron of eighteen planes which set out to bomb the Tyne area.

Bombs Destroy Plane

Near Tyneside they were met by British warplanes. Three R.A.F. machines, they said, engaged their plane in a dog-fight. The Germans were machine-gunned and shot down.

The R.A.F. planes then flew off, but one swooped down to signal to a Danish ship that the Germans were down and in distress.

The British airmen then returned, watched the Germans being picked up, then bombed and destroyed the Nazi plane.

Let Crew Escape

The rescued Germans added that the British 'planes did not bomb their machine until the crew had escaped.

The Danish steamer, says British-United Press, landed the four Germans yesterday at Rudkjobing, near Svendborg, Denmark.

As they were picked up in international waters they will probably be allowed to go back to Germany.

THREE KINGS TO BACK FINNS

THREE Northern Kings are to meet in Stockholm, Sweden's capital, on Wednesday to discuss the Soviet demands on Finland.

The Kings are:—

Gustav of Sweden, who, at eighty-one, is known to the British public chiefly as a tennis player;

Christian of Denmark, who is expected to arrive in Stockholm with his Foreign Minister, Dr. Munch, on Tuesday, and

Haakon of Norway.

President Kallio, of Finland, is to attend the meeting.

Other neutrals may be invited to a later conference.

The conference meets at the invitation of King Gustav. It was he who invited the Kings of Denmark and Norway to Malmo in 1914 to seek means of preserving Scandinavian neutrality.

Meanwhile the Swedish Government is strengthening its defences in Upper Norrland, in North-East Sweden, near the Finnish border.

President Roosevelt revealed in Washington

Continued on Back Page

DAILY MIRROR, Tuesday, Oct. 17, 1939.

Daily Mirror

No. 11,189
ONE PENNY
Registered at the G.P.O as a Newspaper.

FIRST BOMBS ON BRITAIN: 4 NAZIS DOWN, CRUISER HIT

The Boy Heroes of Britain: A Story to Make You Proud (See P. 11)

Fourteen German bombing planes in a daylight raid on British warships in the Firth of Forth, yesterday dropped the first bombs on Britain since the war began.

The enemy first sent scouting planes over Edinburgh and the Forth, then, in the early afternoon the bombers appeared over the Pentland Hills, dive-bombed the famous Forth Bridge, aimed ten or more bombs on warships anchored off Rosyth, great naval base.

One British warship, the cruiser Southampton, was hit as a glancing bomb struck her bows. Splinters caused 35 casualties among men of the Navy.

Four at least of the German raiders were shot down in flames.

No civilians were killed or injured. No property was damaged. A stray dog was killed by falling shrapnel.

In many of the towns round the Forth no air-raid warning was given, and for a time even officers of the defence forces thought the raiders were British planes.

Crowds Watch Battle

In Edinburgh men and women crowded into the streets as the anti-aircraft guns opened fire, stayed to watch one of the most thrilling air combats ever seen over Britain.

One Nazi raider, twisting, turning and diving to dodge out of the bursting shells, swooped to within 200ft. of the roofs, then straightened up and vanished behind a hill with the shells still bursting on his tail.

The attack, launched on Rosyth as an apparent reprisal for the British raid on Kiel, was maintained in a series of raids, always repulsed as our fighters chased the bombers out to sea.

Crashed in Flames

THREE BOMBERS WERE SHOT DOWN BY R.A.F. PLANES; ONE CRASHED IN FLAMES AS IT WAS CAUGHT IN THE FIRE OF OUR ANTI-AIRCRAFT GUNS.

"I was sitting at home with my sister," Miss J. Kerr, of South Queensferry, said "when we heard the noise of many planes I said, 'That's the sound you'll hear when the Germans come.'

"I looked out of my window, and to my amazement saw two big black aeroplanes.

"They dived on Forth Bridge and we saw the bombs hurtling down. Great spouts of water splashed up as the bombs fell, but the bridge was undamaged.

"At once our guns opened fire. Then

Continued on Back Page

35 MEN INJURED IN RAID

OFFICIAL news of the raid, released last night, said:

"To-day, October 16, between 9 a.m. and 1.30 p.m., several German aircraft reconnoitred Rosyth. This afternoon, about 2.30, a series of bombing raids began.

"These were directed at the ships lying in the Forth and were conducted by about a dozen machines.

"All the batteries opened fire upon the raiders and the R.A.F. fighter squadron ascended to engage them.

"No serious damage was done to any of his Majesty's ships. One bomb glanced off the cruiser Southampton causing slight damage and sank the Admiral's barge and pinnace.

"There were three casualties on board the Southampton and seven on board the cruiser Edinburgh from splinters.

"Another bomb fell near the destroyer Mohawk, which was returning to harbour from convoy escort.

"This bomb burst on the water and its splinters caused twenty-five casualties to the men on the deck of the destroyer. Only superficial damage was caused to the vessel, which, like the others, is ready for sea.

"On the other hand, four bombers at least out of the twelve or fourteen were brought down, three of them by fighters of the R.A.F.

"The first contact between R.A.F. aircraft and the enemy raiders took place off May Island, at the entrance to the Firth of Forth, at 2.35 p.m., when two enemy aircraft were intercepted.

"They were driven down by our aircraft from 4,000ft. to within a few feet of the water and chased out to sea. Another enemy aircraft was engaged ten minutes later over Dalkeith. It fell in flames.

"Within a quarter of an hour combat took place off Crail and the second raider crashed into the sea. A third German aircraft was destroyed in the pursuit.

"Two German aviators had been rescued by one of our destroyers, of whom one has since died.

"No civilian casualties have been reported and none occurred in the Royal Air Force."

Navy Sink Nazi Warship

A GERMAN warship was sunk in a battle with British ships and planes off the Norwegian coast, according to fishermen who watched the action.

The story is told in the *Gula Tidende*, of Bergen, Norway. The fishermen, returning to the Norwegian mainland from Vaagsoe Island, say that the battle took place on Saturday. It lasted for two hours.

They heard heavy gunfire and saw columns of smoke, and through a telescope saw one warship engaged in a running fight with three others, which were British, and a number of aircraft. The lone warship appeared to be trying to escape to Norwegian territorial waters.

The fishermen report that the warship was badly damaged and seemed to be settling in the water. They think that the ship sank.

The Nazis indulged in an orgy of naval claims yesterday. Last night the British authorities described them as "absurd invention."

After the German Supreme Command claimed that the U-boat that had sunk the Royal Oak had "severely damaged H.M.S. Repulse and put her out of commission," the German radio claimed that H.M.S. Hood, the largest battleship in the world, had been "severely damaged" when aircraft dropped two 600lb bombs on her in the North Sea.

"Fantastic Claims"

Later, the German Supreme Command issued a "corrected" communique which said that the Repulse had been "torpedoed," but the effect of the alleged action was not given.

A joint communique issued by the Admiralty, the Air Ministry and the Ministry for Home Security last night describes as "an absurd invention" the claim that the Repulse had been damaged.

"In view of the habit of the German wireless of making fantastic claims," the statement adds, "it must be again repeated that neither the Repulse nor any other British warship has been damaged by hostile attack except as mentioned in the statements of the Admiralty."

TANKS LOST IN ATTACK

Germans lost more than twenty tanks and suffered from 500 to 1,000 casualties in yesterday's attack in the Moselle region, it was announced in Paris this morning.

The French, anticipating an attack on a four-mile front, withdrew from their advance positions, and left large numbers of mines in them.

Several hundred Germans, among them men wearing steel vests and visors and carrying machine-guns, advanced. The mines then exploded, killing a large number of them.

The French next opened heavy artillery fire, disorganising the enemy and forcing them to retreat. The French then reoccupied all their advance positions. — British United Press.

Four-mile Front Attack Repulsed—page 2.

DAILY MIRROR, Friday, October 20, 1939.

Daily Mirror

No. 11,192 — ONE PENNY
Registered at the G.P.O. as a Newspaper.

THE TERMS

Terms of the treaty signed with Turkey last night are:

France and Britain come to Turkey's aid if she is attacked; or if she is involved in a war in the Mediterranean as the result of an act of aggression by a European Power.

Turkey will come to the aid of Britain and France if an act of aggression by a European Power involves them in a Mediterranean war; or if Britain and France have to go to war as a result of their guarantees to Greece and Rumania.

Immediate consultations are to take place between the three countries if an act of aggression menaces any one of them.

Nothing in the Treaty can compel Turkey to go to war with Russia.

The pact is to last 15 years.

THE DUKE OF WINDSOR talking to a French General at headquarters "Somewhere in France." The Duke is working as liaison officer with the French Army. Other pictures on back page. *(Pathe Gazette.)*

TURKEY IS OUR NEW ALLY

BRITAIN and France signed a treaty with Turkey in Ankara last night, two days after the Soviet-Turkish negotiations had been broken off in Moscow.

News of the signing was announced by Mr. Chamberlain in dramatic fashion in the House of Commons last night, writes the "Daily Mirror" political correspondent.

He rose suddenly in the middle of a routine debate, asked leave to interrupt. The Speaker agreed.

Bells ringing all over the House brought M.P.s hurrying in to hear the announcement. And when Mr. Chamberlain revealed that the pact had been signed half an hour before, the House broke into the loudest cheer heard since war began.

The Premier explained that the Pact in its present form had been agreed by the three parties three weeks ago. The signing was postponed in the hope that Turkey and Russia would sign a treaty on parallel lines.

The Russian negotiations have been temporarily suspended.

"It has been announced both from Moscow and Ankara," Mr. Chamberlain said, "that Turkey's relations with the Soviet Government continue to rest on a foundation of friendship."

Mr. Attlee, for the Labour Party, and Sir Percy Harris, for the Liberals, congratulated the Government on a major diplomatic success.

Success it is, for the modern Turkey that stands guard over the Dardanelles is a valuable friend, a vital ally.

Her standing army of 200,000 can be expanded at once into mobilised, trained divisions fit for any phase of war.

For Germany the signing of the Pact is a political reverse. It is generally believed that Russia and Turkey would have reached agreement had not Herr von Ribbentrop persuaded Stalin to raise his demands so as to weaken Anglo-Turkish friendship.

The German newspaper *Lokal Anzeiger* warns Turkey: "Germany and Russia are friendly. Turkey's attitude must be evaluated with regard to these friendly relations."

German Plan Shattered

In Berlin, says Associated Press, it is admitted that the pact shatters Germany's plan to enlist the support of the South-Eastern European States, but it is hinted that a coming joint statement by Germany and Russia will change the atmosphere.

But as Germany stood by to see her enemies triumph in the Mediterranean, the Red Army was on the march.

Russian troops yesterday poured into Estonia to man the military bases granted to the Soviet.

As civic guards and police guarded the routes taken by the Russian army, Estonian newspapers and radio stations were silent about the arrival of the troops.

Drinking in the occupied areas was forbidden. A military censorship was applied. The Russian soldiers were forbidden to talk to the inhabitants.

Bulgaria, Turkey's neighbour to the north, was plunged into crisis. The Government that

Cont'd Back Page, Col. 1

Heroism Is Just a Job

"The R.A.F. last night conducted a successful reconnaissance over North-West Germany. The aircraft taking part reached their objectives, and all returned safely."—Air Ministry announcement last night.

THAT is "officialese" for unspectacular heroism. Yesterday Sir Kingsley Wood, Air Minister, visited an R.A.F. aerodrome in France and learned the real story behind such communiques.

Sir Kingsley, paying the first visit to the front by a British Cabinet Minister, spoke to the pilots and crews of planes which have flown hundreds of miles over Germany on reconnaissance flights—sometimes over the great industrial area of the Ruhr.

Flying with German Messerschmidts "blowing hell out of our tail" and anti-aircraft shells spreading white mushrooms of smoke and shells round you is "something of a job," according to one pilot.

He looked as if he ought to have been at school instead of flying one of Britain's big warplanes in bullet-scattered air above the Western Front.

"All Hell Broke Loose . . ."

"Three of us went over in perfect weather," he said. We went into a dirty bit and were forced lower. This was fine for taking pictures, but also fine for the German anti-aircraft guns.

"All hell started to break loose around our plane. She was jumping around from concussion and exploding shells. We had an awful time keeping her trim.

"We had just about succeeded when their fighters hit us. They came down on our tail and opened fire about four wing lengths away. I never stopped to count 'em.

"All I knew was the sky seemed full of them. We dived down to get away and it worked. We lost them, turned and headed back, and didn't waste any time.

"We didn't have any pictures, but we went back a couple of days later and got them."

Another flyer, a big sergeant who had been in the Air Force since 1925, found it downright boring. In a Scottish accent he said:

"We went over in daytime to take pictures. The weather was terrible, and we couldn't

Cont'd Back Page, Col. 3

SAVED 400 AS HAIR BLAZED

FROM OUR OWN CORRESPONDENT

NEW YORK, Thursday.

THE red hair of telephonist Marcia Smith was burned off as, surrounded by flames and smoke, she called hundreds of rooms in a Broadway hotel today.

"The place is on fire.
"Keep cool, but get out quickly."

Her heroism saved 400 guests.

When she had made her last call she fell unconscious.

Firemen wearing gas masks rescued her.

A young man worked the only undamaged lift until he collapsed, overcome by smoke. Dozens of times the lift travelled down the blazing building to the lobby.

He carried 300 guests to safety. The remainder fled by the fire escapes.

JUTLAND GUNFIRE

Heavy gunfire was heard west of Skagen, in Northern Jutland, yesterday afternoon and also last night, according to reports from Skagen.

It is impossible to localise the site of any engagement at present.—British United Press.

CAVALRY OUT ON WEST

FOR the first time in the war cavalry have been in action on the Western Front.

The cavalry, with some infantry support, were left behind to keep contact with the enemy when the Nazis advanced on a four-mile front after the bulk of the troops had been withdrawn.

They then withdrew in accordance with orders, states a French war communique, issued last night.

"This movement was successfully effected over the whole front on a depth which at certain points amounted to almost six miles," says the communique.

"The units involved took their stand as had been planned on a line organised beforehand, far in advance of our system of permanent fortifications, and only suffered very light losses."

But one detachment of an officer and fifty rank and file was out-flanked by the enemy and cut off.

Attacked on all sides, it fought back with desperate courage, inflicting heavy losses on the Germans.

The Front has now been stabilised on the lines which had been planned. A number of prisoners were taken by the French.

Rain is fighting Hitler in West.—See page 3.

We Have Scapa Map —Nazis

According to German circles in Amsterdam, the German Naval Command has had a detailed plan of the minefields protecting Scapa Flow in its possession for several months, says Exchange.

They made this claim in their jubilation over the sinking of the Royal Oak by a German U-boat, which penetrated the defences of Scapa Flow and then successfully escaped.

104

DAILY MIRROR, Saturday, October 21, 1939.

Daily Mirror

No. 11,193 — ONE PENNY
Registered at the G.P.O. as a Newspaper.

TAKE A SMACK AT ADOLF !

CUT THIS PAGE OUT!

Pin it or stick it up on the wall. If you are in a pub, PLEASE ask the landlord FIRST.

A STATEMENT BY CASSANDRA

The Editor has today put this front page at my disposal.

In terms of advertising space it could not be bought for a thousand pounds, but we believe that no effort is too great to make our Fund for sending dartboards to the troops a roaring success. The War Office is co-operating, and judging by the first results the British public is going to help in a big way.

I ask you to send me a donation. In one way, I don't really care whether the amount is big or small, for I know you will give what you can afford.

I know what it's like to be broke, and I know that a penny to one person is the same as a tenner to another.

But I want YOU to help.

✦ ✦ ✦

Forget for a moment that this page is being read by other people.

I'm talking to YOU.

For all I know, you may hate my guts, and loathe the stuff I write. But this time I'm bowling on a good wicket. There's nothing fake about this scheme. I am determined (sorry this sounds a bit like Adolf !) to see that the troops get dartboards—and good ones at that.

As a player myself, I can assure you that the boards we have ordered are absolutely first class.

I'm counting on YOU.

Stamps, coppers, silver, postal orders, notes or cheques.

Surely you can send something—but I know you will !

✦ ✦ ✦

Now just a word to pubs and all people who go there.

Get together and start a little fund for your pub. Seven-and-six will buy one dartboard and six darts.

Get your pub to buy a board for the boys over there.

Now I'll tell you what I'll do.

On every board there is going to be a little metal plate. If you'll send me the money for one board (or more) I'll see that the name of YOUR pub goes on the metal plate. Fair enough ?

That's fine. MONEY, GENTLEMEN, PLEASE !

With all good wishes,

From yours sincerely,

Cassandra.

SIXPENCE, PLEASE !

Any lady or gentleman whose dart falls so wide of Old Handsome that it lands on the above Mister Goering must immediately send at least sixpence to the "Daily Mirror" Cassandra Fund. This is a command—not a request !

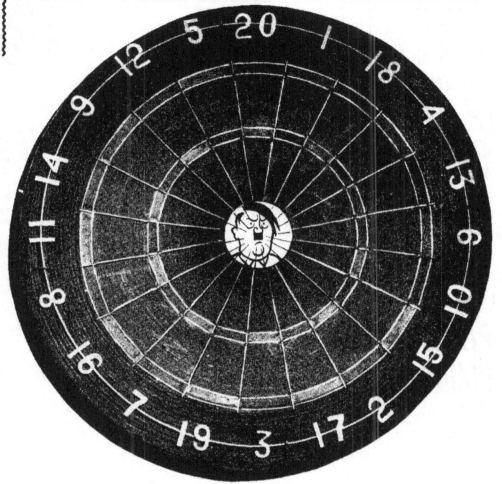

Cut this page out. Pin it up.

And take a smack at Old Nasty !

See that stoopid moustache? See that silly face? See that ridiculous hank of Nazi hair? Well, take a dart and plonk the blighter slick in the middle of his ugly kisser.

WHOP ! GOT 'IM !

Feel better? Of course you do. ANYBODY WHO MISSES THE PERISHER OWES THIS FUND HALF A CROWN, AND NO BACKING OUT. But what about the troops in the trenches? Friends, they are out to paste Adolf good and proper. Leave the job to them. They'll fix him. But all the same, they need relaxation from what is, after all, the toughest job in the world.

They want something to help them forget the mud, the weary waiting, and the strain of war.

What could be better than a game of darts ?

We of the " Daily Mirror " have started a great campaign to send thousands of dartboards to our soldiers, sailors and airmen.

Will YOU help ?

Let's ALL see to it that the chaps who are doing the real work in this war are not going to be bored for lack of equipment for a game of darts.

The money is already coming in—but we want more of it—AND FASTER !

There's no time to lose. Hundreds of thousands of men are already at their action stations—and maybe your husband, your boy, or perhaps your father is with them doing his bit. We know of no game which is more typically British than darts. Every shilling you send brings cheer and comfort to those who have undertaken the hardest part of this struggle.

Every shilling you contribute to this fund is a smack in the eye for Adolf.

Why not have a couple of bob's worth? Thanks friends. Send your donation to: The "Daily Mirror" Cassandra Fund, Rolls Buildings, Fetter-lane, E.C.4.

DAILY MIRROR, Tuesday, October 24, 1939.

Daily Mirror

No. 11,195   ✦ ✦   ONE PENNY
Registered at the G.P.O. as a Newspaper.

4 MEAT MEALS A WEEK—RATION ORDERS

'Jigsaw' Code Kept Secret of Finns

The conversations on which weak but doughty Finland's fate will depend opened at the Kremlin at 6 p.m. last night and ended two and a half hours later.

These talks were held in the utmost secrecy. So that not a word of them should leak out the code message which the Finnish delegation afterwards sent off from Moscow was cut up into small strips and distributed among a number of officials for deciphering. None knows what the others had. It was left to the Foreign Minister, M. Erkko, to co-ordinate the whole.

It is typical of the coolness with which Finland is facing the present situation that, according to a report published by the "Berlinske Aftenavis," M. Erkko spent Sunday swimming and fishing in the Archipelago.

When the Finnish negotiators, Dr. Juho Paasikivi and Social-Democrat Finance Minister Vaino Tanner, arrived in Moscow yesterday, they were met by a few minor Russian officials.

Dr. Paasikivi, now assisted by M. Tanner, was continuing the negotiations he started on October 11 and interrupted four days later to return home and place before the Helsingfors Government Russia's demands.

Ship, Planes, Sink 3 U-Boats

Three more German U-boats have been sent to their doom.

REPORTS received last night tell of one sunk after being holed in an hour's losing battle with an armed merchant ship and two sunk by R.A.F. bombers.

Story of the merchant ship's gallant fight was told by Mr. Robert Whelan, a deckhand, of Elinhurst-crescent, St. Thomas, Swansea. He said they were three days out from the Bristol Channel, bound for America, when the U-boat was sighted.

"We in the gun crew immediately rushed to our gun," he said, "and returned the U-boat's fire. The fight continued for over an hour before we beat off the submarine.

"Two hours later we found that our ship was holed on the water-line while our starboard lifeboat was full of shrapnel holes, so we had to turn round and head back for port.

"In response to an S O S, warships came and escorted us. In the evening the U-boat was sighted again. It was unable to submerge, having been holed by our gun, and was quickly sunk by our escort.

"Only one of our gun crew was injured, and he only slightly."

Patches of Oil

Air Ministry announcements tell of the two other U-boat sinkings, one in the North Sea and one in the Atlantic.

The report of the North Sea attack says:

A reconnaissance aircraft sighted and attacked a submarine in position. A salvo of anti-submarine bombs was dropped ahead of the periscope. The submarine dived steeply.

The air-gunner said definitely that he noticed a second under-water explosion after the explosion of these bombs. The aircraft then turned about, flew over the submarine a second time, and dropped a second salvo.

Patches of oil were observed after the first salvo, and more extensively after the second attack.

Nothing more was seen of the U-boat.

"Direct Hit"

The pilot of the Atlantic patrol plane says:

An enemy submarine was sighted some distance away. It dived and heavy bombs were dropped on it. The first is thought to have been a direct hit.

Dark objects appeared in the water after the attack, and air bubbles rose to the surface.

A second bombing attack was made as near to the same position as possible.

We circled over the area for some time, but nothing further was observed.

As these reports were issued, news is released of the valuable work done in protecting convoys by men and planes of the Auxiliary Air Force—the "Territorials" of the Air.

A large convoy of merchant ships in the

Continued on Back Page

RAIDERS 16 HOURS ADRIFT

HOW he picked up three German airmen—one of them wounded—who had drifted for sixteen hours in a rubber float after being shot down in the North Sea convoy raid, was told last night by a Grimsby trawler skipper.

He also saw the rescue of three other Germans by nearby trawlers.

The pilot of the seaplane told him that Saturday, the day of the raid, was the first anniversary of the birth of his son.

"We saw three German seaplanes pursued by four British fighters," the skipper said. "One of the machines came down on the sea belching smoke and overturned.

"Other trawlers picked up three airmen, then, just before dawn on Sunday, we saw a collapsible rubber float with three young men in it. One was wounded in the knee by a machine-gun bullet, and I dressed his injuries.

"One, a lieutenant, who spoke good English, told me that they had been in the water sixteen hours. We gave them cigarettes, food and dry clothes, and I put a splint on the injured man's leg.

"We brought them back to Grimsby and handed them over to the Naval authorities."

The Nobel Peace Prize!

Whether the Nobel Peace Prize will be awarded as usual this year through the Norwegian Storthing (Parliament) has yet to be decided.

Under the heading, "Unworthy of the Peace Prize?" a Malmo newspaper quotes a member of the Nobel Foundation as saying that "as far as can be judged now," there will probably be no Nobel Festivity this year.

VICTORY SOON, SAYS HITLER

HITLER told the Nazi leaders yesterday that a German victory was assured; boasted that he would soon bring Britain to her knees.

He had to boast, for his Gauleiters, party leaders from all districts of the Reich, had told him the public reaction to the war. They revealed doubts and uneasiness.

But Hitler, demanding sacrifices as the price of German domination of the world, dangled the promise of a quick victory.

In Berlin, says British United Press, it is believed that Hitler is staking his success on intensified air and sea attacks on Britain and British shipping.

Some German officials hint that hostilities will begin in the Mediterranean before there is any real fighting on the Western Front.

In London, says the "Daily Mirror" Political Correspondent, it is believed that Hitler is staging a new attempt to impress neutral opinion. He will create a new German Parliament and hold a plebiscite throughout the country on th issue of peace or war.

Stalin's "No"

Any plebiscite held by the Nazis would, of course, be a dictated vote.

Meanwhile, Hitler's request to Stalin for military aid—includin the supply of 2,000 warplanes—has been rejected, writes the London correspondent of L'Oeuvre. Russia also said "no" to the Nazi request that Soviet trade with Britain and France should cease.

German newspapers were sarcastic yesterday about Mr. Duff Cooper's statement in America that a revolution of the German Right Wing was a possibility.

But no mention was made of the reported purge of German generals.

Among the arrested generals are believed to be General von Bock, retired commander of the First Army; von Hammerstein, ex-chief of the General Staff; and von Stalpnagel, a renowned German military expert.

Ribbentrop speaks in Danzig tonight. "It will be of great political importance," it was said in Berlin.

MEAT rationing is to come into force almost at once. The "Daily Mirror" learned last night that the necessary ten days' notice is about to be given.

The Ministry of Food stated last night that every man, woman and child will receive two coupons a week—and a half coupon will be considered sufficient for the purchase of a really good portion of meat for one meal.

Restaurants, in fact, will take one half coupon on each occasion rationed meat is served with a meal.

Families, however, will be much better off than those who eat all their meals in hotels or restaurants.

Where the ration cards can be pooled, a food expert told the "Daily Mirror" last night, there may easily be sufficient rationed meat to enable it to be served almost every day if cooked in economical fashion.

It is not expected that offal—kidneys, liver, sweetbreads, etc. — will be rationed, nor will rabbit, hare and game, according to present plans.

The weekly ration of ham and bacon will be additional to the meat ration, not, as was at one time expected, part of it.

If You Complain?

It has not yet been decided what steps will be taken if a housewife should complain of the quality of her meat rations. Whether it will be possible to exchange a portion or not is unknown.

Vegetarians may be allowed to exchange their meat coupons for other foods.

Snack bar proprietors are hoping that the scheme will not mean the end of meat sandwiches on their counters.

"We have stock for meat sandwiches which will last for weeks yet," one of them told the Daily Mirror. "We hope that we shall be allowed to go on serving them until our stock runs out. After that we shall be able to serve tinned meats."

All Equal

"This is to ensure that everybody has an opportunity of getting an equal quantity of meat," said a Ministry official. "It is not because of the temporary shortage of imported meat."

A London restaurant proprietor, when told of the two-coupon ration, said his whole menu would now have to be re-organised.

"Fifty per cent. of the meals I serve are with meat," he said. "This will mean we shall have to prepare for far more vegetarian meals.

"There will be an increase in omelettes, spaghetti, salads and tinned foods. But attractive meals can be served without meat."

The Ministry pointed out that, in the last war the ration amounts fluctuated from time to time. At the moment no one could say that this meat ration would be maintained in the same proportion for the duration of war.

AMBASSADOR RECALLED

Japan has recalled her Ambassador in Berlin, Mr. Hiroshi Oshima, it was announced last night. He will be replaced by the Japanese Ambassador to Belgium, Mr. Saburo Kuruso, says Associated Press.

Mr. Oshima has held the post since November last year.

DAILY MIRROR, Thursday, Nov. 2, 1939

Daily Mirror

No. 11,203   ONE PENNY
Registered at the G.P.O. as a Newspaper.

4oz. of Butter 4oz. of Bacon

ANGRY M.P.s PROTEST AT FOOD CUTS

A FIERCE political storm was last night blowing up over the Government's decision on the rationing of butter and bacon.

Four ounces of each will, it was announced, be the weekly allowance per head after a date, still to be fixed, in the middle of December.

The Opposition are planning a bitterly critical motion which will, they hope, embarrass the Government. It is mainly directed against the butter ration of four ounces per head a week.

M.P.s are asking why the Government did not import vast reserves of butter and put it in cold storage at the outbreak of war. The Government claim that it could not be stored is likely to be challenged.

It is also argued that Britain's meagre butter ration will be exploited by the Nazi propaganda department.

Although the German butter ration is only 2.5 ounces a head, it was not expected by M.P.s that our ration would be so small as four ounces.

When he announced the rationing decision in the House of Commons yesterday Mr. W. S. Morrison, the Minister of Food, made this statement about other articles of food:

SUGAR.—Purchases are restricted to 1lb. per head a week. There will be supplies for some months. In the meantime, consumers must register for sugar.

MEAT.—" Adequate supplies should continue to be available."

MARGARINE. — Manufacture has been greatly increased since the war.

COOKING FATS.—Quantity is equal to normal

TEA.—There will be no " pool."—" I hope no such scheme will be needed for a considerable time, if at all."

Explaining why this rationing was needed, Mr. Morrison said that since both bacon and butter were perishable, neither being suitable for storage, no Government reserve of either commodity existed on the outbreak of war.

Books by Post

He pointed out that ration books were printed more than twelve months ago. Consequently they contained coupons for many foodstuffs which it was not necessary to ration now—that is, for meat, margarine, cooking fats and sugar.

For the Labour Opposition, Mr. Alexander declared the Minister's statement "profoundly unsatisfactory." He said the Opposition would demand a day to discuss the whole question.

Broadcasting last night, Mr. Morrison explained that the ration books will be delivered through the post. You must not all expect them to arrive on the same day. If you have not received your book during, say, the next fortnight, you should make inquiry of the Local Food Office. [Full details about what to do are on page 2.]

There will be one coupon each week for

Continued on Back Page

Sunk by U-Boat in U.S. Zone

FOR the first time since America declared that her neutral zone extended to 300 miles of ocean, a German submarine yesterday sank a British merchant ship in U.S. waters.

In Washington last night it was stated that more details are awaited before action is taken. A strong protest is likely to be sent to Berlin.

News of the U-boat attack was first received by the Mackay Radio Corporation of New York, whose operators picked up the call .. SOS .. SOS submarine SOS.

Canadian coastal stations instantly sent out alarm signals, radioed the steamer to send details of her position.

But the doomed ship was silent. The U-boat had struck.

It is now established that the ship, the Coulmore (3,700 tons) of Glasgow, owned by Dornoch Shipping Company, was sunk southeast of Boston and well within America's declared neutral zone.

Rescue was quickly organised. A U.S. ship altered her course and steamed 200 miles to the scene. Three coastguard cutters raced towards the steamer.

Destroyers Join Search

Destroyers and aeroplanes joined in the search.

One of the cutters, the George M. Bibb, radioed last night that she had reached the spot indicated. There was no sign of survivors.

The other two cutters were forced to abandon the search by the southerly gale that swept the sea.

The Liverpool steamer Bronte, of 5,317 tons, was sunk yesterday by a U-boat in the Atlantic. A crew of forty and one passenger, Mr. G. H. Kressel-Williams, an inventor, were on board. All were saved.

One of the crew was fireman Andrew Quinn, aged thirty-two, of Liverpool. Nine days before he had been in the liner Ionic Star that ran aground.

NUFFIELD'S BIG DEFENCE JOB

Lord Nuffield has been appointed Air Ministry Director-General of Maintenance.

He will be responsible to the Air Council—through the Air Member for Supply and Organisation, Air Vice-Marshal Welsh—for the repair of aircraft.

He will also supervise the R.A.F. Supply Services.

Lord Nuffield will be assisted by Mr. Oliver Boden, managing director of Morris Motors, Ltd. Both will receive no salary.

'TREASURE' DIES IN FLAT

TREASURE MUFFET, the girl who should have given evidence in the Birmingham blackmail case today, was last night found dead in a gas-filled room in a flat at Alexandra-road, Hampstead.

Beside her, also dead, was Miss Maire Williams, aged twenty-two, with whom she took the flat a few weeks ago.

Police believe that the women had been dead for several days. The discovery was made by the owner of the apartment house in Alexandra-road, where the women were living.

She saw water dripping from the kitchenette of the flat and went to investigate.

Mrs. Muffet should have attended Handsworth Police Court this morning.

She was to give further evidence in a case in which William Ronald Ward, aged twenty-seven, of Heathfield-road, Handsworth, is charged with attempting to obtain £500 from a Mr. X with menaces.

It had been alleged that Ward threatened to expose Mr. X as a Nazi spy unless he was paid £500.

Giving evidence last Thursday, Mrs. Muffet admitted pretending that she was German and speaking broken English when talking to Mr. X.

Mrs. Mabel (Treasure) Muffet and (left) Miss Maire Williams, who were found dead yesterday in a gas - filled room at Alexandra-road, Hampstead, N.W. Mrs. Muffet was to have given evidence today in a blackmail case at Birmingham.

NEW TRADE TALK WITH RUSSIA

BY OUR POLITICAL CORRESPONDENT

AN important trade deal is now being negotiated between Britain and Russia.

Russia requires wool, cocoa and certain kinds of gum. Britain is prepared to barter these for wood and wood pulp. The talks may extend to other commodities and a far-reaching trade agreement between the two countries may be signed shortly.

Germany's trade delegation now in Moscow announced a surprise last night. They are going home today. It is believed they have reached deadlock.

Count von Schulenberg, the German Ambassador in Moscow is also going back to Berlin today for consultations with Herr Hitler.

ARSENAL GUN PHOTOS LOST

SCOTLAND YARD has been notified of the loss at Woolwich on Tuesday afternoon of a series of photographic negatives belonging to the War Department.

It is stated that the negatives relate to a gun.

The film, it is understood, was given with other packages to a messenger at a military establishment on Woolwich Common with instructions to take them to Woolwich Arsenal.

When the messenger arrived at the Arsenal, the negatives were missing from a roll of documents he was carrying.

On his way to the Arsenal the messenger had travelled in an omnibus and it is thought that the negatives may have been left on that vehicle.

Search is being made by the London Passenger Transport Board of the buses used on that route.

Anyone finding the negatives is asked to take them at once to a military establishment or police station.

DAILY MIRROR, Monday, Nov. 6, 1939.

Daily Mirror

No. 11,206 ✦ ONE PENNY
Registered at the G.P.O. as a Newspaper.

NORWAY TO DEFY NAZIS: INTERN CREW

TO LEAVE THE FRONT

A CENSUS is being taken in the Amalgamated Engineering Union of members " who have brains."

Those who are at the front are to be withdrawn to serve as tradesmen in the Forces or returned to home employment.

This was revealed by Mr. Fred Smith, general secretary of the union, in a speech at Swansea, South Wales.

Mr. Smith said that the union had " an undertaking " to that effect.

Labour Waste

Not only production of munitions but the export trade had to be kept going, he urged.

This, unlike others, was an engineering war. The union had found that a great number of their young men had been put into the line. No differentiation was wanted between them and others, but while the country required skilled engineers it was throwing away good labour if they were not utilised where required.

The Director of Mobilisation had thanked the union for its assistance, said Mr. Smith. "We will go on assisting the prosecution of the war to a successful issue," he said, "but we do not want to give 100 per cent. men to a 15 per cent. job."

KILLS BRIDE 'FOR THRILL'

FROM OUR OWN CORRESPONDENT

NEW YORK, Sunday.

"I'VE wanted the thrill of killing a person for some time. When I married Caroline I saw my chance," Robinson Hibberd, Springfield (Mass.), champion jitterbug, calmly told the police.

Thus twenty-year-old Hibberd callously confessed that he had murdered the bride to whom he had been wed only eight days.

He killed his eighteen-year-old wife while her bridal bouquet was still fresh in the refrigerator.

Just for a "thrill" he stabbed her to death as she lay asleep in bed, and afterwards dismembered her body.

"Luckiest Bride"

Shocked detectives who took Hibberd's confession call his New England's most revolting crime.

Hibberd's lively dancing to swing music made him the hero of all the girls in the local dance hall.

They adored him. When he married Caroline they called her the luckiest bride in the world.

At the police station Hibberd betrayed no emotion until he was shown the bouquet that his bride had so carefully kept fresh.

Then his self-control broke down. He hid his face in his hands and wept

NORWAY LAST NIGHT DEFIED THE MIGHT OF GERMANY, REFUSED TO LIBERATE THE PRIZE CREW ON BOARD THE CAPTURED U.S. STEAMER CITY OF FLINT, AND PUBLISHED A STATEMENT OF THE LEGAL POSITION.

While the steamer remained at anchor off Bergen, the Norwegian Government revealed that the German commander aboard had refused to leave the port.

" I have my orders from my Government," he said, " and I refuse to carry out your instructions to leave this port."

The Norwegians had then no choice. They decided, in accordance with neutral practice, to free the ship and intern the prize crew.

Germany at once lodged an official protest, couched in the strongest language. For a time it appeared that Norway, afraid of Nazi vengeance, might submit to the German demands.

But, within a few hours, it was announced that Norway had rejected the demand, had decided to take her stand on international law and to dare Germany to do her worst.

The official Norwegian report disclosed, too, that the German claim that they had brought the steamer to port because one of the American seamen was ill was easily revealed as a trick when Norwegian doctors went aboard.

Meanwhile the crew of the City of Flint are tired of being kept afloat. Shore leave has been forbidden.

They complain that they haven't seen a newspaper since the ship was captured by the Deutschland nearly a month ago.

Many members of the crew looked longingly towards the shore as reporters went alongside in a motor-boat last night.

"Where are you going now?" one reporter shouted.

"Brother, your guess is better than ours," said a seaman. "We heard on the radio last night we were going to Britain. Then we heard from another programme that we were going straight back to America.

Asked about their detention in Murmansk, another seaman said that the Russian port was full of ships, including many German prizes.

"It Was a Relief"

"We were there five days, and it was cold. The Russians paid no attention to us and gave us no protection.

"We heard we were going to be freed. Then we heard we were going to be taken to Germany. It was a relief when we finally got away, even if the Germans had us."

Mrs. Harriman, the U.S. Minister in Oslo, is expected to arrive in Bergen today for a conference with Captain Gainard, the U.S. skipper of the City of Flint.

—British United Press and Associated Press.

"Norway's rejection of the German protest over the City of Flint creates an entirely new situation and makes the problem considerably more acute," it was said in Nazi political quarters in Berlin last night.

Norway's two strong men: Johann ✶ Nygaardsvold (above), once a labourer in a sawmill, now Socialist Premier; and (left) King Haakon VII, 6 feet 3 inches tall, 67 years old.

Hitler to Buy in U.S.

—If He Can

A GERMAN plan to outwit the Allies in the American market by buying as many U.S. planes as they can was disclosed in Paris last night.

General Kuehl, a chief of the Nazi Air Force, is expected to head a mission to New York to carry through a big deal with American manufacturers.

Goering, it is reported, is urging Hitler to put large funds at his disposal for the U.S. deal, and promises him that all bombers bought in America will be flown direct to Germany.

But the plan is doomed to failure.

It is probably intended to gull the German public, says the Daily Mirror New York correspondent, and to attempt to minimise the great help now coming to the Allies.

Officials of American aircraft companies say it will be impossible for Germany to buy in America—even if she has the money.

No aeroplane manufacturer would dare to sell to Germany. The anti-Nazi movement is too strong.

If one manufacturer did take the risk, this is what would happen:—

1. Washington would bring pressure on the manufacturer not to sell to Germany because she is the aggressor nation. Sales to Japan were completely stopped this way.

2. United States Air Force would vigorously oppose sales to Germany.

It is doubtful, too, whether American firms would even sell war materials to Russia owing to her association with Germany.

Planes on Way

Meanwhile millions of pounds worth of aeroplanes and war materials are moving across America on their way to Britain and France.

Ten thousand men in Californian aircraft factories are starting work on day and night shifts.

In ports all along America's eastern seaboard British and French freighters are being hastily loaded with goods for the Allies. Nazi representatives in the United States, learning of the vast stocks of American war materials that are now available for the Allies, are crestfallen.

This, indeed, must be Hitler's unhappiest day since war started.

News of the President's signature of the "cash-and-carry" Neutrality Bill was flashed over the radio and millions of Americans sympathetic to the Allies celebrated. All over New York could be heard the happy words. "He's signed it." New York stock exchange prices rocketed in expectation of £20,000,000 Allied war orders. Practically every aviation stock soared to new heights.

CROWD ATTACK MOSLEY'S CAR

SIR OSWALD MOSLEY and his supporters were mobbed by the crowd at the close of a British Fascist Union meeting in a Wilmslow (Cheshire) cinema yesterday. Three people were injured.

As Sir Oswald's car swung round the corner of the cinema and drove past the fighting mob, one man ran alongside battering the car bonnet with his walking-stick.

Stones flew through the air, smashing the windows of two buses which moved off with Sir Oswald's supporters clambering aboard to escape the crowd's fury.

Holding a handkerchief to his face, a spectator, Mr. Thomas McGann, of Hawthornwalk, Wilmslow, told the Daily Mirror: "I got this with a razor."

As a contingent of Sir Oswald's supporters marched down the road to where one bus stopped to wait for them they were followed and surrounded by the crowd. It was several minutes before the road was cleared.

No arrests were made.

Goering Planning Gas War

Instructions issued yesterday by Goering the Nazi air chief, " for the safety of the population," suggest that Germany has not abandoned her plans for bombing civilians and using gas.

He is well aware that German towns run no risk unless British or French towns are attacked by German planes.

Yet Goering—says the Exchange—has ordered an investigation into the proper method of equipping air raid shelters, and issued a warning that the sandbagging of windows is not sufficient protection against gas.

DAILY MIRROR, Thursday, Nov. 9, 1939.

Daily Mirror

No. 11,209   ONE PENNY
Registered at the G.P.O. as a Newspaper.

HITLER ESCAPES ASSASSINATION BOMB, SIX DEAD

SHE WANTS TO BE WED
War Office Says, NO

Miss Joan Richardson (right), of Warrenpoint, Co. Down, asked for a permit to go to Singapore to marry Lieutenant Digby Morris (below).

Director of Movements at the War Office said: "Nothing doin'" — or words to that effect.

And now the War Minister is to be asked in Parliament to say "Yes."

(See story on page 3.)

A FEW minutes after Hitler had left the Munich Beer Hall where he spoke last night, an explosion wrecked part of the premises.

The cause is still not known, but all the facts point to an attempt to assassinate the Fuehrer in the very hall where Nazism was born.

Six people were killed and sixty injured. Among the Party leaders present were Goebbels, Hess, Julius Streicher, the Jew-baiter, and Dr. Ley. It is not known if any of them were hurt.

It was admitted that the occurrence was not an accident, but the work of an "explosive body," presumably a bomb.

Hitler remained in the beer cellar for some time after the ceremony. The explosion occurred twenty-seven minutes after he had finished speaking.

The Munich police said they were not permitted to disclose the number of casualties, says British United Press.

Hitler's speech was a tirade against Britain.

He blamed Britain for the war, shouted at British lies . . . British trickery . . . British envy . . . British culture . . British hate.

And in one passage of defiance he declared: "Germany never, never will capitulate. On the day that war broke out I gave Goering orders to prepare for a war of five years. Not that I believe that this war will last for five years, but because if it does last so long we shall not give in."

Hitler began by saying that the beer cellar Putsch, although a failure, was the start of the National-Socialist movement.

Recalling the defeat of 1918, he ascribed this to the failure of the Government of those days in allowing itself to be dragged into a war in unfavourable circumstances, and added:—

"The enemies of 1914-18 are the same as those of to-day."

Hitler said that the German soldier of 1914-1918 was unsurpassed by any enemy soldier.

"For Civilisation"

In 1914 it was said that Britain fought for justice and had done so for the past three centuries. She had received as a reward from the Lord forty million square kilometres and four hundred and eighty million people to be ruled by England.

England said she fought for civilisation, but only in the slum areas, the distressed areas and in Whitechapel was this civilisation of which England talked to be found.

England said she had fought for humanity. Then she said she did not fight against the German people, only against the German Government. That was said by Churchill and Chamberlain, who wanted to separate the German people from their Government.

"In 1918 the victors spoke of a just peace. England and France promised to disarm.

"If forty-four millions of people have succeeded.

Continued on Back Page

Continued on Back Page

2 DOWN IN CRAZY AIR DUEL

FIGHTING only 100ft. above the wave-tops, an R.A.F. pilot yesterday brought down two Nazi planes in one of the most thrilling air scraps of the war.

Two British planes, on reconnaissance over the North Sea, met three German machines and at once attacked.

One R.A.F. machine brought down a Nazi plane after five dives in quick succession, then turned and put out the second with two more dives just as his ammunition was exhausted.

"After the second dive attack," said the British pilot later, "the German rear gunner's cockpit was seen to be empty."

"After the fifth dive," added the pilot, "the enemy aircraft was seen going down partly out of control."

Met Second Attack

While this fight was going on the rear gunner of the British plane had seen the second German flying-boat coming up behind.

He signalled to the pilot. "That can wait," said the pilot. "It is still 1,000 yards away."

And he waited till he had downed his man before he turned to meet the second.

He made two attacks, and saw bullet holes appear in the nose of the enemy flying-boat. These bursts silenced the enemy's front guns.

"By this time, however, I had used all my front gun ammunition," the pilot added, "so I made three fairly tight circuits to give my rear gunner a shot."

The gunner's shooting was as accurate as the pilot had been. His bursts wrecked the wings and engines of the flying-boat.

Another R.A.F. plane signalled that he had destroyed a Nazi machine only one minute after reporting he had made contact.

Five Miles Up

And in France, a young New Zealand flyer, fighting higher than man has ever fought before, scored another victory for the R.A.F.

From five miles up over the Maginot Line he sent a Dornier 17, one of Germany's fastest reconnaissance machines, diving to earth.

The plane crashed in the middle of a French village several miles from the locality of the fight, and buried its nose 10ft. deep in the main street, bursting into flames.

Holland Widens Floods

HOLLAND and Belgium, fearful of a sudden attack by Hitler despite their offer to act as peace mediators, last night strengthened their defences.

Holland it is stated, has extended the flooded areas which will act as her "last barrier." At the same time it is reported from the Dutch frontier that German troops are at work preparing pontoons which could be used for the passage of flooded areas.

Belgium called up about 5,000 more men and the military authorities requisitioned many omnibuses.

This is described as the "completion of a measure already announced."

Meanwhile, the Germans are building pontoons near the frontier, and all troops on leave since the end of the Polish campaign have been recalled. Germans on the frontier zone are said to have gone into the interior.

Shock troops withdrawn from the east are now stationed on the Dutch-German frontier and are strongly armed with armoured cars and machine-guns.

Possibilities of Nazi aggression against Holland and Belgium are fully recognised by the British Government, writes the Daily Mirror Political Correspondent. It would bring Nazi air bases much nearer to our shores.

Whitehall believes that the mediation gesture by King Leopold and Queen Wilhelmina was a stroke of diplomacy which anticipated a possible Nazi ultimatum followed by an invasion of the Low Countries.

Mr. Chamberlain is expected to make a very brief reference to the matter during his speech at today's luncheon given by the Lord Mayor of London at the Mansion House.

Semi-official Berlin comment was that the peace appeal had "no great prospects of success."

"NO WORK, NO KISSES"—WIVES

FROM OUR OWN CORRESPONDENT
NEW YORK, Wednesday.

SHOUTING, "No work, no kisses!" wives of Detroit striking motor-car workers started a campaign today to make them go back to work.

Hundreds of wives have vowed they will deny their husbands affection until they stop the strike.

The "No kisses" campaign was started by Mrs. Clara Schindler, in emulation of Lysistrata, heroine of a Greek comedy, who led warriors' wives into withholding love until their men stopped fighting.

Mrs. Schindler told me on the phone: "We wives think the strike is silly, so we decided to take a lesson from Lysistrata.

"If the men stay on strike they will get no affection. We believe this will break the strike and bring them to their senses."

109

DAILY MIRROR, Saturday, Nov. 11, 1939

Daily Mirror

No. 11,211 ♦ ONE PENNY

Registered at the G.P.O. as a Newspaper.

"TILL MONDAY": NAZI LIMIT FOR DUTCH

Lights Are Going Out...

HOLLAND'S defence measures were intensified yesterday. All lighthouses along the Dutch north coast have been extinguished.

All lightships have been brought into port except the "Noord Hinder" at the mouth of the Maas. Enemy planes cannot now be guided by lights along the coast.

In the interior of the country, roads running eastward are being hastily blocked, to force cars to crawl round the barriers.—Exchange.

"The lights are going out all over Europe," Earl (then Sir Edward) Grey said in 1914. "Few in our time will see them lit again."

THE NAZI GOVERNMENT HAS DELIVERED A VIRTUAL ULTIMATUM TO HOLLAND —A DEMAND FOR SEA AND AIR BASES— WHICH MUST BE ANSWERED BEFORE MONDAY. IT IS BELIEVED IN BELGIUM THAT HOLLAND WILL ANSWER "NO."

The demands, says the "Daily Mirror" correspondent in Brussels, were the real reason King Leopold of the Belgians made his night dash to see Queen Wilhelmina at the meeting that produced the joint peace appeal.

The facts behind the move were revealed in Brussels yesterday at a secret meeting of Belgian M.P.s.

The German demands on Holland were for a free port in Amsterdam and for the establishment of Nazi air bases in the provinces of Friesland and Groningen. An answer before Monday was requested.

King Leopold made it clear to the Dutch that if Holland accepted the Nazi demands, his army would have to occupy the southern Dutch province of Zeeland, and part of Limburg, the frontier province which projects into Belgium.

The Belgian occupation of Zeeland would incorporate Flushing and the mouth of the Escaut, which is Belgium's main communication with the North Sea.

In either case, should a German invasion of Dutch territory take place, Belgium would throw open her frontiers to French troops.

Dutch and Belgian officials continued to deny last night reports that the joint peace offer was made under threat, or that it was issued as a way out of a dilemma.

In Paris it was reported that the German "ultimatum" had been delivered to Holland by the German Ambassador at The Hague.

He refused, according to the Paris reports, to put the Nazi demands in writing.

A neutrality speech last night by M. van Kleffens, Dutch Foreign Minister, was construed as another attempt to stave off the Nazi pressure.

Addressing the Dutch Lower House, he said

Continued on Back Page

Continued on Back Page

Saved Her Baby—Was Fined £3

OFFICIALDOM. That's what's going to win this war, boys. Officialdom and the strict application of the law, regardless of circumstances.

✦ ✦ ✦

Mrs. Anne Fleming knows now how the war is going to be won: how justice can be tempered with discretion.

She is a young wife who lives in Renfrew, and her baby Annette, six months old, is subject to fits.

When, in the night, she heard a short cry and the helpless choking sob of a child, she ran to the baby's room, lifted her from her cot . . . and switched on the light.

✦ ✦ ✦

The baby was in a fit. For minutes Mrs. Fleming tended her child. Then she remembered the lights. She turned to pull down the blind. Too late. The police were at the door and Mrs. Fleming's name and address were duly taken.

✦ ✦ ✦

At Paisley Sheriff Court Mrs. Fleming was introduced to the majesty of the law. The story was soon told. And Sheriff Hamilton turned to the accused, and gravely asked: "Have you no thought for the community?"

Mrs. Fleming doesn't know very much about the law. "But in another minute I might have lost my baby," she explained. She pleaded in vain.

✦ ✦ ✦

"It seems," said the Sheriff, "that some people never think of others."

And he fined her £3.

✦ ✦ ✦

Mrs. Fleming's husband is a fitter in an engineering shop. He has just gone back to work after a three weeks' illness. And £3 is a lot of money.

They've got the first thirty bob, and they're saving the rest as quickly as they can.

Now Mrs. Fleming has asked an M.P. to raise the case in the House of Commons.

"Being fined makes me feel like a criminal," she said last night. "Surely I did only what every other mother would have done."

✦ ✦ ✦

Tut! Tut! Mrs. Fleming. Are you still unrepentant? Don't you remember these grave judicial words: "Have you no thought for the community?"

And don't you know that this is how the war is going to be won?

Window of the War Office at 6.10 p.m. yesterday. (Black-out time 5.48 p.m.).

But they "doused the glim" two minutes later. The War Office was Whitehall's only offender last night.

They're learning the lesson of the light leaks.

Get Your New Pool Coupons in "Daily Mirror"

THE first of the new war-time football pool coupons will be published in the "Daily Mirror" next Wednesday, bringing the delights of the homes, aways and draws to your fireside once again. Completed coupons should be posted on Wednesday night to ensure safe receipt by Unity Pools, as the new comoine is being called.

Because of war-time restrictions, which make it impossible for a newsagent to order more copies of a paper than he can be sure of selling, the only way to be certain of obtaining your "Daily Mirror"—and your pools coupons—is to place a regular order. Do it now.

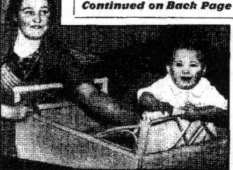

Mrs. Fleming with her six-month-old baby, Annette.

ENEMY PLANE SUNK AT SEA

TWO coastal command aircraft of the Royal Air Force yesterday engaged a Nazi plane—a Dornier flying-boat—off the East Coast of England, the Air Ministry announced last night.

They forced the enemy aircraft down on the water. A dinghy was seen to be launched from the plane and the crew got into it.

The aircraft was then seen to sink.

A second enemy aircraft then appeared and was promptly engaged, but it escaped in the clouds.

Raider Driven Off

People rushed out of their homes when they heard anti-aircraft guns firing at a German reconnaissance plane off the south-east coast of England yesterday.

Three British fighters suddenly appeared, but before they made contact the raider sought shelter in the clouds and scurried off across the Channel.

A German plane, believed to be a Heinkel bomber, flew over the Shetland Islands yesterday presumably on reconnaissance duty.

After anti-aircraft fire it flew off. Air raid warnings were given by mistake yesterday in several towns in South Wales and at a pilot training centre in the Home Counties.

Homeward bound City workers last night mistook the blaring of an electric motor-horn which had jammed for an air raid warning at Mornington-crescent, N.W. Some people went to nearby shelters.

Daily Mirror

No. 11,215 ONE PENNY
Registered at the G.P.O. as a Newspaper.

YOUR BACON

Soon you may be eating "mutton bacon" and eggs for breakfast. What is it? It's both mutton and bacon—and it certainly puzzled most M.P.s in the House of Commons yesterday.

Mr. F. A. Macquisten, M.P. for Argyll, was responsible for the mutton-bacon mystery. He mentioned "mutton bacon" in a question, and was told by Mr. A. T. Lennox Boyd, Parliamentary Secretary to the Ministry of Food, that he was arranging for an experimental cure of it.

It is mainly a "local" product, and is not generally known. Mr. Macquisten, however, declared that "any farmer's wife in Perthshire will show the bacon people how to cure it."

The "bacon people" did not know. Farmers and their wives in Perthshire, appealed to, declared that they had never seen any and did not know how to make it.

Then M.P.s themselves solved the mystery. M.P.s from Wales and some parts of Scotland know it well. On the hill farms of Wales it is still a common practice to dry a leg of mutton, salt it, and hang it up just as a side of bacon is hung up. Thin slices are cut from it and fried.

When Mr. Macquisten first tasted it in Scotland many years ago he commented: "This bacon has a curious colour and taste." His wife told him: "It is not bacon—it is mutton."

MAY BE..

GRACIE, YOU DESERVED A V.C.

GRACIE came to France and Gracie sang. She started singing long before she got to the concert hall.

As she went shopping yesterday morning in a little town behind the lines, soldiers recognised her, clamoured round her for autographs. And as she signed, she sang.

The soldiers sang, too, and Gracie, to the tune of "Sally," was escorted back to her hotel by a hundred singing, swinging troops. Her day had begun.

Before it was over every British soldier in France was singing; those still at their posts who listened on the radio and the 5,000 who roared out her choruses while half England heard . . . and sang, too.

The 5,000 were the lucky ones. They had won seats by ballot for Gracie's two concerts. Over 100,000 men in advanced positions in the line drew lots for the coveted places.

Well were the winners rewarded.

A dozen songs Gracie sang; the old favourites and the new. Every one was acclaimed. Whistles, shouts, encores, hand-clapping. "Sing on, Gracie; sing on."

And the girl from Lancashire, with pain racking her body and emotion surging in her heart, poured out the songs the men of England love.

And all the old tricks; the quick back-chat shout, the jest that brought the rippling laugh, and then the kind of song that stirs the tears so near to laughter.

It was a new one this time:—

"*I'm sending a letter to Santa Claus*
A letter I hope he will see;
He'll get a lot of letters for playthings
From other girls and boys;
But I want my soldier daddy
Better than all the toys—
So I'm sending a letter to Santa Claus
To bring daddy safe home to me."

There was a hush as it ended, as though thousands of daddies were thinking of thousands of boys and girls and wives and homes, then the deafening applause.

War Forgotten

War was forgotten; war and Hitler and Goebbels and Goering and mud and discomfort.

But Gracie, in almost her only topical note, sang a new line to the Biggest Aspidistra in the World:

We are going to hang old Hitler
From the very highest bough
Of the biggest aspidistra in the world.

And the troops remembered there was a war on—and laughed again.

For Gracie it was a day and night of agony, though sing she must. Was it by chance that a tenor first sang the Prologue to Pagliacci?

"The doctor said I wouldn't do it, but I did," she said, as she rested on a couch, between the concerts.

"I've never had such a lump in my throat since I was little Gracie Fields, unknown, singing to troops in England in the last war."

"But I wouldn't miss this for anything."

Continued on Back Page

THREATEN FINNS WITH POLES' FATE

AS the Finnish delegation arrived back in Helsinki yesterday after six weeks of fruitless talks with the Kremlin, the *Pravda*, official Communist Party newspaper, appeared in Moscow with a suggestion that Finland would meet the same fate as Poland.

The newspaper published a cartoon showing Colonel Beck, former Polish Foreign Minister, and General Sikorski, new Polish Premier, entering a French hotel in rags and remarking: "Let's wait for Erkko."

M. Erkko is the Finnish Foreign Minister. The Polish Government is now established in France.

Associated Press, British United Press and Exchange.

DUCE'S "ARMED PEACE"

"Fascist peace is an armed peace," declared Signor Mussolini in Rome last night. He was appearing on the balcony of the Palazzo Venezia in response to shouts of "Duce, Duce" from 60,000 people in the Venezia-square, most of them members of students' guilds.

"In accordance with Fascist custom and for reasons of precaution," he said, "keep your rifles alongside your books."—British United Press.

Send Your Pools Coupon Off Today

QUEEN TO RE-FILM

BY A SPECIAL CORRESPONDENT

THE news-film of the Queen broadcasting to women of the Empire from her drawing-room at Buckingham Palace will not be allowed to go abroad in its present form.

People in the Dominions who have never seen the Queen in person or heard her voice have been eagerly awaiting this first talkie short ever to be made of her Majesty. Now they will have to wait for the re-edited edition.

When her Majesty saw the film she realised that re-editing was advisable. The original was recalled for that purpose.

More Back-Ground Needed

It is thought that more background must be built into the short for such an important event.

Arrangements for the re-editing are to be made as speedily as possible, and the Queen has promised full co-operation.

The United States and the Dominions are disappointed at the delay, but their distributors are consoling themselves with the thought that these improvements will assure an even greater success for this royal movie abroad.

CRUISER CAPTURES GERMAN STEAMER

A GERMAN steamer believed to be the Leander (989 tons), with twenty to thirty men aboard, has been taken into a West Country port as a prize.

It is thought that the ship put into Vigo, Spain, when the war broke out and that the crew decided to make a dash for Germany after being unable to get food.

The vessel was sighted by a British cruiser

Raids "Only Starting"

NAZI LEADERS, STUNG INTO ACTIVITY BY THE POPULAR DEMAND FOR ACTION THAT WILL QUICKLY END THE WAR BROKE YESTERDAY INTO A STORM OF THREATS AGAINST BRITAIN.

"Our air raids on the Shetlands, Scapa Flow and the Firth of Forth are only the very beginning of a campaign of surprise attacks on Britain," declared the official German news agency last night.

And Party leaders in Berlin spoke of a secret new aeroplane which "can reach England in an hour and a half."

At the same time it was unofficially declared in Berlin that a new attack will be made on Britain's sea-borne trade. Any neutral ship carrying coal from Britain will be sunk by U-boats.

This, it was emphasised, would force neutrals to buy coal elsewhere.

Herr von Ribbentrop formally handed Hitler's reply to the peace proposal of Queen Wilhelmina and King Leopold to the Dutch and Belgian envoys in Berlin last night.

Must Act Soon

He told them that after the "brusque rejection" of the mediation offer by Britain and France, Germany considered that the proposals were dead.

But Hitler, robbed of a chance to seize peace on his own terms, must strike, and strike quickly. He knows—and the German people know—that time is against him.

There was tension throughout Germany yesterday as reports spread that the next Nazi drive would be to the Balkans.

But Berlin was silent. Although Germans believe that the Army must march again, the way to the East is still barred.

Russia stands in the way. Italy, still pursuing a Balkan policy, dare not be offended. In Istanbul, Herr von Papen, the discredited Nazi envoy to Turkey, began a new line of propaganda.

"Germany plans, after the war," he said, "to set up a European commonwealth."

Just what that means we didn't say. In Germany the newspapers report that all are anxious for the war to begin, for the drive to start against Britain!

But in the black-out anti-Nazi slogans appear on the Berlin walls. Secret pamphlets are being distributed. Socialists and Communists are still in opposition.

Bavarian and Austrian monarchists are working together and gathering strength.

Hitler knows that he must win soon—or never.

Daily Mirror

No. 11,216   ONE PENNY
Registered at the G.P.O. as a Newspaper.

HITLER SEES EX-PRINCE: IS DEFIED

FROM OUR SPECIAL CORRESPONDENT

PARIS, Thursday.

HITLER SUMMONED THE EX-CROWN PRINCE TO HIS STUDY IN THE WILHELMSTRASSE IN BERLIN AND COMMANDED HIM TO SIGN A PRO-NAZI DECLARATION. LITTLE WILLIE REFUSED.

The meeting, I learn from sources hitherto reliable, was a stormy one. The Fuehrer, especially since the Munich bomb exploded, is alarmed at reports of a monarchist revolution to overthrow the Nazi regime.

The ex-Crown Prince was summoned from his estate at Cecilienhof, near Potsdam, where he has been under open arrest for the past fourteen days.

The meeting took place yesterday at noon. Hitler accused Prince Wilhelm of supporting and secretly abetting the plot to restore the monarchy.

In a blaze of anger he revealed to him that his Gestapo agents had many records of conversations between monarchist leaders.

"Death will be the punishment for every traitor," Hitler roared.

Finally, he told the ex-Crown Prince that he must sign a "loyalty pledge," a document he refused to sign some months ago.

The Prince refused. He said he was unable to sign without his father's permission, and already the ex-Kaiser had ordered him not to sign.

After ninety minutes the ex-Crown Prince was escorted back to his estate still under open arrest.

✦ ✦ ✦

All day representatives of the Army, Air Force, Navy, the Nazi Party and the Government visited the Berlin Chancellery to confer with Hitler or members of his entourage (says the British United Press).

In Berlin the real war aims of Germany were revealed. An authorised spokesman said: "Our aim is to fight until British supremacy is destroyed.

"It is no longer a question of German peace terms. We are far beyond that. There will be no terms until our victory is won."

Hitler's own newspaper, the Volkischer Beobachter, says: "Britain, mortal enemy of the Reich, must be brought down with all the resources of the 84,000,000 German people."

Queen Phones Leopold

At The Hague, Queen Wilhelmina had a number of telephone talks with King Leopold. The Dutch Cabinet met, and when the Ministers parted the Minister for Defence reported on Hitler's irreconcilable attitude.

Belgium reacted to Hitler's negative reply to the Leopold-Wilhelmina mediation offer with a decision to make no new peace move for the time being.

A Foreign Office spokesman said that the Belgian Government must now "wait and see," and did not contemplate any fresh step to bring the belligerents together.

THEY WANT A KING—NOT 'ADOLF THE OX'

The Gestapo are searching for persons who are distributing anti-Hitler leaflets throughout Bavaria.

These leaflets, states a Dutch report, are identical with those distributed in 1934 bearing the wording, "We prefer a king by the grace of God to the ox in Berchtesgaden."—Exchange.

CAPONE IS FREE AFTER SEVEN YEARS

Al Lost, Even His Hair

By JOHN WALTERS ("Daily Mirror" Special Correspondent)

NEW YORK, Thursday.

AN invalid, frightened out of his wits, was met by his relatives to-day at the gates of the little gaol at Lewisburg, Pennsylvania. Al Capone, once king of Chicago's underworld, was a free man again.

Free, but changed. His waiting friends scarcely recognised the completely bald, partly paralysed half-wit who stumbled forward to meet them.

Capone, sentenced to eleven years in prison for evasion of income tax, has served nearly seven years. Last Sunday he was specially disguised by theatrical make-up experts in the dreaded prison of the Alcatraz.

Then, surrounded by G-men, he was taken in a machine-gun guarded railway coach to Lewisburg.

He was whisked away today to Baltimore Hospital for treatment and observation. From there he will go to his luxurious mansion in Florida, with its twenty-five bedrooms and great gardens . . . and its host of manservants trained to shoot straight.

Vengeance Threat

But he cannot move in the open yet. Gangsters, relatives and friends of the men Capone's gang shot down in the old but not forgotten battles in the beer-running days, have sworn that Al shall die.

In Chicago, Capone's old friends have begun a new campaign. With the slogan, "Make Chicago safe for Al," they threaten to wipe out his enemies.

They will fight without a leader. Seven years of gaol have changed the bejewelled, swaggering Italian.

In the sea-bound fortress off the Californian coast the deposed Tsar became a shoemaker and a tailor.

His soft, white hands grew hard and horny; his brain grew soft. The "tough guy" was almost a model prisoner.

Often he was attacked by fellow convicts;

Continued on Back Page

M.P.s' FOOD— £2,500 MORE

SO that M.P.s may eat and drink properly during working hours, the public will have to pay £2,500 extra.

This works out at more than £4 a member a year.

Sir John Simon, Chancellor of the Exchequer, stated in a written reply to Mr. Bracewell Smith (Con., Dulwich) yesterday that the Chairman of the House of Commons Kitchen Committee had asked for assistance from public funds to provide refreshments and meals for members at a reasonable cost during the abnormal conditions now obtaining.

The Committee was facing a serious loss, and he had decided to present a supplementary estimate after Christmas for £2,500 to assist the Committee to carry on until the end of the present financial year.

Since the war began the cost of living index figure has risen by 14 points, about 8.75 per cent.

This was announced by the Ministry of Labour last night in a statement showing that the increase during October was 4 points—about 2½ per cent.—being 69 per cent. above the level of July, 1914, as compared with 65 per cent. at September 30.

For food alone, the index figure at November 1 was 54 per cent. above the level of July, 1914, showing a rise of 2½ per cent. since September 30. This rise was due largely to increases in the prices of bacon and eggs. Meat and butter come next.

RAIDER SINKS BRITISH SHIP

ONE of the two Nazi raiders, Deutschland and Admiral Scheer, last reported in the North Atlantic and the Pacific respectively, has sunk a British tanker, the Africa Shell, off the coast of Mozambique, East Africa—inside Portuguese territorial waters.

All the crew are reported to be safe at Inhambane, 200 miles north of Lourenco Marques.

According to their statements, reported in the newspaper "Noticias," the German raider ordered the ship to stop two and a half miles from the coast, near Zavala, in the Inhambane district. The raider took off the crew, made the captain a prisoner and then sank the tanker.

Deutschland's exploits so far are:—Sunk the British ship Stonegate, the Norwegian ship Lorentz W. Hansen and captured the U.S. City of Flint.

The Brussels wireless announces that a German steamer was scuttled near Iceland on the approach of a British warship. All the crew were rescued.

A submarine, believed to be a German, has been seen near Manzanillo (Mexico), an important Pacific port.—Associated Press and Exchange.

MORE GRACIE FOR TROOPS

Gracie Fields will come back to sing again for the British Expeditionary Force as soon as she possibly can. She will return from Capri probably early in January.

She had signed to go to Hollywood to act in another film as soon as she is well, but she has cabled to America to make new plans which will allow her to give more concerts behind the lines.—British United Press.

DAILY MIRROR, Saturday, Nov. 18, 1939.

Daily Mirror

No. 11,217   ONE PENNY
Registered at the G.P.O. as a Newspaper.

NEW 'SHARE-ALL' PACT SIGNED BY ALLIES

'Daddy's Safe: Is Yours?'

FROM OUR SPECIAL CORRESPONDENT
PLYMOUTH, Friday.

NOREEN EXALL, aged ten, of Halcyon-road, Plymouth, ran all the way home from school to-day.

She had something important to tell her mother. In the school playground she had been playing with another little girl, Mary Pryne, of Plymouth.

"My daddy's on the same ship as yours," Mary had told her. "Mummy got a telegram from him this morning saying he has been saved. Has your daddy sent one?"

When Noreen reached home her mother was getting dinner ready. No telegram had arrived. Noreen breathlessly told her mother the news. Mrs. Exall at once put on her hat and coat and hurried to the naval barracks.

They told her that an explosion had occurred on her husband's ship, but if she had not received a telegram to say that he was involved she could rest assured that he was safe.

Anxiously she made her way home.

Inside the letter-box a telegram was waiting for her

"Daddy Won't Come Back"

It was from the Admiralty telling her that her husband was dead. She read it. Then with tears in her eyes turned to her three little girls waiting patiently to see if their daddy had sent them a telegram.

"Daddy won't come back any more." their mother said

Three sad little girls went to school this afternoon and broke the news to Mary Pryne that their mummy, too, had got a telegram.

"But it's not like yours," they told her.

Stoker Tom Exall, aged forty-three, had been in the Navy twenty-six years. He lost his two best pals, Tom Toomey and Dan Buckley, when the Courageous went down. They all came from Cork, in Ireland, and met when serving on the same ship.

Mrs. Exall is left with three children, Noreen, aged ten, Margaret, aged seven, and Eileen, aged six.

Picture on back page.

An Hour Earlier Blackout

Summer Time ends at midnight and all clocks must be put BACK one hour tonight.

The return to Greenwich Mean Time will bring a further hour of black-out dangers and discomforts.

On Monday the black-out ends at 6.57 a.m. It starts again at 4.34 p.m., when people are still at work.

HERE SHE IS

..BACK TO B.B.C. AS ANNOUNCER

MISS ELIZABETH COWELL (see her above) is a driver in the W.A.A.F. For three years she was television announcer (see her on the right) with Jasmine Bligh.

Now, after a lapse of six years, the B.B.C. is going to have a woman announcer.

And it has asked the Air Ministry to release Miss Cowell so that she may return to the microphone.

♦ ♦ ♦

The B.B.C. has had only one woman broadcast announcer before—Mrs. Sheila Borrett, who was engaged experimentally in 1933.

"It is not intended—for the present at any rate—that Miss Cowell will announce news," said the B.B.C. last night.

CHEAPER WAR BABY WIRES

THE B.E.F.'s front-line daddies will in future learn by telegram the glad news that "It's a boy," or "Twins; mother and babies well."

By arrangement with the War Office the Army postal authorities are to provide cheap-rate telegrams from the folks at home to the boys in the battle zone.

Tommy in turn will be able to send cheap telegrams back to Blighty. This telegram service will be available only for really important messages of urgent consequence to the soldier in the field or to his relatives in the United Kingdom.

The cheap rate will apply in the case of grave illness or sudden death.—British United Press.

INGRID AWAITS BABY

There was general rejoicing in Denmark yesterday when it was learned that Princess Ingrid, wife of Crown Prince Frederick, is expecting a baby in April.

WHEN THE SUPREME WAR COUNCIL MET SECRETLY IN LONDON YESTERDAY, BRITAIN AND FRANCE JOINED THE CLOSEST ALLIANCE EVER MADE BETWEEN TWO NATIONS— A PACT TO SHARE EQUALLY THE SUPPLIES AND TO ACCEPT EQUALLY THE SHORTAGES OF WAR.

The French leaders, M. Daladier, General Gamelin, Admiral Darlan and General Vuillemin flew from France early yesterday, and within an hour of their arrival they joined Mr. Chamberlain, Lord Halifax, Sir Kingsley Wood and Lord Chatfield in a closely guarded London building.

The conference lasted three hours. When it ended a joint statement was issued by the two Prime Ministers. It said:—

Arrangements already put into effect by the two Governments have now been strengthened and completed in such a way as to ensure common action in the following fields:—

Air; munitions and raw materials; oil; food; shipping; economic warfare.

The new measures adopted by the two Governments will provide for the best use in the common interest of the resources of both countries in raw materials, means of production and tonnage.

Joint Imports

They will also provide for the equal distribution between them of any limitations, should circumstances render necessary a reduction of the programmes of imports.

The two countries will in future draw up their import programmes jointly, and will avoid competition in purchases which they have to make abroad in carrying out those programmes.

The execution of these tasks has been entrusted to permanent Anglo-French Executive Committees, under an Anglo-French Co-ordinating Committee, which are being set up immediately.

The agreements reached, which can, if required, be extended to other fields, afford further evidence of the determination of the two countries to co-ordinate their war efforts to the fullest possible extent.

3 Years Ahead

By this means arrangements have been carried into effect two months after the beginning of hostilities for the organisation of a common action by the two countries, which was achieved during the last conflict only at the end of the third year of the war.

The most interesting feature of the pact is the announcement that limitations will be equally borne.

It is not yet known whether this means that both Britain and France will adopt the same standards of rationing, but it is clear that one country will not enjoy a surplus of any commodity if the other lacks it.

Mr. Hore-Belisha, Secretary for War, is spending a few days in France.

Mr. Hore-Belisha plans to visit the British troops and to see something of the French positions, including the part of the French line which is under Lord Gort's command.

Later the War Minister will go to Paris, where on Monday he will meet M. Daladier, General Gamelin and other French political and military leaders.

R.A.F. SNAP NAZI NAVY BASE SECRETS

An Air Ministry bulletin issued last night stated:—

"Daylight reconnaissance over North-West Germany were carried out today by aircraft of the Royal Air Force. In spite of heavy A.A. fire, an important German naval base was successfully photographed and other valuable information was obtained."

DAILY MIRROR, Monday, Nov. 20, 1939

Daily Mirror

No. 11,218 ✦ ONE PENNY
Registered at the G.P.O. as a Newspaper.

BABIES ARE NOTHING TO HIM

THESE TWO BONNY PIC-CANINNIES WERE PICKED UP IN THE SEA WHEN THE DUTCH LINER SIMON BOLIVAR WENT DOWN IN THE NORTH SEA, SUNK BY TWO GERMAN MINES.

The babies look like twins, about six months old. The one on the left is seriously injured in the right eye. It is shockingly disfigured and completely closed.

The children will never see their parents again. They died with the mined ship.

Survivors tell of mothers moaning for lost children; of children shrieking for fathers and mothers swept away as the ship blew up; of men and women fighting to save themselves and their loved ones in a sea of choking oil.

It is nothing to Hitler. This is his view of a humane war. It is nothing to him that women and children die in a war that is not theirs.

The British Admiralty has branded the Nazis with this deed that outrages all the rules of war.

Berlin newspapers declare that the mines were British — as though Britain would lay mines in the path of her own and valuable neutral shipping.

But truth is as little valued by Hitler as human life.

IT IS NOTHING TO HIM.

FOUR MORE SHIPS MINED

FOUR more ships have been sunk by German mines, it was announced last night.

They are the B.O. Borjesson (1,586 tons), Swedish; Blackhill (2,492 tons), British; Grazia (5,857 tons), Italian, and the Kaunas Lithuanian (1,520 tons).

The first three were sunk off the East Coast in circumstances similar to those of the Simon Bolivar.

Sixteen of the seventeen men aboard the Kaunas, which was on her way to Britain, were saved by a fishing-boat and taken to a Belgian port.

Six of the nineteen men on board the B.O. Borgessen died and five were injured.

Injured Men on Raft

"The explosion occurred in the darkness in the early hours," said one of the survivors.

"It smashed the engines as though they were made of cardboard, blew some of the boards through the ship's sides and, I think, killed some of the men below.

"We collected the injured men as well as we could and placed them on a raft. About three hours after the explosion the ship went down. Twelve of us, including the seven who were hurt, floated off on the raft. The thirteenth man got away floating on some of the wreckage.

"We were drifting for an hour or so, then we were sighted by a trawler, which picked up our raft. The other man was picked up by another trawler."

The Grazia sank within fifteen minutes of the explosion.

Two ships, a lifeboat and an aeroplane searched the sea for more than two hours, and twenty-three survivors were picked up.

Hope was abandoned for the five remaining members of the crew.

More Pictures and full story of the Simon Bolivar disaster on pages ten, eleven and sixteen.

DAILY MIRROR, Tuesday, Nov. 21, 1939

Daily Mirror

No. 11,219   ONE PENNY

Registered at the G.P.O. as a Newspaper.

RAIDER NEAR LONDON IN BLACK-OUT

A Heinkel bomber.

Met in Bus, Agree to Wed

A day after meeting a young seaman on a bus, Miss Margaret Baker (right) agreed to marry him, but their romance led to Bow-street Police Court, London.

There yesterday the seaman, Edward Victor Biggs, aged twenty-two, of Milton-road, Weston-super-Mare, was committed for trial. He was accused of stealing from her a diamond brooch, a cigarette case and other jewellery worth £300.

Miss Baker, a secretary, of South Audley-street, Mayfair, said she fell asleep and was wakened by Biggs, who took her to a restaurant and then walked home with her. He left her at her door and they arranged to go to church together next day.

He explained his rough clothing by saying that he had been in a car accident and had changed clothes with a labourer. Later, she missed the jewellery.

(See story on page 7.)

NAZIS KILL 55 POLES IN PRISON

FIFTY-FIVE Poles, including the town's mayor, have been massacred by the Nazis at Innoworclaw.

They had been thrown into prison when their town was captured early in the war.

A detachment of soldiers was marched to the prison and all the fifty-five men were put up against a wall and shot.

A German proclamation last night, reports the *Daily Mirror* radio station, orders all unmarried Polish women to be conscripted for labour service.

Czech students sent to concentration camps now number 1,200, it was officially admitted in Prague yesterday, says Associated Press.

The Czech secret radio station yesterday threatened: "A time will come when for each Czech life, ten Nazis will pay with their lives."

M. Sramek, a member of the former Czech Government, speaking over the Paris radio to his people, said: "We know your suffering, but the hour of freedom will come. Strengthen your faith and hold out."

5 SHIPS SUNK

THE sinking of five more steamers including four known to be British, was reported yesterday as the Nazis continued their atrocity campaign against merchant ships of all nations by means of magnetic mines and torpedoes.

Last to be revealed was the wreck of the London steamer Arlington Court (4,915 tons) in the Atlantic.

Twenty-two of the crew were picked up by the Dutch motor vessel Algenib.

The chief engineer died, apparently from exhaustion, while in the ship's lifeboat before the rescuers arrived and was buried at sea.

Eleven other members of the crew put off in a second boat, but became separated from their companions. Although the Dutch vessel searched, there was no trace of them.

Doctors Stand by

The twenty-two survivors—some are injured and others are suffering from exposure—will be landed today. Doctors and ambulances are standing by.

In three days Nazi Germany has been responsible for the sinking of eleven ships, four of them neutral.

Ten of them were sunk off the East Coast of England. Nine were mined. One was torpedoed.

The other sinkings revealed yesterday were:
Grimsby trawler Wigmore (345 tons), crew of sixteen missing.
London steamer Pensilva (4,258 tons) (torpedoed), all crew safe.
An unnamed steamer, seventeen landed, six teen missing, feared drowned.
London collier Torchbearer (1,267 tons); four survivors of crew of thirteen landed.

Continued on Back Page

ENEMY AIR RAIDERS APPEARED OVER THE OUTSKIRTS OF LONDON YESTERDAY FOR THE FIRST TIME SINCE WAR BEGAN. NO BOMBS WERE DROPPED.

In East Kent last night sirens shrieked a warning when unidentified planes appeared in the night sky. British fighter planes raced to find and fight the raiders.

No guns were fired and two hours later the "All clear" signal was given.

Earlier, our anti-aircraft guns burst into action when a daylight German raider soared over the Thames estuary.

It was first seen flying at a great height over the Sussex coast. It turned eastwards towards London.

As it approached it was met by a bombardment from the guns. Puffs of smoke broke around it.

The enemy plane—"a large white Heinkel bomber," one observer described it—continued on its way until British fighters came into view.

Then it turned and raced back. The fighters chased it out to sea.

In Essex and Kent many people narrowly escaped injury as fragments of exploded British shells fell.

While pupils of a recently-built £30,000 central school played outside, shell splinters hit the gymnasium and crashed through the roof.

The gymnasium was empty.

Shrapnel in Wash-Tub

A few yards away District Nurse Winifred Alden was at home alone when a heavy shrapnell splinter hurtled through the roof, bringing down slates, plaster and laths.

One woman at her washtub in the garden was startled when shrapnell whizzed passed her head and fell in the washtub.

The night raid over East Kent sent people in four towns hurrying for shelter. In one, thousands of men and women walked to tunnel shelters 90ft. below ground. Invalids, wrapped in blankets, were carried into the tunnels.

Cinema audiences were told of the raid and invited to leave for shelter. In one cinema only A.R.P. workers walked out. The show went on.

The sirens sounded just as one district council was meeting. Business went on and members heard a report that the local A.R.P. arrangements were in perfect order.

Nazi Story of Raid

The raiders' activities were officially announced in Berlin last night when the German News Agency said:

"Despite storms, German reconnaissance planes flew over Scapa Flow, Scotland, the South Coast of England and the North Coast of France to-day.

"Valuable results were obtained.

"In the London area pursuit planes and anti-aircraft fire attacked the German planes, but great height enabled them to escape."

A German bomber that tried to attack a British destroyer in the North Sea was driven off.

In Essex women watched a mystery plane, thought to be German trying to write smoke signs in the sky.

CONSCRIPTION IN JERSEY

The Jersey States yesterday adopted a National Service Act, by which all men from eighteen to forty-one will become liable to military duty with the British Forces as soon as the measure has received Royal Sanction.

CHRISTMAS— NO CURFEW FOR SHOPS

BLACK-OUT closing hours for shops are to be suspended for a week before Christmas, and there's a chance that shop windows may be lit, too.

The Home Secretary announced the lifting of the curfew last night. Illuminated windows depend on whether Home Office arrangements for modified lighting are completed in time.

In any case shops will be open until late just as usual at Christmas.

An official of the Home Office told the *Daily Mirror* last night:

"The Home Secretary's order will certainly help Christmas shoppers.

"If the lighting arrangements are complete it will mean that shops may have their windows lighted and people will be able to 'window gaze' as usual."

The Home Secretary's order does not affect in any way the provisions of the Shops Act relating to the shop assistants' half-holiday, the regulation of the hours of young persons and the closing of shops on the weekly half-holiday.

GOERING'S WIFE QUITTED GERMANY

FRAU GOERING, wife of Marshal Goering, has given birth to a daughter—but not in Germany.

The man who commands the world's most invincible air force did not feel that his own country was safe enough, so he sent his wife to Lausanne, in Switzerland.

She remained in the most fashionable hotel for three weeks, out of range of the noisy R.A.F. reconnaissance planes, until the baby was born. Even a Swiss newspaper has commented: "Why was this German child not born on German soil?"

Now everyone is wondering why Marshal Goering did not think his own country was good enough.

Any explanation, Dr. Goebbels?

DAILY MIRROR, Thursday, Nov. 23, 1939

Daily Mirror

No. 11,221
ONE PENNY
Registered at the G.P.O. as a Newspaper

DESTROYER HITS A MINE— 40 MISSING

H.M.S. Gipsy—beached after striking a mine.

4 RAIDS IN A DAY—ONE NAZI DOWN

FOUR GERMAN AIR RAIDS WERE MADE OVER BRITAIN YESTERDAY. IN THE LAST RAID, AT 10 O'CLOCK LAST NIGHT, ONE NAZI PLANE WAS SHOT DOWN IN THE SEA OFF THE ESSEX COAST.

A few minutes before the alarm sounded, anti-aircraft guns burst into action and the beams of hundreds of searchlights lit the sky.

For a few seconds a racing plane was caught in the shafts of light. Machine-gun fire and the roar of aircraft engines were heard.

At the same time shore searchlights swept the sea to make sure that enemy sea action was not being combined with air attack.

The Air Ministry announced last night: "Enemy aircraft approached the south-east coast. Anti-aircraft guns opened fire and R.A.F. fighters were sent to intercept them.

"One enemy aircraft was shot down into the sea by anti-aircraft fire. A second enemy aircraft was engaged and driven off by our fighters."

Biggest attack was on the Shetland Islands, where six Nazi planes dropped bombs. A British flying-boat lying in the water was attacked by bombs.

The Nazi plane swooped so low that the crew could be seen plainly.

Flying Boat Set on Fire

The flying-boat burst into flames. Her crew of seven leaped into the water and swam to the shore.

The raiders also attacked a small inter-island mail steamer. One bomb fell some yards astern, and others went wide.

In Berlin last night, cables British United Press, an official announcement said:—

"This afternoon German planes attacked British naval craft near the Shetland Islands. The German planes, diving low, machine-gunned and set on fire one British flying boat.

The second raid on Britain was a single machine flight over the Thames estuary. The Nazi escaped the anti-aircraft barrage, then sped over South Essex.

British planes engaged the enemy, drove him down so low that for a time it seemed certain he would hit the roof-tops. All the time the fighters harried him.

The third raid was carried out over the East Coast. A twin-engined black Nazi plane was fired on by our anti-aircraft guns.

It climbed quickly into the clouds.

★ NAZIS TO 'VIOLATE AIR'

According to a Paris report the Nazis will use Britain's plan to seize German exports in neutral ships as an excuse for attacking Britain and Holland.

Goering is said to have urged at yesterday's conference of war chiefs that as Britain had "violated the seas," the Nazis were justified in "violating the air."

★ "31 Mines Adrift"—

The American Navy warned shipping yesterday that thirty-one mines were adrift in the North Sea. Reports were relayed by the United States cruiser Trenton, flagship of the American special squadron in Europe, from warnings broadcast by belligerent nations (states Associated Press). ★

SHOT FOILED NAZI ESCAPE

SHOTS fired by a sentry prevented three German seamen escaping from a Scottish internment camp yesterday.

This was the third escape attempt in four days. Two prisoners who escaped on Monday were captured last night.

"I saw a German prisoner in a cemetery nearby. He had scrambled in among the tombstones," a workman told the "Daily Mirror."

A man who lives on the top floor of a block of flats had a good view of what happened, said: "Two sentries in a look-out tower were peering into the darkness and had their rifles at the ready. One of them fired."

Asked for Food

A young man and woman returning from a cinema took refuge in a house when the firing began.

The two German prisoners who escaped on Monday were recaptured after they had called at a house and asked the woman occupier for food.

The woman, Mrs. Mathison, said a man, wearing a beret and a raincoat over dungarees, asked in broken English if she could give him and his companion something to eat.

Suspecting he was one of the escaped Germans, she put some food in a box and after the man had gone, told her son who telephoned the police.

The fugitives were seen making their way through the fields to the main road. Mr. Mathison, jnr., and a constable jumped into a motor-car, sped down the main road, and captured the two men.

TWO MORE U-BOATS SUNK

A French torpedo boat has sunk two U-boats. The torpedo boat sank one submarine and three days later contacted another, and sent that to the bottom too.

Both U-boats were "spotted" by naval aircraft.—British United Press.

HUNDREDS OF PEOPLE, AWAKENED BY AN EXPLOSION, HURRIED TO THE QUAYSIDE OF AN EAST COAST TOWN AND SAW SEARCHLIGHTS PLAYING ON THE BRITISH DESTROYER GIPSY, SINKING AFTER SHE HAD STRUCK A MINE.

ABOUT FORTY RATINGS ARE MISSING AND TWENTY-ONE OFFICERS AND MEN HAVE BEEN REPORTED INJURED, THE ADMIRALTY ANNOUNCED LAST NIGHT.

In the glare of the searchlights crowds saw more than 100 men rescued and landed by small boats which had raced out from the quayside.

Shortly before, the Gipsy had returned to port with three Nazi airmen found floating on a rubber raft in the North Sea after their plane had been shot down by anti-aircraft fire.

Her errand of mercy completed, she swung out to sea again. Suddenly there was a sheet of flame and an explosion which shook the town.

Nazi mine-layers had claimed their second British destroyer. The Gipsy was beached.

Led Swim to Safety

One vessel lying at anchor picked up thirty survivors who were swimming strongly against an ebb tide.

The men were being led by a powerful swimmer, who continually encouraged them with shouts of "Come on, boys. Here we are."

"The explosion shook the windows and made the chairs dance about the floor," said a householder who was awakened by the noise. "I rushed to the front. Other people were pouring from their homes to see what had happened.

"We could see a vessel showing up vividly in the glare of the searchlights from surrounding craft."

"Smaller boats took off the crew as the destroyer, almost broken in two, sank in shallow water."

Many sailors, amazingly cheerful after their ordeal, were brought singing into port.

They were wearing all kinds of clothing—dressing gowns and bathing suits—and one man, clad in a black and white football shirt, shouted as he stepped ashore! "All right, chaps. I am playing for Newcastle tomorrow."

Another, limping, refused help. "I don't

Continued on Back Page

GERMANS LOSE NINE PLANES

THE Germans suffered losses in the air yesterday.

Seven Nazis were shot down by fighters, one crashed in the fire of anti-aircraft guns, one riddled with bullets, fell near Ostend.

The last plane, a bomber, had been driven off by French fighters as it attempted to raid a Channel port. It tried to fly back over Belgium, but broke up in the air.

Two French fighters were lost. Both pilots attempted to escape by parachute. One succeeded. The other was killed when his parachute failed to open.

French fighters brought down three Messerschmitts, one Dornier bomber and one unidentified plane. British airmen shot down a Heinkel III bomber and a machine of unknown classification.

There were no British casualties.

The Air Ministry officially announced last night that the R.A.F. successfully carried out flights, on Monday and Tuesday, over Stuttgart, Frankfurt, Hamburg and Bremen.

Captain Payne Best (wearing monocle) and Captain Stevens.

NAZIS FAKE BOMB TRIAL

NAZI secret police are rapidly manufacturing evidence to stage a grand public trial on the scale of the Reichstag fire frame-up.

The trial, attended by all the publicity which the Reich's gigantic propaganda machine can give it, will attempt to fix the blame for the explosion in the beer cellar on the British Government.

The delay in extracting a confession from Georg Elser, held by the Gestapo on a charge of putting the bomb in the cellar attic, recalls the delay which also occurred before the Dutchman Van der Lubbe "confessed" to firing the Reichstag.

Fought Kidnappers

"Incontestable evidence" linking the two Englishmen. Captain Richard Henry Stevens, an official of the British Passport Control Office at The Hague, and Captain Payne Best with the bombing is now being promised shortly by officials in Berlin.

It is explained that the investigation is still going on, and therefore it would be unwise to publish details which might prove premature.

Captain Stevens who, with Captain Best, was kidnapped over the Dutch border at Venlo by Nazi S.S. troops, has been murdered, according to a report reaching Amsterdam.

Information from Germany states that Captain Stevens and Captain Payne Best resisted their kidnappers and were beaten unmercifully in the car, which was racing to the Nazi Customs House close at hand.

Contd. on Back Page

DAILY MIRROR, Friday, Dec. 1, 1939

Daily Mirror

No. 11,228 ♦ ONE PENNY
Registered at the G.P.O. as a Newspaper.

FINLAND YIELDS TO REDS: GOVT. GO

FINLAND'S GOVERNMENT RESIGNED LAST NIGHT WHILE THE STREETS OF BOMBED HELSINKI STILL BLAZED.

A Russian ultimatum, reported in Copenhagen, had threatened to raze the capital to the ground unless Finland capitulated completely by 3 a.m. this morning.

For hours the Cabinet met in secret session. Then at midnight came the resignation.

THE NEW GOVERNMENT WILL PROBABLY ATTEMPT TO NEGOTIATE PEACE TERMS WITH RUSSIA.

As the one-day war ended Finland's tiny fleet of two coastal defence ships and a few gunboats and submarines was at sea, seeking battle with the Red Fleet in the Gulf of Finland.

And rescue work was still going on in Helsinki and other big towns raided by the Red bombers.

The Finnish capital last night was in darkness; lit only by the flames rising from burning buildings. One Russian bomb had wrecked the hydro-electric works.

Women and children crowded into the railway station. But only a few of them could be evacuated. There are not enough trains to serve the civilian population.

Home for Christmas

Christmas leave for the British Expeditionary Force will probably start on December 17.

♦

Free passes and quick transport will be arranged. As many men as possible will be released at Christmas time itself.

Moscow Radio 'Did Not Know'

The first mention of the Russian invasion of Finland in the Moscow broadcast in English was made at ten o'clock last night, fourteen hours after Red troops had crossed the border.

In the eight-thirty broadcast in English no news of the invasion was given. The announcer emphasised the desire for " friendly collaboration with the people of Finland " and referred to " eternal friendship with a sovereign State with whom we have no desire to interfere."

When, at last, the Moscow English broadcast mentioned the invasion the message began a " Berlin news agency reports . . ."

German newspapers contained only a few lines about the invasion. " We await confirmation from Moscow " was the reason.

All day the Soviet radio stations (broadcasting in Russian) were silent on the invasion of Finland. Then, half an hour after they had closed down, the stations reopened and an announcer said : " Some important news has come in and will be read. A report is expected on the Soviet-Finnish hostilities."

Red Troops Fire on Hungarians

Reports from the Ruthenian frontier last night said that Russian soldiers had opened fire on Hungarian sentries, according to the Associated Press.

It was learned that there had been tension at the Soviet-Ruthenian frontier because a shipment of propaganda leaflets intended for the Ruthenians had been confiscated by the Hungarian authorities.

Ruthenia, which was a part of the Czechoslovak Republic, was taken by Hungary after the Munich agreement last year.

Finns' Neighbours Alarmed

Alarmed, Sweden, Norway and Denmark looked to their defences, but officially maintained a non-committal attitude of neutrality.

The general public, however, made no effort to disguise their feelings.

Swedes crowded about newspaper offices excitedly commenting on the news.

Women burst into tears when they heard that bombs had rained on Helsinki.

A Swedish Foreign Office spokesman said that Sweden was already in a state of preparedness and no new measures had been taken.

Members of the Swedish, Norwegian and Danish Cabinets conferred on the situation.

Denmark was tremendously excited. Crowds gathered in the streets in Copenhagen, snatching newspapers, while groups stood indignantly commenting on the bulletins.

Rumours are current in Norway that Moscow is demanding three naval bases on the north coast of Norway.

Copenhagen talks of reports that Russia has demanded three Norwegian ports along the Arctic coast.

DALADIER FACES CRISIS—WINS

EDOUARD DALADIER, " Strong Man " of France, faced crisis in the French Chamber yesterday when Socialist M.P.s held up the Bill to give him full powers to conduct the war.

Daladier, the Premier, demanded that France should be ruled by decree.

The Socialists—despite a declaration by Herriot, ex-Premier and " Speaker " of the Chamber, that rejection would be a serious blow to the morale of the nation and the Army—insisted that Parliament should be called every month to approve the decrees.

The Finance Committee itself had sponsored this move.

For hours the debate went on. Then Daladier acted. He cancelled a broadcast to the nation timed for 8 p.m., retired to his private room, and refused to meet any of the Socialist leaders.

The Chamber was suspended. Consultations went on among deputies and leaders.

Finally, with the deputies again in their places, Daladier mounted the tribune and personally staked the life of his Government.

He made it a question of confidence in the Government and their conduct of the war.

By 318 votes to 175 the Chamber gave its approval that he should rule France by decree.

Daladier, the Strong Man, had won again.

WOMEN HELD AS NAZI HOSTAGES

POLICE in Germany are holding a score of British women as hostages till the German Foreign Office finds out whether any German women have been arrested in Britain.

A few Australian women were arrested last week but later released.

Meanwhile, about twenty British Consular officials are still being held pending an arrangement for the exchange of German Consular officials.—British United Press.

3 WARSHIPS IN PORT, DAMAGED

THREE British warships—a cruiser, a torpedo-boat and a damaged submarine— have put into a Norwegian port pleading stress of weather and damage.

This was announced by the Norwegian Admiralty yesterday, says British United Press.

The submarine is stated in Oslo to have been disabled in Wednesday's sea battle, reported to have been between British ships and German aircraft.

But it is pointed out in London that the gales in the North Sea during the last few days have been the worst for many years and it is possible that the submarine, having developed minor defects, was being taken under escort to a port where, presumably, she would remain for repairs.

The British Admiralty has made no statement.

Under international law, warships of belligerents can put into neutral ports pleading " stress of weather " or damage, but undamaged warships must leave within twenty-four hours.

The first ship appeared off Mosjaroey, near Stavanger, at 7 a.m., followed by another towing the submarine.

Stalin's " lightning war " from the air had extended far beyond Helsinki. Towns deep in the Arctic region were rocked and partially destroyed by raiding Red bombers.

Twelve Streets Ablaze

But the capital was the chief sufferer. In the south-west area of Helsinki, twelve streets were blazing.

Windows were shattered. Men, women and children died in the wreckage of crashing buildings.

FIRST REPORTS GAVE THE TOTAL DEAD AS 200, BUT LATE LAST NIGHT IT WAS OFFICIALLY ANNOUNCED THAT EIGHTY PEOPLE HAD BEEN KILLED. " RESCUE WORK," IT WAS ADDED, " IS STILL CONTINUING."

The Helsinki Radio announcer, speaking as calmly as though he were relating the results of the day's racing, broadcast a message picked up by the Daily Mirror short wave station. He said :

" Russian troops which crossed the frontier have been repulsed in several places. Only in the Karelian Isthmus did they succeed in occupying a part of Finnish territory.

" The Russians have used tanks. Bombing went on continuously.

Six towns have been heavily bombed, houses and even hospitals were hit.

Planes Brought Down

" In one of these towns four civilians were killed and thirteen were wounded.

" One heavy bomb has been dropped on Helsinki, but several incendiary bombs were also dropped.

" Three Russian bombers have been brought down. The Russians tried without success to bomb a railway junction but never drove off. The people of Finland remain calm."

Later the Finnish Defence Ministry announced that two Russian tanks had been destroyed. Midnight reports gave the number of Russian tanks destroyed or captured as eight.

The special correspondent of a Swedish newspaper, in a dispatch from Helsinki, said: " I never saw worse scenes in Madrid or Barcelona. There were bombs of the 500lb. type mixed with incendiary matter. One of the big ones fell in a street near the Russian

Continued on Back Page

U.S. May Break with Russia

A source close to President Roosevelt told the " Daily Mirror " New York correspondent: " Don't be surprised if the United States breaks off diplomatic relations with Russia within the next few hours. Everything points that way."

President Roosevelt returned from Georgia to Washington yesterday and immediately conferred with his Foreign Minister, Secretary of State Hull, and with Assistant War Secretary Johnson.

The President is indignant that Russia spurned the American offer of mediation in the Finnish dispute.

DAILY MIRROR, Monday, Dec. 4, 1939.

Daily Mirror

No. 11,230 ♦ ♦ ♦ ONE PENNY
Registered at the G.P.O. as a Newspaper.

Women Bomb Finns

RUSSIAN women pilots bombed and machine - gunned helpless women and children in the raids on Helsinki and other towns in the south of Finland.

Finns clearing bodies from a Soviet bomber, shot down in Helsinki after killing twenty people with machine-gun fire, were amazed to find that one was that of a woman.

She was one of many crack women aviators who took part in the raids, lasting two days.

Hundreds of civilians were killed and wounded and thousands fled into the snow-bound countryside rather than face the terror in the towns.

Russia has boasted of the prowess of her women pilots ever since the Red air force was opened to women as a career years ago.

Finnish pathologists are making post-mortem examinations on bodies of other Russian bomber crews badly burned and mutilated in crashing, to see how many of them were women.

Poison Gas Lie

Finland last night faced a new Soviet menace —the lie from Moscow that the Finns are using poison gas.

Fears grew in Helsinki that Stalin is adopting the German technique of inventing poison gas atrocity stories as an excuse for using it against opponents.

The new Finnish Government, led by Premier M Ryti, denounced allegations made in *Pravda*, the Moscow Communist newspaper, that the Finns had used poison gas from the outbreak of the war.

Nikolai Virta, correspondent of *Pravda* on the Karelian frontier, declared that he saw chloropicrin gas used by the Finns.

Chemists of the Red Army, Virta added, were able to neutralise it, and Russian bombers " soon liquidated the depots from which the gas was being distributed."

Before the Germans used poison gas in the last war, they spread false stories of the gas used by the Allies

The Nazis, after invading Poland, accused the Poles of using " poison gas made in Britain " against German troops

Britain at once denied the allegations and warned the world that the Nazis were preparing to break international law in this war the same way as the Huns did in the last

League to Meet

The League Council Assembly has been called to meet a Geneva on Friday, at Finland's request, to discuss arbitration of the Soviet-Finnish conflict.

The statement to be made to the League is aimed at strengthening world opinion.

Meanwhile long lines of sad-faced women and children moved into the rocky interior of Finland last night with a few blankets and belongings while workers sandbagged the city for what was expected to be terrific air attacks on Helsinki.

The German ship Donau was loaded with some 500 Germans, a few Russians and about fifty Italians for evacuation to Tallinn.

It was feared generally that the departure of the ship would be the signal for renewed bombardment.

It was believed that the ship's presence in harbour was the only reason for holding off from bombing during the week-end.

The ship is due to leave today.

Russian troops launched a fierce attack on Petsamo, which the Finns recaptured on Saturday after taking Red soldiers by surprise.

Associated Press, British United Press and Exchange

THE NAVY LURES 3 U-BOATS TO DOOM

THREE MORE OF HITLER'S PIRATE FLEET OF U-BOATS HAVE BEEN SUNK. TWO WERE CAUGHT BY AN ADMIRALTY TRAWLER, AND THE THIRD WAS LURED TO ITS DOOM IN A TRAP SET BY BRITISH WARSHIPS.

Residents in several holiday resorts, awakened by the blasts of depth charges soon after midnight, ran to the foreshore.

Searchlights swept the sky and the roar of the high-powered engines of the searching craft heightened the illusion that enemy warplanes were in action.

But the explanation of the detonations was soon obvious. Large crowds saw depth charges throw huge fountains of water into the air.

This success was due to the resource of the crew of a small fishing smack, who had seen the submarine slipping stealthily along the coast in bright moonlight.

Knowing that no British submarine was stationed in the area, the fishermen hastened to the nearest port, where they reported to the naval authorities.

The U-boat commander, lulled into a false sense of security, made his way towards his objective and was almost ready to carry out his mission when, at a pre-arranged signal, warships and searching craft swooped on her in deep water.

The raider had no chance of escape and in the morning a trawler could be seen from the shore mounting guard over the spot where the submarine was sunk

—Then National Anthem

No damage of any kind was received by the British warships, whose crews celebrated the end of another of Germany's pirate fleet by singing the National Anthem.

An hotel manager and his wife were listening to the wireless when the action began.

" It was just after midnight," said the wife, " when a terrific explosion shook the hotel. The floor boards quivered under our feet.

"We ran to the sea front. It was a clear night with a particularly bright moon and we could easily see patrol boats dashing about.

" Inside an hour we heard about a dozen explosions, which seemed to be under the water. The first awakened many people in the hotel and for a time we thought an air raid was in progress."

For three hours the hunt went on, then there was peace. And, at daybreak, a floating patch of oil and hundreds of dead fish was all the evidence that remained.

An Admiralty armed trawler, formerly owned by the Crampin Steam Fishing Co. of Grimsby, is believed to have sunk one, if not two, U-boats.

The trawler was patrolling the North Sea when she located two submarines Both were attacked with depth charges.

In one instance there was no doubt in the men's minds that the submarine had been destroyed.

In the second case oil patches and bubbles on the water after the explosions indicated that the submarine had been accounted for, although the evidence was not as conclusive as in the first case.

German Liner Scuttled

The Royal Navy, in its relentless combing of the seas for the Nazi vessels that venture out of port, has brought in two more German ships as prizes They are the Ellbek (2,185 tons) and the 215-ton trawler Sophie Busse. Both are now in British ports.

The German liner Watussi (9,521 tons) was scuttled off Cape Point after she had refused to go to Simonstown at the orders of South African bombers which intercepted her.

When first challenged the Watussi refused to reveal its identity, continued on its course Warning bombs were dropped.

Smoke rose from the ship as boats full of women and children were lowered. The airmen stopped bombing. Survivors were picked up.

GERMAN NAVY IS BOMBED

R.A.F. bombers successfully attacked German warships near Heligoland yesterday.

Direct hits were made with heavy bombs.

The British planes—a strong formation—met considerable anti-aircraft fire.

They shot down the only enemy fighter encountered—a Messerschmitt.

And all our planes returned safely.

The Air Ministry also announces that an R.A.F. plane patrolling the North Sea bombed and destroyed an enemy submarine surprised on the surface yesterday. A direct hit was obtained on the base of the conning tower.

NO ARMISTICE BID BY POPE, SAYS VATICAN

Berlin reports that the Pope has proposed a Christmas armistice are denied in authoritative Vatican circles

It was pointed out that it was hardly likely such a proposal would be made in view of the relative calm on the Western Front

An armistice at sea would be meaningless on account of floating mines it was added.— British United Press.

2 MORE ITALIAN SUBMARINES

Two more submarines for the Italian Navy were launched yesterday. Each is of 1,000 tons, is equipped with eight torpedo tubes, two guns and four machine guns, and has a surface speed of eighteen knots.—British United Press.

SOS TRICK TO TRAP SHIPS

BURNING distress flares, hoping to trap trawlers that respond to them, is the latest dastardly method employed by German submarines in their campaign of frightfulness against Fleetwood trawlers.

This new ruse was revealed yesterday when the trawler Roman arrived back from a fishing voyage.

The Roman, in charge of Skipper Charles Seeting, was steaming to the fishing grounds when distress flares were sighted in the darkness by men on watch at 2 a.m.

" We called the skipper and as he had been warned previously to keep a look-out as U-boats were in the vicinity, he decided to investigate," a member of the trawler's crew told the *Daily Mirror*.

" We did not want to desert a ship in distress or leave shipwrecked men in the Atlantic, so we steamed cautiously towards the distress signals.

Trailed Five Hours

" When we were about one hundred yards away the outline of a submarine on the surface came into view. Our engines were immediately stopped and orders given to steam away in the direction we had come.

" It is well known that submarines will not attack trawlers in the darkness, because they cannot see whether a trawler is armed. If there is one thing U-boat commanders do not like it is a gun.

" For five hours the submarine followed us in the darkness.

" As daylight came we were approaching an area where naval vessels were, but the submarine commander, rather than meet naval ships, submerged and disappeared. We never saw the submarine again."

This is the second time the Roman has been confronted with U-boats. Early in the war she encountered one which left her unmolested.

1 DEAD, 3 HURT IN SHOP EXPLOSION

A woman was fatally and three children seriously injured when an explosion, believed due to gas, wrecked the house and shop in Downsquare, Hetton, Co. Durham, of Mr. Thomas Milburn on Saturday.

The victims were: Mrs. Annie Adamson (forty-five), married daughter of Mr. Milburn; Teresa Oldham (seven), of Henry-street; Thomas Fishburn (six), of Lady-street, and Charles Gibson (five), of William-street. All were taken to Sunderland Infirmary, where Mrs. Adamson died.

Mr. Fishburn, who was in the doorway of the shop, was blown into the street and suffered from shock.

Windows and doors were blown out and the ceiling fell, and Mrs. Adamson, who was serving in the shop, was buried in the debris.

The three children were struck by flying glass and masonry. The boy Gibson was yesterday reported to be very ill.

A portion of the ceiling fell in the house next door.

118

DAILY MIRROR, Thursday, Dec. 7, 1939.

Daily Mirror

No. 11,233.   ONE PENNY
Registered at the G.P.O. as a Newspaper.

BRITISH PLANES, ARMS SENT TO FINLAND

MORRISON WARNS

" Our first business still is to settle accounts with the Nazi regime, which has been a persistent nuisance to the peace of Europe for years.

" Our fifth column must not be permitted to exploit our annoyance with the Soviet Union by promoting an alliance between Britain and Nazi tyranny against the U.S.S.R." — Mr. Herbert Morrison on page 8.

By THE EDITOR

IT WAS ANNOUNCED IN LONDON LAST NIGHT THAT BRITAIN IS TO SEND ARMS TO FINLAND. BRITISH MANUFACTURERS HAVE BEEN AUTHORISED TO SEND TWENTY FIGHTER PLANES TO THE FINNS.

It was also announced in London that Germany is sending arms — Czech arms—to Finland.

The Fifth Column—Hitler's friends in this country, and there are many in high places—will seize on these two statements, both issued in London, and use them to further their plans of an Anglo-German Alliance.

I WARN YOU AGAINST SUCH PLANS.

Already in these announcements the names of Britain and Germany are linked together in a common cause.

Tremendous efforts will be made by the Fifth Column to strengthen that link.

There is no menace to us from Russia—yet. Let us deal with that when—and if—it arises.

There is a great and terrible menace from Germany

Hitler's one aim is to destroy the British Empire and degrade its people.

If an Anglo-German alliance were to succeed, he would do it. He will promise friendship, then trick us as he has tricked everyone. No faith can rest on this man's word

To save ourselves and the world we must fight Germany, beat her, break her.

In no circumstances must we form an alliance with her.

IF WE DO WE ARE DOOMED.

One thing more: can we afford to send planes and arms to Finland ? Our own need is great. We require every plane and every gun for the great struggle in which we are engaged.

LET US KEEP OUR ENERGIES AND OUR STRENGTH FOR OUR ONE PURPOSE—VICTORY OVER GERMANY.

KING TESTS R.A.F.

THE King gave R.A.F. men an "action test" on the Western Front yesterday.

Standing in the control tower of an R.A.F. station, where a squadron is always on the alert for an emergency—the sighting of an enemy plane—the King decided to see how long it would take them to get into the air. For his test it was assumed that ten German aeroplanes were overhead.

He gave the word of command through the telephone from the control room and in less than thirty seconds three fighters were in the air and roaring over the aerodrome.

It was the second day of the King's tour. He spoke with a twenty-four-year-old pilot who claimed the first enemy victim, and will probably have a second German plane credited to him.

"Jolly Good Show," He Said

The King asked him how long his first air battle had taken. When he was told that it was a matter of seconds he exclaimed: "Jolly good show !" and shook the pilot's hand.

In contrast to Tuesday's tour, when he ate at a village estaminet, the King had lunch yesterday at a fine old French chateau which the Duke of Wellington visited after the Battle of Waterloo.

After a meal of Lancashire hot-pot—again the King refused the sweet, mince-pie this time—the royal party inspected troops lined up outside.

The King laughed heartily when a dog became mixed up with the party, and actually "joined" the staff officers. All attempts to send it away failed and finally the dog was allowed to walk along beside the King.

Films of the King's visit to his troops in the field are to be shown to his people.

Once, yesterday, a photographer got in front of Lord Gort, the Commander-in-Chief, and apologised. "Don't worry about me," said Lord Gort. "I'm in no hurry."

" Daily Mirror " and British United Press.

Growth of 'Red Tape' Terrifies Bishop

" I am really terrified at the growth of the spirit of bureaucracy," said the Bishop of Bristol, Dr. C. Salisbury Woodward, last night.

Criticising what he called " the increase of red tape," he said :

" Bureaucracy means a little body of people in Whitehall — quite out of touch with the Tom, Dick or Harry in the street—who have power to lay down regulations, control industries, and to a large extent commandeer our lives."

R.A.F. RAIDS—NAZIS GIVE NEWS FIRST

R.A.F. planes yesterday raided the Frisian Islands and Schleswig Holstein. The first news of the raid came from Berlin radio station.

It alleged that British planes flew over Denmark. Strong "anti-aircraft fire forced the British planes to turn north."

Three hours after the Berlin announcement the news of the raid was given out by the Air Ministry.

On Sunday, when British planes bombed Heligoland, the German radio was the first to give the news.

Berlin reported that no material damage was done. This was later corrected by the assertion that only a fishing boat was sunk.

Actually at least one direct hit was registered on a German cruiser.

GOERING'S WIFE MOVES ON

Frau Goering has left Lausanne with her baby, Edda, for Shorfheide, says the *Paris Soir.* The child has not been registered as of Swiss nationality.

Only twelve people saw Mr. Leslie Roy Derrick, a cinema commissionaire of twenty-nine, wed sixty-nine-year-old Mrs. May Annie Harris yesterday at Peasedown St. John, near Bath. (Story on page two.)

DANCING AFTER 11 p.m.

BLACK-OUT gloom is getting thinner Two bright spots in today's news are that public dance halls are to stay open later and that there is to be more Sunday opening of cinemas.

Public dance halls are to be open after 11 p.m. during the Christmas holiday, writes the *Daily Mirror* Political Correspondent. If the experiment is a success it will be continued.

This decision is understood to affect every part of the country.

Chief Constables will have the power to ban extensions, but such action will be discouraged by the Government unless there is substantial reason.

County and Borough Councils are to be given power under the Emergency Powers (Defence) Act to authorise Sunday opening of cinemas in their districts.

Mr. J. W. Brown, General Secretary of the Civil Service Clerical Association, told 1,000 evacuated Civil Servants at a north-west town last night that dances at a local hotel have been prohibited by the Office of Works.

" If the order is not withdrawn, I'll go and organise a dance in that ballroom myself," he said.

STALIN WILL MARCH

Fifty aeroplanes were flown yesterday to Finland from Italy. War material was also sent from Hungary and Yugoslavia.

" There is every evidence that Russia intends to invade Sweden and Norway," said H. R. Knickerbocker, famous American journalist, on his arrival in New York yesterday from Europe.

" Stalin wants Swedish ore. Hitler won't like it, but one day he may have to pay Russia for that ore and like it."

MORE, BUT DEARER, PETROL

More petrol may be available for private motorists in the New Year, but it is likely to cost more.

Tomorrow a deputation of M.P.s is to urge the Chancellor of Exchequer to reduce the horse power tax of 25s. on private cars.

Daily Mirror

No. 11,235   ONE PENNY

Registered at the G.P.O. as a Newspaper.

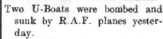
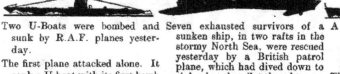

Two U-Boats were bombed and sunk by R.A.F. planes yesterday.

The first plane attacked alone. It sank a U-boat with its first bomb and dropped another as the enemy sank in a whirl of oil.

The second submarine was bombed from the air and dispatched by the depth charges of two British destroyers.

Seven exhausted survivors of a sunken ship, in two rafts in the stormy North Sea, were rescued yesterday by a British patrol plane, which had dived down to sink what the pilot thought were two floating mines.

A British destroyer, H.M.S. Jersey (1,690 tons) has been torpedoed by a U-boat. Two officers and eight men are lost, twelve are injured.

The Jersey has been safely brought into harbour.

U-BOAT STRIKES —IS SUNK

THE British destroyer Jersey (1,690 tons) was torpedoed by a German submarine yesterday. Two officers and eight ratings are lost and believed to he dead. Twelve men are injured.

The Jersey remained afloat and is now safe in harbour.

It is reported that, immediately after the attack, the U-boat was bombed and shattered by a patrolling British plane.

Two destroyers dropped depth charges, making certain of her destruction.

She was the second U-boat to be sunk yesterday by an R.A.F. bomber.

The first was sunk by two direct hits and went to the bottom five minutes after she had been sighted.

The plane, on patrol in near-Arctic seas, saw the U-boat on the surface, dived to the attack. As the submarine crew made desperate efforts to submerge, a bomb fell within a yard of the conning tower.

"Nearly Vertical"

The explosion seemed to shatter the superstructure, and the U-boat plunged by the bows, its stern high out of the water. The turbulent sea around the stricken submarine was blackened with oil.

"The stern," says the pilot, "slowly subsided again, and as the U-boat sank, I released a second bomb, which exploded on the spot More oil and bubbles appeared.

"I stayed over the U-boat until the bows rose right out of the water and the hull stood nearly vertical. A moment later she went down, stern first, and vanished."

It was officially announced last night that the British destroyer which sank after hitting a German mine on Monday, November 13, was H.M.S. Blanche. One man was killed and one reported missing after the sinking.

Spanish Adventures

According to the August Navy List, Blanche was re-commissioned at Chatham on July 1, 1939.

She had many adventures while engaged on patrol during the Spanish civil war.

In 1936 she was bombed near Melilla, and in April, 1937, with her sister ships, Brazen and Beagle, she was involved in an incident with General Franco's warships and planes off the Spanish coast.

The three destroyers hastened to the aid of the steamer Thorpehall, held up by the cruiser Almirante Cervera off Bilbao, and steamed in line ahead between the two ships as far as the three-mile limit.

Captain C. Caslon, of H.M.S. Blanche, was later commended for the way in which he had dealt with "an unexpectedly difficult situation," having cleared for action and steaming straight for the Spanish cruiser, by which he was greatly outgunned.

Blanche, with another of her sister ships, was again bombed in the following year when airmen mistook her identity. She was not damaged.

Nazis "Ready for 30-Year War"

"We are ready even for a thirty years' war," said a broadcast from all Nazi stations last night, says the "Daily Mirror" radio station.

"We wait patiently for the right moment for decisive action," it was added. "The Fuehrer will choose it."

In a radio speech after the opening of the Adolf Hitler canal in Upper Silesia, Gauleiter Wagner said: "This is only the beginning of the Fuehrer's plans. We will have channels in the Balkans down to the Black Sea—if not this year, certainly in the future."

KIDNAPPED— NOTE FROM CAR

FROM OUR OWN CORRESPONDENT

NEW YORK, Friday.

A NOTE scribbled by a girl and thrown from a car led to a police chase which ended in the capture of her kidnapper, it was stated at Pittsburg U.S., today.

Sobbing, still terrorised, pretty Virginia Snyder, twenty-one, told the story of a wild thousand-mile ride across the United States as the captive of her love-crazed kidnapper.

Virginia, who is an expectant mother, said she accepted a ride in the car of John Spahr, thirty-nine, as she was going to Meadville, Pennsylvania.

Instead of stopping in Meadville, Spahr dashed through the city and kept driving westward, threatening to kill Virginia if she made an outcry. For days he never let the girl out of his sight.

Although she never got a chance to call for help, Virginia managed to scribble notes on scraps of paper and toss them from the car. One of these notes was found, and Spahr was arrested when he and the girl were 1,000 miles from their starting point.

Spahr was sentenced to three years' imprisonment.

FORTH BRIDGE BOMB

AN attempt to damage the Forth Bridge with a "bomb" thrown from a train was being investigated by the Scottish police and military authorities last night.

The 2.20 p.m. train, from Dundee to Glasgow, was slowly crossing the bridge when an object was thrown from a carriage on to the bridge.

Train Held Up and Carriages Searched

As it fell it burst into flames, but no damage was done to the permanent way and traffic was not impeded.

The remains of the object were recovered for examination by experts. It is not yet known whether it was a crude form of incendiary bomb.

When the train reached Dalmeny station, the next stop, the incident was reported, and the authorities held the train while carriages were searched and passengers questioned.

No arrest had been made late last night.

PLANE SOS SAVES 7 IN RAFT

SEVEN men on two lashed rafts, prepared to die in a storm that swept across the North Sea. Their ship had been sunk; they were exhausted; no help was at hand.

Six hundred feet above, the pilot of an R.A.F. patrol plane, flying home to his base in Scotland, saw two tiny objects tossing in the waves.

He decided they were floating enemy mines and dived down to sink them with gunfire. But as he came down he thought they might be fish crates washed from a trawler.

Then he looked through his glasses, saw two rafts, four men on one, three on the other. Wild seas were sweeping over the small rafts, and all that the aircraft, which was not a seaplane, could do, was to search for a ship to come to the rescue.

Ten miles away, the Danish vessel Ivar was intercepted, and the wireless operator tried to communicate with her by lamp. For ten minutes the aircraft flashed signals, but the merchantman did not alter course.

The aircraft went back to the rafts, but in the heavy seas and thick mist, could not locate them at first. The pilot began another systematic search and at last found the rafts.

Almost at the same moment the wireless operator was able to attract the attention of the Norwegian ship Lyng and the crew of the aircraft fired coloured Verey lights into the sea to show the position of the rafts.

By this time the Ivar was also coming to the scene, steaming fast.

Guided, Yard by Yard

The plane flew a few feet above the rafts. It was seen that the men were in extreme exhaustion, but each man was able to raise an arm and wave.

When the Ivar was 800 yards off the men on one of the rafts fired what seemed to be their last distress signal. So terrible was the weather that even at this distance the signal could not be seen by the merchant vessel.

It seemed to the R.A.F. men that the ship would miss the derelict sailors. The pilot therefore flew above the bows of the Ivar and took her to the spot yard by yard.

When the ship had been guided to the length of a football pitch from the rafts, a small boat was lowered in the violent sea.

BRITISH SHIP SUNK: 43 DIE

A BRITISH cargo liner, the Royal Mail steamer, Navasota. was sunk by a German submarine in the Atlantic yesterday. Forty-three of her crew are lost.

The London steamer Merel struck a mine off the south-east coast and sank in four minutes. Only two of her crew of seventeen were saved. Both were injured. A third man was picked up. He was dead.

One of the crew of a motor boat which put out on hearing the explosion stated afterwards that the Merel "must have been blown to smithereens." This boat failed to find any survivors.

Joseph M. Neville, of Plymouth-road, Canning Town, one of the Merel's two men who was rescued, said:

"The fore part of the ship had been blown to pieces. No one in that part of the ship could have stood a chance."

His shipmate who was saved is Frank Read, of Harpham-road, Holloway, London, N.

Sunk Destroyer

The Newcastle steamer, Thomas Walton, was torpedoed in a Norwegian fjord. Fourteen of her crew were killed.

And two trawlers returned to port and reported that they had been machine-gunned by German aeroplanes.

A British warship rescued thirty-five members of the Navasota's crew and landed them at a south country port yesterday. Nine others were picked up by a merchant vessel and were taken to another port.

The story of the sinking of the Navasota was told to the Daily Mirror by one of the survivors, Samuel Erving, of Alton-road, Tuebrook, Liverpool.

He said: "We left Britain without a cargo. It was early in the afternoon when the torpedo

Continued on Back Page

120

Daily Mirror

No. 11,239.

Registered at the G.P.O. as a Newspaper.

ONE PENNY

RUNNING BATTLE WITH NAZI SEA RAIDER

H.M.S. Achilles (above) and the Admiral Scheer (right).

A TERRIFIC SEA BATTLE IS IN PROGRESS THIS MORN-ING OFF THE COAST OF SOUTH AMERICA, WHERE TWO BRITISH CRUISERS ARE ENGAGED IN A RUNNING FIGHT WITH THE NAZI SEA RAIDER ADMIRAL SCHEER.

The fight began at six o'clock yesterday, when a British force consisting of the six 8in. gun cruiser Exeter and the small cruisers Ajax and Achilles, found the Admiral Scheer.

For four hours the three British cruisers engaged the Admiral Scheer in a running battle.

The German's heavy guns—she carries six 11in. guns—boomed out to keep the pursuers beyond range.

But the attackers came on.

The Admiral Scheer was hit again and again. But weight of armaments told.

Exeter Falls Out

By 10 a.m. the Exeter had been so damaged that her speed was reduced. She fell out of the action.

The Achilles and the Ajax continued the chase. Admiral Scheer, by now badly damaged, appeared to be trying to seek shelter in the River Plate.

For a time there was silence. Then, at 8.15 last night guns were heard twelve miles off the South American coast.

The lighthouse-keeper at Punta del Este saw a warship on the horizon. It was the Admiral Scheer.

And, miles behind, streaked the two British cruisers.

News of the battle was flashed all over South America by radio.

Listeners sat by their sets as if hearing a round-by-round description of a boxing match.

Guns Roar Again

The German warship passed out of sight of land and for a time the gunfire ceased.

Then, after a brief pause, the roar of guns was heard again from the ocean.

An Admiralty statement issued at two o'clock this morning tells the story of the first running fight.

The British force, it says, is commanded by Commodore H. H. Harwood.

The message adds: "The pursuit continues."

The Achilles, launched in 1932, was one of the three cruisers authorised in the 1930 programme. She is of the Leander class of medium-sized cruisers built in accordance with the London Treaty.

The Achilles in 1933 established a world's record for long distance steaming at high speed by a warship of her class by travelling 1,100 nautical miles in thirty-nine hours, maintaining an average of 29 knots, or about 33 statute miles an hour.

LEAGUE—RUSSIA LAUGHS

BY A SPECIAL CORRESPONDENT

THROW Russia out of the League; turn the League secretariat into a "general staff" to organise the supply of military material and humanitarian aid to Finland.

With these recommendations the Special Committee of the League decided last night to ask the Assembly to take the strongest measures taken against any State since sanctions were applied against Italy.

And, like the sanctions campaign, the Leagues move will be futile. Russia is laughing at Geneva.

She knows how helpless is the League. It can do nothing to save Finland.

One representative heard the recommendations with ironic surprise. He was Dr. Wellington Koo, of China.

He has attended session after session urging League help against Japan, whose aggression is certainly not less flagrant than that of Russia.

And session after session he has been met with polite words and murmured sympathies.

"Danger to Us?"

Since Russia can be expelled only by a unanimous vote of the Council, something has had to be done about China, who refuses to vote out the one nation befriend her.

So it has been decided to take the vote on expulsion before China is elected to the Council.

One interesting feature of the new "sanctions" recommendation is that "non-member nations" are invited to co-operate.

The phrase means U.S.A.

It is reported in London that President Roosevelt inspired Finland's appeal to the League, and that large American supplies of war material have been promised to the Finns.

In the British House of Commons yesterday Sir Kingsley Wood, the Air Minister, agreed that export licences had been granted for the supply of British planes to Finland.

Mr. G. Strauss: Isn't there a danger of this action getting us involved in another war?

There was no reply.

As the League talked yesterday, M. Nicholas Gorelkin, Russian Ambassador to Rome, was on his way home to Moscow.

He is probably the first of many Soviet envoys to make the trip to Moscow.

Italy has openly announced her decision to help Finland. It is reported in Paris that Russia will withdraw Ambassadors from all countries supporting League action against her.

IN THE NORTH SEA

U-Boat Sunk, Nazi Cruiser Torpedoed

A GERMAN cruiser has been torpedoed in the North Sea and a U-boat sunk—both by the British submarine which sighted the Bremen.

This was announced by the Admiralty this morning.

And the R.A.F. yesterday won a North Sea fight.

Two aircraft of the R.A.F. coastal command attacked two enemy Dornier flying boats over the North Sea.

Both enemy rear gunners were hit and both enemy aircraft damaged by machine-gun fire.

FIVE SAVED FROM MINED STEAMER

A NORWEGIAN steamer arrived at Olesund last night with one survivor of the British steamer Deptford, torpedoed in Norwegian waters. Two other members of the crew of thirty-five were picked up but died of exhaustion, says British United Press.

It is believed that four more of the crew were saved by another ship.

Three of the five survivors of the Leith collier Marwick Head, mined in the North Sea, are in an east coast hospital.

Most seriously injured is the master, John Thain, of Port Gordon, Banffshire. Others are James Coulgreen, of Port Gordon, and Angus MacEachin, of Edinburgh. Five men lost their lives.

The Swedish tanker Algoe, 978 tons, struck a mine yesterday inside the territorial limit off Falsterbo close to where another Swedish boat, the Toroe, sank on Tuesday. Five of the crew and the pilot were injured.

The Estonian steamer Estonia, which left Tallinn for Stockholm on Saturday with 185 passengers, mostly Polish Jews, is reported seized by the Germans.

GERMANS TAKE TEN PRISONERS

GERMANY took the initiative again on the Western Front yesterday.

In the Saar area, according to the French communique, the enemy carried out a raid and captured "some ten prisoners."

Rome radio last night, reporting increased activity on the Western Front, said that the initiative is on the German side.

German shock troops attacked especially those points between the Saar and Moselle where the French are building new heavy fortifications.

♦ ♦ ♦

German Ship Home

ANOTHER German liner, the 22,000-ton New York, has reached a German harbour after eluding the British Navy on a voyage from Murmansk, the ice-free port in Arctic Russia.

When war broke out she was on her way from Hamburg to New York, but changed her route and reached Murmansk.

Now she has safely returned to Hamburg.

WOOED WITH KICKS

FROM OUR OWN CORRESPONDENT

New York, Wednesday.

THREE years of unwelcome wooing, which began with a kiss, went on with slaps and kicks and ended with a dynamite bomb, were described to a Court here today by a pretty twenty-six-year-old teacher, Mary Miller.

A school supervisor is charged with setting a dynamite bomb to kill Mary because she refused to wed him.

She said: "He would blacken my eyes and kick me and then beg me to marry him. His idea of showing affection was to drag me around by my hair."

Daily Mirror

No. 11,241   ONE PENNY

Registered at the G.P.O. as a Newspaper.

SPEE TO LEAVE BY TOMORROW

Mrs. Yvette Harwood with her children, Slade and Gillian—and the postal order.

THE ADMIRAL GRAF SPEE WAS ORDERED BY THE URUGUAYAN GOVERNMENT LAST NIGHT TO LEAVE THE PORT OF MONTEVIDEO BY 11.30 (GREENWICH TIME) TOMORROW NIGHT.

THIS WILL BE EIGHT O'CLOCK LOCAL TIME—AND IT WILL BE BROAD DAYLIGHT AT THAT HOUR.

One of the British cruisers which battered the Admiral Graf Spee, the Achilles, has gone inside the harbour at Montevideo and is anchored near her

The Admiral Graf Spee, battered and holed by British guns, can still navigate, but could not fight the warships awaiting her

There are five British warships patrolling outside the harbour, and one of the biggest French battleships, the Dunkerque (26,500 tons) is reported from Buenos Aires to be on her way.

According to the Buenos Aires message, the Graf Spee is expected to put to sea in spite of the fact that her 11in. guns were put out of action by a British shell that hit the fire-control tower

Her anti-aircraft guns, searchlights and range-finder are damaged, too.

Nazis Sending Aid

In Montevideo it is reported that units of the German fleet, including ocean-going submarines, may try to reach the River Plate region before the Graf Spee sails.

The German freighter Tacoma began yesterday to transfer fuel oil to the Graf Spee, and the warship was expected to load 1,290 tons.

She could navigate—a point stressed by the British authorities in asking Uruguay to order her to leave at once or submit to internment.

Germany claims the right to repair her pocket battleship—and then twenty-four hours' grace. One report stated that the Nazis had asked for thirty hours' grace.

"Intern Her" Demand

Britain increased diplomatic pressure on Uruguay last night for internment or ejection of the Graf Spee from its refuge.

A British legation spokesman confirmed that his Government had presented a first request to Senor Guani which, stripped of diplomatic phrases, amounted to a demand that the Graf Spee be interned.

The contents of a second Note were not disclosed, but informed quarters said it was in the nature of an additional protest that the Graf Spee had been allowed to remain more than twenty-four hours, take on supplies and equipment, and repair damage.

A British spokesman admitted that Article Seven of the Uruguayan Neutrality Decree of August 14, 1914, which was incorporated in the present neutrality law provided "a sort of loophole."

Four Killed in Achilles

The Article says that Uruguay may grant to damaged vessels permission to remain longer than twenty-four hours to make necessary repairs.

But the second British Note complained that the Graf Spee, in taking on supplies and apparently repairing her fighting equipment, was "going far beyond the intent either of The Hague Convention or Uruguayan neutrality action."

Meanwhile, cruising at a bare fourteen knots, the British cruiser Exeter, hero of the battle, is expected soon to reach an Argentine port

Unconfirmed reports said that the Exeter had asked for dry dock facilities and 100 beds to be prepared in the hospital for the wounded.

Thirty-six German sailors were buried with full military honours in the German cemetery yesterday.

The Admiralty last night announced four killed and three wounded in H.M.S. Achilles.

Mr. Clement Davies.

GET A MOVE ON

—M.P. Tells Premier

ONE Government M.P. came out in open revolt against the Cabinet yesterday because of its handling of the war.

Mr. Clement Davies, K.C., Liberal National M.P. for Montgomeryshire, wrote to Mr Chamberlain last night intimating that he could no longer support the Government.

In his letter he complained of the many failures of the Government to take the measures necessary for the vigorous prosecution of the war

He had reached the opinion, he said, that the Government has not "the resolution, policy or energy to meet this crisis."

Mr Davies, who is fifty-five years old, and a director of Lever Bros. and Unilever, in a statement later said

"I am not a defeatist; I am certain of our victory But I want to see more planning, more energy, more drive.

"I want to see a small war cabinet of men devoting their whole time, all day and every day, to major issues.

"That cannot be done even by half-timers, still less can it be done by men who have full-time executive tasks.

Call in Unions

"I want to see the production of our supplies guided and fostered by men who know the industry and speak the language of the factories and workshops.

"Call in the trade union leaders and the manufacturers—not merely to advise, but to do the jobs.

"What is the food situation today? What is the position as to animal and poultry foods? Have we to expect more rationing and stricter rationing? If so, tell the people the truth. This nation can face facts. It hates camouflage.

"There is too much 'hush-hush.' This is not a private war of any individual in any position, however eminent he may be in any office.

"We want policy firm and clear, we want resolution and courage to put that policy into effect, we want direction, we want drive. We want them now "

DAY'S 6 NAZI SEA VICTIMS

THE sinking of two British tankers, mined in the North Sea, with, it is feared, heavy loss of life, announced late last night, brought the total number of British and neutral ships lost by enemy action yesterday to six.

The British Fleet claimed two successes yesterday—the Dusseldorf, which put out of Valparaiso on Thursday, was sunk off Chili, and the cargo ship Adolf Leonhardt was scuttled to avoid capture.

The mined tankers were the Athel Templar (8,939 tons) of Liverpool, and Inverlane (8,900) of Dublin. The survivors have been landed at north east coast ports.

An apprentice on the Athel Templar said Both tankers were mined within about half an hour

"The Inverlane went up in flames and the men would not have a chance. I understand there were only seven survivors.

Was Carrying Oil

"We got away three of our lifeboats and the two men who are missing must have been killed in the explosion. We carried a crew of forty and there were thirty-eight of us saved."

The Athel Templar was later salved by tugs and beached.

The Duseldorf was reported to be carrying 7,000 tons of crude oil.

The crew of forty of the Adolf Leonhardt were picked up by the British cruiser which intercepted her

H.M. trawler James Ludford has been sunk by a mine with the loss, it is feared, of two officers and fifteen ratings, it was announced by the Admiralty last night.

The Norwegian steamer Foejna (2,000 tons) bound for Scotland was reported lost yesterday with eighteen men

All but one of the crew of the London tanker San Alberto (7,397 tons) were saved when she was damaged by enemy action and sank.

The Belgian steamer Rosa (1,103 tons) has been sunk by an explosion off the north-east coast.

Foreign messages from Associated Press.

Another Mrs. Harwood

Mrs. Harwood, wife of Commodore Harwood, commander of the ship that chased the battered Graf Spee into Montevideo, is England's proudest wife.

She has reason to be. England, too, is proud of her husband whose gallant action impressed the world.

There is another Mrs. Harwood—no relative of the Commodore. She is Mrs. Yvette Harwood, of the Heights, Northolt Park, Middlesex.

Is England proud of its treatment of her ?

Her husband is a soldier. They have three children.

When war broke out and her husband joined his Territorial unit, Mrs. Harwood applied for the supplementary allowance paid to soldiers' wives in special cases.

So far, after twelve weeks, she has received one payment—a postal order for one shilling.

That wasn't quite all, for the official envelope contained a message with the Comptroller's compliments !

"My husband is an engineer," Mrs. Harwood said to a "Daily Mirror" reporter last night. "In peace time his salary was £4 a week.

Pay Halved

"Now, under the Army allowance scale, I get two guineas a week.

"My children are aged eight, four and four months.

"Like most young people we had many commitments.

"We are buying our house—with rates, it costs 27s. a week—and I have to pay for furniture and insurance.

"Ours is an all-electric house, and today the electricity company have notified me that the supply will be cut off if I do not pay my bill."

Mrs. Harwood is not in good health. For years she has had to attend a London hospital for treatment twice a week.

Her baby, suffering from strained muscles since birth, has also had to be taken to hospital regularly. Fares amount to 6s. a week.

"I don't know," Mrs. Harwood said, "if the 1s. I have received is meant to cover my husband's twelve weeks' service. I don't know if there is more money to come.

"But one thing I do know. My children are not going to starve."

Is Britain proud of its treatment of this Mrs. Harwood, the wife and mother who got a bob for twelve weeks ?

DAILY MIRROR, Monday, Dec. 18, 1939.

Daily Mirror

No. 11,242   ONE PENNY
Registered at the G.P.O. as a Newspaper.

SCUTTLED
GRAF SPEE SINKS IN 3 MINUTES

ADMIRAL GRAF SPEE, the 10,000-ton Nazi pocket battleship chased into Montevideo Harbour by three British cruisers, sailed last night on her last voyage.

Her officers, refusing fight with the Allied ships patrolling outside territorial waters, scuttled her three miles out of Montevideo.

Three explosions shook the Graf Spee. Flames leaped from her magazine. She went down in three minutes.

She sank in 25ft. of water, directly in the path of a shipping lane for shallow draft boats between Montevideo and Buenos Aires.

With smoke pouring from her burning hull, the pocket battleship went down, leaving the top of her bow and the greater part of her superstructure out of the water.

"Captain Stays"

As she sank, flames reached her munitions store, and a new series of explosions tore her apart. The Germans had made sure that the pride of their fleet could not be salvaged.

HER CREW WERE ALL SAVED, WITH THE EXCEPTION OF HER CAPTAIN, WHOSE FATE IS NOT YET KNOWN. IT IS BELIEVED THAT HE BLEW HIMSELF UP WITH HIS SHIP.

"We do not know where the commander of the Graf Spee is, but a German captain stays with his ship," said the German Legation in Montevideo.

Later the Legation announced: " The captain of the Graf Spee has left a letter behind him."

It was clear, when the Graf Spee sailed, that it had been decided to scuttle.

Seven hundred of her crew were transferred to the German cargo steamer Tacoma, which had earlier refuelled the battleship.

Then, amid tense excitement among the thousands of people lining the quay and the river banks, the pocket battleship weighed anchor.

Would She Dare?

All day a furious diplomatic war had waged. The British envoy had lodged a note with the Uruguayan Foreign Office; the Germans had fought to delay the expiry of the time limit.

But at nine o'clock the Admiral Graf Spee moved out of her anchorage. For a time the great crowd stood in suspense.

An excited radio announcer, reporting the incident to all America, voiced the question all were asking.

Would she dare to sail out to open sea, where a cluster of Allied ships waited to send her to the bottom; or would she run for Buenos Aires to steal a further twenty-four hours' respite?

She cleared the harbour, turned up-river towards Buenos Aires, then stopped in midstream.

There she turned and headed to the southeast and the sea.

With Nazi flags flying fore and aft, she moved down river. Five British warplanes appeared and dipped in salute to a doomed ship.

In German Tradition

As she moved down river, six of her own launches followed in her wake, evidence that plans had been made to sink the ship and save the crew.

Then, as the sun set over the River Plate, the roar of an explosion was heard. The Graf Spee, in the true tradition of the German Navy, had been sunk by her own men.

When the roar of the explosion echoed in Montevideo Harbour, merchant ships sounded their sirens in a chorus of delight.

The crowd, who did not disguise their hatred of the Nazis, rushed to vantage points to watch the battleship settle in the water.

A fleet of ships—tugs, launches, lighters, an

Continued on Back Page

The Graf Spee.

B.E.F. MEN KILLED

FIRST British casualties—dead and wounded—were officially reported from the Western Front. They are few in number.

Most occurred when a night patrol set out from the Maginot Line to reconnoitre No Man's Land.

The patrol felt its way slowly through wooded country for nearly three miles.

It was bitterly cold. Over their battle dress the British wore brown leather jerkins or great coats. An N.C.O. with sixteen years' Army experience led them.

Snow had fallen, and the muddy ground had a treacherous frosting of ice that cracked under each step the soldiers took in their hip-high rubber boots.

Suddenly they met an enemy patrol. Shots were exchanged. Several men fell.

Working heroically, the rest of the patrol collected their wounded comrades and made several journeys back to the British lines with them.

Carried in Coats

One badly wounded man was carried in on a blanket.

Others were carried in their companions' greatcoats.

The leader of the patrol was wounded in both arms.

The wounded were first treated at a casualty clearing station, and were then taken back to a French hospital.

According to an American war correspondent, the patrol was armed with a "Tommy-gun," a submachine-gun similar to that used by American gangsters.

Generally speaking, the active sector of the line held by the British has been quiet.

The French beat back several enemy " shock raids " yesterday.

British United Press and Exchange.

P.O. 'PHONE GIRL IS SHOT DEAD

EVELYN BROTHERTON, an eighteen-year-old telephone operator, was killed by a revolver bullet as she sat working at Harpenden (Herts) Post Office.

The revolver of a soldier guarding the premises on Saturday night was discharged accidentally, and the bullet hit the switchboard in the telephone room in an upper floor.

Ricochetting off, the bullet struck Miss Brotherton above the right eye, and she fell dead.

Miss Brotherton, who was the daughter of a retired police officer, lived in Sandridge-road, St. Albans.

DUTCH QUEEN AIDS FINNS

Queen Wilhelmina has contributed £200 to the Dutch Red Cross to be used for humanitarian purposes in Finland.

The funds collected by the Dutch Red Cross organisation will be handed over to the Finnish Red Cross.—Associated Press

---

NAVY LOST 72 IN THE FIGHT

Sixty-one were killed in the cruiser Exeter during the battle with the Graf Spee, the Admiralty announced last night. Twenty-three were wounded.

Casualties in H.M.S. Ajax were seven killed and five wounded ; and in the Achilles (previously announced) four killed and three wounded.

Casualty list : Back page.

PENSIONERS MAY GET 5s. MORE

EARLY in the New Year old-age pensioners and unemployed are expected to get increased benefits to meet the higher cost of living, writes the *Daily Mirror* Political Correspondent.

In trade union circles it is suggested that pensioners may get 3s. to 5s. more and that the unemployed may get a smaller increase

Claims for increases are being closely investigated. Sir John Simon promised M.P.s just before the House rose that he would announce his decision as soon as possible after employers and trade unions had been consulted.

Already hundreds of thousands of workers have gained small increases to meet the rise in the cost of living.

NAZI BOMBER SINKS SHIP

ENEMY aircraft appeared at several points off the coast late yesterday afternoon and sank one vessel.

The Greenhithe (Kent) motor ship Serenity (244 tons) was machine gunned and then bombed by two Nazi aeroplanes about eight miles from shore.

One bomb made a direct hit and totally disabled the Serenity, but the crew, who took to the boats and were picked up by a fishing boat, were all landed uninjured. British aeroplanes drove off the two Nazi raiders, and people further along the coast said that one of the raiders was destroyed.

One of the crew of the Serenity said that the German planes dropped eighteen bombs.

"We abandoned ship and the planes continued bombing until the Serenity sank," he added.

Inhabitants of an isolated cliff farm on the lonely North-East Coast had a grandstand view of an exciting half-hour encounter between German aeroplanes and a number of British

A farmer said: "We saw six or seven little vessels which appeared to be mine-sweeping as if they were the advance guard of a convoy going south.

"Suddenly two big black planes swooped down from the sky from a great height and began attacking the boats. I saw great columns of water being thrown up around the boats and there were a number of deafening explosions.

"There were also flashings from the ships, as if they were firing back.

"Then two R.A.F. planes appeared coming from the land at a great speed. The black planes turned tail and made off out to sea. I heard the sharp rat-tat-tat of machine-gun fire and about twenty minutes afterwards both R.A.F. planes returned."

Daily Mirror

No. 11,243   ONE PENNY

Registered at the G.P.O. as a Newspaper

THE CANADIANS ARE HERE

WE ARE TELLING THIS NEWS—ALTHOUGH THE WAR OFFICE AND THE CENSOR HAD BANNED IT UNTIL TO-MORROW.

FOR, IN SPITE OF THAT BAN, THE FIRST LORD OF THE ADMIRALTY, MR. CHURCHILL, CHOSE TO STEAL THE LIMELIGHT OF OTHER GOVERNMENT DEPARTMENTS AND MADE THE STORY PUBLIC LAST NIGHT. AND WHEN THE WORLD KNEW—THEN THE CENSOR RELEASED IT.

Canadian troops landing from the first tenders. As they came ashore they shouted " Hey, hey—the gang's all here ! " (See other picture on back page.)

Escorted and guarded by the great ships of the Grand Fleet—as Mr. Churchill revealed on the radio last night—the first fighting troops from Canada have landed on British soil.

Among the men are Americans who crossed the Canadian border to enlist unofficially in the war against Hitler.

FROM OUR SPECIAL CORRESPONDENT

A WESTERN PORT.

A WILD skirl of bagpipes shrilled from the great grey transport across the waters to the watchers on the quay.

Then, drowning the pipes, drowning the roar of the aircraft on their beat round the ship, we heard the shrill cry coming over the waves: " Yahoo."

The Canadians had come to Britain.

They had left their ploughs on the prairie country, they had carefully closed their ledgers in city offices, they had stowed away their traps at little stations far in the Arctic circle.

And they had voyaged thousands of miles—some of them knowing the sea for the first time in their lives, to throw their weight into the fight against Nazidom.

They sang as they came—" Hey, hey, the gang's all here." They screamed out the towns from which they had journeyed. Again and again they gave their characteristic call—" Yahoo."

Soon that call will be striking dread in the hearts of enemy soldiers at the front.

As the tender neared the shore, hats were tossed in the air, girls blew kisses to the young soldiers, children shrieked excitedly and flapped handkerchiefs.

Welcomed by Mr. Eden

Leaning against the boat's rail were two with darker skins than their neighbours. Their narrow eyes were blue and bewildered. They were Canadian Indians.

Now the tender touched the quay and men and girls perilously bridged the narrow gulf over the water to grasp the soldiers' hands

Down came the gangway and the men swarmed ashore.

Quickly they were lined up on the quayside, row upon row of them in their battle-dress, to be welcomed to these shores by Mr. Anthony Eden, and to receive a message from the King.

" On behalf of the people of this country," it said, " I extend the warmest welcome to the first contingent of the Canadian forces to reach these shores. The British Army will be proud to have as comrades in arms the successors of those who came from Canada in the Great War and fought with a heroism that has never been forgotten. Signed, " George, King and Emperor."

The Canadians are under the command of Major-General A. G. L. McNaughton, who is fifty-two, a leading figure in imperial research

" It will be my greatest pleasure one of these days," he told me, " to report to Lord Gort and say, 'I am at your orders.'"

12 NAZI 7 R.A.F. PLANES LOST

BIGGEST air battle of the war was fought out yesterday over Heligoland and Wilhelmshaven.

R.A.F. bombers, scouting over German waters to find and attack Nazi warships, were met by a strong force of enemy fighter planes, and brought down half of them after a stern fight lasting for hours.

The Air Ministry announced last night: "Twelve Messerschmitts were shot down, whilst seven of our bombers are at present unaccounted for."

Later the Ministry stated: "Reports indicate that twelve enemy aircraft destroyed represented some 50 per cent. of the total enemy fighter forces engaged."

The importance which the German High Command attaches to the preservation of their diminishing fleet is emphasised by the strenuous resistance offered to these R.A.F. reconnaissances.

Their hope of destroying enemy warships at sea failed because the enemy had gone into hiding.

The Germans announced the aerial combat is a great Nazi victory.

The official announcement in Berlin said:—

" In the afternoon of December 18 the British attempted a large-scale raid with forty-four of the most modern bombing planes.

" The enemy formations attempted to attack at several points on the North Sea coast, but were intercepted in their approach by German fighter planes north of Heligoland.

" Several bitter air battles over the inner Heligoland Bight occurred, according to present reports, in the course of which thirty-four British planes were shot down.

" This figure does not include losses which the remaining British planes in all probability suffered on the return flight.

To Wilhelmshaven

" A few of the Englishmen were successful in breaking through to Wilhelmshaven. They were covered by anti-aircraft gunfire, and indiscriminately dropped three bombs, which fell into a field without doing damage.

" Two German planes crashed, but the crews escaped by parachute.

" The successful German fighters belonged to the Schumacher Fighter Squadron, which on December 14 had sent the enemy home with 50 per cent. loss, shooting down ten out of twenty British attacking planes."

That was the version—" grossly exaggerated," the Air Ministry said—issued for the German public, and officials in Berlin tried to hide their chagrin over the Nazi sea losses by boasting of their air victory.

" This is revenge for the Graf Spee," they said. " The news has come just at the right time."

THREE LIFEBOATS OUT

After some air activity off the East Coast, three lifeboats put out last night

GERMAN CRUISER SUNK AMID MINES

Picking her way through minefields, dangerous shoals, and a screen of six destroyers a British " baby " submarine has torpedoed and sunk a 6,000-ton German cruiser in the Nazi naval base at the mouth of the River Elbe.

BRITAIN'S audacious under-water raider is the 540-ton Ursula, whose chief is Lieutenant-Commander G. C Phillips. He has a crew of twenty-seven

The Admiralty announcement of the Ursula's feat came less than twelve hours after the pocket battleship Admiral Graf Spee had been ignominiously scuttled outside Montevideo Harbour. Calmly, the Admiralty stated:

" H.M. submarine Ursula reports that she sank one Koln class cruiser at the mouth of the Elbe on Thursday, December 14. The cruiser was screened by six German destroyers."

And yesterday, also, came the news that the German steamer Antiochia (3,106 tons) was scuttled by her crew while being pursued in the North Atlantic.

Recalls Scapa Feat

The Ursula has emulated the exploit of the U-boat which penetrated the defences of Scapa Flow and torpedoed the Royal Oak on September 17.

On the south of the strongly-fortified mouth of the Elbe lies the German harbour of Cuxhaven, and on the opposite side the naval base of Brunsbuttel, scene of the R.A.F.'s first heroic attack on enemy naval forces on the second day of the war.

The torpedoed cruiser was a miniature Graf Spee. The Koln class—comprising the Koln, the Konigsberg and the Karlsruhe—carries nine 5.9 guns, and has a speed of 32 knots.

It is not yet known which has been sunk. Naturally, the Nazis officially deny that a British submarine has sunk any German cruiser.

But it was admitted that the underwater explosion mentioned in last Thursday's German

Continued on Back Page

Why Has The News Been Held ?

The publication to-day—and not to-morrow as arranged—of the news of the landing of the Canadians reveals once again the utter lack of unity and co-ordination between Government Departments.

The " Daily Mirror," in common with other newspapers, knew that the Canadians were here—safely.

There was no sensible reason why the news should not have been published yesterday.

The troops were here, out of danger.

Hundreds saw them land.

In a very few hours the news had spread to thousands.

The War Office and the Censor decided to hold it up until to-morrow.

But they forgot to tell the Admiralty that it was a secret.

So Mr. Churchill told last night.

Innocently, of course.

Or are we doing these Government officials an injustice ?

Did the War Office and the Censor keep the news from the public so that it might add a touch of colour to Mr. Churchill's speech ?

It may have added to the colour of the speech—and we are all interested in Mr. Churchill's speeches.

BUT

The nation should be told the news at once. It should not be saved up to colour Mr. Churchill's speeches.

It is also unpleasant to think that many details of the damage to our ships at Montevideo appear also to have been saved for Mr. Churchill's effort.

This senseless suppression of news that can be of no value to the enemy, and that you have the right to know, will have to stop.

After all, we are fighting one form of dictatorship.

WE DON'T WANT TO ACQUIRE ANOTHER.

RUSSIANS FIRE ON NAZIS

The German steamer Pillau (1,308 tons) arrived at Gaevle, north of Stockholm, yesterday and the crew said she had been attacked by a Russian submarine which fired thirty shells at her south of the Landsort lighthouse, near Stockholm.

The Pillau was not damaged. The captain is reporting the incident to the German Minister—British United Press.

DAILY MIRROR, Saturday, Dec. 23, 1939.

Daily Mirror

No. 11,247   ♦   ONE PENNY
Registered at the G.P.O. as a Newspaper.

R.A.F. HERO'S ESCAPE

LOSING blood from a shot wound, a 14st. R.A.F. gunner, his plane's wings in tatters, was brought back safely by his plane's crew after he had shot down five Messerschmitts, crack German planes.

This story of the battle over Heligoland Bight in which twelve German planes were brought down, was revealed last night.

The air gunner is now in hospital progressing favourably.

In the battle he was shot through the thigh, and the rest of the plane's crew all played their part in saving his life on the return journey.

Both wings of the plane were in tatters, and the fuselage was riddled with bullet holes. One wing had burst into flames, but the fire did not last long.

Carried from Plane

Despite the damage the aircraft "flew as well as ever." An armour-piercing bullet tore the sole from the boot of a member of the crew, but he escaped with a graze and a burn.

When the aircraft returned, the pilots and airmen made an escalator of their backs to remove the gunner from the machine.

The bullet which pierced his thigh missed both bone and artery, but he lost a great deal of blood on the long and extremely cold flight home.

Naval Honours

Officers and men of the submarine Spearfish have been honoured by the King for "courage, seamanship and resolution in bringing their ship safe home after many prolonged and violent enemy attacks which almost put her out of action."

These are the awards, announced last night:

Distinguished Service Cross: Lieutenant John Henry Eaden, R.N., commanding officer.

Distinguished Service Medal: Chief Engineroom Artificer Stanley N. Peel; Petty Officer Alfred F. Blackmore.

"These two men were specially commended by their commanding officer for their conduct.

Continued on Back Page

PETROL PRICE UP TO 1s. 10d.

THE price of petrol will be increased by a halfpenny from today, bringing it up to 1s. 10d. a gallon—the highest since February, 1924, when it was 1s. 11d.

Also from today the wholesale price of petrol in bulk to dealers and non-rebated commercial users will be 1s. 6½d net.

Until further notice, commercial consumers who are currently paying full retail price, when calling at Petroleum Board depots for supplies into the tanks of their vehicles, will continue to be charged at retail price. All others calling at the depots will be charged a flat price of 1s. 5d. per gallon.

The charges, which have been agreed to by the Government, apply to deliveries in England, Wales and South Scotland. In other areas, such as the north of Scotland, the corresponding differentials will continue.

The Petroleum Board state that the object of the alterations has been to increase the dealer's retail margin.

The net return to the Petroleum Board will not be increased.

To All Our Readers This Christmastide We Say
BE STRONG AND OF GOOD CHEER

CHRISTMAS. AND AGAIN THE TIME HAS COME WHEN THE GREETING, "A MERRY CHRISTMAS"—THE WORDS MEN HAVE USED THROUGH THE CENTURIES—SEEMS FOR A MOMENT EMPTY OF MEANING.

Hitler has done his best to make this a sad Christmas.

BUT HE HAS FAILED.

He has failed because in every way he underestimates the British people.

And if he thinks he is going to interfere with a British Christmas—that is just another mistake he has made.

✦ ✦ ✦

True, the youth of the Empire is scattered in war; many children wisely evacuated to new and safer homes.

Around the firesides there will be reunions; but there will be many who will be there only in thought.

The pictures in the fire will be of absent men and women —on guard for Britain: doing their job.

We will have visions of them all.

At sea the Navy and Merchant Navy keeping their ceaseless watch in mine-strewn waters, heroes every hour.

On land the troops facing the German lines, the anti-aircraft men at their posts.

In the air, the flyers maintaining their tireless vigil in the clouds.

We shall think of them.

✦ ✦ ✦

And let us remember also those who have made the great sacrifice, and their saddened homes.

Those sacrifices can never have been made in vain if we all play our part, resolute and determined to see this thing through until truth and right and liberty are established once more again.

So this Christmas of 1939 let there be a smile on your lips and in your heart confidence.

✦ ✦ ✦

And next Christmas?

Well, that is looking a long way ahead.

Remember the tasks that lie ahead of us.

But down the coming year we will march on in our own British way—to sure and certain triumph over evil.

Then the next Christmas can be a real riotous merry one.

✦

FLYING ATLANTIC TO ATTEND PARTY

SIX-YEAR-OLD Helen Halford and her brother, John, who is four, children of an R.A.F. pilot, are to fly the Atlantic to attend a party.

They will board the transatlantic Clipper on Christmas Day and two days later they will be at their home in Broughton, near Stockbridge, Hants.

Mrs. Halford, their mother, told the *Daily Mirror* last night: "It will probably be a thrill for them—it will certainly be a great thrill for us.

"They went over in the Queen Mary to stay with my sister in New York when war began.

"A nurse will accompany them on the flight.

"I'm flying to Paris beforehand, and I'll be at Lisbon to greet them as they step from the plane.

"We are going to give them a party when they get home. It is a pity they won't be here for Christmas, but they couldn't get seats on the Christmas plane.

"I don't know whether they will bring Christmas presents for us—I should hardly think so, for luggage must be so light on the Clipper.

"Their best Christmas gift, and ours, too, will be our being together again."

More Pay

Wage increases which will cost the main line companies £1,000,000 a year have been granted to railwaymen.

The increase means a 5os. a week minimum for adults in traffic grades in London.

A REALLY FOUL REILLY-FFOULL'S XMAS IS REALLY FOUL! STAP ME!!

WHAT A TIME WE'LL HAVE WITH THE MISTLETOE—SUCH GREAT BOYS TOO!

I HOPE THERE IS NO MUD IN YOUR XMAS PUD— BUT MUD IN YOUR EYE AND ALL THAT!

AHOY TROOPS! COMPLIMINTS OF SEASINGS, WIT' ALL THE BRASS FITTINGS, YER'S TRULY—POPEYE!

YIPPEE! CHRISTMAS LEAVE COMES BUT ONCT A YEAR! YIPPEE! YIPPEE!!

Daily Mirror

No. 11,250 ✦ ONE PENNY
Registered at the G.P.O. as a Newspaper.

No U.S. Aid to Finns

The United States is not supplying any arms or munitions to help Finland fight the Russians. The Finnish Mission in the United States, anxious to arrange immediate deliveries of important war materials, are being told that the American fighting forces need all available stocks themselves.

The U.S. authorities further state that their Army and Navy arms establishments cannot fill foreign orders, and that private arms and munitions factories are at present unable to meet the demands of their own Government, without contracting for immediate deliveries to foreign nations.

YOUR RATION GUIDE

NEW rationing plans were announced yesterday. And this is the situation now—the housewives' complete guide at a glance:

FROM JANUARY 8
Everyone is entitled to :—
SUGAR : Twelve ounces.
BACON and HAM : Four ounces.
BUTTER : Four ounces.

NOT BEFORE FEBRUARY
MEAT : Amount to be announced.
NOT RATIONED : Liver, hearts, kidneys, tongue, tripe, sausages, brawn, pies, meat paste, rabbits, poultry, game and fish.
EXTRAS : For marmalade making, three pounds of sugar for every two pounds of oranges (similarly for jam) ; ten pounds per colony for beekeepers.

The sugar ration may be increased later.
For meat, the public should register with retailers not later than January 8. Rations will be "well up to ordinary requirements." The weight will vary with the customer's choice of quality

The scheme for the control of livestock and home produced meat will start on January 15.

To Satisfy "Sweet Tooth"

The Ministry of Food said yesterday that there is to be an "appropriate" ration of sugar for manufacturing sweets, chocolate, etc.

It appealed to the public not to increase demands for sugar before rationing starts.

Issues of sugar to retailers up to January 8 will not be more than sufficient for sales of 3lb. per head a week—the present unofficial ration.

In Germany, the sugar ration is 8½oz. a week, but their jam is also rationed at 3½oz. for adults, and 5½oz. for children.

It is pointed out that although sugar is an important source of energy, this is available in alternative foods, especially in potatoes and other vegetables.

The Ministry is confident that the housewife will think of numerous ways of satisfying the "sweet tooth" in the home.

The Minister of Food, Mr. W. S. Morrison, last night explained these points.

The sugar rationing will take account of special cases — housewives who want to make preserves, beekeepers, brewers.

"Anyone who wants to make marmalade," said Mr. Morrison, "will buy the oranges required and show the invoice at the Food Office, where any extra allowance will be made available on the basis of 3lb. of sugar for every 2lb. of oranges.

"We hope there will be similar extra supplies for the jam-making season."

Under the meat and livestock scheme, the Ministry will purchase not only all imported meat, but also all livestock offered by farmers.

Continued on Back Page

GIRL N.C.O. IS SHOT DEAD

A GIRL A.T.S. SERGEANT, WEARING PYJAMAS AND DRESSING-GOWN, WAS FOUND SHOT DEAD BY HER FATHER IN THEIR GARDEN YESTERDAY.

She was Miss Vivienne de Meric, twenty-five, of Bradford Peverell, near Dorchester.

Hearing a shot in the garden, her father, Captain V. de Meric, one of the food officers at the Western Area Food Office, Bristol, hurried into the garden.

He found his daughter Vivienne, an attractive brunette, lying on the ground. To his horror he found that she was dead.

Gun at Her Side

She had a severe head wound. A sporting gun, which had recently been fired, was at her side.

She was clad only in pyjamas and a dressing gown.

"Miss Meric seemed quite happy when she went to her bedroom on Wednesday night," the *Daily Mirror* was informed last night.

"She was a sergeant serving with the A.T.S. at Dorchester.

"She was popular and members of her unit are mystified by her death."

Captain de Meric was too distressed by his daughter's death to see anyone.

He will, it is understood, be a witness at the inquest, which will be held at Dorchester today.

Messages of sympathy were sent to him by his daughter's friends in the Service and in civil life.

Monks Give Their Blood for Friend

Two Cistercian monks, who rarely go out into the world, have made a special journey to give blood transfusions in a vain effort to save the life of a friend.

The Lord Abbot gave them permission to travel from Mount St. Bernard Abbey, Coalville, Leicester, to Leicester Infirmary in the hope of saving the life of Mr. S. Edwards.

HOMES SWEPT OUT TO SEA

TOWERING waves smashed against seaside houses and, with screaming people trapped inside, swept them out to sea in the earthquake on the Black Sea coast of Turkey.

Ships were torn loose and vanished with the wreckage of homes.

This was revealed yesterday in reports reaching the Turkish capital of Ankara, where the Government decided to make a world appeal for funds to tackle the aftermath of the earthquake disaster.

It is now known that 42,000 people are dead or hurt in the city of Erzinjan alone—practically all its population.

Whole families were crushed in their beds. Hundreds escaped from crashing houses, only to be trapped and burned to death in fires caused by broken gas mains and shattered oil lamps.

Freezing to Death

Every big building collapsed, including the barracks, where all the officers, ninety cadets and many soldiers were killed.

Twelve towns and eighty villages are in blazing ruins, and thousands of scantily-clad homeless refugees are encamped in the frozen countryside.

Reports of two new shocks came through yesterday as Turkish M.P.s were naming a commission to seek international aid.

General Ismet Inonu, President of Turkey, rushed to the area to direct rescue work. With the temperature at 22 below zero, Fahrenheit, many of the thousands who fled to the fields have been frozen to death.
Associated Press and British United Press.

STALIN TRIES A NEW GENERAL, NOW

STALIN has appointed a new chief of the Leningrad military district—General G. M. Shtern, one of the youngest and most able of the Soviet Generals—it was reliably reported in Moscow last night (says Associated Press).

Shtern, who is forty, replaces General Meretskov, who was reported to have been dismissed after a recall to the Kremlin to explain his troops' lack of progress against Finland.

He was blamed, it was stated, for trying to secure too quick a victory.

(2,000 Italians Aid Finns : Page 2)

Nails !
Human fingernails just one year old !

Juliette, who runs what she calls the "Hollywood Nail Hospital"! grew them to prove that a girl's nails can be strong and not brittle.

Then she gave them their first birthday party and had them shorn. With relief, we suspect.
(See story and more pictures on page 5.)

WED IN HOUR TO WIN BET

A WAGER, jokingly accepted at a Christmas Eve party, was the cause of a wedding ceremony arranged and completed within an hour.

The couple are Mr. Matthew Bland, twenty-five-year-old taxi owner, of Grantham, Lincs, and Miss Mary Meads, twenty-three, supervisor in a local stores.

Last night Mr. Bland told the *Daily Mirror* the story of his "marriage of minutes."

"Mary and I had been engaged for some time, and on Christmas Eve a friend told me that, since I drove so many people to the church to be married, it was about time I was married myself.

"On the spur of the moment I accepted a bet that I would be married to Mary by 4 p.m. on the following day.

"O.K., I'll Be Ready"

"All next day I was busy driving wedding couples to church in my taxi, and quite forgot about the wager until I was waiting for my seventh couple to come out from the ceremony.

"After that service, I went to the vicar and arranged to be married at 4 o'clock. It was then about 3.15 p.m.

"So I drove my customers to the wedding reception, then dashed home, telephoned mother, changed and rushed round to tell Mary we were to be married in half an hour. All she said was, 'O.K., darling, I'll be ready.'

"I told my brother-in-law, Mr. Albert Chapman, to be ready to be my best man at St. Wulfran's Church in twenty minutes.

"Meanwhile, my mother had arranged a grand spread for the reception at my home in Belton-lane, and when we got back seventy guests were waiting.

"But in the middle of the celebration I was called away to drive a honeymoon couple to Nottingham. When I got back I found the drawing room full of presents and notes of congratulation."

GERMAN SHIP SCUTTLED

After being chased by a British warship, the German steamer, Gluecksbarg (2,880 tons) has scuttled herself, according to Paris radio reports from Madrid.

The ship, carrying sugar and other foodstuffs for Germany, sank near San Legere de Barameda.—Exchange.

PRISONERS' ESCAPE BID

FOUR soldiers, manacled in pairs, made a dash for freedom from a train at Byfleet, Surrey yesterday.

Jumping from a compartment as the train stopped, the men eluded their guards, and ran across "live" electric rails.

They climbed a wooden fence and disappeared.

Police joined in the hunt. The four men were later captured on the station.

THE REDS ARE HOT

Moscow had a celebration yesterday because, as they announced from all radio stations. It was the fifteenth anniversary of central heating in the U.S.S.R.

Made in the USA
Middletown, DE
08 March 2019